CREDITS

No book is ever done by one person and this book is no exception. Many people contributed in some small but nonetheless important way and if I don't mention you by name please forgive me. A notoriously bad memory is my excuse. However, there are some people that I do want to give a public thank you to because their efforts on my behalf were timely or above and beyond what one would normally expect even from good friends. Some of these good people are in business. I will deal with them first lest you tire of reading the credits and they miss out on getting the business from you that I feel they justly deserve.

About a year ago, I discovered a company that does almost unbelievable high quality polishing at almost unbelievable bargain prices. This company, Mag Masters (714-541-9777) is run by Tom Kidd and his wife Liz, and now gets all my polishing business even if it does involve a drive a third of the way across California. A special thanks and a commendation for high-quality work must also go to Keith Wilson at Wilson Manifolds in Fort Lauderdale (305-771-6216) and Brad and Ruth Urban of the Carb Shop (909-481-5816). Brad's patience for letting me turn the shop upside down was stretched, but we made it didn't we Brad? Many people at Holley also put their ten cents worth (and often more) in so thanks a lot fellas, you helped make my job easier.

Also, some other big names in the carb business that I have to thank are David (used to be Dave when he was younger) Braswell of Braswell Carburetion (602-579-9176) for support over many years and Barry Grant and Vic Moore of BG Fuel Systems (706-864-8544). Another long-suffering helper was Sam Davis of Gold Coast Coating (805-987-9060) who painstakingly did most of our major coating exercises over the last few years.

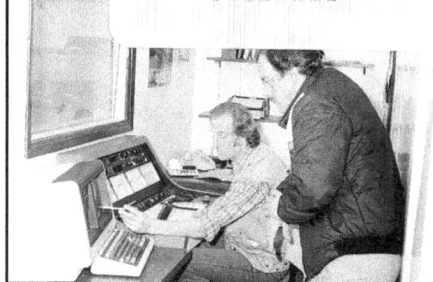

The Vizard "office" consists of a dyno cell where he conducts rigorously exacting dyno tests...

On the personal side, I would like to thank my good friend Roger Helgesen for his unfailing encouragement, support and access to his near photographic memory. Thanks to my dear wife, Josephine, for her patience and willingness to help with those less-than-exciting book building chores that inevitably crop up. To Terry Watson and Gil Mink must go thanks for helping out with some new (to me) computer programs and equipment so I could do better-looking drawings. Editor John Baechtel for being a neat guy to work with. Ric "Doc" LeClair for his time and suggestions setting up and doing many of the photos, and last, but not least to my now old friend Allan Nimmo. Yes Al, thanks for the welding!

ABOUT THE AUTHOR

.... and a small but comprehensively equipped machine shop. Part of the machine shop is a full cylinder head facility where David flow tests heads and manifolds, and modifies them as required. It is the hours that are spent in this shop that give him the first-hand experience to pass on to the reader.

David Vizard has a background originating in the aerospace industry. He is a university lecturer and a consulting high-performance engineer with a great deal of hard-core research as well as considerable, personal "hands on" engine and race car building experience. He has been successful with road, dirt and drag race engines and has amassed an enviable race win record. In one season, when a tally was kept, the eight engines he built amassed a combined 169 1st places, track records and championship wins. This included five championship wins, two seconds and a fourth place. One well known European factory team achieved a 100% win record two seasons in a row using engine specs developed by the man often known as "Vizard the Wizard." For his R & D work, David Vizard uses a 1000 horsepower computer controlled engine dynamometer and a 1200 horsepower chassis dynamometer. To develop cylinder heads and induction systems, he uses a computer-supported flow bench along with a workshop having extensive machining and fabricating capabilities. This allows him to personally experiment with new ideas and to test products, concepts and procedures covered in this book. Unless otherwise noted, all test results, tables, drawings and photographs in this book are by the author. Apart from this and other publications in the *How to Build Horsepower* series David Vizard has written more than 3,200 magazine articles and more than 25 books on the subject of high performance.

Author, David Vizard, in the Vizard engine room assembling another potent powerplant according to the Vizard horsepower philosophy.

When time allows, Vizard, an avid road and drag racer, goes racing and frequently wins, but by his own admission he spends far too little time at the track.

About S-A Design's *How to Build Horsepower* Series

If you read nothing else when you pick up this book be sure to read this.

This book is intended for performance enthusiasts, pro or otherwise. It fills the educational gap between high school and university. It covers not only the author's practical and theoretical experience but also the many professionals with whom he associates. Theory is only dealt with as far as required to provide a working understanding of the principles involved. The book's #1 goal is to help get your car past the finish line first. By presenting powerful, yet easy to understand information that can be quickly applied to your car's engine we will improve your position in the highly competitive world of automotive performance. Guaranteed!

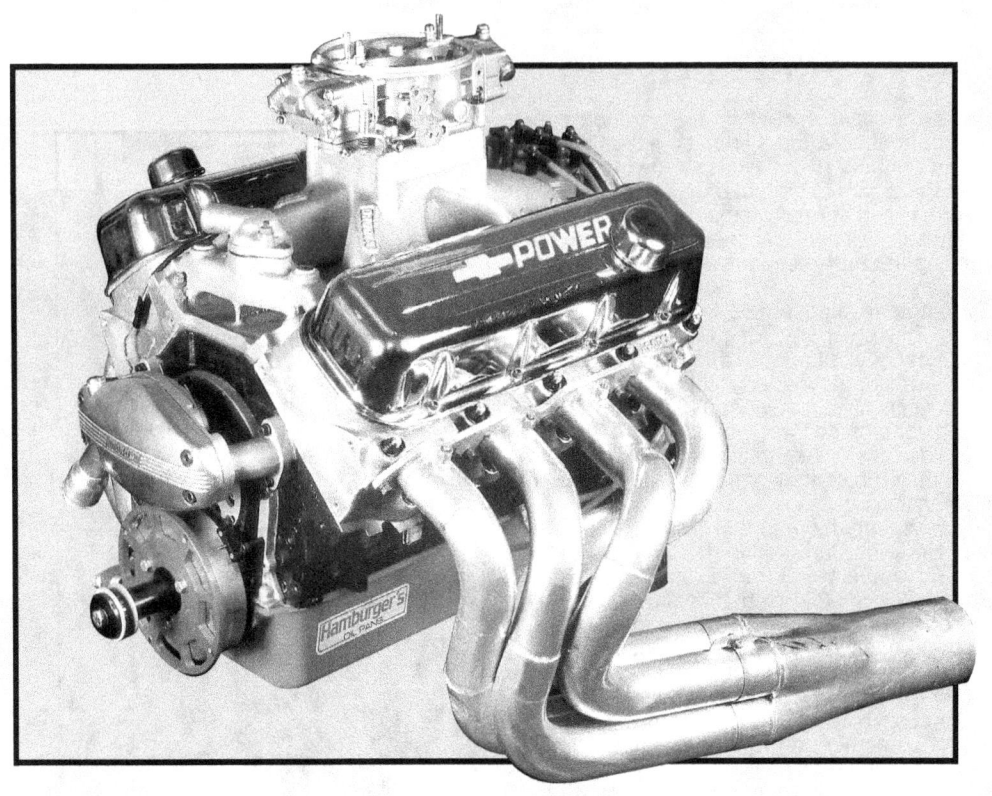

The text, photographs, drawings and other artwork (hereafter referred to as information) contained in this publication is sold without any warranty as to its usability or performance. In all cases, original manufacturer's recommendations, procedures and instructions supersede and take precedence over descriptions herein. Specific component design and mechanical procedures – and the qualifications of individual readers – are beyond the control of the publisher, therefore the publisher disclaims all liability, either expressed or implied, for use of the information in this publication. All risk for its use is entirely assumed by the purchaser/user. In no event will Cartech, Inc., or the author be liable for any indirect, special or consequential damages, including but not limited to personal injury or any other damages, arising out of the use or misuse of any information in this publication.

This book is an independent publication, and the authors and/or publisher thereof are not in any way associated with, and are not authorized to act on behalf of any of the manufacturers included in this book. The publisher reserves the right to revise this publication or change its content from time to time without obligation to notify any persons of such revisions.

HOW TO BUILD HORSEPOWER: VOL. 2
CARBURETORS AND INTAKE MANIFOLDS
By DAVID VIZARD

Copyright © 1996 by David Vizard. All rights reserved. All text and photographs in this publication are the property of David Vizard unless otherwise noted or credited. Selected sidebar photography picked up from other CARTECH® publications. It is unlawful to reproduce – or copy in any way – resell, or redistribute this information without the expressed written permission of the author. Printed in U.S.A.

EDITED BY
JOHN BAECHTEL
COPY EDITING BY
LISA HANKS
PRODUCTION BY
JOHN BAECHTEL

ISBN 978-1-61325-029-7
Product No. SA52P

CARTECH®, INC., 39966 Grand Ave., North Branch, MN 55056
www.cartechbooks.com

CONTENTS

CHAPTER 1, PERFORMANCE FILTRATION 4
- SIGNIFICANT PRESSURES AND FLOWS 4
- FILTER FLOW 4
- BOOSTER BUFFETING 5
- HIGH SPEED AIRFLOW 6
- IMPROVING EFFICIENCY 6
- POWER PRODUCTION 7
- POWER AND TEMPERATURE 7
- HIGH OUTPUT FILTRATION 7
- FILTER CLOGGING 8
- PERFORMANCE AND COST 9
- FILTER TESTS 10
- ELEMENT SIZING TIPS 11

CHAPTER 2, CASES, COOL AIR AND RAMMING 12
- SHORT AND TALL STACKS 13
- CALCULATING RAM PRESSURE 14
- PRESSURE POTENTIAL 14
- PRESSURE BALANCE 15
- RAM AIR TIPS 17
- COOL AIR TIPS 18
- PRESSURE VERSUS DENSITY 19

CHAPTER 3, BASIC CARBURETOR FUNCTION 20
- THE VENTURI 20
- CORRECTIONS 21
- TRIMMING THE FUEL CURVE 21
- THE EMULSION TUBE 22
- EMULSION TUBE SELECTION 22
- POWER VALVES AND MIXTURE SPREAD 23
- LEAN CRUISE MIX 24
- IDLE SYSTEM 24
- TRANSITION CIRCUIT 25
- ACCELERATOR PUMP CIRCUIT 25
- COLD START SYSTEM 25

CHAPTER 4, PROPERTIES OF MIXTURES 28
- LEAN BURN 29
- INTAKE MANIFOLD BASICS 30
- CYLINDER HEADS 31
- ATOMIZATION AND POWER 32
- PUMP FUEL COMPARISON 33
- UNLEADED HIGH OCTANE 34
- OCTANES TESTED 35
- FUEL DISTRIBUTION 36
- RACE FUELS 37
- ALCOHOL FUELS 38
- CARB CALIBRATION 39
- CHASSIS DYNOS 40
- PLUG READING 40
- OXYGEN SENSORS 40
- AIR FUEL RATIO REQUIREMENTS 42
- FUEL SUPPLY 43
- FUEL FLOW REQUIREMENTS 43
- FLOW AND PRESSURE 44
- BYPASS SYSTEMS AND PRESSURE REGULATORS 45

CHAPTER 5, INDUCTION BASICS 46
- INDUCTION PRESSURE PULSE TUNING 46
- BASICS 46
- HELMHOLTZ PLENUM 51
- LENGTH AND VOLUME 55
- PORT AREA 52

CHAPTER 6, HOLLEY CARBURETORS 54
- SPREAD BORES 54
- 4150 AND 4160 SERIES CARBURETORS 56
- 4010 SERIES CARBURETORS 57
- 4011 SERIES CARBURETORS 58
- 4500 SERIES DOMINATORS 58
- CARBURETOR CFM AND ENGINE DEMAND 59
- AIRFLOW CAPACITY INFLUENCES 60
- COMPUTING REQUIRED AIRFLOW 60
- CARB CFM CORRECTION FACTOR 60
- MINIMIZING MANIFOLD PRESSURE LOSSES 61
- CARB FLOW VERSUS TEST PRESSURE DROP 62
- RECOMMENDED READING 63
- EFFECTIVE USE OF MORE CFM 64
- CALIBRATING HOLLEY CARBURETORS 65

CHAPTER 7, PERFORMANCE MODS FOR HOLLEYS
- AIR FLOW 66
- BOOSTER GAIN 68
- IDLE AND CRUISE QUALITY 70
- TRANSITION CIRCUIT MODIFICATIONS 71
- FLOAT BOWL MODIFICATIONS 71
- RAPID RECALIBRATION METHODS 72
- HOLLEY'S ELECTRONIC CALIBRATION 72
- WEBER JET PLATES 74
- CARB SHOP SPEED BLOCKS 74
- FINE TUNING WITH WEATHER CHANGES 75
- DENSITY TUNING 75
- WEATHER STATION/COMPUTERS 76
- BOOSTER PERFORMANCE 77
- FLOWING MORE AIR 78
- FOUR CORNER IDLE 79
- TRANSITION CIRCUIT FUEL METERING MODS 80
- OTHER CONSIDERATIONS 81

CHAPTER 8, PERFORMANCE MODS FOR Q-JETS 82
- AIR FLOW AND BOOSTERS 83
- MORE FLOW AND MORE SIGNAL 84
- IDLE SYSTEM MODS 85
- TRANSITION AND CRUISE CIRCUITS 86
- IDLE SYSTEM 87
- TRANSITION AND CRUISE CALIBRATION 87
- MAIN CIRCUIT 87
- ACCELERATOR PUMP CIRCUITS 89
- THE AIR VALVE 90

CHAPTER 9, OTHER PERFORMANCE CARBS 92
- CARTER AND ITS DESCENDANTS 92
- PREDATOR CARBS 92
- SU CARBS 93
- MODIFYING SU CARBS 94
- RAM PIPES 95
- LENGTH TUNING 96
- DELLORTOS, MIKUNIS AND WEBERS 97
- IR CARBURETION IN PRACTICE 99
- CALIBRATION TECHNIQUES 100
- IDLE SYSTEM 102
- ACCELERATOR PUMP CIRCUIT 102
- CHOKE SIZING 103

CHAPTER 10, MANIFOLD DESIGN BASICS 104
- POWER AND HEAT 104
- CR INCREASE 106
- ALUMINUM VERSUS IRON 106
- MANIFOLD DESIGN 107
- REDUCED CARB CAPACITY 108
- BUYING THE RIGHT MANIFOLD 109
- FUEL DISTRIBUTION 110
- WALL AND PORT FUEL FLOW 111
- VORTEX GENERATORS 111

CHAPTER 11, HIGH PERFORMANCE INTAKE SYSTEMS 112
- MANIFOLD CHANGE 112
- MORE CUBIC INCHES 114
- SMALL ENGINES 115
- IR SYSTEMS AND V8s 115
- MANIFOLD COMPARISONS 117

CHAPTER 12, MODIFYING AND BUILDING MANIFOLDS 118
- MODIFYING STOCK MANIFOLDS 119
- MODIFYING SINGLE PLANE MANIFOLDS 120
- PLENUM AND PORT ENTRANCE 121
- PORT EXTENSIONS 121
- MANIFOLD FLOOR AND PORT FORM 122
- PORT DESIGN 122
- TUNNEL RAM MANIFOLDS 123
- TUNNEL RAM PLENUM VOLUMES 123
- SHEET METAL MANIFOLDS 123
- PORT TAPER 123
- BUILDING A PERFORMANCE MANIFOLD 124
- CUSTOM MANIFOLDS 125

CHAPTER 13, SOURCES 128

How To Build HORSEPOWER: Chapter 1

Carburetors & Intake Manifolds
Performance Filtration

It's amazing how an item as common as an air filter can be so misunderstood and misused by so many people seeking performance. This wide misconception permeates from the top professional ranks at Super Speedways right down to the weekend dirt track racers, bracket racers and street rodders. To put things into perspective, let's make one thing clear. By applying the latest technology, the use of a regular type air filter on an engine will not reduce horsepower, as is often believed. The state of art has advanced in recent years to where the reverse is true.

The words you've just read were the introduction to a *Popular Hot Rodding* magazine article in 1979, and as of 1995, the situation has not significantly changed. Many professional racers are still making fundamental filtration system mistakes and likewise amateurs, who follow what the top dogs do. If you believe what you see, one would think air filtration in many fields of motor sport was of minor importance. Not so, and for what it's worth, drag racers are among the worst offenders. There are significant power gains to be had from a better understanding of a vehicle's filtration system. Even on a mundane, low-horsepower small-block V8, it is entirely possible to find 20 horsepower from simple, and usually inexpensive, changes to the filtration. If cost-effectiveness alone is considered, filtration modifications often represent the best horsepower-gain-per-dollar-spent ratio of almost any modification you can make.

SIGNIFICANT PRESSURES & FLOW

To determine where losses may occur in a filtration system, it helps to analyze the case and element as separate, but interrelated, entities. To do its job effectively, a filtration system must perform in three areas. First, it must clean the air of dust particles down to micron size. Second, it must do so with a minimal restriction, and third and most overlooked, it must minimize booster (auxiliary venturi) buffeting. To see how all these requirements can be met, let's start by investigating various filter elements and their effects on air flow.

FILTER FLOW

An air filter element's flow capability is dependent on both its size and the material from which it's made. A visual check of a filter assembly will not tell you if the combination of size and efficiency will satisfy the engine's requirements. If it's stock, chances are it won't. To check the overall effectiveness of both case and element only requires a simple water manometer as shown in Fig. 1-1. This can be made of a clear windshield washer hose secured to a wooden scale by means of clear tape or tacks. Provisions must be made to tap into the air filter case in two places. The first should be on the carb side of the element to measure the pressure drop just prior to the carburetor. The other tapping should be in the main body of the case outside the filter element. This will record the pressure drop caused by the case design.

The technique for testing is simple. Find a reasonably steep hill and power up at full throttle in, say, second gear from a relatively slow speed. Have an assistant check the manometer at certain key RPM points, say 2, 3, 4 and 5000 RPM. At each point, note the total inches of difference between the two legs of the U tube. When testing most stock cases, it's unlikely an 18-inch manometer will suffice past mid-range RPM due to the cases' restrictive designs. This situation

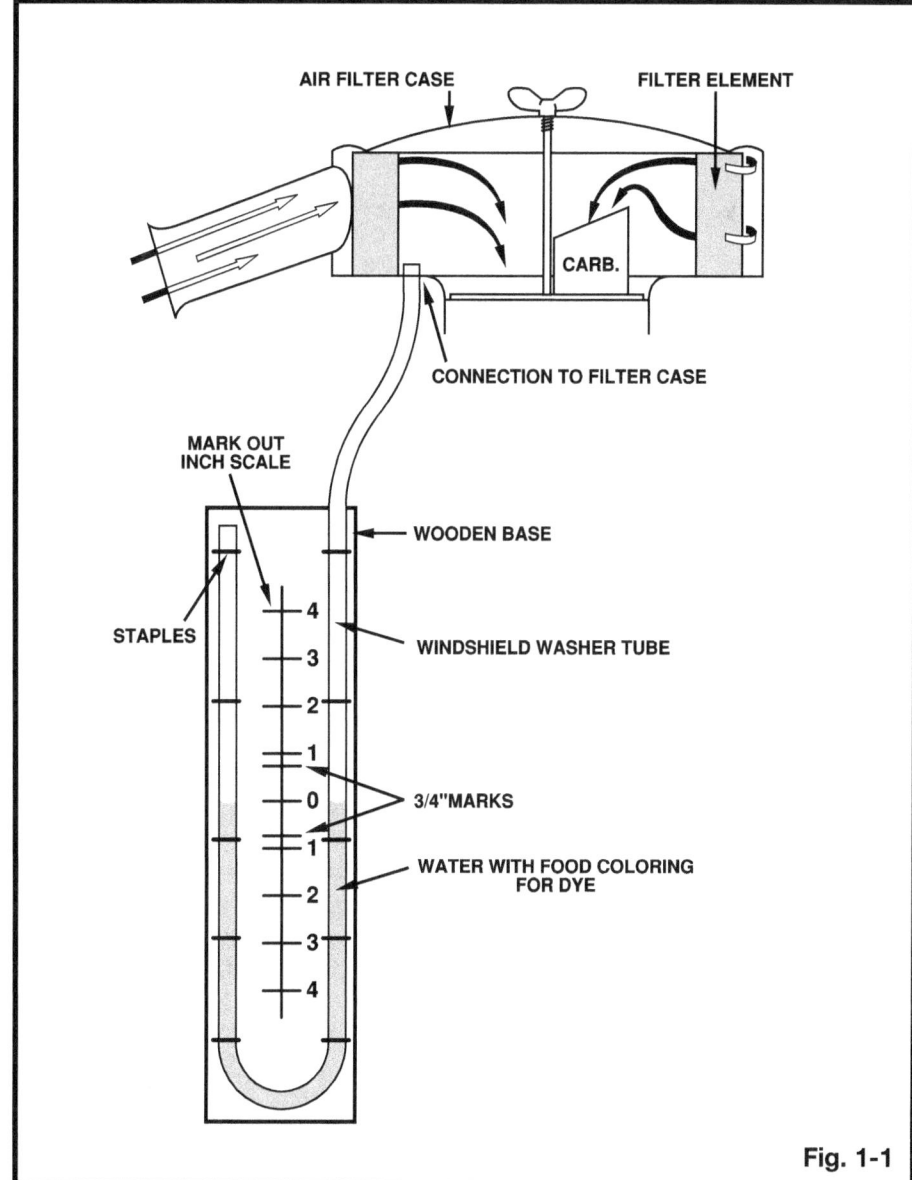

Fig. 1-1

An accurate assessment of the filter assembly flow capability in relation to the engine's requirement can be made using the simple manometer setup shown here. A connection inside the element shows overall effectiveness and a connection outside the element will test case performance. The ¾ inch marks above and below the zero represent the maximum for a competition engine. Although not shown here, this manometer needs to be about 18 inches high.

It takes very little time on a flow bench to establish just how restrictive most production air filters are. This is especially so for the bigger domestic V6 and V8 engines, where considerable horsepower can be lost to excessive flow restriction.

will be aggravated even with a small accumulation of dust on a stock paper element. To determine if this is a deficiency of element or case, tap into the case outside the element and re-test. As for the previous test, the manometer is likely to top out before the engine reaches its maximum RPM. However, case designs range from very good to very bad. For instance, the dual snorkel GM truck and high-performance car cases are very effective and show a minimal pressure drop. On the other hand, the small diameter snorkel on many of the heated intakes used on later emission vehicles are extremely restrictive. Not only do they impede the air flow in the first instance, but they also heat the air to levels that are unacceptably high temperature for a performance engine.

Though it appears to be a complete analysis of the system, a manometer check as described here doesn't check for a filter lid that is too close to the carburetor mouth. For a typical two- or four-barrel carb, the filter case lid should be a minimum of three inches from the air horn or mouth of the carb.

Manometer pressure measurements inevitably prompt the question as to how much of a pressure drop is acceptable. In an ideal world, the answer would be none. In practice, things are a little different and dyno testing has shown that with 1½-inches of water across the filter, any power loss that occurs is barely measurable on the dyno. To put things into perspective, such a pressure drop represents only a 0.36% reduction of air pressure at the carb. This means that on the dyno, a 500 horsepower motor would only experience a 1.8 horsepower drop in output over no filter, an amount usually too small to reliably measure even on the best dynos.

BOOSTER BUFFETING

Earlier it was stated that an air filter could be used without a penalty in output. Although in the example just given a 1.8 horsepower drop out of 500 represents a power reduction, it is one which, in practice, is usually offset by the positive aspects of having a filter installed. If the carb is situated in a high-speed, air stream a great deal of buffeting can occur at the carb entry. This upsets the operation of the carb's booster or auxiliary venturis. Their proper function is important to the delivery of the correct air/fuel ratio and fuel atomization. The installation of a filter, especially on a carb exposed to a high-speed air stream (Fig. 1-2), steadies the air flow into the carb, allowing it to function as if it were in still air. Track times have shown this to be very important on vehicles as wide ranging as Formula Fords to sedans to econo-dragsters.

How to Build Horsepower, Vol. 2

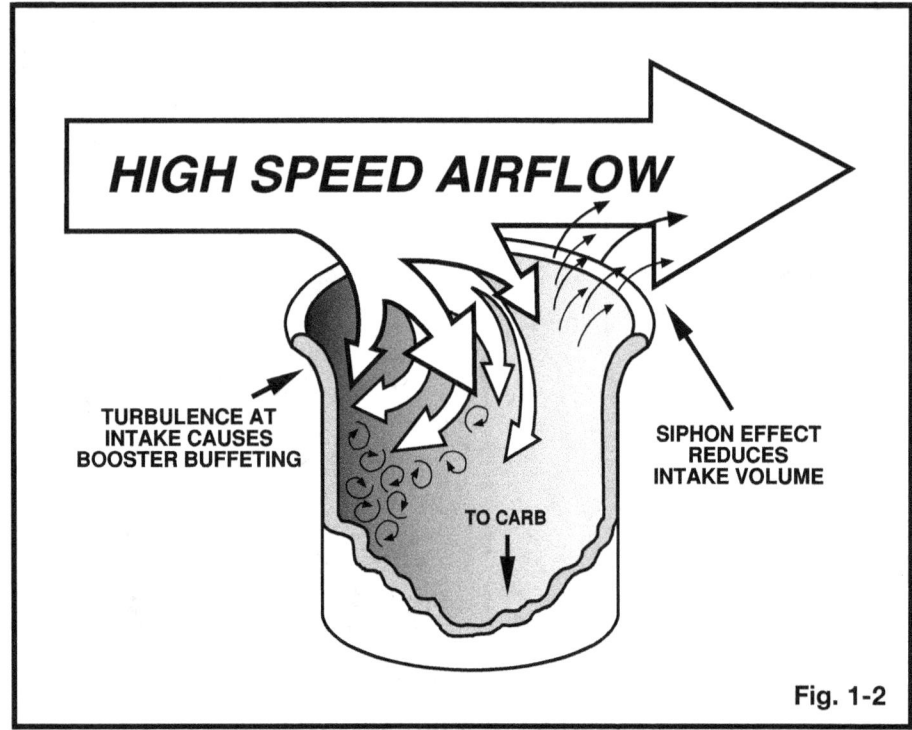

An exposed carburetor intake suffers from "booster buffeting" and a mild suction effect in much the same way as the jet in a spray gun. The combined effect of these two factors can significantly cut power at high speed.

IMPROVING EFFICIENCY

There is a substantial filtration and flow margin between the best and worst filter elements available. Unfortunately, the amount of bogus information in advertising claims, especially in some segments of the performance market, clouds the issue. Fortunately, as far as flow is concerned, it's easy to sort truth from fiction by conducting appropriate tests on a special high-capacity SuperFlow flow bench.

Sample elements of a common size from various manufacturers were obtained from parts stores. All were 12-inches in diameter x 3-½-inches high. When flow tested, they produced the results seen in Fig. 1-3. It doesn't take much to see that the K & N cotton wire type filter was head and shoulders above the rest and the Fram filter with its cotton barrier pre-filter proved less than practical for a high-output engine. Our recommendations, as of 1995, are Motorcraft for the best-buy in paper elements. If you want the best-flowing high filtration element then you have no other choice but to use a K & N filter element.

Basically, all the paper filters on the market are required to pass certain SAE or ISO dust tests. You may reasonably assume that all paper filters will perform the job of filtration in line with the minimums demanded by the auto manufacturers.

At this point, we have narrowed down what can be used for a performance filter to little more than the paper Motorcraft or K & N. We know the Motorcraft does actually filter, as it is capable of passing the relevant dust tests but how about the K & N? Experienced desert racers have proven that a K & N is one of the few, if not the only, filter element that will keep their engines in good shape for a 1000-mile desert race. Even the best paper filters fail to do this unless they are changed every 100 to 200 miles!

POWER PRODUCTION

As far as increasing power with increasing flow is concerned, a law of diminishing returns applies, and there is a limit beyond which the engine requires no further air filter capacity. However, because of the restrictive nature of stock cases and elements, we can, initially at least, expect relatively big gains in output. Typical gains are shown in Fig. 1-4. Baseline tests produced 210.5 horsepower at 4000 RPM and 310.3 ft-lbs. of torque at 2900 RPM. Still utilizing the stock case, the Motorcraft element was replaced with a K & N element. Some mixture leaning was seen when the change was made, but it was not sufficient to invalidate the test. The added filter air flow allowed the engine to produce 213.6 horsepower, an increase of 3.1 horsepower. A point worth making here concerns the mixture change. On many vehicles, factory fuel calibration has been made to suit the more restrictive characteristics of a paper element. The significantly greater flow capability of a K & N element can, in some instances, cause the mixture to lean out sufficiently for the engine to produce less horsepower. You must recalibrate the carb/injection to return the mixture to its original setting. When recalibrated as required, V8 engines often deliver as much as a 10 to 15 horsepower increase.

The air filter case used in the tests of Fig. 1-4 had a relatively small and restrictive snorkel tube. Flow was further restricted by a vacuum-actuated flapper valve which, at full-throttle bypassed the hot air supply from the exhaust manifold in favor of cooler air from the end of the

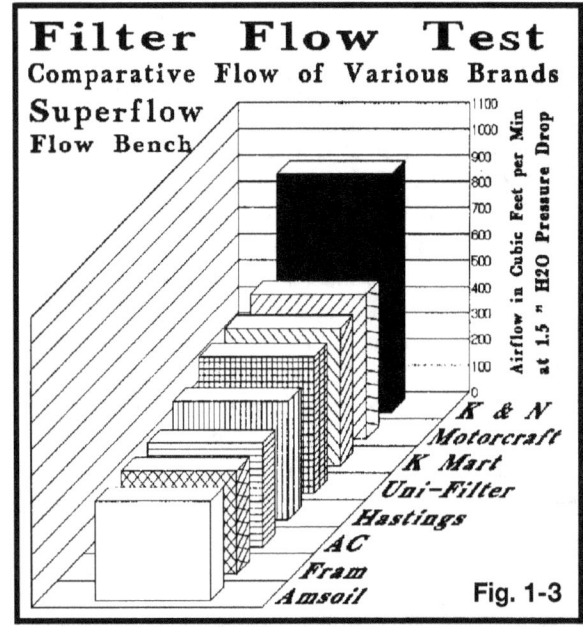

Shown here are the test results of a selection of new elements, all of the same size, in order of ascending effectiveness. The Amsoil and Unifilter are both foam-type elements, whereas all the others, with the exception of the K & N, are paper. From this test it is apparent that, as of 1995, K & N has no real competition.

Air Filter Comparison

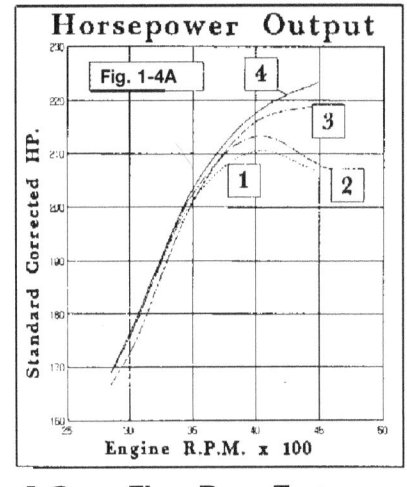
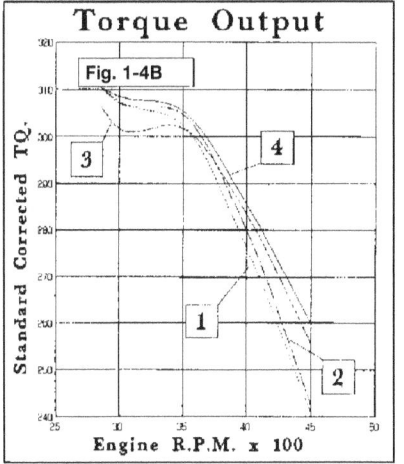

A SuperFlow Dyno Test

Fig. 1-4

Curve #1 shows the output from a 305 test engine with a stock case and a Motorcraft element. Curve #2 was produced by replacing the Motorcraft element with a stock replacement K & N element. Curve #3 was produced by installing a K & N element ½ inch taller than stock. When the stock case was replaced by a K & N 360-degree case and element, it resulted in a peak gain of 13 horsepower as shown by curve #4.

snorkel. Not only was the snorkel restrictive, but the lid of the case was too close to the mouth of the carburetor, thus further restricting flow. Installing a ½-inch taller element not only moved the lid farther from the mouth of the carburetor, but also produced a large annular slot around the edge of the filter case, providing the needed additional flow area to counter the restrictive snorkel. Test #3 Fig.1-4 shows the results. Peak power climbed by almost 9 horsepower, but torque dropped, in spite of the fact that the mixture was re-set to suit. The reason for this is that the snorkel of the stock case provides a degree of inertial ramming. Around 2500 to 3000 RPM, the snorkel is able to deliver the volume of air the engine needs. At this RPM, the air velocity in the snorkel is sufficient to cause a slight ramming to the carburetor. Raising the filter lid increased top end flow at the expense of low- and mid-range inertial ramming.

For test #4 the stock air filter was completely removed and replaced by a 360-degree K & N high-performance filter and case assembly. The high flow capability of this assembly produced no measurable intake restriction. As a result, the engine's peak power rose to 223.5 horsepower, 13 horsepower more than that achieved with the stock case and element.

POWER & TEMPERATURE

The test 305 just dealt with was hardly high-performance, yet induction system mods showed worthwhile results. These improvements were achieved solely by increased engine air flow. But air flow is only half the picture, the other half is temperature. Many emission-type cars have filter assemblies designed to hold intake temperature at a constant level. Changes in air temperature cause mixture fluctuations on carbureted engines. This is because a carburetor meters fuel by virtue of the volume of air passing through it. In other words, it's a volume-sensitive device. Ideally, we need a carburetor that is mass sensitive. Three hundred cubic feet of hot air through a carburetor draws just about the same amount of fuel as 300 cubic feet of cold air. The point is that cold air, being denser, contains far more oxygen and needs proportionally more fuel. It isn't practical to cool engine air to a constant level to eliminate density variations, but it is practical to heat it to a level higher than normally seen. The heated air means less power, but it allows more precise carburetor calibrations to meet emission requirements. To show how much cool air can be worth, consider the test results of a small block Chevy equipped 1980 Firebird with a "hood shaker" type air box. The hood shaker on this year of Firebird is totally cosmetic, lacking the air door of earlier models. On this particular installation, the factory employed a relatively large air filter so restriction from the element was fairly minimal. The installed output for this engine was 145 horsepower. Installing a K & N filter produced a 5 horsepower gain at the rear wheels, but opening up the dummy hood scoop for cool air produced an additional 14 horsepower along with a 9% increase in torque all through the rev range. The torque increase is a typical result of cooling the air. The engine reacts exactly as if it had more cubic inches and therefore produces more torque. Re-working the filtration system on this Firebird took about an hour and cost only the price of a K & N filter, yet it delivered close to 20 horsepower and 20 ft.-lbs.

Many performance cars have a cold air induction system. Before making any changes to such a system you should establish the amount of restriction occurring in the air filter case. Often the cold air pick-up steps up power by more than its restriction drops it. This means that before spending money on an air filter that draws on hot, under-hood air, try modifying the existing cold air pick-up for greater flow. Many late model cold air pick-ups equipped with a suitably sized K & N filter will deliver more installed horsepower than a 360-degree aftermarket filter and no cold air pick-up.

HIGH-OUTPUT FILTRATION

So much for stock or near-stock motors and the effect elements can have on them, let's now turn our attention to some higher output engines and see how critical the element is in such a situation. Fig.1-5 is representative of a well tuned, high out-

These 3-twos look good, but one cloud of dust and the engine's rings are history. This setup can still look just as eye catching if the right filter case is used.

How to Build Horsepower, Vol. 2

Race engines are expensive and always lose power when they ingest dirt. From this, it seems totally logical to equip an expensive, powerful race engine with an effective filter.

put street motor. This hydraulic-cammed, single four barrel 350 V8 engine was good for over 430 horsepower. In sizing the filter, it was assumed that anyone with enough performance knowledge to achieve this level of power output is unlikely to consider a totally inadequate air filter. A sensibly sized air filter, typical of those chosen by a capable street rodder was used to baseline the tests so as not to distort the results. A number of filter elements were run on the engine, but to avoid clouding the issue, the results from only three elements are shown, these being the lowest, middle and top flowing contenders. The element size chosen was 11.5 inches in diameter x 3.5 inches high. As can be seen from the graph, the K & N filter outpowered it's opposition consistently by 4 to 6 horsepower, in spite of the fact we're on the down side of a diminishing return curve of the relatively large size of filter employed for the test.

FILTER CLOGGING

So far all of the testing relating to the filters has dealt with brand-new, out-of-the-box items. In reality, filter performance starts to decay the moment you drive out of the workshop because dust and dirt plugs them up. The way filters react to dirt loading depends mostly on their structure. It is easy to fall into the trap of thinking that dirt is dirt and will plug all filters in the same fashion, thus reducing them all to a single common denominator. This proves to be a total fallacy. Fig.1-6 shows flow ratings of various filters, both new and used. The first point to note is that in a dusty climate, even the best paper filters can be reduced in performance to that of the worst in as little as 5000 miles. This assumes typical atmospheric conditions. One passage through a dust storm can cause a paper filter to accumulate enough dust to warrant it's replacement. The K & N filter shows a much lower clog rate than the other elements tested. One would think that if an element was heavily loaded, say $\frac{1}{8}$ inch or more, the dirt itself would become the major flow restriction. If such was the case, a layer of dirt should reduce all elements to a common, low flow level. The flow bench shows this is not the case, and the reason why lies in the contrasting filtration mechanism employed by the K & N element as opposed to a regular paper element.

A typical paper element filters air principally by two means. Primary filtration is mechanical by virtue of the fact that paper has microscopic holes in it. This allows nothing larger than the size of the holes to pass through the element. Secondary filtration is by virtue of the slight tackiness of the paper. The problem with this type of filtration is that it works very much like the plug hole in the bathtub. Pull the plug out and everything in the tub sooner or later makes a dive for the plug hole. When an object larger than the hole arrives, it simply plugs it up and flow ceases. In a like manner, a plugged hole in a paper element is now removed from the air supply system. The K & N appears to work on a substantially different principle. When our tests revealed a K & N packed with $\frac{3}{16}$ inch of dust still flowed like a new Motorcraft paper element it raised a serious question. How could this be so? A first guess was that a K & N may be working on an electro-static charge principle. Namely, that a charge building up on the wire and cotton barrier attracts dust to the barrier rather than to the holes. Holding a K & N element up to the light reveals holes about 1,000 times larger than the particles size arrested. Tests to establish the existence of a suitably high electro-static charge were a great disappointment. During operation our tests showed less than two volts across the element rather than the several thousand anticipated. Another theory had to be used to explain the K & N filtration mechanism.

The best to-date, though not proven, is that the fine strands of oil-soaked cotton vibrate due to the pulsing flow generated by the engine. This vibration sweeps the air and the minute particles are picked up by the oil-laden strands and subsequently held in place. This means the dust particles accumulate not in the holes but on the matrix of the element itself so dust particles do not directly clog the passage of air through the filter. It sounds like a good theory and strong supporting evidence comes from the results of SAE/ISO dust tests. During such tests a K & N element rarely shows more than about 98% dust filtration efficiency. However, in use on an engine under desert conditions it is clearly far superior to a paper element filter, which may have shown 99% efficiency on such a test. Official industry dust tests are conducted under steady flow conditions rather than the pulsing flow seen in an engine. This leads us to believe there is reduced fiber sweeping activity by the K & N element, hence the reduced filtering efficiency shown by steady-state flow tests.

SECOND OPINION

Better than 98% of the test results shown in our *How to Build Horsepower* publications contain our own independent tests. Although we are very sure of the validity of our filter tests, it is nice to have further independent supporting evidence as to their accuracy. Just such a test

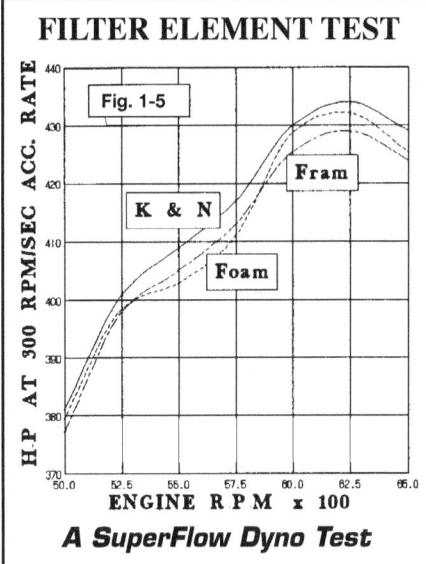

As can be seen from these test results, the filter element you choose for your high-performance engine can significantly affect the final power output.

was published in England by *Performance Tuning* magazine. The author, Vish Seshadri, presented some very thorough comparative tests of three brands of foam filters, one paper and one K & N. Vish Seshadri is in the business of selling automotive products through his company distribution network. He was approached by a manufacturer that wanted him to sell its filter in the U.K. To ascertain the quality of the product, he took a sample along with it's principle competitors for testing at the Motor Industry's Research Association. The results of these tests are shown on the next page.

PERFORMANCE AND COST

We have looked at the negative aspects of paper elements, so now is an appropriate time to put K & Ns under the magnifying glass. As far as strikes against K & N are concerned, not many exist. However, one you will come across early on is initial cost. It is far from the cheapest filter but there again, anything of sufficient quality for Rolls Royce's industrial division or a world championship-winning Formula I Car is unlikely to be produced down to a price. However, though initial cost may be high overall, economics still favor the K & N. A major advantage of a K & N is that it is a permanent filter rather than a throw away item. Once acquired, it will last the life of a drag, street or road race driven car and then some. Not only will this save you the cost of further filter purchases, but it will also give longer ring and valve seat life for more power. Mileage is also increased because a K & N element prevents the problem of fuel enrichment caused by filter clogging. For an off-road car, the balance between the cost of a new engine must be weighed against the price of a new filter for each race. With as much dirt as the filter has to arrest, the possibility of getting dirt on the inside of the filter during cleaning totally justifies installing a brand new K & N.

For oval track dirt cars some of the clay track compositions can play havoc with any and all filters. Fine, wet clay will seal any filter, including a K & N, sometimes in as little as one event. Often the fact that the filter is loaded with fine clay is difficult to see, so under such circumstances certain steps need to be taken to preserve both the longevity and power of your expensive race engine. For a solution, try these moves. First, use a dispos-

The cosmetics of these ram pipes should be considered irrelevant. They are still ...

able K & N foam cover over the element. With two of these, you can wash and rotate as required between races. Second, shield the element behind a deflector so nothing can directly impinge on it. Incidentally, the aforementioned are good moves for off-road vehicles as well. Lastly, replace the element if any doubt exists as to whether it's becoming clay sealed.

With all this information on air filters, you are now in the position to make a wise selection. To sum up, it is safe to say you have two choices: K & N or others. As of 1995 at least, your second choice will always be inferior, period.

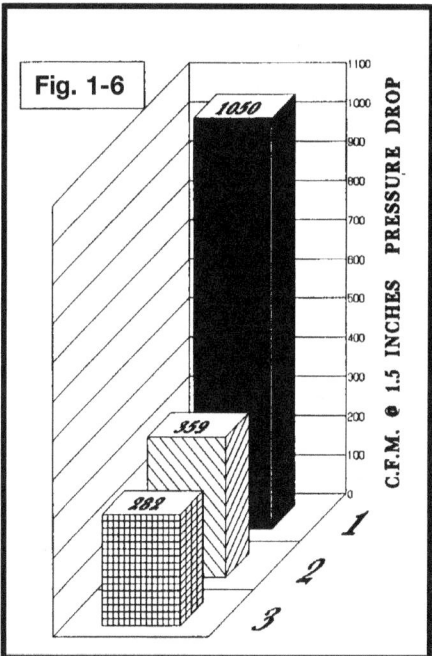

The K & N element exhibits a very low clog rate. #1 is the flow of a new K & N. #2 is the same part # after 80,000 miles without any servicing. Approximately 25% of this mileage was on unmade forestry roads. After this extended use, the K & N still flowed the same as a new Motorcraft filter and 25% better than a new Fram filter.

... performing as they should inside these filter cases. If these don't have quite the performance image you are looking for, then you can build your own case as shown below.

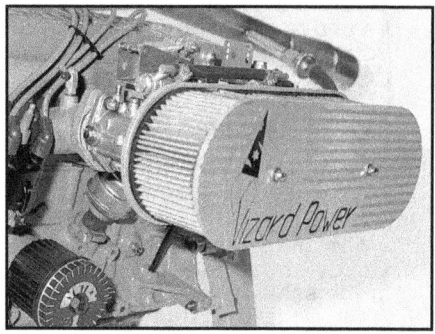

Try making your own filter case as the author did here. This allowed an even bigger filter to be accommodated thus reducing the effect of any filter clogging that might take place during a long rally or off-road event.

HORSEPOWER Quick Facts & References

ISO 5011 FILTER TESTS

Vish Seshadri is in the synthetic lubricants business in England. His company imports and supplies some top race teams as well as servicing industrial clients. All lubricants are intended to eliminate wear, but no matter how good they are, they will always turn to some form of grinding paste if mixed with grit. The immediate effect of this will be to accelerate wear on rings, bores and valve seats with an increased rate of bearing wear occurring shortly thereafter. Selling expensive, functional high-tech lubricants that were supposed to show significant wear reductions and didn't, prompted a serious investigation. This was the situation Vish Seshadri was in. He was dissatisfied with the filtration performance and the resulting higher than expected wear rates on his clients' engines. These ranged from heavy industrial units to race engines. Though air filter recommendations were made, they were not always acted upon. This prompted the testing that resulted in a feature in the English magazine, *Performance Tuning*. Flow bench tests on a SuperFlow 300 established the flow ratings while dust tests were done at the Motor Industries Research Association (M.I.R.A.) at Lindley near Coventry. This huge plant is run at the expense of member motor companies, which essentially means it's funded by most of the big European motor giants. The test procedures adopted were basically to ISO 5011, which is based on the SAE J726 procedure and commonly accepted throughout the motor industry.

The types of elements tested were a regular paper, several foam and the cotton/wire K & N type element. The foam elements were produced by Pipercross and I.T.G., which are both British companies. The U. S. was represented by Unifilter, which asked, after the test results were in, to be left out of the article. We can only surmise as to how they fared! However, in spite of threatened lawsuits, the rest of the feature went ahead more or less as planned.

Now for the flow test results.

Test #1

Filter Brand		External Dimensions (mm) (Height x Length x Width)	Flow Rate (CFM @ 1.5 in. H_2O)
K & N Challenger		130 x 190 x 158	440
Pipercross 300		130 x 190 x 150	378 (dry)
I.T.G. Megaflow		130 x 190 x 150	351 (dry)
K & N Challenger		65 x 190 x 157	345
Pipercross KK300		65 x 190 x 150	274 (dry)
As above but oiled for greater dust retention		65 x 190 x 150	233
I.T.G. Megaflow		72 x 190 x 150	236 (dry)
As above but oiled for greater dust retention		72 x 190 x 150	224
Typical service station sourced paper element			228
K & N oval		82 x 179 x 114	323
Pipercross PL200		82 x 190 x 150	225 (dry)
K & N	Ford XR2i flat panel element		366
Motorcraft	Ford XR3I flat panel element		311
Pipercross PP38	Ford XR3I flat panel element		228 (oiled)

As can be seen from these tests, even though there was a little variation in sizes, the K & N dominated in terms of air flow. The results of the dust tests are equally interesting, as can be seen from the following results.

Test #2

Filter Brand	External Dimensions (mm)	Efficiency %
K & N Challenger	65 x 190 x 157	97.5
Pipercross KK300	65 x 190 x 150	50.8
As above but oiled for greater dust retention	65 x 190 x 150	93.9
Paper sample #1	65 x 175 dia.	98.6
Paper sample #2	65 x 175 dia.	98.2
I.T.G. Megaflow	72 x 190 x 150	25.9
As above but oiled for greater dust retention	72 x 190 x 150	70.7
K & N oval	82 x 179 x 114	97.6
Pipercross PL200	82 x 190 x 150	44.5

The above figures show that a typical motor manufacturer approved paper element to be the best on steady-state flow dust test. Some brands of paper elements will actually make it to 99%, but at the other end of the scale, plenty of cheap paper elements barely make the low nineties. As the main text explains, a steady-state dust test for comparative purposes does put the K & N element at a disadvantage because its mode of operation requires a pulsating flow. In practice, under the arduous conditions of off-road racing, it proves far better than even the best paper elements. As for the foam filters, these proved totally inadequate when dry and barely passable when oiled. When oiled, they don't flow particularly well.

ELEMENT SIZING FOR A HIGH-PERFORMANCE ENGINE

When maximum horsepower is the objective, the determination of the filter element's dimensions is of significant importance. Two factors dictate an air filter units air flow, these being the shape and area. When dealing with a performance element such as K & N, we can make use of the substantial R & D the company has done toward determining the right element for a given application. This allows us to select, first time around, an element of sufficient area for both the flow and dirt holding capacity based solely on the element's external dimensions.

SHAPE

Flow bench tests have shown that with typical two- and four-barrel automotive carburetors, air filters flow more when the diameter is relatively large by comparison with their height. That means an air filter 8 inches in diameter x 2-½ inches high will generally flow more air than an air filter that is 5 inches in diameter x 4 inches high, though both have the same area. Although there will be exceptions, the basic rule of thumb is that, space permitting, the diameter of an element should be four to five times the height. When we are dealing with typical two- and four-barrel carbs, the lid of the filter should never be closer than three inches to the carb mouth or choke horn.

On single throat carburetors or injector stacks where one air filter per throat is used, a taller element can often be used to an advantage. The element diameter in relation to the carburetor bore is important and should typically be at least three times as big. When space constraints cause compromises, an element of adequate area may be greater in length than diameter.

SIZING

Once the filter shape has been decided the size of the filter must be calculated. This is the most important aspect of a high-performance filtration system. A filter that is too small will restrict flow to the engine with the consequent loss of power. No more than 1½ inches of water pressure drop across the air filter element at full throttle, maximum power RPM, is acceptable. This represents an efficiency of 99.63%. Two factors dictate the filter size required: the displacement of the engine and the RPM it turns to develop peak horsepower. If we assume the basic 1½ inches of water pressure drop is maximum, then a typical K & N air filter will flow 6.03 cubic feet of air per minute per square inch of effective area. By comparison, even the best paper elements make only 4.95 CFM per square inch and dry synthetic foam is 4.38, a figure that is substantially reduced by the necessary oiling.

With units in inches, the effective area of a filter in the context we are dealing with here is equal to:
Diameter x 3.14 x (height - 0.75)

The reason for subtracting the 0.75 is due to "edge effects" Close to the edges very little air flows, so this part of the filter is lost for use.

To determine minimum filter area 'A' for typical street usage, apply the following formula:

$$A = \frac{CID \times RPM}{25{,}500}$$

Once the area has been determined, it becomes a simple procedure to search through a K & N catalog and, using the dimensions given, find an appropriate element.

An element selected this way would be fine for street use, but for off-road, the element should be one and one half to two times the area to compensate for heavy dirt loading. For long distance off-road racing, large remote mounted air filters are the most desirable set-up. For race vehicles on a hard track, the element needs to be sized about 50% larger than the formula just given. Inevitably the formula will give an odd size for an answer, so select the nearest size larger.

Another way to determine the area of the K & N filter your engine requires is by the horsepower/area method. If the horsepower of the engine is known, then it can be assumed that, for the street, a K & N will support 7 horsepower per square inch of installed area. Where power is critical, but the need to hold large volumes of dust is not, as in the case of road or drag racing, work with 4 to 4½ horsepower per square inch. Lastly, when filter loading is a potential problem, such as off-road or dirt track racing, work on 3 to a maximum of 4 horsepower per square inch. Having set out all these parameters, one rule overrides all. If space exists for a larger element than predicted, use it. When it comes to filters, bigger is always better!

How To Build HORSEPOWER: Chapter 2

Carburetors & Intake Manifolds
Cases, Cool Air & Ramming

After selecting an effective element, the next step toward achieving an effective filtration system is full utilization of the element by marrying it to a high flow case design. Failure here will limit the quantity of clean air delivered to the engine. The previous chapter explained why a performance filtration system should deliver cold air to the engine. If, for some reason, this proves impractical the next best option is a good free-flowing installation such as a 360-degree-type shown nearby. Because of the various types of carburetors and engines involved, numerous variations are possible. For aerodynamic reasons, many cars have low hood clearance and this can limit the height of the filter assembly. To compensate for this on a typical V8 powered car, what is commonly known as a drop down case can be used. This allows a taller element to be installed without raising the overall height.

Because of the wide variety of cases available, it pays to spend time at your local speed shop to determine which is likely to be the easiest to install. Whichever case you chose, remember it must house an element of sufficient area for the engine's airflow requirement. Also, the lid must not be positioned too near the mouth of the carburetor. About three inches should be considered a minimum for a typical four barrel carb or one and a half times the throttle bore for most other carbs.

Any device that seeks to improve the airflow into a Holley carburetor must eliminate the sharp edges the air must otherwise negotiate. The K & N Stub Stack does just that, and as a result, is worth some 30 CFM on a stock 850.

12 *How to Build Horsepower, Vol. 2*

SHORT STACKS

Having effectively conducted air to the mouth of the carburetor, we find, in most two- and four-barrel installations, it is forced to make an abrupt turn into it. For Quadrajet, Carter, or for that matter, a spread bore Holley, there isn't much we can do short of physically reshaping the carburetor mouth. On the other hand, if your engine is equipped with one of the square bore Holleys or an Edelbrock carb, then a practical solution to aid air entry into the carb is to use a K & N Stub Stack. This concept mimics the ram stacks found on exotic European carbs such as Webers and Dellortos. Our tests show installing a Stub Stack on a Holley to be worth between 20 to 30 CFM of additional flow. What this is worth in terms of horsepower depends on how short the carburetor was on flow in the first place. For instance, an 850-equipped 300-inch motor probably has all the carburetion it can use. Increasing that to 890 CFM with a Stub Stack is unlikely to show a significant power increase. Conversely, even a mild 400 inch with a 650 carb is likely to be under carbureted. Adding a Stub Stack will boost an otherwise stock 650 to about 670, which can easily return a 15 horsepower increase. In some instances, the full increase won't be realized fully without some carb re-jetting if it was previously optimal. Even if the carb was optimally jetted, in instances the additional airflow caused by the Stub Stack also produces a proportional increase in fuel flow, thus avoiding a lean out condition. However, to be sure of the mixture ratio after the installation of a Stub Stack, each situation should be dealt with on its own merits.

For street use, a Stub Stack on a Holley allows the selection of a carburetor biased toward the small side for good low-end output and economy, while giving the top-end power benefits of a larger carburetor. For a competition engine where budget restraints prevent the purchase of an all out race carb, the use of a Stub Stack can really pay off. Its use allows the engine builder to select a carburetor favoring mid-range power while the Stub Stack provides the added airflow needed for good top-end output. Fig.2-1 shows the results of some tests conducted on a record setting circle track engine built by Darryl Buehl of Magnum Aircraft Engines in Ontario, California. In this test, which was run on our dyno, a Stub Stack proved to be worth about 22 horsepower. Such a gain was not unexpected bearing in mind a race engine on a single four barrel is almost always starved of air. For an average 300 horsepower V8, benefits from a Stub Stack typically run to the tune of 5 to 7 horsepower.

TALL STACKS

The Stub Stack is so named because of its short, low profile. This being the case, those tall stacks often seen on boats, street rods and race cars can justifiably be termed Super Stacks, although, as we shall see, rather more due to their height than function. Judging by the number sold and installed, most people are working under the assumption that these Super Stacks increase power. Unfortunately, this is rarely the case. If looks count for anything, then fine, but they deliver negligible additional air to the engine. Looking into an installed Super Stack reveals the same major flow obstructions exist. They contributed nothing to streamlining the

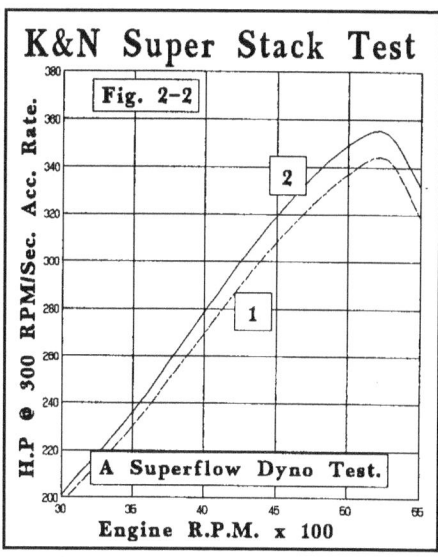

Curve #1 is the output produced by a 650 Holley equipped with an unmodified Super Stack. This curve was virtually the same as tests done without the Super Stack thus showing its contribution to the engine's output was negligible. By adapting a Stub Stack into the Super Stack, curve #2 was produced. Essentially an increase of some 10 ft/lbs throughout the rev range was seen.

These tall Super Stacks look impressive but do not increase airflow without...

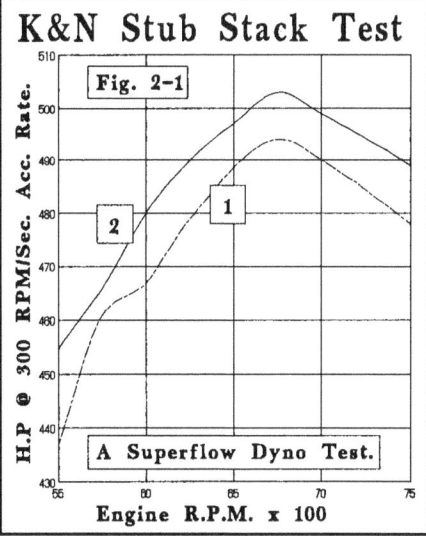

Here are the results of a 650 Holley run with (2) and without (1) a Stub Stack on a 9:1 circle track motor. Power increases throughout the working RPM band ranged from 10 to 14 HP. This result is a conservative one. We know of several tests at reputable dyno shops that have seen increases as high as 22 HP.

... the help of a Stub Stack such as the one seen here. This has been turned on the OD to fit.

How to Build Horsepower, Vol. 2

carb entry. However, there still remains several justifiable reasons for using them. A good one that springs to mind concerns boat engines. Keeping the engine air intake as far away from the water as possible is a good way to cut the chances of hydraulicing the motor. To make it functional in terms of airflow, a Stub Stack needs to be turned down and installed into the Super Stack as shown on page 15.

All the effort to get the Super Stack working could be undone if you failed to read and act upon the information in the previous chapter. Many Super Stacks are sold with small and totally inadequate filters elements. Worse yet, some come equipped with a perforated sheet steel or wire grid top. Neither type of top has any useful filtering capability, but these tops do cause a substantial airflow reduction, which makes them a totally useless item for any performance engine. We've already discussed at some length why an inadequate filter should not be used, so unless you're bent on invalidating all efforts directed toward finding more horsepower, you should avoid installing any of the aforementioned on the end of a Super Stack. At the risk of being repetitive this leaves only one functional option, an adequately sized K & N. Fig.2-2, shows easily achievable power gains by utilizing a properly prepped Super Stack on a typical high-output street motor. Although these gains are worthwhile, there is one significant factor that does not show up on the dyno test. Because of a Super Stack's height, it will stick through the hood and pick up cool air, so it can be expected to deliver more power than an under-the-hood 360-degree case. This means the potential in use gains for a Super Stack are greater than indicated by our dyno tests. This leaves only the problem of pushing a relatively unstreamlined object of some 1½ square feet through the air, thereby increasing drag. These factors need to be weighed with the intended purpose of the vehicle. For a boat or rear-engined drag car such as an econo-rail, a Super Stack represents a minimal increase in drag and a simple way of supplying the engine with cool, filtered air.

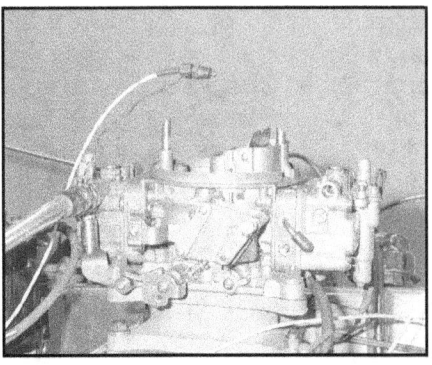

Here is a carb without a Stub Stack. Note the temperature sensor for horsepower correction purposes. Two points to note on this subject. The first is that the sensor is placed well away from the error producing effect of exhaust heat. Second, it is a rapid response type so it does not store heat and give false readings by over-correcting the initial power figures. Making the change from no flow aiding devices, as seen here to...

... this setup here produced, on this street motor, an 8 horsepower increase. This is typical for street engines, but on race engines we have seen, on occasions, up to 22 horsepower.

STAYING COOL UNDER PRESSURE

The volume of air drawn into an engine depends largely on its capacity. But, as we have already seen, an engine's potential to produce power depends upon the mass of the air it inhales, and there's more to that than just cubes! In our efforts to get more power from an engine, we bore and stroke, install more carburetion, flow the heads and so on. These mods may help the engine breathe more deeply but how often do we see cars built to reap the benefits of optimizing air intake pressure and temperature. They are a minority at the race track and almost nonexistent on the street. But by picking up the coldest air possible and then ramming it into the induction system, we can significantly improve

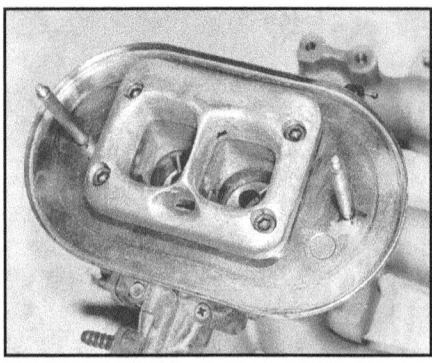

In classes where induction is limited to a two-barrel carb, some form of Stub Stack is essential for maximum output. The entry device shown here was worth 5 horsepower on one of our 2 liter Pinto circle track engines.

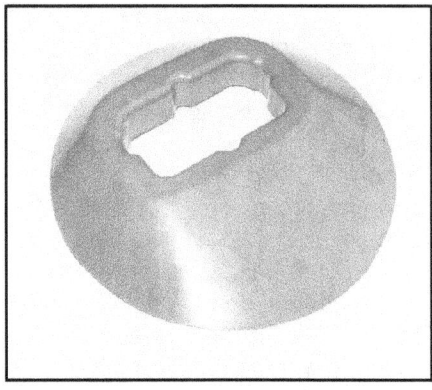

For race engines using the two-barrel Holley, there are options other than the K & N two-barrel Stub Stack. Shown here is the Brzezinski Racing Products Carb Hat. Like all the Brzezinski products we have dyno tested this item proves to be very functional.

the charge weight drawn into the engine's cylinders. We touched on the subject of cold air in the last chapter and saw how effective it could be. Now let us investigate in greater detail the combined effects of ram and cold air.

PRESSURE POTENTIAL

Putting a hand out of a car window while traveling at even a moderate speed reveals a significant force acting upon it. In engineering terms, the pressure brought about by bringing a stream of air to a dead stop is known as the static pressure head. It is this phenomena that we can use to ram an induction system.

Two factors affect the ram air pressure—air speed and air density. The pressure changes in proportion to the air density, but changes as the square of the speed. If, when using ram induction, the speed of the car is doubled, the ram pressure generated increases by a factor of four. That's the good news. The bad news is that it takes a lot of speed to get a worthwhile degree of ramming. The formula in Fig. 2-3 can be used to calculate the ram pressure generated under ideal conditions by the car's speed. Calculating the pressure produced

---

Ram Pressure PSI = $\dfrac{Ad \times V^2}{4287}$

Where Ad = atmospheric density

At sea level this is 0.076 lbs./cu. ft.

V = Speed in MPH

This formula gives the maximum ram pressure that can be generated by forward motion. If the race track is at any significant altitude or the air temperature is high, the ramming pressure will drop in direct proportion to the drop in air density.

by a car moving at 100 MPH shows that under ideal circumstances the ram effect amounts to 0.177 PSI. That is a 1.22% increase over normal atmospheric pressure. As speeds increase, the picture begins to look better. For instance, at 150 MPH the ramming pressure could reach 0.4 PSI and at 200 MPH some 0.7 PSI could be realized.

Now these may not seem earth shattering increases, but on a Pro Stock drag racer this equates to some 60 bhp on the fast end of the drag strip! A worthwhile gain, you'll agree, but unless the pitfalls are appreciated, ram induction can easily produce negative results. A good example of a fully functional ram air system was built by John Lingenfelter and used on his econo-rail. The ram air unit consisted of an air box containing a tall 10-inch diameter K & N filter element. This set-up netted an ET improvement of 4/100 second along with an increase of 1½ miles an hour. This translates to about a 20 horsepower increase in engine output over a simple unrammed cold air system.

THE DOWNSIDE

The biggest problems associated with ram induction occur when carbs, rather than fuel injectors, are used. First, its important to understand that a carburetor is nothing more than a self-powered, low pressure fuel injection system. To put the "low" into perspective, the fuel metering pressures involved often amount to no more than 1 PSI.

To make maximum power, the fuel/air ratio must operate within tolerances of about 6%. If the mixture ratio is forced outside this narrow envelope, power losses can outweigh any possible gains from ram induction.

In most cases, the fuel mixture difficulties occur at the carb's auxiliary venturi, or as it is more appropriately know in the states, the booster venturi.

The purpose of this venturi is to amplify the pressure drop that is produced across the main venturi. This produces a stronger draw on the fuel being pulled into the engine from the main jet well. However, the system is very susceptible to outside influences. A carb intake that is directly exposed to moving air experiences considerable booster buffeting. This buffeting can, at the speeds of a typical race car, cause erratic pressure changes equal to as much as 30 to 40% of those that would normally be experienced by the booster when it is running in still air. This buffeting causes substantial mixture metering errors, which lead to a measurable loss of power. The cure for the unwanted effects of buffeting is to install a high-flow air filter element into the system.

With a forward facing ram air system, some thought must be given to wet weather driving. If a paper filter element is used, the airflow will drop dramatically when the element gets wet. The scenario from here is that the element collapses and the engine attempts to devour it! The fix is to use a K & N-type element, as these have proved capable of withstanding a heavy water splash on race boats with minimal loss of flow.

PRESSURE BALANCE

Booster buffeting is not the only problem we must contend with. If ram induction increases the pressure at the mouth of the carb, but doesn't produce a corresponding pressure rise in the float bowl, the mixture will become lean because the extra air will not draw a sufficient amount of extra fuel. The way around this problem is to connect the air space above the fuel in a float bowl to the air box being ram-fed (Fig. 2-4). On DCOE-type carbs, there are built-in holes beside the bell mouths connected to the float bowls, which achieve this provided they are covered by the air box plenum chamber. If you go this route with this type of carb, be sure to seal the jet cover lid on the top of the carb.

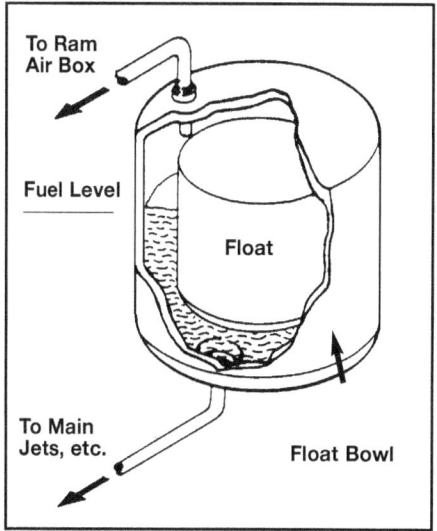

Fig. 2-4 Here is the principle of maintaining the float bowl to booster pressure differential to compensate for any forward ramming pressure generated. Without this compensation, the mixture will lean out as speeds increase.

COOL POWER

As air temperature drops, its density increases. The rate of change is about a 1% increase in density for every 6°F of temperature reduction.

The air entering a production engine's induction system can easily reach 180°F. But by drawing cold air from an outside source, the air temperature at the carb mouth can drop by as much as 75° to 80° F.

Testing the effect that a filter case and element has on volumetric efficiency involves housing the entire assembly within this case, affectionately know in our shop as the air filter coffin. Once the lid...

...is on, all the air must pass through the airflow measuring turbine thus measuring the airflow reduction caused by the case and filter. The unit tested here with the modified Stub Stack showed an increase in airflow and volumetric efficiency. More power with clean air — <u>drag racers please note!</u>

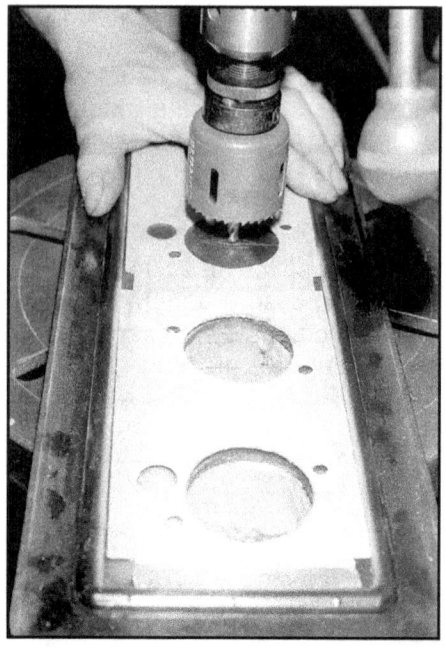

Many race and performance car induction systems are very much one offs. To aid the fit of an air filter, Advanced Performance Technology (APT) of Riverside, California produces a number of filter and case kits that can be customized to fit many foreign and domestic compact cars and some V8 applications. The first step is to cut the holes for the carb barrels in the back plate.

This represents an increase in air density of a little over 12%. The affect this will have on power will be much the same as 1.77 PSI of supercharge pressure, and offers the chance of a 12% increase in torque and power. <u>Best results are obtained if all precautions are taken to preserve the reduced temperature all the way into the cylinders</u>, and the increased air density is fully exploited by maintaining the correct fuel/air ratio.

In practice however, the power gain extracted from reducing the temperature at the intake by about 80°F is only 60 to 70% of the theoretical advantage. So where does the discrepancy occur? While you may succeed in supplying cool air to the carb mouth, the air will pick up heat during its passage down the inlet tract past the port walls and hot intake valves. Air that's 80°F cooler at the carb mouth may only be 50°F cooler at the time it enters the cylinders. This being the case, we need to take steps to keep the heat out of the intake charge as it progresses through the intake system.

The case is then attached to the carb bodies, as seen here, and the element placed in position.

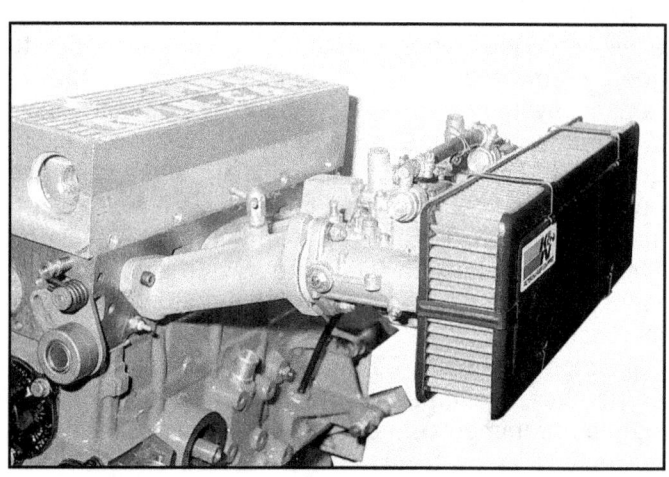

The lid is then positioned and the metal securing clips hold everything in place. For about an hour's work, you get more power, cleaner air, which equates to a considerably longer engine life, and, significantly less induction roar.

How to Build Horsepower, Vol. 2

RAM AIR IN PRACTICE

Horsepower Quick Facts & References

Producing a successful ram air box requires a little thought, but there are a number of effective options. The most unobtrusive is to duct air from the front of the car. This is a good way to do the job for two reasons. First, this is normally a high-pressure area, and so helps raise induction pressure. Second, an intake at this point marginally cuts aerodynamic drag.

Collecting ram air from the front of the car, however, normally means relatively long ducting to reach the carb. This can negate some of the potential gains unless the ducting is thermally insulated. Aluminum ducting is not a good choice, nor is corrugated piping of any sort as it is highly flow-resistant and energy absorbent.

The most effective ducting is hard plastic piping joined, where flexibility is required, by the shortest possible run of rubber hose and hose clamps. All this must feed into the air box/filter housing through as large an opening as can be accommodated. Another factor is the ducting bore, which must be 3.5 inches or more.

NACA DUCT IN HOOD

Although a NACA duct as shown here does not become fully effective until speeds of some 300 MPH, it is still a viable option for an air intake system. It is easy to make and offers a low drag penalty.

So much for the unobtrusive front end air intake. Now lets look at the racier hood scoop. The first question is obvious. How big does the scoop mouth need to be? If it's too big, we'll offset power gains by increased drag; too small, and the engine will end up starved of air, and power will be reduced. A good guide is to make a realistic estimate of the engine's output and work on 20 bhp per square inch of intake area.

Once the opening area has been decided, the entry itself needs to be a suitable shape. You may be tempted to make the intake in the form of a NACA duct (Fig. 2-5). This form of duct was originally developed for aircraft use during World War II. The idea was to allow air to be drawn from a surface for cooling or engine induction with a minimum drag penalty. This form of duct is often seen on purpose-built formula-cars. Although functionally better than many other alternatives, they are not really effective until speeds of about 300 MPH plus!

For engine air, a better proposition is to build an intake duct along the lines shown in Fig. 2-6. The key factors to success are a correctly sized opening area, a smooth form around the intake opening, adequate volume and the inclusion of a filter element. Pay attention to all these points and not only will your engine benefit from ram air induction, but you'll also be able to take advantage of the cold air it'll be drawing in.

If the scoop/ram air set-up required is predominately for street use, a forward facing air inlet is, for the most part, unnecessary, as the vehicle spends most of the time at speeds that produce insignificant ram effect. In actuality, putting a lot of miles on a vehicle with a forward opening means the filter picks up dust and element-clogging bugs quicker. Rotating the scoop so the opening is near the windshield, usually within six inches, puts the air pick-up point in the high pressure zone created in front of the wind shield. This is virtually as effective as a forward facing scoop, but it minimizes the negative effects of dust, dirt, bugs and rain.

The biggest advantage of a hood-mounted scoop for the street is garnered from the fact that the engine is not breathing air at underhood temperature. This is a very important point for a heavy, slow-moving vehicle such as a truck in a towing or off-road situation. Slow forward speeds means the engine compartment is not purged of the hot air very quickly. This causes the temperature to rise further, while power of course, follows an opposite trend.

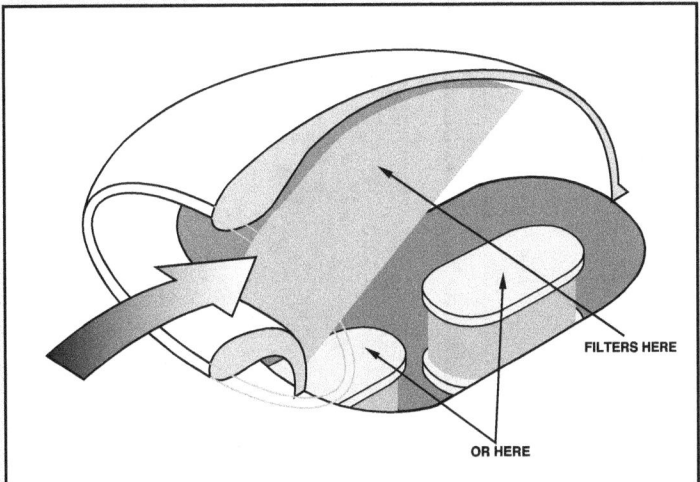

FILTERS HERE
OR HERE

This scoop design represents a functional approach to the problem of effective induction ramming. The first point to note is, the form around the opening. This and the area of the opening can affect the units efficiency. To ensure clean air is fed to the engine a high-flow filter must be used somewhere in the system. It is shown here in two possible locations. Last, the duct/air box system must be sealed to the carbs so that the high-pressure air does not simply vent into the engine compartment.

How to Build Horsepower, Vol. 2

Photo courtesy of Rod Saboury

A ram/cold air induction system such as the one seen here is not simply go fast decoration. Picking up cold air boosts torque, regardless of speed, so it is beneficial throughout the length of the strip. The ram effect, however, only begins to have some measurable effect above about 100 MPH. With Pro Stock cars running close to 200 mph, a ram intake can be worth several MPH in the lights.

HORSEPOWER Quick Facts & References

COOL AIR IN PRACTICE

If cold air is successfully picked up via a scoop, your next job will be to prevent the charge being unduly heated between the carb mouth and intake valve. The first step toward achieving this is to isolate the carb from all heat sources. This means a heat shield between the carb body and the exhaust if they're both in close proximity. Even if they're not separating the carb from the usually higher under-hood air temperature and drafting cold, outside air over the carb is a good move. The cooling effect this has on the carb or injection system means it can be further enhanced by also cooling the fuel. The easiest way to do this is to employ what is normally known as a cool can (Fig. 2-7). A coiled tube of heat-conductive material such as copper is passed through a container holding a mixture of alcohol and ice, or dry ice. If you go this route and fail to make more power, then the fault lies with the carb's atomization capabilities—a subject we shall deal with in a later chapter.

With Weber-style carbs, a potential atomization problem can be exaggerated if the interchangeable venturis selected are too big for the engine, or if the booster (auxiliary) venturis are not producing adequate signal amplification. On a fuel-injected engine, the problem of inadequate fuel atomization is minimal to nonexistent.

Having persuaded the carb to deliver a cold charge, the next problem to deal with is the thermal effect the intake manifold can have on the mixture. A major problem here is that most intake manifolds are constructed from aluminum, which conducts heat from the engine and dumps it into the intake charge.

If you must use an aluminum intake, then do yourself a big favor and put a thermal barrier coating on the inside and polish the outside. On a V8 that has the underside of the manifold exposed to hot oil a thermal barrier or an oil shield is recommended at this point. If your engine utilizes a tubular steel manifold of the type popular in Europe then have it polished and chromed. The high shine does a great job of reflecting the heat and keeping the charge temperature down. This move can often be more effective than you would at first think. On small capacity race cars, which are always under-powered for a fast track, we have seen as much as four-tenths of a second off a lap.

If a low air temperature has so far been retained to the point of the ports in the cylinder head, all that remains is to finish the job. This would normally entail applying a thermal barrier coating to both the port walls and to the combustion face of the intake valves.

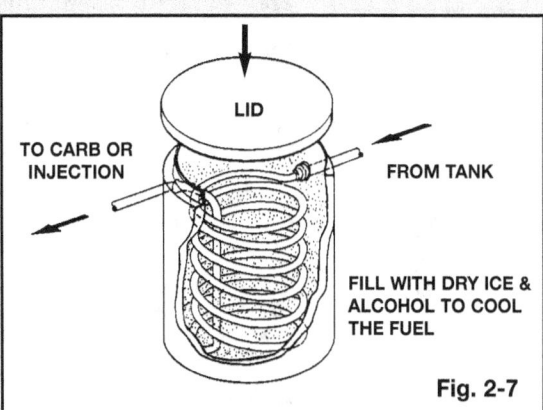

This is the basis of a cool can. It is most effective when steps are taken to prevent excess heat getting into the intake charge from other sources such as manifold heat.

FINISHING TOUCHES

If efforts at applying cool ram air induction are successful, there will be side effects that must be addressed. The first, and most obvious, is that the carb or fuel injection will need to deliver more fuel to go with the additional charge weight entering the cylinders.

Second, the ignition timing may need to be reset. There are two conflicting factors at work here. The reduced charge temperature initially causes the mixture to burn more slowly, thus requiring more ignition advance. On the other hand, the increased charge density means it will tend to burn faster, therefore needing less advance. In many cases these conflicting requirements largely cancel out. However, this cannot be counted on, so each engine must be dealt with as a special case.

A final point concerning the engine spec relates to induction length tuning. If the engine's original induction length gave what were considered optimal results before a thermal control program was undertaken, then, to produce the same results the system will need to be shorter, because pressure waves travel slower in cooler air.

Applying cold air induction to a production car is a very positive move. Even the more restrictive factory systems are worth about 5% increase in torque on a typical 80°F day.

PRESSURE vs DENSITY

Forward facing hood scoops may look very racy, but the ramming effect produced doesn't necessarily contribute as much to the performance as does the use of cooler air. The chart below shows the effect of both ram air induction and cold air induction. Picking up cold air doesn't have quite the monster power look of a ram air system, but it is a lot more effective. Bear that in mind when designing your next induction system.

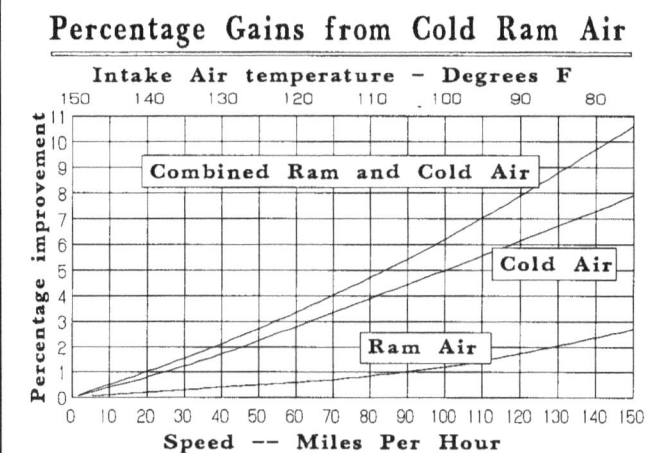

This air box from Air inlet Systems in Hamilton Ontario, Canada, is, in the author's opinion, one of the best filter cases available. It accommodates a large K & N filter and can be connected to a high pressure source of cool air. There is not a lot else one could ask for in an air filter inlet system.

Hood scoop systems must be completely sealed from under-hood air, and care must be taken that adequate clearance exists above the carb inlet. Even this well-sealed setup would benefit from a Stub Stack or other type of radiused entry.

Inducing cold air is a good start toward improving torque, but it is also important to try and maintain a low air temperature as long as possible. Installing a thermally insulating spacer between the carb and manifold can help do this. Normally, the high conductivity of an aluminum manifold together with a highly conductive carb body causes fuel temperature to rise substantially. This drops the engine's VE. The insulating carb spacer can reduce this VE loss.

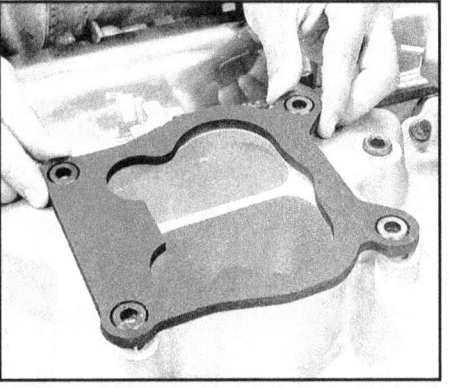

On a street car you can use commercially available carb insulating gaskets. They do a good job, but understand that the carb will never be as cool as you wish because it still transfers heat through the bolts or studs. Actual hard running cools the carb best because the high speed air pulls heat from the carburetor. This air initially enters the motor hot, but a cooler temperature quickly prevails if the throttles remain open for any length of time.

How to Build Horsepower, Vol. 2

How To Build HORSEPOWER: Chapter 3

Carburetors & Intake Manifolds

Basic Carburetor Function

To get the best from a high performance or race engine it is very important to have a working understanding of the carburetor. With the exception of its most basic functional parts like the throttle, the venturi, choke and a couple other minor details, the actual calibration and fuel circuitry seems to be a mystery for many engine builders. A hard look at the most successful engine builders often reveals a high priority on understanding the working principles of a fixed jet carburetor such as a Holley. Understanding these principles has proved to be a tool of great value for deciphering the fuel circuits of carburetors *regardless of type*—allowing the knowledgeable engine builder to swim where others would sink.

The Venturi

There is really no better place to start toward understanding a carb than the heart of the carburetor itself, the venturi. A venturi is no more than a streamlined orifice which has properties useful to the carburetor designer. Fig. 3-1, is a schematic showing what happens in a venturi as air passes through. At the minor diameter of the venturi, the air speeds up, and in so doing, the pressure at that point drops. This causes the liquid to be drawn farther up the tube connected to the minor venturi diameter than at any other point. The faster the air flow, the greater the draw on the connected tube.

Once the consequences of air flow through a venturi are appreciated, we can move along to the basic carburetor main jet function as shown in Fig. 3-2. If the fuel level in the reservoir is kept at the same level as the discharge nozzle in the venturi, then any pressure drop occurring here will cause fuel to flow. This crude means of mixing air and fuel only needs the addition of a main jet and a butterfly valve (Fig. 3-3) controlling air demand to produce the basis of a carburetor.

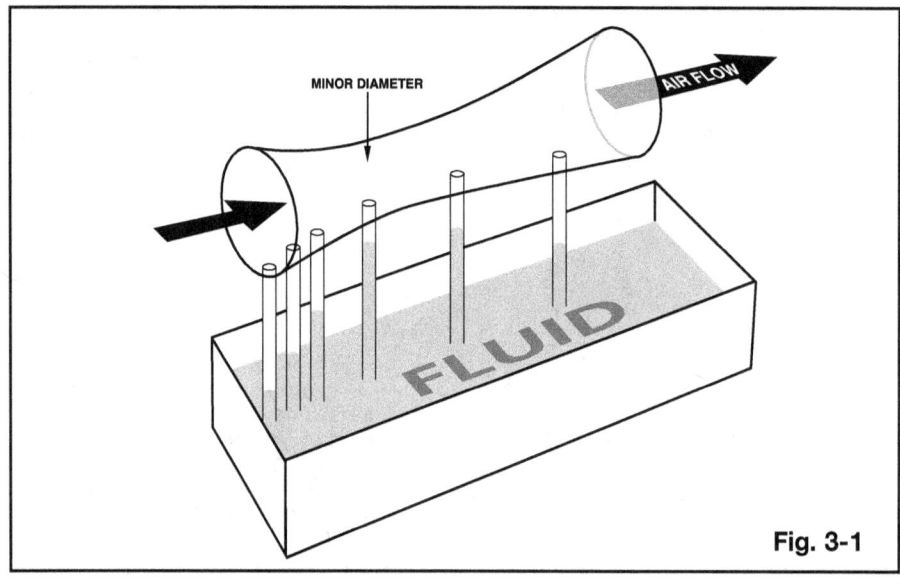

Fig. 3-1

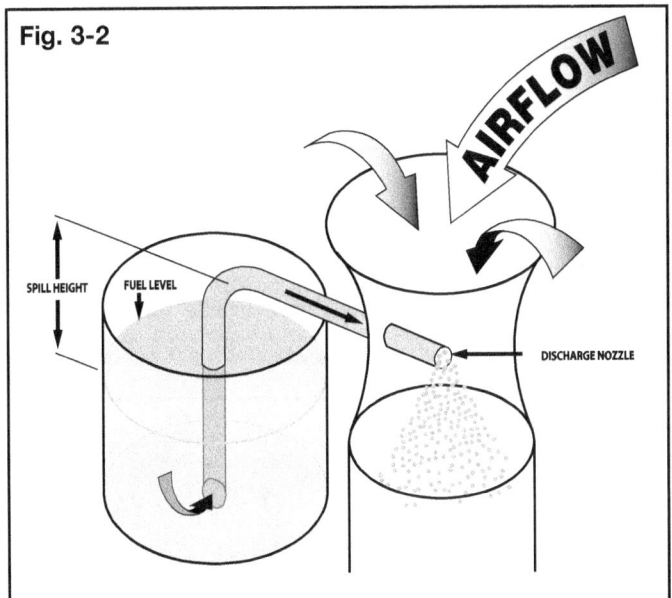

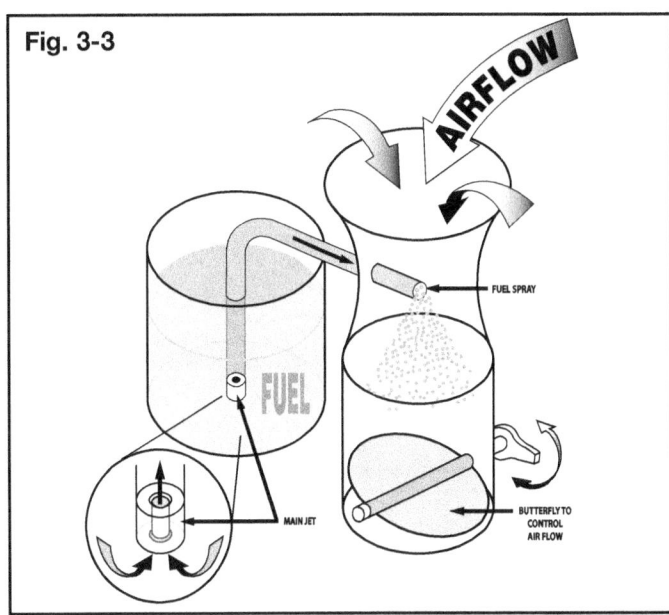

Most high-volume production carbs such as Holleys, have fixed size venturis. However, where production volumes are lower...

Correction

At this point it looks like we have a functional carburetor. If so, why do real world ones seem so complicated by comparison? Although the carb in Fig. 3-3 would work, it would only do so at a fixed speed and if the balance of fuel levels between the reservoir and discharge nozzle were not upset by movement. To avoid spillage of fuel from the main jet into the venturi the fuel level must be set about a ¼ to ⅜ of an inch lower than the discharge point in the venturi. This is called the "spill height." Because of this and the fact that air is compressible and fuel is not, we find that when fuel finally does start to flow from the discharge point into the venturi, its flow rate increases faster than air flow. The result is that as demand increases, the mixture becomes progressively richer. Some sort of solution to this problem is obviously needed, and the technique used is to dilute the fuel with air prior to its arrival at the discharge orifice in the venturi. The problem is how to do this in such a way that it controls the air/fuel ratio or mixture so it is always within prescribed limits. This is done by introducing air into the fuel along the lines shown in Fig. 3-4 (next page). Introducing a calibrated air bleed at this point bleeds off a portion of the venturi signal to the fuel jet. This has two positive effects. First, it produces an air/fuel emulsion which atomizes far more readily, and secondly it allows a measure of control over high speed main jet enrichment.

Trimming the Fuel Curve

The form of fuel delivery in relation to the air is commonly known as the "fuel curve," and the addition of an air jet has allowed us to reduce the mixture strength for any given main jet size. In practice, what is needed is an air bleed system that becomes more active as air flow through the venturi increases. This can be achieved in a number of ways, the simplest being to position the air bleed at the venturi entrance where a slight pressure rise occurs. By picking the right spot and appropriately sizing the air corrector jet, the amount of air bled into the fuel becomes progressively larger and counters the increasing richness normally seen in an uncorrected system. On the face of it this system fix looks pretty good, a little juggling here and there and we appear to be in business. Unfortunately, this type of carburetor assumes steady air flow and does not take into account that a high performance or race engine can have a strongly pulsating intake air flow. At certain RPMs, resonant pressure waves will affect the flow at the main jet to the air corrector jet differently, thus upsetting the mixture calibration. Abnormally strong reversionary pulses can occur when intake, cam and exhaust in a race engine are poorly matched. Air may momentarily

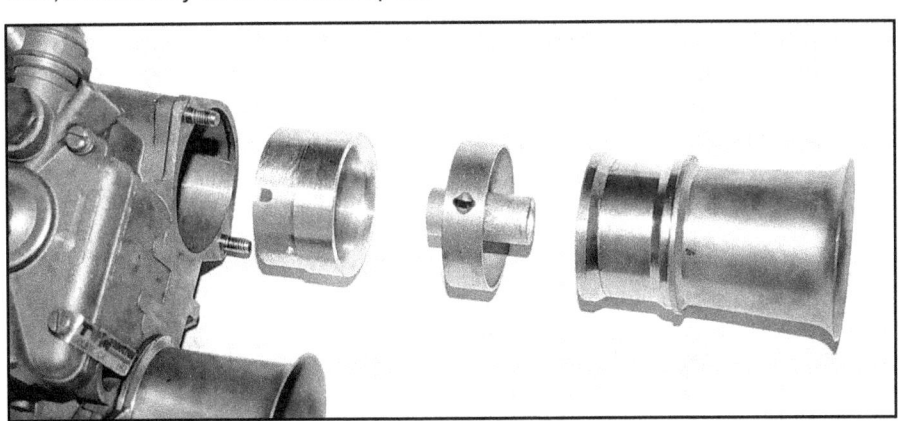

...some carb manufacturers, such as Dellorto and Weber, find it easier to make only a few throttle body sizes and have replaceable venturis so the best size can be selected.

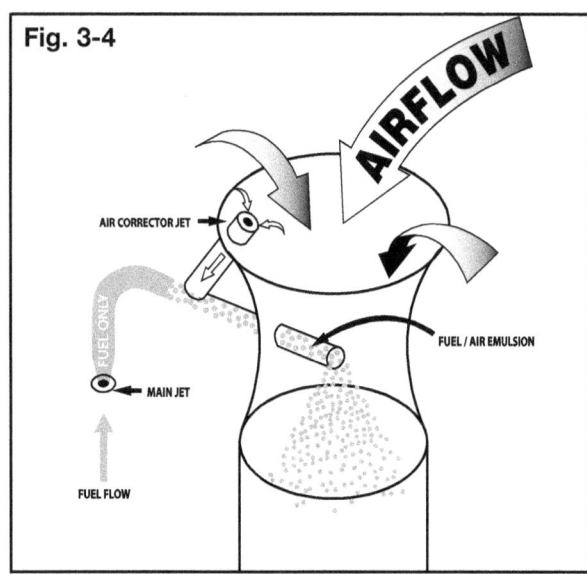

Fig. 3-4

The Emulsion Tube

The emulsion well is an aptly named section of the carburetor, and under static conditions it sees the same fuel level as exists in the float bowl. Fuel enters the well via the main jet and exits via the discharge nozzle in the venturi. In essence, the well is nothing more than a substantial expansion of the tube that joins the main jet to the discharge nozzle. With that basic concept of the well in mind, let us add an emulsion tube and air corrector. The function of the air corrector is just as described earlier, it produces air dilution of the fuel to compensate for the RPM-induced overrichness of an uncorrected main jet. From Fig. 3-5 you can see that the air corrector is now connected directly to the bore of the emulsion tube. If the emulsion tube were to have no holes in its walls, the air corrector would be unconnected to the main jet and so have no effect on the mixture. Now let us add some holes to the emulsion tube as per the drawing. What happens now is that at static conditions, fuel fills up the emulsion tube until it gets to the same level as the fuel in the well in the float chamber. When the engine is running at low RPM, fuel in the main jet/emulsion well is drawn off by the suction produced by the venturi at the discharge nozzle. This causes the fuel in the well to drop slightly and the fuel in the emulsion tube to drop a greater amount. However, so long as no holes in the tube are uncovered the fuel being discharged at the nozzle will not be diluted by any air.

Let's now increase the RPM and consequently the engine's air demand. The situation is now similar to that being shown in the drawing. The air being drawn into the emulsion tube has caused the fuel level in it to drop below the first series of holes. There is now a measure of air bleeding into the well, forming an air/fuel emulsion, and by this means the mixture is leaned out. At this point, you may begin to discern how the emulsion tube functions. By varying the pattern of the holes in the emulsion tube it will be possible to vary the fuel curve delivered by the carburetor to suit the engine's characteristics. If we're dealing with a typical V8, it will, in most cases, use one four-barrel carburetor to feed all eight cylinders. Often,

reverse direction through the venturi. A pressure drop occurs at the venturi regardless of the flow direction. This means when the air reverses flow, it picks up fuel in addition to that picked up in the forward direction. When the correct flow direction is resumed, yet more fuel is picked up. While all this is going on, the air corrector will inevitably have added less air than needed so the mixture will go rich. The bottom line is that a far more sophisticated air correction system is needed. Now it is time to introduce a calibration item, the design and selection of which is often viewed as a black art. This is the emulsion tube, but to cover its function we also need to consider the main jet well and associated air corrector. We will need to look at these parts as a single working component. Fig. 3-5 is a schematic of a simple system. Because it is important to understand exactly what's going on here, we will take things one step at a time.

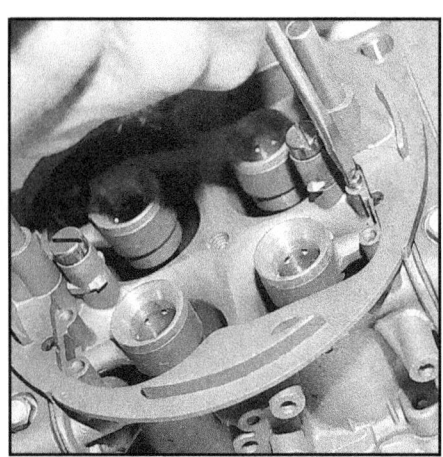

Air corrector jets or air bleeds for the Holly are positioned here. The outer ones, are for the idle circuit and the inner ones, the main circuit.

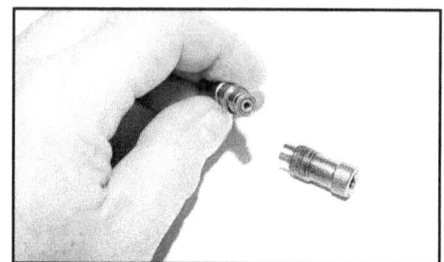

The Weber air correction system for the main jet circuit is like other carbs of this ilk, housed in the top of the emulsion tube and ...

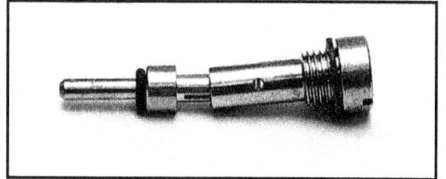

...the idle air corrector is built into the idle jet holder.

the type of manifold used, is of the plenum variety, where all 8 cylinders can draw from all four barrels. Under normal circumstances, the air flow pulses through the carburetor are relatively well damped or smoothed, either by the number of overlapping induction pulses or by the manifold's plenum volume. This aspect cuts the sensitivity of the emulsion tube to the system it has to work with. In other words, since the carb sees almost a constant flow, the need for much in the way of emulsion tube fudging to get the mixture right is minimal. This is fortunate because it means that as long as a unit based on the carburetor manufacturer's recommendations is selected, it is unlikely to be far off what is needed. However, what may need to be done to get the calibration of the main circuit right, is to deal with main jets and to a lesser extent, air correctors.

If the emulsion tube design for a four barrel can be considered simple, the same cannot be said for one barrel per cylinder installations. The heavily pulsating flow makes emulsion tube design for a given application far more critical. If you intend to run a carburetor set-up, such as Dellortos, Webers or Mikunis, chances are you will need to go through an emulsion tube selection routine. Without the information you are about to read, your selection will be strictly on a hit-and-miss basis.

Emulsion Tube Selection

Refer back to the drawing of Fig. 3-5 showing the function of the emulsion tube and well assembly. Here you can see that

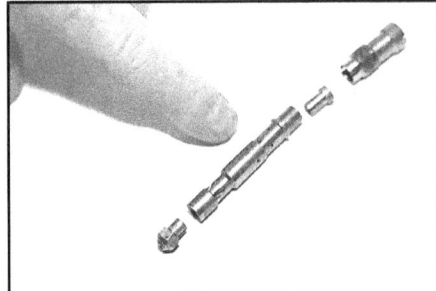

Emulsion tubes for IR type induction systems are complex affairs because of the pulsating nature of the induction stroke. As airflow becomes less...

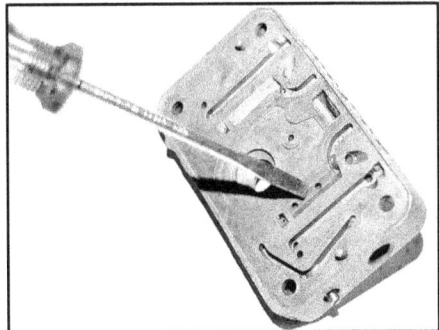

...pulsating and more even because a number of cylinders are connected to common plenum, the emulsion tube becomes less critical and simpler to determine. On a Holley, the channel here is in effect an emulsion tube, although some have a more conventional one in the main jet well.

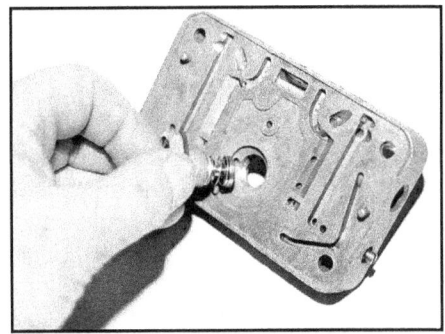

The power valve, when connected to a vacuum source, is held closed. When the throttle is opened wide, the vacuum goes away and the power valve opens to allow auxiliary jets to introduce more fuel to the system, thus giving the full power rich mixture required.

the emulsion tube now has a series of holes getting more plentiful toward the lower end. What this does, in essence, is introduce more and more air into the fuel as air demand increases to combat the increasing richness that would otherwise exist. The function of the air corrector jet in the assembly is to control just how much or little the mixture is leaned out.

The components we've looked at are the main jet, the well, the emulsion tube and air corrector. Starting at the main jet, it will be pretty obvious that putting in a bigger main jet will make the mixture richer everywhere in the rev range and a smaller main jet will lean it out. The effect of the emulsion tube will depend on the hole pattern. The more holes there are at the lower end of the emulsion tube, the more it will lean out top end mixture. The higher up the emulsion tube the holes occur, the sooner the effect of the air corrector comes in. The effect of the air corrector itself is to lean out the mixture the more it is increased and to richen the mixture when reduced in size. Its effect being greater as RPM increases, but the measure of control is also influenced by the hole pattern in the emulsion tube.

Although it was mentioned earlier, one other aspect you must appreciate is that the emulsion tube serves another useful purpose apart from its metering function. It is so named because it turns the fuel in the well into an emulsion of air and fuel. An emulsion atomizes far better than straight fuel when it's discharged from the nozzle in the venturi.

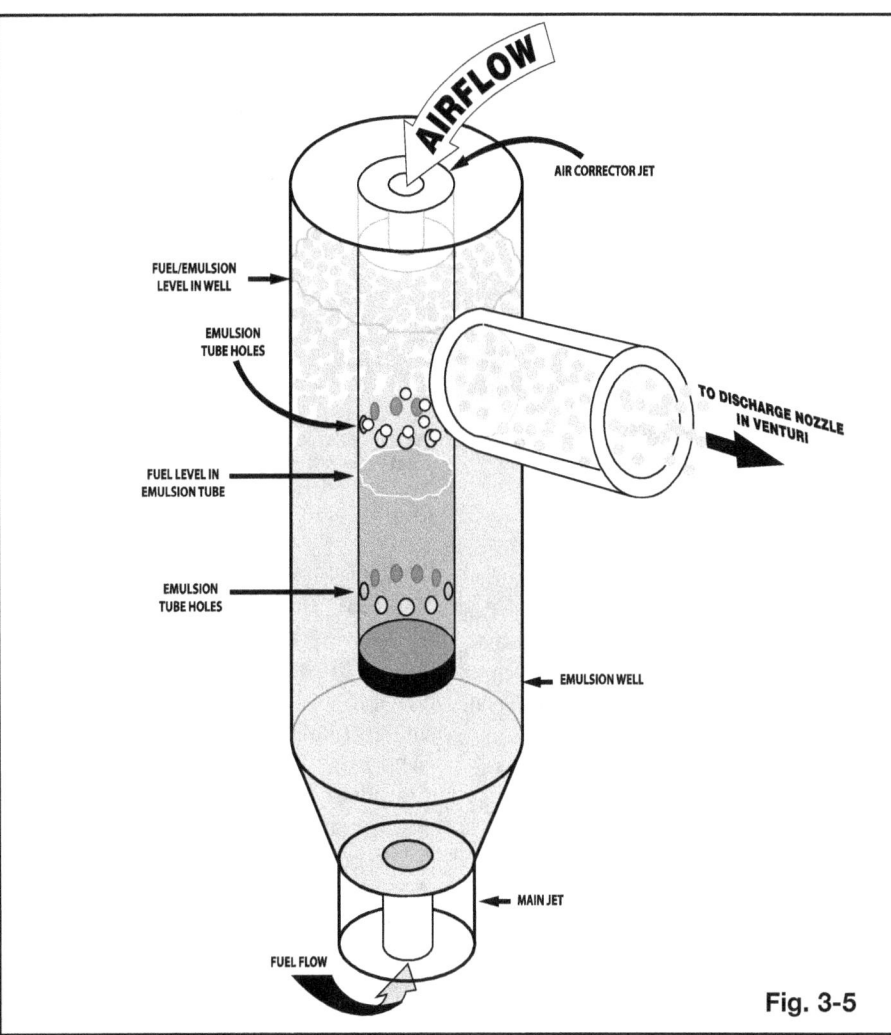

Fig. 3-5

Fuel should be delivered to an engine in fine enough droplets to produce complete vaporization of the charge toward the end of the compression stroke. Any vaporization taking place in the manifold takes up more room and cuts the volumetric efficiency of the engine. It's a good idea to keep in mind the atomization aspect of an emulsion tube/air corrector assembly, because it can prove significant in the performance of your engine.

The Power Valve & Mixture Spread

For a typical single four-barrel equipped V8 engine to produce maximum horsepower, the gasoline air/fuel ratio, by weight, needs to be around 12.5:1 to 12.9:1. That is 12.5 lbs. of air to 1 lb. of fuel. If perfect fuel distribution is achieved, the optimum ratio tends to be a little leaner at around 13.0/1 to 13.1:1. The chemically correct mixture varies slightly dependent on the fuel blend, but, is typically around 14.7:1 to 15:1. From this you can see that to

The booster or auxiliary venturi amplifies the signal produced at the main venturi. In most carbs, such as the Holley shown here, this is a factory fixed entity. With some carbs...

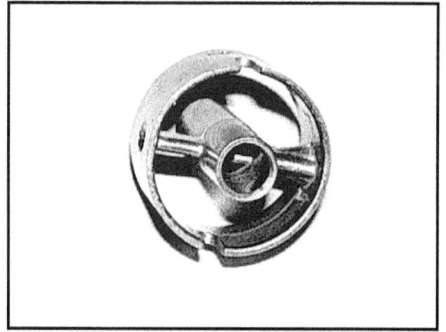

...such as Webers, Dellortos and a few others, the type of booster venturi can be selected by the end user. With variations in gain and atomization characteristics, this allows a higher degree of tuning to an engine's individual requirements.

deliver maximum power the air/fuel ratio must be on the rich side, i.e. only 13 lbs. of air to 1 lb. of fuel means there is now excess fuel in relation to the air. The major reason an engine makes maximum power with a rich mixture is that the excess fuel cools the air, allowing a denser charge to enter the cylinders. Second, and to lesser extent, it also makes up for manifold distribution and fuel droplet size problems.

Lean Cruise MixTURE

A full-power rich mixture at cruise would produce very poor fuel consumption. With a fixed jet carb, such as the Holley, the main jets are used not to calibrate for maximum power, but to set the air/fuel ratio for good part throttle fuel economy. For this, a lean mixture, typically around 16-17:1 air/fuel ratio is required. However, using a mixture ratio this lean can cost a considerable amount of horsepower at full throttle. Fig. 3-6 shows how the horsepower changes as the air/fuel ratio is varied. To get the best results at both part and full throttle, the carburetor must be capable of varying the mixture ratio between lean for economy and rich for full power. To satisfy these demands the carb must be able to deliver leaner ratio's for cruise, idle and any circumstances which don't require a maximum power rich mixture ratio. This can be done in a number of ways, but the method typically employed is to have what is known as a power valve enrichment circuit. This device is essentially nothing more than an additional main jet that is brought into operation by a vacuum sensitive switch. When an engine is operating at part throttle, a considerable amount of vacuum exists in the intake manifold. This vacuum is used to keep the power valve closed so fuel flow to this extra main jet is shut off. Opening the throttle causes the vacuum in the intake manifold to largely disappear. When this happens, it is obvious that the driver is demanding power. Under these conditions, the vacuum supplied to the power valve disappears, allowing this additional main jet to open. This jet, known on Holley carbs as a Power Valve Restriction Channel (PVRC), allows more fuel to be fed into the metering well, supplying fuel in addition to that passing through the main jet. Net result: an instant enrichment of the mixture. The drawing, Fig. 3-7, shows the power valve system built into our basic carburetor.

Back to Venturis

To get an adequate signal from the venturi at low RPM, it is necessary to make the venturi relatively small. This means at high engine RPM, it is virtually strangling the engine and preventing anything like the engine's true maximum power from being developed. Fortunately, there is at least a partial solution to this problem and it takes the form of a booster venturi. The solution employs a second venturi located with its end at about the same position as the point maximum depression occurs in the main venturi. This causes the air to go through the booster venturi faster than through the main venturi, providing an increased signal. A good booster design can increase the signal developed at the main venturi by 50 to 100%. By employing a booster venturi, the carburetor designer can increase the size of the main venturi to deal with top end flow requirements without the big compromise in low speed performance. Some carburetors, such as certain models of Q-Jet, employ a triple venturi, in-as-much as the booster venturi has an additional booster within it.

Idle System

From the foregoing, it won't come as much of a surprise to realize that a venturi, even with a triple booster, isn't going to meter the fuel accurately enough for an engine at idle where the air demand is minimal. Because of the minimal air flow rates at idle, a carburetor circuit specifically tailored for the needs of low RPM/high vacuum is necessary. Hence, the idle circuit of a carburetor. Fig. 3-8 shows the breakdown of a typical idle circuit. The signal required to draw the fuel from the float bowl is supplied by the engine. With the throttle plate closed, there is a considerable amount of vacuum existing in the intake manifold. This vacuum is used to draw fuel from the float bowl, or the main jet well, via an idle jet. This same passage is also joined by an air bleed, so an emulsion is formed. This emulsion is then routed down to an orifice below the butterfly, which is controlled in size by a tapered needle. From this, you can see that screwing the needle in will reduce the amount of fuel passing out through the orifice and backing it out will increase it. (Although there are some Holley carburetors which control the air to operate in the reverse mode). From this diagram you can see that most of the air required for the engine to idle is going past the butterfly and only a small amount of air is passing via the air bleed into the fuel to form an emulsion. This system works just fine until the throttle is opened slightly. When an increase in air flow takes place, the vacuum in the manifold drops. Net result: the engine stalls. So the idle circuit tends to be self-canceling, and is only any good when the engine is truly idling and doing nothing else. It is, in essence, a totally steady-state circuit and, unless it can be modified in some way, will not cope with anything other than idle circumstances.

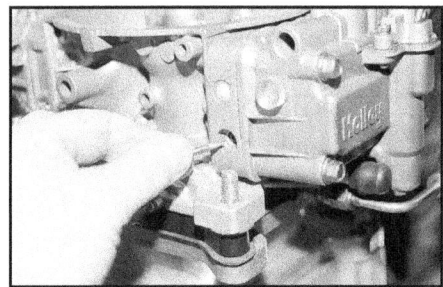

The use of a tapered screw to set the idle mixture is almost universal amongst carburetor designs and little difference will be found from one brand to another.

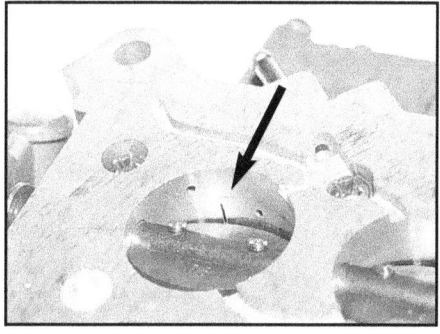

The transition, or progression as it is termed in Europe, from the idle circuit to the main circuit is accomplished by means of a transition slot on most U.S. carb designs and a...

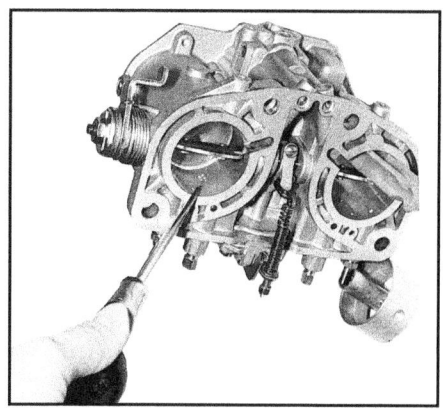

...series of holes on most European carbs. Whichever way it is done, the operational principles are the same.

Transition Circuit

The transition circuit takes care of the engine's fuel and air requirements just off idle. It is incorporated into the idle circuit for a smooth progression from idle to small throttle cruise conditions. This modifies the idle circuit by drilling into the idle circuit fuel supply hole just above the position that the butterfly will be at idle. In reality, some carburetors employ drilled holes at this point and others, such as Holley, utilize a slot as per Fig. 3-9. When the throttle is closed at the idle position, vacuum from underneath the butterfly not only draws fuel through the idle circuit but also pulls in air through the transition slot to better emulsify the fuel being discharged from the idle orifice. As the butterfly opens, it begins to uncover the transition slot, and, instead of drawing in air, it starts to draw more fuel. This change over from air to fuel occurs because the length of the slot above the butterfly is reduced so less air is drawn through it. However, a great deal more air is passing around the now more open butterfly. As we continue to open the butterfly so the amount of fuel drawn in from the transition slot increases, and to a certain extent, so does the fuel being discharged by the idle orifice. By the time the butterfly has reached the end of the transition slot, sufficient air is being drawn into the system to bring the main jet into action. Although the transition circuit on most carburetors is simple in function, it is very important because most street driving, especially in traffic, is done from the middle to the end of the transition circuit. If this circuit isn't correctly calibrated it will bring about poor drivability and high fuel consumption. In most systems the idle jet is the biggest influence on the transition circuit calibration. In this respect the idle jet is probably misnamed since most of the mixture at idle is controlled by the idle mixture adjustment screw.

Accelerator Pump Jet Circuit

Under idling conditions, a considerable amount of vacuum exists in the intake manifold. This vacuum reduces the boiling point of the fuel, causing the fuel to vaporize much easier under high-vacuum conditions than under low conditions. This is a very useful aspect as it helps fuel distribution at idle considerably. The same situation applies at cruise. When running down the freeway at 2 to 3000 RPM and 15 to 17-inches of vacuum, a lot of the fuel being drawn into the engine is vaporized before it reaches the cylinders. However, when you stand on the throttle suddenly, the fuel that is held in suspension in the air in vapor form suddenly condenses on the walls of the intake manifold. Although a fresh charge of air is entering the engine and carrying its associate fuel, for a moment the engine goes very lean because the fuel that was in the manifold air is now on the manifold walls and for a moment at least, going nowhere. This causes an enormous flat spot which, unless countered, cannot be driven through. To offset fuel condensing on the walls of the intake manifold, an accelerator pump system is added. What this does is physically squirt in additional fuel to cover the would-be hole in the carburetion. Fig. 3-10 is a basic schematic of a typical pump jet system. Here a piston is shown injecting the fuel, but most often a diaphragm, such as on Holleys is used. Calibration of the accelerator pump fuel system is not only by means of jets to control the rate at which it goes in, but also with various springs, cams, and piston/diaphragm sizes to control the amount that's injected.

The Cold Start System

All cold start systems work by enriching the fuel/air ratio until the engine warms up enough for fuel to be sufficiently vaporized for more effective combustion. The simplest cold start system is the "choke," (Fig. 3-11) so called because it literally chokes the air supply to the engine.

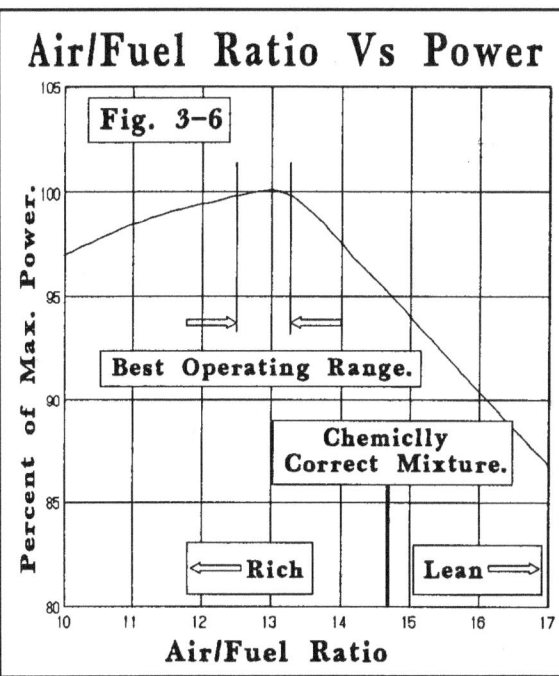

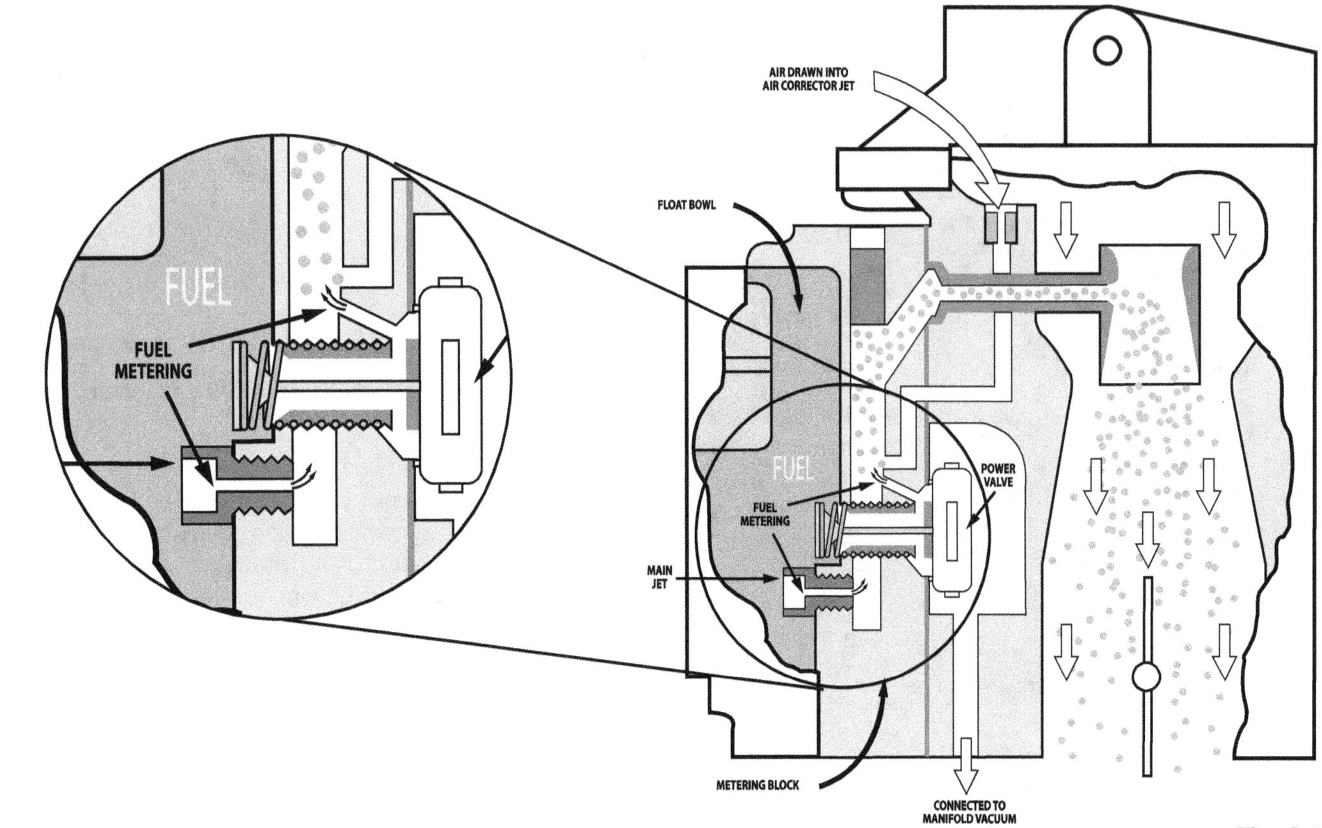

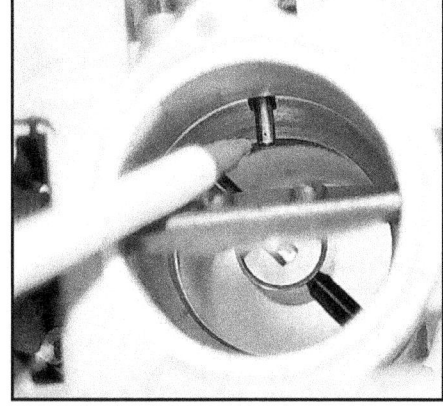

Fig. 3-7

This causes the engine to draw harder on the transition and main jet circuit, resulting in less air flow and more fuel flow for a richer mixture. Any complexity we may see in the choke system stems from making it automatic in operation. When self-operated, the choke may be applied and shut off by either an exhaust heat activated bi-metal strip system or, as many of the newer carbs are, by an electrically heated system. Since none of these choke systems contribute to performance, no great detail will be gone into concerning their function. Suffice to say that several other SA books cover in detail the overhaul of these systems on popular carbs such as the Holley.

The use of a diaphragm as the means of injecting fuel into the engine to cover the acceleration lean out is about the most common way of doing the job. Fuel from here...

... enters the induction system via these pump jets, which are required to be appropriately sized.

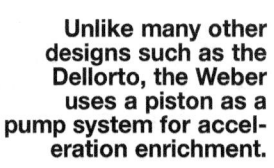

On carbs intended for IR usage, the pump jets can also act as a high speed fuel bleed, which at high airflow values starts to feed fuel into the system for power enrichment.

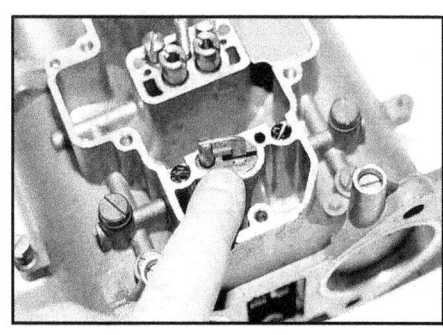

Unlike many other designs such as the Dellorto, the Weber uses a piston as a pump system for acceleration enrichment.

26   *How to Build Horsepower, Vol. 2*

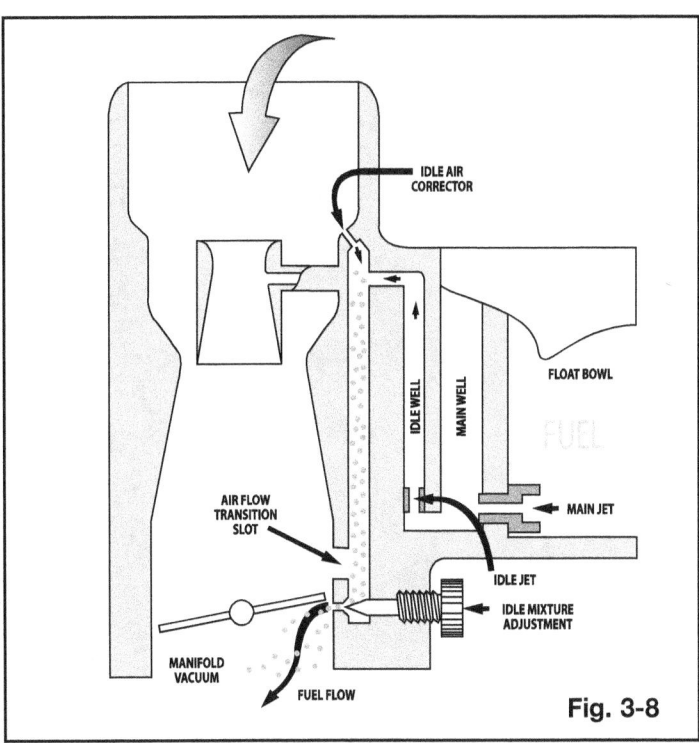

Fig. 3-8

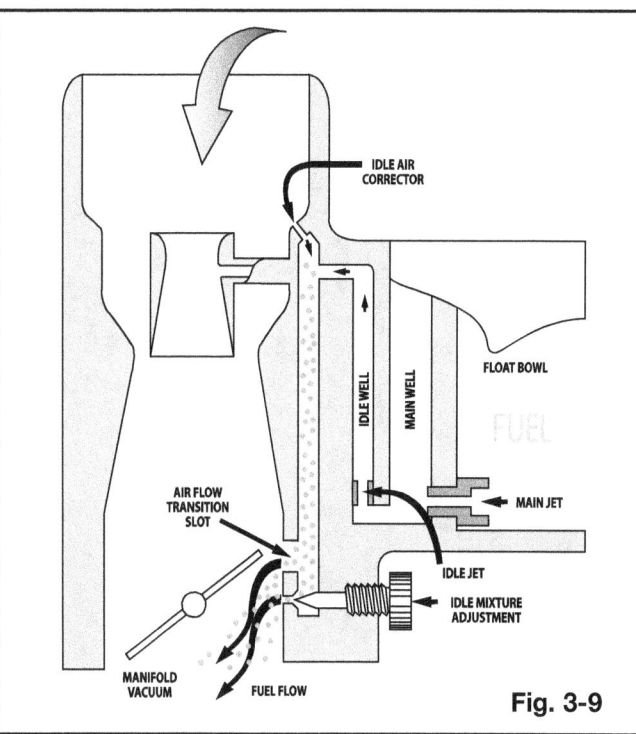

Fig. 3-9

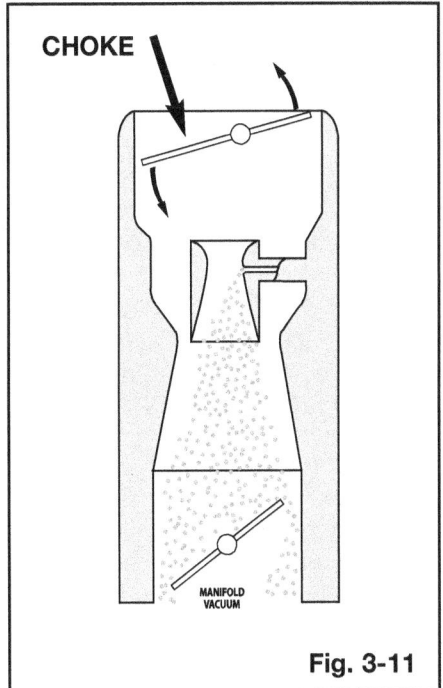

Fig. 3-11

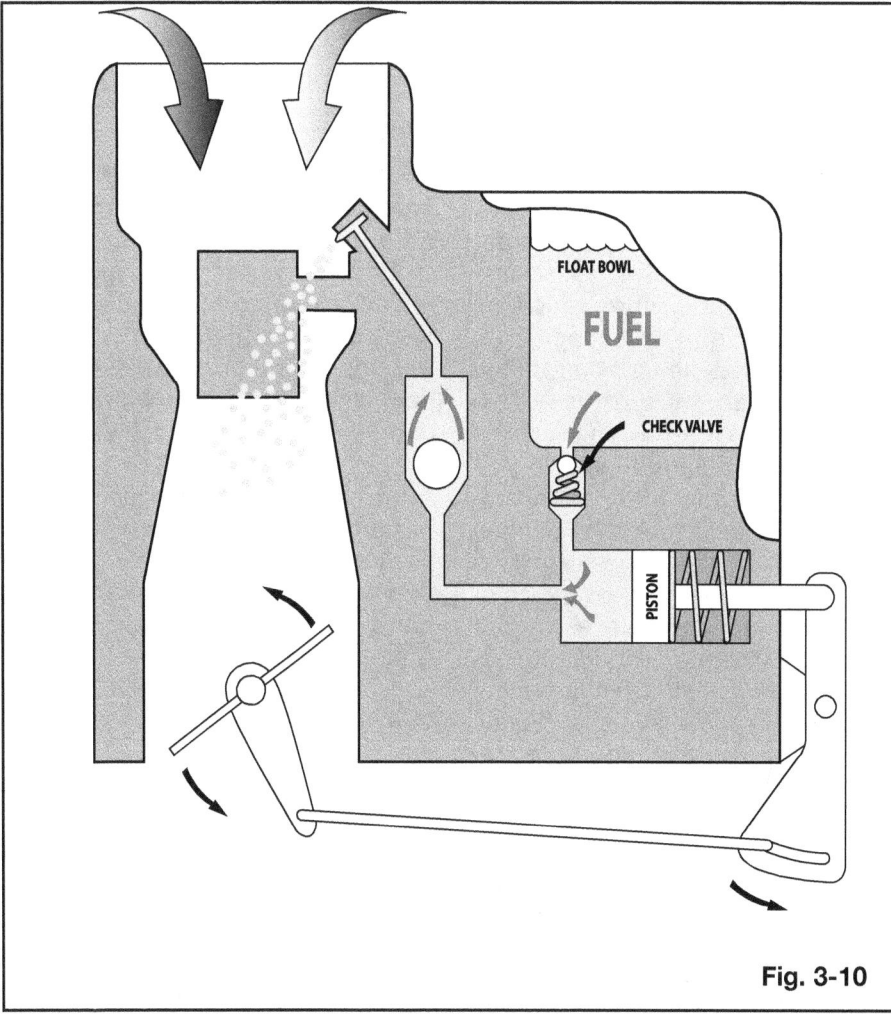

Fig. 3-10

On carbs like the high-performance Webers, the cold start system is not a choke. The mixture is actually enriched by means of a jet system, that is manually brought into operation for cold starting purposes. Although these systems can be calibrated, they rarely need anything other than the original "as produced" calibration settings.

How To Build HORSEPOWER: Chapter 4
Carburetors & Intake Manifolds
Properties of Mixtures

For optimal operation under all driving conditions the carburetor must deliver three distinctly different mixture ratios as depicted in Fig. 4-1. Except for a race only vehicle the maximum economy lean mixture is where most driving is done. This can be best described as the leanest mixture that will effectively burn producing, the least fuel consumption for the power developed. Next, is the chemically correct or stoichiometric mixture. This is a mixture ratio in which just enough fuel is supplied to the air, so that in the combustion process, it combines with all of the available oxygen. After combustion,, there should, theoretically be neither free oxygen nor fuel left. Knowing exactly what this ratio may be is, in the real world, a little difficult because fuels vary in their make-up. If we were to consider a fuel made entirely of one type of petroleum distillate such as Iso-octane or Toluene, then calculating the chemically correct mixture would be a straightforward chemistry problem. However, fuels are made up of many different types of sub-fuels, which not only vary from manufacturer to manufacturer, but also with location and seasons. For most practical purposes, we can consider that the chemically correct mixture for a typical gasoline is around 14.7 to 15:1. At this point having the chemically correct mixture might look to be the way to go for maximum power, but this proves not to be the case, for two basic reasons. The first is due to the carburetor and manifold's inability to evenly distribute the fuel throughout the air charge. This makes it necessary to add more fuel than would otherwise be required, to insure that every molecule of air has nearby fuel to burn. The second reason relates to the intake charge temperature. By adding more fuel to the air than is required for the combustion process alone, a useful degree of intake tract and charge cooling takes place producing a denser intake charge. As would be expected a limit exists on how much extra fuel the engine can usefully use. As

No matter how good the carb or supply source is, or whether it is supposedly pre-calibrated or not. if you assume it needs calibration you will, 99 times out of a hundred, be right.

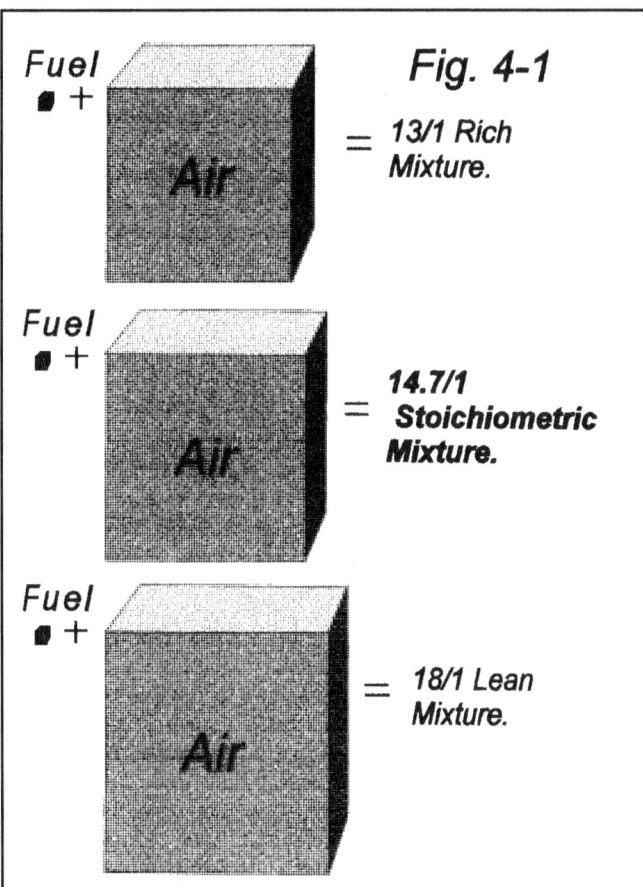

Fig. 4-1

Fuel + Air = 13/1 Rich Mixture.

Fuel + Air = 14.7/1 Stoichiometric Mixture.

Fuel + Air = 18/1 Lean Mixture.

Although air fuel ratios are quoted in weight, this drawing shows what the typical weights of fuel and air look like, size for size. As can be seen, fuel represents a relatively small volume compared with the relevant volume of air. For a rich mixture, there is too much fuel for the volume of air inhaled into the engine, so after combustion, the exhaust contains unburned fuel. When there is 10 to 15% excess fuel, maximum power is developed. At stoichiometric, the mixture is exactly the right proportions for complete combustion, as all the fuel and oxygen chemically combine in the combustion process. When the mixture is lean, there is surplus oxygen remaining in the exhaust, and it is under these conditions that maximum fuel economy is achieved.

Sometimes carb calibration means changing more than just the main circuits, so it will pay to understand how carbs work in case you have to do your own figuring.

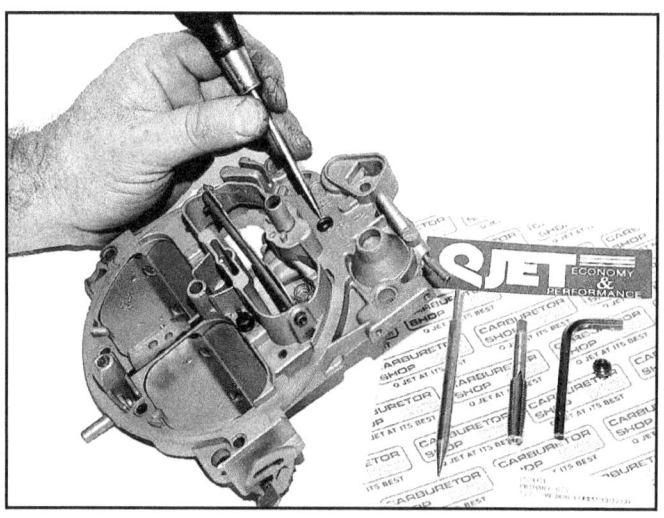

By making some simple mods on the Q-Jet, the part throttle cruise mixture can be made adjustable. In which case, getting the right mixture is just a question of keeping track of the MPG and...

can be seen from Fig. 3-6 in the last chapter, the power drop-off as the mixture goes too rich, occurs, at least at first, slower than the power drop-off from the lean mixture. This means it is better to err a little on the rich side rather than lean.

LEAN BURN

Although the chemically correct mixture represents a total combustion situation, it is, other than a useful reference point, of little value to us. The two points in the mixture curve that are important to us are best economy and maximum power mixtures. Because of its complexities, and the fact that it has the most influence on the size of our fuel bill, we will deal with the

Where calibration is done by both component selection and adjustment, as in a Rochester Quadrajet, achieving acceptable calibration becomes easier if you have close to the right needles to start with. The Carb Shop specializes in Q-Jets and can, given the spec of your engine, determine needle requirements pretty closely. From here on in, adjustment usually gets the job done.

...optimizing it. On board computers, such as this unit here, were popular in the eighties and made the job of optimizing MPG fast, as they could give an instantaneous MPG readout at any particular speed.

How to Build Horsepower, Vol. 2

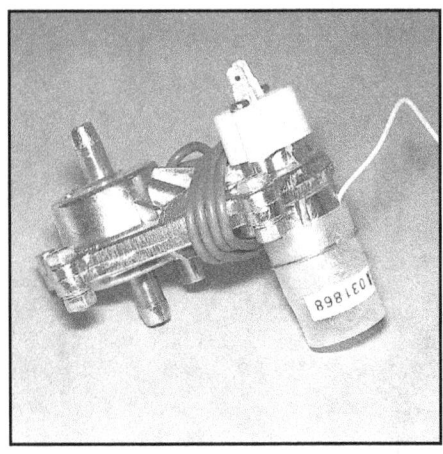

The key to the on-board computer's ability to give fuel-related data was the use of an inexpensive and relatively accurate fuel flow measuring device.

Achieving idle mixture balance with an IR system can be a difficult and lengthy procedure. However, when correctly set up, the idle quality usually justifies the effort. There are several ways to make this job easier and one of the most common in Europe was to use...

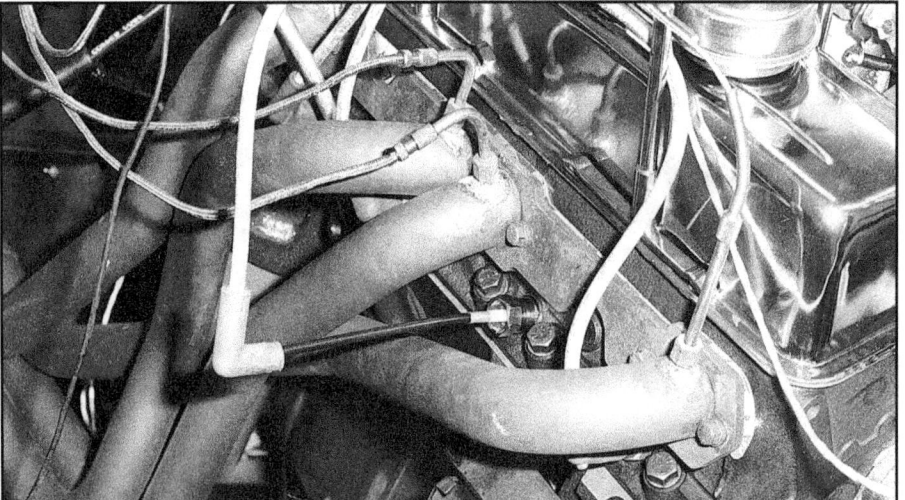

... a Color Tune plug as seen here. This plug was made of high temperature glass and allowed the user to see the combustion flame color. Lean mixtures produce a blue flame. At the point the mixture becomes stoichiometric the flame becomes white. As it goes richer still, it becomes yellow. This device, now no longer in production, can never give an incorrect reading at the color change points. The author uses a Color Tune to check the calibration of other more common, and usually more complex, mixture devices, such as infrared red, mass flow sensors and the readout of oxygen sensing mixture devices. A similar but slightly less precise effect can be achieved by drilling a small hole in the exhaust pipe near the header flange and observing the color of the exhaust flame.

maximum economy mixture and associated factors first. As you might expect, there is no clear-cut maximum economy mixture applicable to all engines. It is subject to change due to many external variables, and if delved into in intricate detail, the list of these is almost endless. Yet, the main points are relatively straightforward to cover. Starting at the carburetor, we'll deal with those factors that have the greatest influence on economy.

Let's start with mixture quality. The principle subjects under this heading are fuel atomization and distribution. It's not hard to imagine that, if the fuel went into the cylinder in one glob, then, irrespective of whether the mixture ratio was correct or not, the fuel would not burn very effectively. The main function of the carburetor is to mix the fuel as finely and evenly as possible with the air passing through it. As far as fuel economy is concerned, tests indicate that the finer the fuel droplets delivered, the better. The most obvious reason for this is that it allows a leaner fuel/air ratio to be successfully burned. Apart from this there is another significant reason why trying to burn the leanest air/fuel ratio possible pays off.

At this point, we will assume that an improved mixture quality has allowed a leaning of the mixture. This means at any given speed, the air flow will be unchanged, but less fuel will be passing into the engine. At this throttle setting, we will now find there is insufficient fuel for the engine to deliver the required power to maintain its speed. To compensate, the throttle must be pushed a little more open. At this slightly wider throttle opening, there still won't be the previous amount of fuel flow, but the cylinders will have more air to work with. Remember, air is the working medium for an internal combustion engine. It is the heating of this air and its subsequent expansion that pushes the piston down the bore. The extra air induced means the effective compression ratio of the engine, as opposed to its measured compression ratio, will be higher. Higher effective compression ratios mean higher thermal efficiencies, which in plain language means better fuel efficiency.

INTAKE MANIFOLD BASICS

Moving on from the carburetor to the manifold, we find a number of factors affect just how lean a charge the engine will burn. The first and most obvious is the fuel distribution characteristics of the manifold. Because of their greater mass, fuel droplets do not follow quite the same path as the air. However, the smaller the droplets, the nearer fuel and air paths coincide. This leads to a more even distribution within the charge. In many respects, adding intake heat helps this situation. What this does is turn a certain percentage of the charge into a vapor, which has the same distribution characteristics as air. At first sight, vaporizing the fuel might look like a good way to not only get more fuel economy but also more power. But this is not the case. When a droplet of fuel is vaporized, it takes up more than a hundred times the volume it did in liquid form. The vapor occupies more space in the manifold

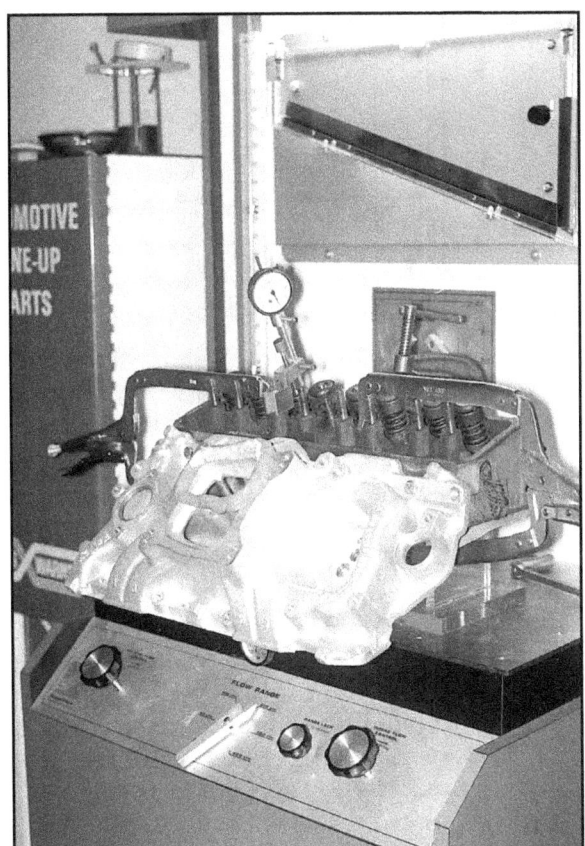

Much of what goes into manifold design is due to the basic shortcomings of the carb. Divided plenums, pressure balance ports, dual ports, plenum packers, turtles, etc., are all more or less Band-Aid fixes to compensate. They are only functional so long as problems exist and for the most part..

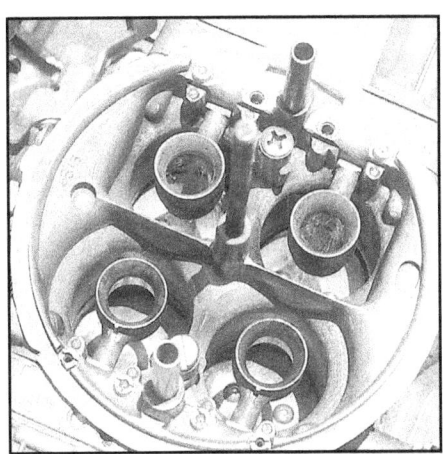

... they do. Seen here is the fuel discharge from one of Holley's best boosters. Engine RPM is down around the 2000 mark. Note that the fuel is hardly what could be described as 'atomized'. Fortunately, the heat conducted from the heads of an otherwise unheated aluminum intake manifold vaporized sufficient fuel to start satisfactory, if less-than-optimum combustion.

and this in turn reduces the volumetric efficiency of the engine. In other words, the engine now inhales less air. By vaporizing the fuel, the engine is supplied with a more easily ignitable charge, which enhances combustion efficiency. The bottom line here is that the engine will deliver a better ratio of power to fuel used, but its outright power would be significantly down. In engineering terms, the measure of an engine's fuel efficiency is known as the Brake Specific Fuel Consumption or BSFC. In English units it is measured in pounds per horsepower per hour.

Simply adding heat to the manifold is far from the whole story. The form of the manifold itself plays a significant part in how well the carburetor atomizes the fuel. High heat and vacuum usually take care of all the idle and low speed drivability problems a carbureted induction system may otherwise have. But for higher RPM and power levels, the situation changes. Manifold design can strongly influence booster fuel atomization. Better results are seen if the booster receives a sharp induction pulse rather than one damped by a large intake manifold volume. Essentially, this means small runners and plenums tend to encourage the carburetor to deliver more finely atomized fuel. This is one of the reasons two plane manifolds, as opposed to single plane, tend to produce better low-end output and fuel economy, as the volume seen by any one cylinder of the engine during its induction stroke is less. Another is that there is a reduced tendency for exhaust dilution to take place during the overlap period because there is far less overlapping of the individual induction strokes. Additionally, on a two plane manifold any one cylinder only sees half the carb capacity, so peak air speed through the carb is increased. The result of dividing the carburetor on a two plane manifold is reduced low-speed, part throttle exhaust dilution, better fuel atomization and usually, slightly improved fuel distribution. In the absence of any other fix for inadequate atomization, both these factors allow a leaner fuel/air ratio to be effectively used. However, we must keep in mind that we are now using manifold designs, which may be compromised in other areas, to compensate for the carb's inability to adequately atomize fuel at low speed.

CYLINDER HEADS

The cylinder head presents all sorts of design complexities, which affect how lean a fuel/air charge can be burned. Understanding the basics will most certainly help get the best from your engine. First, consider the intake port. A large intake port cross sectional area not only contributes to the overall induction volume, thus damping the intake pulse at the booster, but also produces a lower port velocity. At low RPM, smaller ports giving higher velocities are better at holding fuel in suspension in the air. High velocity ports are also better at shredding puddled fuel back into the air from the port's short turn radius, corners of the valve seat, etc.

Both the swirl and the squish action generated from the pistons close approach to the quench area become more critical as fuel droplet size increases. The importance of good fuel atomization at the carburetor cannot be overstressed, basically because the typical intake port, and to a lesser extent, chamber is characteristically bad at maintaining atomization. Even if the fuel is finely atomized at the booster, the manifold and intake ports tend to cause fuel to coagulate into larger droplets. But fine atomization from the booster is far from a lost cause. The more finely the fuel is atomized in the first place, the better, even though it is degraded by the time it arrives in the cylinders.

Just to sum up the aspects of atomization, for best part throttle and low RPM use let's run through the basics involved. First, effective booster design, small venturis and high velocities improve atomization and mixture quality. In general, smaller plenum volumes and port runners improve the atomiza-

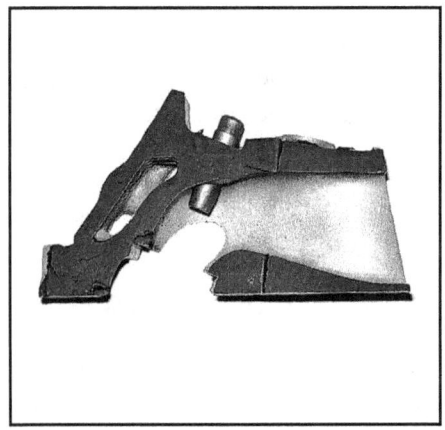

The size and shape of the intake port can have a significant influence on mixture quality arriving at the combustion chamber. Abrupt changes in area and direction should as far as possible be avoided. However, a smooth radius on the short side turn required for improved airflow usually reduces mixture quality. A rough surface here and a ledge as usually left by machining is best for fuel shearing. A sharp edge in this area is usually worth the odd 2 to 3% improvement in MPG.

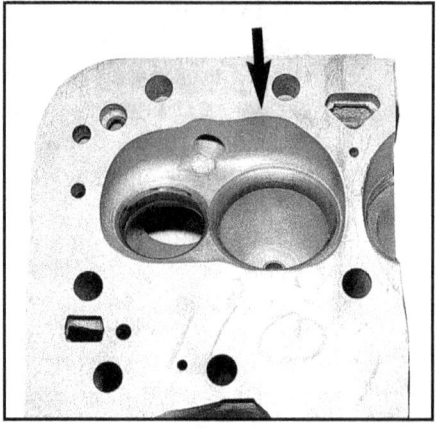

Raw fuel that enters the cylinder of a typical small block Chevrolet combustion chamber usually ends up splattered over the combustion chamber wall in the indicated area—leaving a rough or corrugated surface here can help re-introduce fuel into the air.

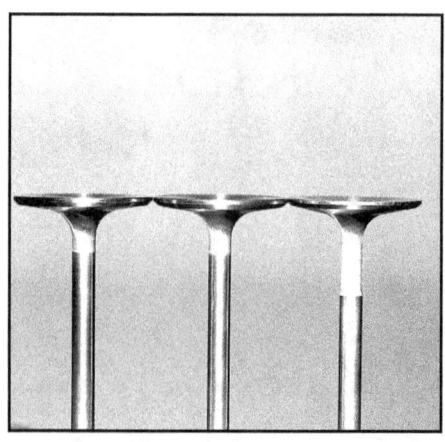

The shape of the valves can also influence the wet flow pattern arriving in the cylinder. With low angle ports common to most production pushrod engines, the flatter the valve profile the better. As the port is raised, the back of the valve needs to become more angled.

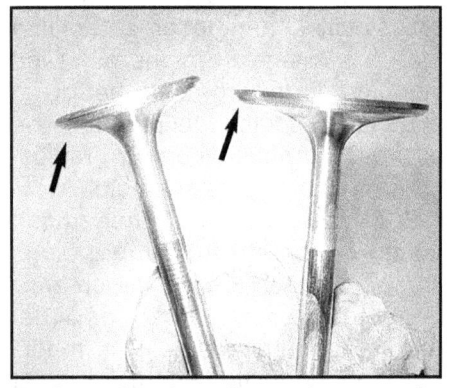

Back-cutting the valves to improve airflow is probably better than joining the back face of the valve to the seat with a radius. The point where the back-cut angle meets the seat provides a ridge for fuel shearing and helps break up the fuel as it enters the cylinder.

tion at the booster and have a tendency to degrade the quality of the mixture less than large plenums and runners. Lastly, small, high swirl intake ports in the cylinder head are better at maintaining mixture quality going into the cylinder than large cross-sectional area, low swirl ports. All the foregoing have a distinct affect on how well the engine operates at part throttle under cruise and full throttle low rpm conditions. They also have an effect on how responsive the engine is to the throttle.

What we have just discussed gives a working overview of the variables that determine the limiting lean mixture ratio. As can be seen, it can be a highly variable number. A typical, well set up engine can usually run lean mixture ratios up to about the 18:1 mark. However, attention to detail throughout the induction and ignition systems can produce what qualifies as a lean burn engine with mixture ratios as lean as 22:1, effectively ignitable. When building specifically for economy, it is possible to effectively use ratio's as lean as 28:1.

ATOMIZATION & POWER

Good fuel atomization and high port velocities that tend to maintain atomization produce a snappy engine. For full power, however, another set of criteria begin to come into play. Obviously small venturis and minimally sized ports are going to restrict the engine's breathing ability, hence the need to select a carburetor, intake manifold and cylinder head design that will be the best compromise for the required usage. For a street vehicle, carburetor sizing and intake manifold selection will obviously need to be dictated so as to produce an acceptable amount of mileage and drivability consistent with the desired top end power. For a race vehicle, mileage only becomes a problem on long distance races, and even so, it must remain subordinate to outright horsepower. For a drag racer, fuel consumption is irrelevant. Maximum power is everything. But even if maximum power is the sole intent, fuel atomization must still be good in the desired RPM operating range. Even if large carburetors are used, along with large plenums and cross-sectional area of manifolds, these sizes must be consistent with the engine's potential output capability. If the carburetor and intake manifold combination selected is too big for the job and mixture quality suffers, then power is likely to drop by more than the potential gain from better breathing.

No doubt you've heard many times that selecting a carburetor that is too big for the job hurts low end power. We now know it hurts low-end power because poor fuel atomization reduces the mixture quality and cuts combustion efficiency. If you can accept that mixture preparation is as important as mixture ratio, you will be one big step in front of the competition. Fortunately, mixture preparation gets easier as RPMs increase, and the hardest situations to satisfy are those conditions where speeds through the venturi are low because the engine is throttled back. Before leaving the subject of mixture preparation and part throttle operations, it is worthwhile pointing out that when a high intake manifold vacuum exists, it is much easier to vaporize the fuel because the boiling point of the

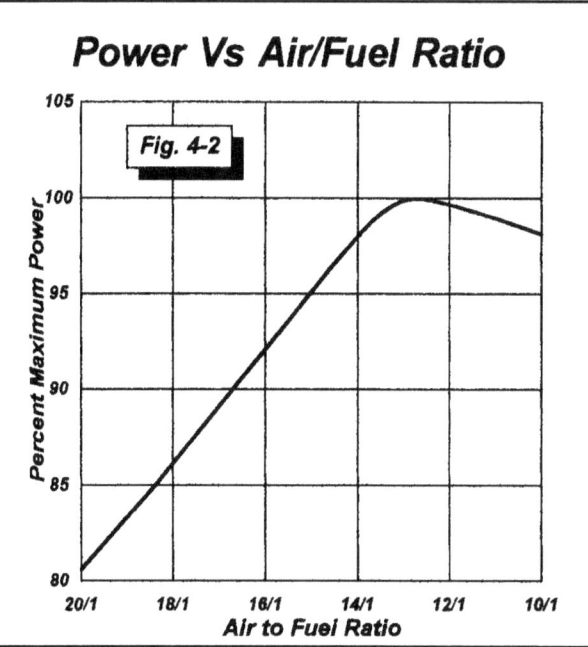

As shown in this graph, the power drops off faster on the lean side of maximum power than it does on the rich side. This means that any tuning should err toward the rich side, as any error in the calibration will have less effect on power. The target zone is generally between 12.7:1 and 13.1:1. Anywhere between these two ratio's, the change in power is not generally measurable. However, if the engine is for long-distance racing the running at the leaner of these two ratios will produce significantly better fuel consumption.

fuel drops as air pressure drops. If the fuel preparation from the carburetor is good enough, it is possible to do away with the hot spot in the intake manifold. Once the engine is warm, there will be no disadvantage to this, even cruising at light throttle openings. The only realistic disadvantage will be that the engine will need the choke on longer during warm-up.

Mixture ratios for maximum power fall within a much tighter range than those for maximum economy. Since what is needed is so much more closely defined, it is not essential to dyno the engine to be able to set the mixture reasonably close to optimum. We have already seen from Fig. 4-2, that being a little over-rich does not hurt power significantly. If operation falls within this reasonably wide operating window, the engine will deliver within the odd percent or two of maximum power. Obviously, it's best if we get the mixture right on, but achieving optimal results usually requires power testing in some form or another. This can be on a chassis or engine dyno or, since speed equates to power, on the drag strip. For maximum power, we are looking for an air/fuel ratio between 12.7:1 to 13:1. Usually, those engines which have the manifold system delivering better mixture distribution tend to operate at a slightly leaner air/fuel ratio. But if this variable is removed from the equation, we then find the mixture ratio for maximum power is close to 13:1. This is almost irrespective of the type of cylinder head, camshaft, induction or exhaust system involved. The only exception to this is an engine having too much compression, and extra fuel must be used to suppress detonation. In such instances, we are dealing with something that comes under the heading of "a miscalculation."

**PUMP FUELS
BRAND 'A' VS BRAND 'B'**

Having looked at the importance of mixture ratios and the quality of the mixture, let's now look at the quality of the fuels we're likely to put into the fuel tanks of our performance machines. Chances are, you have seen it in print more than once that there isn't a lot of difference between fuel Brand 'A' and Brand 'B' in terms of power potential. Although the quality of fuels is continually being improved, there still exists a considerable difference between a top-notch fuel and an indifferent one. Some tests we conducted in a high-compression engine serve to emphasize the point. The basis of the tests was to establish whether the octane value of the fuel was in fact a guide to its power potential in a high-compression engine. In other words, would a 91 octane Brand 'A' fuel produce the same as a 91 octane Brand 'B' fuel in terms of power in a high-compression engine? The answer without a shadow of a doubt was no, and the differences were anything but minimal. Under certain circumstances, the best fuels produced in excess of 25% more power than the worst. Admittedly, the greatest differences between the best and worst fuel becomes greater as compression ratios increase. The high 14.7:1 compression on the test engine did serve to magnify the differences between the fuels. Nonetheless, dyno testing at more normal compression ratios also revealed differences in output.

The octane values of a fuel is normally tested on what is known as a C.F.R. engine. This is a large single cylinder engine on which the compression ratio can be varied. In essence, the ability of a fuel to resist detonation is tested by raising the compression ratio until it just begins to detonate. This value is compared with the detonation level of a mixture of two basic fuels: Normal Heptane (N-Heptane), which detonates very easily and has an arbitrary rating of zero; and Iso-octane, which does not detonate very readily and has been assigned the value of 100 for its detonation resistance. If a fuel detonates at the same level as a blend of 92% Iso-octane and 8% N-Heptane, then it's known as a 92 octane fuel. If it detonates at the same level as 100% Iso-octane, then it's 100 octane fuel. However,

Here is the selection of fuels the author tested in a high compression engine to see if they were indeed "virtually all the same" as has so often been claimed by popular monthlies. The results speak for themselves.

How to Build Horsepower, Vol. 2   **33**

If the engine compartment is hot, a polished manifold becomes a performance aid as well as a cosmetic attribute. The surface reflects the heat from the rest of the engine compartment. If the engine compartment is cool, then it becomes a question of cosmetics only.

The effectiveness of exhaust scavenging has a profound effect on the carburetion and the complexity of the calibration. Hard scavenging exhaust systems, like this one on the author's 230 HP Pinto (2 liter type as opposed to 2.3), require a great deal of care and patience to determine the best emulsion tube/air corrector/booster combination for optimal atomization and fuel delivery accuracy.

there are other factors that influence the level at which a fuel detonates, other than compression. The principle one of these is temperature, with a secondary factor being RPM. In Europe, the octane number used is the Research Octane Number. The United States is different. The octane values shown at a service station pump are the R + M/2 octane values. This number is derived from two distinct octane value tests and results in the Research Octane Number (RON) and the Motor Octane Number (MON). The Research Octane Number is arrived at by running the C.F.R. engine at 600 RPM with an intake temperature of 150°F. The Motor Octane Number is produced by running the engine at 900 RPM with the intake temperature at 300°F. Some fuel fractions may resist detonation very well when induced into the engine at low temperature, but do not show very good results at high temperature. Conversely, some fractions may be okay or mediocre at low temperature, yet not degrade significantly as the temperature increases. Normally, a typical service station pump gasoline shows a Research Octane Number about eight points higher than its Motor Octane Number. The difference between the two is known as the fuel's temperature sensitivity. A highly sensitive fuel may show 10 points difference, whereas an insensitive one may only show six. This information is added not just for casual interest but to explain why induction temperatures and the fuel selected are important to the power output of your engine.

UNLEADED HIGH OCTANE

Many of the high octane unleaded fuels that came onto the market during the mid-to late 1980s achieve these higher values by having them "brewed" in. In other words, the fuel fractions involved were selected from those which had naturally higher octane values. The old technique, when adding lead was a common practice, was to simply add enough lead to bring the fuel up to the required octane. With lead usage restricted, it became necessary to produce fuels that were naturally higher octane in their own right. For instance, Toluene has a high octane and is a relatively common fuel fraction in today's gasoline. By stepping up the amount of Toluene in the blend, the octane can be raised. However, in many cases some of the blends used may have raised the Research Octane Number significantly, but barely changed the Motor Octane Number at all. The net result is the

How important is jetting on a set of sophisticated carbs, such as these 48 Webers? Essentially, you are looking at eight independent carbs here. Having the jetting out is at least twice as disastrous as it would be for a typical four-barrel carbureted engine. Add to this the potentially superior calibration available, and it not hard to imagine loosing 50 to 75 horsepower due to mis-calibration. This being the case, it makes sense to take the trouble to calibrate this type of carb properly.

Getting the mixture "right" by plug reading is not so much an art but more a fallacy. If you believe this is all you need to get the mixture spot on, or even close enough to make no difference, you are 30 years behind the times, and in today's performance world, that won't cut it.

R + M/2 value increases, but the Motor Octane Number, which is the level at which most street vehicles run, changes hardly at all. So the fuel's resistance to detonation in service on the road, improves little, if any. We are not saying this was or is the case for all fuels, but marketing is marketing. If a fuel company can put a 92 octane label on their pumps, instead of 91, without raising their price, they are likely to have an edge on their 91 octane competition.

OCTANES TESTED

The main objective of our tests were to see how much variance there was between fuels of similar octane. Bearing in mind the C.F.R. engine simply tested for octane values, not power output, it was necessary to devise a test which more realistically applied to the vehicles we drove on the street. In reality, the octane value of the fuel is not the final issue, horsepower is. This means if a 90 octane blend produces more horsepower than a 92 octane fuel, then it makes sense to use it rather than the lower power 92 octane fuel. The question is, does octane value alone dictate the results in a high compression engine or is there more to it than that? To establish this one way or another, we built a special engine. It employed a 14.7:1 compression ratio and a short duration cam with a tight

Although many dynos are equipped with exhaust temperature sensors to indicate mixture distribution, it has to be said that this technique is, in most instances, no better than plug reading. On the IR carbureted engine on the previous page, all the calibration components were tried in every carb barrel. In spite of this the same calibration in a different hole would show as much as 600°F difference. Hardly a precise calibration method! In addition to that, it is too slow to pick up resonant surge mixture changes or the effect of accelerator pumps.

lobe center line angle. The idea was to run this engine, a small-block Chevy, at a steady 3000 RPM and measure its output using a variety of well-known fuel brands. At the high CR employed, all service station pump fuels will detonate in this engine. The test involved advancing the ignition timing until the engine was just about to detonate. At this point ,power figures would be taken. Obviously, the best fuel is the one that produced the most horsepower and, as we had previously supposed, this may not necessarily be the one with the highest octane.

Since the effective octane value of a fuel can change with temperature, tests were done at three different intake temperatures. For this, three identical manifolds were prepared. One with exhaust heat, one with the exhaust heat riser blocked and one with a water-cooled heat riser passage. This last manifold was fed with water at 50°F. This resulted in three distinctly different intake temperatures at the intake ports. Eight different brands of premium fuel were tested, and Daeco race gas at 110 Octane (R+M/2) was used as a reference fuel. This fuel was chosen because for many years its specification has remained unchanged, and it is blended to very close tolerances, so two barrels of fuel purchased six months apart are likely to produce virtually identical results under comparative conditions. With i's high octane level, the test engine's ignition timing could be optimized for maximum power without reaching the fue'ls detonation threshold. Having established the Daeco fuel power level for each intake test temperature, the other fuels were run to see how closely they could approach it.

The results of these test are shown in Fig. 4-3. Some obvious facets show up in these tests, namely that the Sunoco Ultra, which had the highest pump octane of the fuels tested, did not produce the highest horsepower when the heated intake manifold was used. It didn't show its true value in terms of power delivered for octane capability until it was used in the cooler intake manifolds. Even then, Texaco with its significantly lesser octane value, was still a good match for it. However, the trends throughout these tests are obvious. The high-

The most effective way to-date, short of spending an unbelievable fortune, that the author has found to verify air/fuel ratio is the use of oxygen (Lambda) sensors in each exhaust pipe. By allowing more precise stagger jetting to reduce inter-cylinder fuel distribution differences, this usually works out to be a 20 horsepower speed trick even on the best previous setups.

The oxygen sensor mixture readouts can be made removable so they can go from car to dyno. The value of installing such a setup in the vehicle is that a video camera can be used to see what happens to the mixture when the car leaves the line at 2.2 G or goes through a banked or flat corner. Oxygen sensors beat exhaust temperature probes by a long mile!

er the intake temperature is, the more sensitive modern fuels become in terms of the results they deliver. In other words, the trend among modern fuels (as of 1995) is that they do not tolerate high intake temperatures as well as the old leaded fuels and they tend to become detonation limited sooner. The moral here is that with modern fuels we need to concentrate more on keeping induction and engine temperatures down so as to better utilize the existing octane values of the fuel.

FUEL DISTRIBUTION

It's easy to make the assumption that fuel distribution is simply a function of manifold design and that the distribution of any liquid within that manifold is mechanically governed by the shape of the manifold. If the liquid introduced into the manifold were always liquid, this would tend to be largely true. But a fuel's volatility can vary. Each fuel 'fraction' evaporates at a different temperature. If a curve of temperatures against remaining volume of fuel is plotted, it produces what is known as a distillation curve. Fuel manufacturers vary the constituents of their fuel depending upon the season and geographic location. For instance, a winter fuel has more low temperature evaporating constituents than a summer one to aid cold starting. For high-performance engines, the amount of fuel that evaporates prior to entering the cylinders can have an influence on the distribution. When what is called the "light front end" hydrocarbons evaporate, they flow in the manifold in exactly the same manner as the air. Hence, fuel distribution problems in relation to vaporized fuel largely disappear. This means the more fuel that is evaporated, the more the mixture ratio between cylinders is evened up. This sounds like it should be

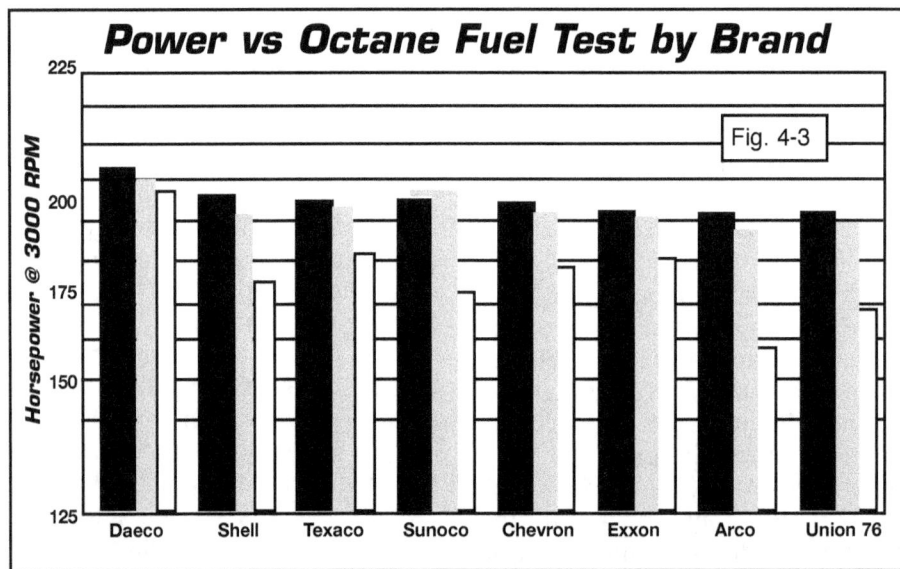

These tests were done using three different intake charge temperatures. The water cooled intake, which showed the best results in all cases, had the intake temperature artificially lowered by running water at 48 to 50°F through cooling passages in the manifold, and therefore represents an artificial condition. The unheated intake manifold, the middle of each set of three, is an unheated manifold and closely represents a race engine intake temperature. The right hand column of each set is the heated manifold and is typical of most street driven engines. The baseline fuel for this test was 105 (R+M/2) octane Daeco race gasoline, which even with the 14.7:1 CR of the test engine, allowed optimal spark timing. Shell 92 octane fuel was the next best when tested with the water-cooled manifold, but it fared worse than several of the other fuels, including the 91 octane Texaco, when tested at the more normally used operating temperature. With the exception of the 93.5 octane Sunoco, all the fuels degraded as the temperature increased. Some fuels, such as Arco 91 octane and to a lesser extent Union 76 91 octane, experienced a strong negative reaction to increased intake temperature. Of the street blends, Chevron 92 octane and Exxon 91 octane fuel showed the least variance between hot and cold intakes. What these tests serve to illustrate is that R+M/2 octane values only represent a possible power advantage at cooler intake temperatures. These results should convince any race engine builder of the value of reducing intake charge temperatures.

good for power, but we have to weigh it against the loss of volumetric efficiency caused by the vaporization. However, if a suitable compromise can be struck, a fuel with enough light front end hydrocarbons could have a tendency to even up mixtures amongst cylinders and improve horsepower. Yet, the better our manifolding gets, the less likely the engine is to need this. Among very high compression V8 race engines using a single four-barrel, there does seem a tendency to prefer fuels having a little more volatility than those on injection or with two fours on a Tunnel Ram intake. Often, achieving a very high compression, especially on small cubic inch engines, means a big dome on the piston. This can compromise chamber shape and cut the burning efficiency of the charge. Usually, the biggest problem with a chamber having a high dome is getting the burn started in a favorable fashion. Evaporated fuels are easier to ignite and once an initial flame front is functioning, the burning of the rest of the charge becomes a little easier.

RACE FUELS

It's often assumed that race fuels will automatically produce more horsepower than service station pump fuel. This is not necessarily the case. The reason for using a race fuel as opposed to a regular pump fuel can be numerous, but the main over-riding factor stems from the fact that race fuels have higher octane values than pump fuels. Most race gasolines are leaded, though we have seen the emergence of unleaded racing gasoline from Union 76 and other well-known companies. Depending upon the type of fuel, various race gas blends can produce octane levels up to a claimed 119 octane. Although there is absolutely no point in using an octane value higher than the engine needs, such octane levels are unlikely to detonate under any normal circumstances. For the most part, the biggest gain in horsepower from a race gas comes from the ability to utilize compression ratios of 11:1 to as high as 17:1.

All too often dyno tests are done without sufficient care to the continuing condition of the engine or fuel and ignition optimization. A primary consideration is to monitor the state of the engine. Apart from regular compression and leak down checks, a blow-by test should also be added to the agenda. If the engine employs some means of generating a crankcase depression, we substitute decaying crankcase vacuum as a prime indicator of engine condition.

CUSTOM BLENDS

Fuel blends can be tailored to produce minor advantages other than just octane values. Let's look at some of these so we have a clearer picture of the potential of race fuel. First, let's consider the energy content of the fuel. Basically, a typical gasoline is fed into the

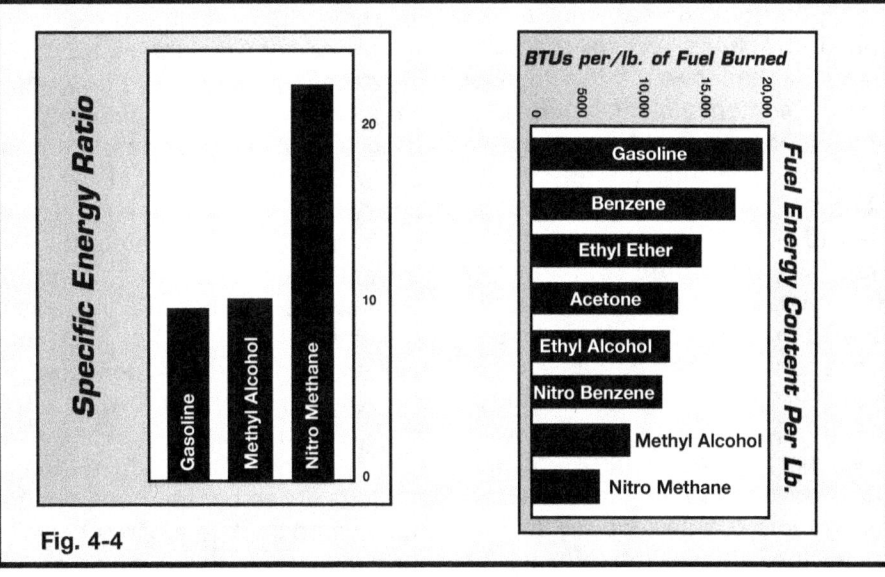

Fig. 4-4

Gasoline is a very effective fuel in terms of its energy content per pound, as the chart above shows. It delivers way more heat than the nitro methane used in top fuel dragster motors. For a race engine, it's disadvantage lies in the fact that it requires only a comparatively small amount of fuel for a given amount of air to produce the required fuel/air ratio. This means it is good for fuel economy but falls short of the power that can be produced by some other well-known fuels. If we look at the amount of fuel required to burn with 1 lb. of air, we see a different picture emerge. Because Methyl Alcohol (Methanol) requires a mixture three times richer for complete combustion, the fact that it has only a little over a third of the energy content is more than offset. When mixed at its maximum power ratio, Methyl Alcohol has some 6% more energy content than gasoline, as is shown in the chart above. If we consider the same situation for Nitro Methane, we find that it has 230% more energy content than gasoline.

Always test engines in a way that is representative of the installation in the vehicle. If air filters are to be used (and why wouldn't they?) test with them installed.

Exhaust systems should have zero back-pressure, and the end of the tuned-length should dump into an open chamber at least 8 times the volume of one cylinder or more if we are dealing with overlapping pulses as per a V8. For more info on exhaust systems read the *How to Build Horsepower* high performance exhaust system book published by S-A Design.

engine for no other reason then to heat the air the cylinder contains. It is the expansion of the air due to its heating that pushes the piston down the bore. Principally, the pressure developed in the cylinder is due to the ability of the gasoline to heat the air, and the amount it can potentially heat the air is called the fuel's energy content. Gasoline has one of the highest energy contents of any monopropellant liquid fuel. This is a fuel that must be burned with oxygen from the atmosphere. To give an idea of the effectiveness of gasoline, let's compare it with some of the other well known fuels as the Chart Fig. 4-4 shows. You can see it has, on a per pound basis, more real energy content than nitromethane, alcohol, etc. Such exotic fuels only score in terms of outright power potential because so much more fuel is required to produce the correct mixture for a given amount of air. The bottom line here is it is difficult to produce a fuel with more energy content and more fuel efficiency than the gasoline we get from the service station pump. Even race gasolines have only marginally more energy content per pound, thus limiting their potential to produce additional horsepower by whatever difference in energy content can be brewed into them.

Another factor of importance is the specific gravity of the fuel, that is, the fuel's density. When burned, a fuel and air charge must be mixed in the correct proportion by weight, but our carburetors mix it in proportion to volume. So if fuels are changed and have differing specific gravities, the carburetor should be re-calibrated to deliver the correct weight of fuel. For instance, let's say we've been running on a gasoline having a 0.7 specific gravity. This means it is 7/10 the weight of water. And the mixture delivered to the engine has been precisely calibrated by the correct jetting of the carburetor. If we now change to a fuel that has a specific gravity of 0.74, a greater weight of fuel will be delivered to the engine. Yet there will be no change in the air flow, so the mixture will now show rich although the jetting has not changed. To get the mixture back to a correct level, it will be necessary to install smaller jets. If the energy content and burning characteristics of the new fuel are identical to the previous fuel, it will be seen that since less fuel by volume is fed to the engine, the heavier fuel will produce more miles per gallon. This may not be important for a drag racer, but it certainly is for a Winston Cup or 24 Hour Le Mans racer.

ALCOHOL FUELS

Many types of race cars use alcohol-based fuels, and although we tend to think of this in relation to drag racing, probably by far the greatest number of alcohol-fueled cars are circulating the smaller paved and dirt circle tracks. Basically, alcohol-fueled engines fall into two groups: carbureted for Seda -style racing and injected for Sprinters. As a fuel, alcohol has pros and cons when compared with gasoline. As can be seen from the energy content chart, alcohol has less energy per pound than gasoline, but it is a well known fact that it makes more horsepower. The reason for this is that it requires about three times the amount of fuel to get the correct air/fuel ratio for proper combustion. Apart from this, alcohol has a substantial cooling effect on the intake charge due to its high latent heat of evaporation. This means alcohol tends to absorb a lot of heat during it's evaporation process. This, plus the fact copious amounts of fuel is being thrown into the engine, means cool intake charges. Basically, an engine fueled on alcohol should produce a theoretical increase in torque output of 12 to 15% throughout the RPM range. This will of course equate to a 12 to 15% increase in power. Yet for these gains to be achieved, everything depends on using the alcohol fuel correctly. If we're considering Sprinters with their fuel injection system, then the problem of delivering fuel to the engine in the appropriate manner and quantities is largely eradicated by the fact such systems are designed from the outset for the job at hand.

For now, let's concentrate on carbureted alcohol-fueled engines. First, the alcohol carburetor of choice is the Holley. Though Holley has produced an alcohol-fueled carburetor, the most favored carburetors are those Holleys built by the independent carburetor specialists. Early efforts at using Holleys on alcohol revealed two main problems with

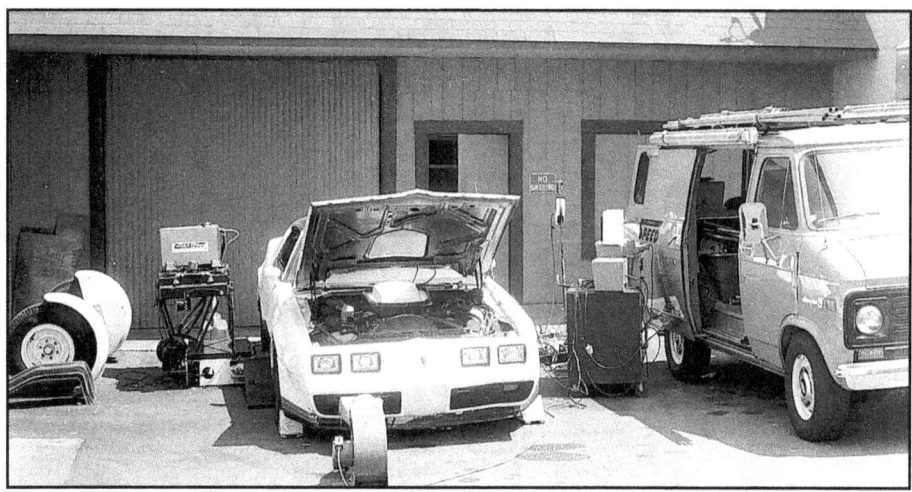

For many, getting on an engine dyno is not very convenient. The transportable chassis dyno as per this one run by Evanspeed in California may be the wave of the future. Proprietor Dave Evens will visit your premises within a radius of about 50 miles, but if it is rented by a car club or the like for a number of dyno tunes, he will transport the dyno over considerable distances to the premises.

The Evenspeed Dyno constructed by Dave Evens utilizes a water brake, and the absorber heat is disposed of by this radiator and fan. The capacity of the radiator system is the limitation of this type of brake. In practice, about 300 horsepower is the limit, although for a short period with a heavy car, 350 can be handled. This may not seem like much considering the numbers that are bandied around in the popular press. Take it from us, only the best 350 inch street motors peg this dyno—much to the surprise of most owners.

the conversion. The first was supplying enough fuel to the float bowl to meet demand. To increase the fuel flow up to 300% higher than gasoline led to some pretty esoteric and overengineered systems. At the end of the day, it only needed a purpose designed needle valve, such as the one designed by the author for Braswell Carburetion in Tucson, to get the job done. Once float bowl fuel delivery problems were taken care of, the next major problem is that an alcohol carburetor needs a really strong booster signal, as fuel atomization is far more critical. The reason for this is that there is a lot more fuel that can puddle. Second, alcohol has a single evaporating temperature. The basic temperature of evaporation for alcohol is significantly higher than the evaporation temperature for gasoline's front end hydrocarbons. Because of alcohol's rapid cooling rates, intake manifold temperatures are lower so the job of generating a good mixture quality and fuel distribution becomes much more difficult than with gasoline. This means the need for good atomization becomes greater. Again, the responsibility for good atomization falls largely upon booster design. Not only must the booster have a high signal to pull in a lot of fuel, but also, this high signal is needed to aid atomization.

CARB CALIBRATION

An engine's most important performance calibration is the correct jetting of the carb. This usually presents the hot rodder with some problems. Two major issues tend to dominate the situation here: first, figuring out which carburetor circuit needs adjustment to fix an incorrect mixture, and second, where and when in the engine RPM range the problem occurs. The first part of the problem can usually be fixed by reading up on the carb you have to understand what each circuit does. But the second part of the problem is not corrected so easily. Although many racers fail to get it right, there is no real difficulty to getting carb calibration spot on. In the past, the racer's "tried and tested" method for carb calibration was to make a hot pass down the strip and adjust the jetting until the highest speeds were obtained. Don't kid yourself that this is a sure-fire method Even if you are an old hand at carb adjustment, optimizing fuel delivery could take 50 and maybe as many as a 100 passes to get the best performance. Then such things as atmospheric pressure and temperature can effect how well those calibrations hold. If the carb calibration was done on a hot day and the car raced in the cool of evening, jetting is likely to be as much as a size or two off. Jetting at the track tends only to sort the mixture under one condition: wide open throttle. It doesn't take into account what happens at part throttle, which for a street machine is where the engine operates most of the time.

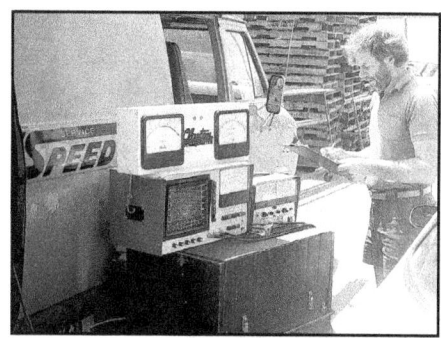

Another advantage of calibrating the carburetion and ignition on a chassis dyno is that a typical session will, with the right operator and equipment, reveal most, if not all the minor system faults and allow them to be rectified before they become big problems.

CHASSIS DYNOS

If you've built and broken in a new engine, the best way to calibrate the carb, along with all the other adjustable features of your engine is to get on a chassis dyno

How to Build Horsepower, Vol. 2   **39**

For a serious racer's chassis dyno, the Dynojet unit is, as of 1996, the power king. Capable of dynoing cars with up to 1200 wheel horsepower, it is in a league of its own. This dyno, which can be had as either an 'in floor' type or as a fully portable unit, uses heavy...

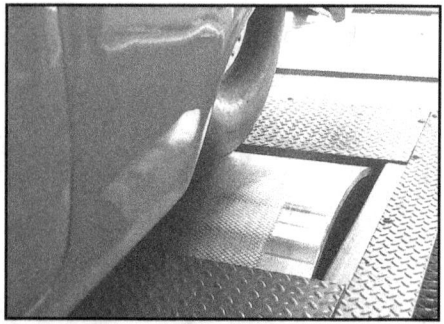

...48 inch diameter rollers to absorb the power. Once a run is made, the vehicle can either be left to coast down or the brakes can be applied to turn the roller kinetic energy into heat. Another unusual and innovative feature of this dyno...

is the fact that, with a manual transmission car it can produce steady state flywheel power figures, usually within the 1% accuracy of a regular engine dyno. When using this type of dyno, the author has found it to be extremely repeatable. When the engine itself is consistent run to run, the dyno output graphs superimpose one over the other with no discernible difference.

and have everything of power output set up by a competent engine tuner. Dynos capable of testing smaller engined cars are common but if you have a stout V8, things get a little more difficult. A good but totally streetable 400-inch motor can top well 400 horsepower at the wheels. At the time of writing, only the Dynojet chassis dyno with some 1200 horsepower capability would hold such a vehicle and they are rare. However if you can find a dyno of adequate capacity for your vehicle the technique for carburetor calibration is relatively straightforward. A conventional mixture analyzer is installed in the exhaust pipe and the vehicle is run on the rollers as if it were on the road. Full power mixture curves, as well as part-throttle, can be analyzed and the relevant circuit of the carb adjusted to deliver an optimal air/fuel ratio under the conditions tested. With a competent operator, a chassis dyno carb calibration session can be extremely effective.

PLUG READING

Plug reading is a popular past time among many racer and engine builders. A plug pulled from the motor will be passed around and declared to be this or that, but watch next time you are at the track and see this about to happen. No one will have an opinion that is far out of line with the norm. Why? No one wants to be the odd man out and be wrong. Plug reading for mixture is an acquired art and at best its an approximation. Assuming a carburetor is calibrated approximately correctly because plug readings look okay is a mistake most people make. In reality, even if the plugs look about the right color, 9 out of 10 carburetors are delivering a mixture that can short change even a 300-inch street motor of as much as 20 horsepower of its full capability. Probably 2 out of 10 are as much as 40 horsepower off. To put the worth of a good dyno tune in perspective, consider the fact that one will cost about the same as a good carb. If the dyno finds 20 horsepower, and they usually find a lot more, we're talking about power gains equal to or better than the carb which you had no trouble finding the cash for. The beauty of having your engine set up correctly is it inevitably does more miles per gallon, drives better and goes faster. Chances are, over the next 18 months or so you will get your money back in fuel cost savings and you'll have the benefits of the extra power.

OXYGEN SENSORS

Setting up on the chassis dyno makes a lot of sense, but what if one isn't within a hundred miles of you or the ones that are convenient aren't into performance tune-ups? Now you have to calibrate the carb yourself. Paying for time on a drag strip and simply making passes down the strip can turn out to be pretty expensive. Setting up carburetor calibration anywhere but on a chassis dyno with the correct instrumentation can fall well short of optimum unless you have some means of determining whether the mixture is rich or lean. As we have just discussed, plug reading is not okay even for experts and it is far from infallible. To do the job properly, you need to have some form of mixture analyzer. Essentially, portable mixture analyzers that

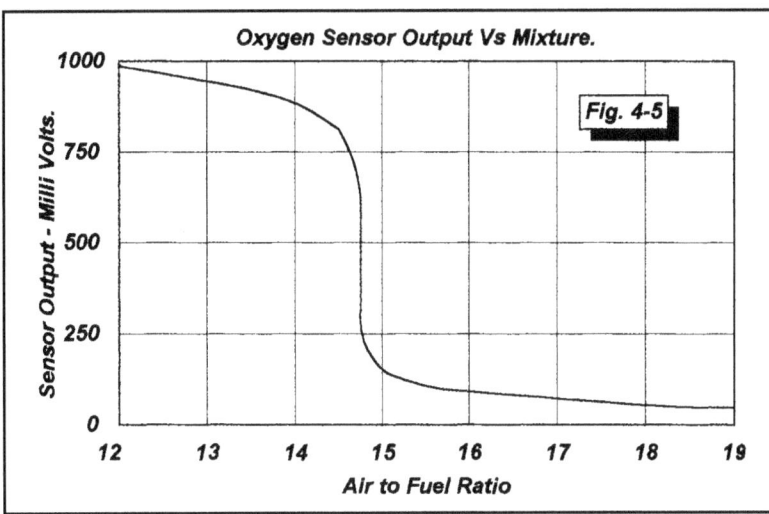

Many pro engine builders reject the oxygen sensor as an accurate means of calibrating carb jetting. The reason most often quoted is that they do not operate in the range that the fuel/air ratio must be for max power. Here is why they are wrong. Shown here is the typical output from what is commonly known as an oxygen sensor, but correctly called a Lambda sensor. The characteristic that allows it to function as a mixture analyzer, measuring ratios richer than stoichiometric is the fact that it operates in two modes. If it only operated as an oxygen sensor, there would be no change in output once the mixture became richer than about 14.7:1 since there would be no oxygen to sense. What saves the day, is the fact that below 14.7:1 the Lambda sensor, in effect becomes a temperature sensor. As mixture ratios become richer below the 14.7:1 point so the exhaust tends to cool off. Over the temperature range we are concerned with the output of the sensor rises with dropping temperature. It is this characteristic that allows the Lambda sensor to provide us with a simple and more accurate means of setting the mixture than plug reading.

But if you are not altogether happy with the accuracy over the cooling range there is another method that even the Lambda sensor's greatest detractors can hardly deny is a functional method of arriving at accurate mixture ratios on all cylinders. This second technique is to calibrate all the jets so that the sensors show a 14.7:1 ratio. Having arrived at this point, if all the jets are now increased in size by 14%, the fuel air ratio will be 13:1. If you are working with a Holley don't forget the jet area also includes the power valve restriction channel. Lambda sensors have yet to be accepted by the pros, but their time will come. They are so much better than plug reading (dodgy at best), and their quick response even allows accurate calibration of accelerator pump circuits.

sample the exhaust as per chassis dyno installations have been around for years. The only problem with such an analyzer is a slow response time and it is necessary to hold the throttle at a given setting for at least 15 seconds to get an idea of what the mixture is.

With the advent of the Lambda-sensor in emission systems, a new breed of mixture analyzer hit the scene. A Lambda-sensor, or its more common name, an oxygen sensor, allows the exhaust to be analyzed in a much more rapid fashion. At first sight, it may seem that an oxygen sensor would only work up until the point where no oxygen existed in the exhaust, which would be at the chemically correct mixture. In practice, however, the oxygen sensor has a wider range of output than is affected by a mixture that has oxygen present. Fig. 4-5 shows a typical output of an oxygen sensor. If this output is suitably processed by an electronic package, it can measure mixtures from about 17:1 down to as rich as 12:1. This is an adequate range to do almost all carburetor calibrations except those for outright lean burn type fuel economy. If you intend calibrating your carb precisely, the first step is to get an oxygen sensing mixture analyzer such as those marketed by K & N, Autotronics, Edelbrock and Howell Injection. These mixture analyzers, which should be used with unleaded gas if they are to have a life of more than a couple of hours, have a very rapid response time and can even be used to analyze pump jet circuits, an almost impossible task with the conventional infrared gas sampler. The Lambda sensor mixture analyzer is very simple to install. The most complex part is the drilling of the hole in the exhaust system and brazing in the threaded adapter nut to allow the insertion of the sensor. From here on wiring takes all of five minutes.

Most of my experience has been with the K & N units, which I normally mount on the steering column. The technique to calibrate the carb is to monitor the mixture in relation to throttle position and RPM, then correct the relevant circuit. If the carb is a Holley, the circuit that will probably present the most problem as to when it's functioning or not, will be the one operated by the power valve. For this, you will need to install a vacuum gauge to an engine manifold vacuum source. Calibrating a Holley's main jet and the Power Valve Restriction Channel represent two distinctly different operational areas. Although most tuners calibrate the main jet for full power, this should be done on the Power Valve Restriction Channel. This will come into operation when the vacuum drops below the value stamped on the power valve. You will need the vacuum gauge to determine for sure when the power valve has opened and brought the PVRC into operation. Let's run through a brief example here. We'll say you have a power valve that comes in at 6.5 inches of mercury. When the power valve opens, the PVRC now passes extra fuel to enrich the mixture to full power rich status. If the mixture was correct for cruise prior to this, then the main jet was right. But if the mixture was not correct when the power valve comes in, it is the PVRC that needs to be re-sized appropriately, not the main jet. The main jet should be calibrated to give a good economy figure with the power valve coming in to give maximum horsepower.

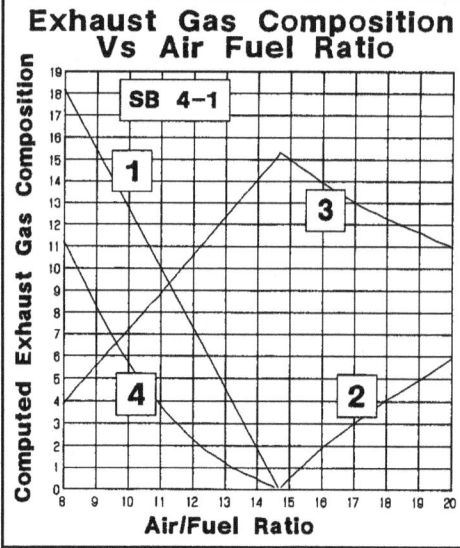

Curve #1 Carbon Monoxide (CO)
Curve #2 Oxygen (O)
Curve #3 Carbon Dioxide (CO2)
Curve #4 Hydrogen (H)

If an engine is set up on a chassis dyno, chances are that the exhaust gas analyzer will read out in percentage of CO. This graph shows the computed percent composition of the exhaust by volume. For maximum power, the CO reading on the exhaust gas analyzer should be about 6%.

AIR FUEL RATIO REQUIREMENTS

A study of this graph will show what is needed in the way of air/fuel ratios under various operating conditions. The first aspect to appreciate from this graph is that the quality and intensity of the spark is a major influence on the mixture's ignitability at the leaner ratios. With a suitably high powered ignition and a well developed head in terms of mixture swirl/agitation, the author has run ratio's as lean as 28:1 with manifold vacuums in the 16 inch range. In practice, we find that as of 1996, most engines run close to the conventional ignition curve. Above about 20 inches of manifold vacuum, there appears to be a trend for the lean limit of combustion to drop off and richer mixtures are required. This is because as the throttle is closed and vacuum increases the amount of exhaust dilution caused by reverse flowing exhaust makes the mixture less ignitable. This graph shows air fuel ratios for an engine in operation rather than at idle. For a conventional ignition, the mixture at idle will often need to be as much as a full 2 ratios richer than shown here. The difference between a lean burn engine and the conventional ignition engine for the smoothest idle may only be 2 to 3 ratio's leaner.

For full throttle driving, the range of mixture ratios and manifold operating conditions falls into area A. Ratios of 12.8:1 to 13:1 are common to most engines, but the situation is influenced by mixture distribution and to a lesser extent, fuel droplet size. In addition to this, maximum power can often be made on a little less fuel, although experience has shown that in some instances, the reverse has also applied. During transient conditions when the accelerator pump is in operation, ratios as rich as 12.5:1 are common. Indeed, the greater the starting vacuum at the commencement of throttle opening, and the faster the throttle is opened, the richer the mixture needs to be. In some cases the mixture ratio may need to be momentarily as rich as 10:1.

Area B is the operating range for fast driving short of full throttle. Since full power is not being used, a full power rich mixture would be nothing more than a waste of fuel. This area is also the range into which the mixture needs to move when the accelerator pump comes into action during typical cruise driving.

Area C represents the mid- to high-speed cruise conditions, as typified by vehicles on a unrestricted highway, such as the Autobahn in Germany, or a light truck with a relatively heavy load on the freeway.

Area D is typical of a vehicle at 65 to 70 MPH on the freeway. Here only about 15% of the engine's output is required, so mileage becomes the criteria, not power.

In addition to all these possible optimum fuel air ratios for power and economy, we must add the requirements for clean exhaust. Very often it is necessary to run mixtures near stoichiometric (chemically correct), so as to achieve the best results from the catalytic converter.

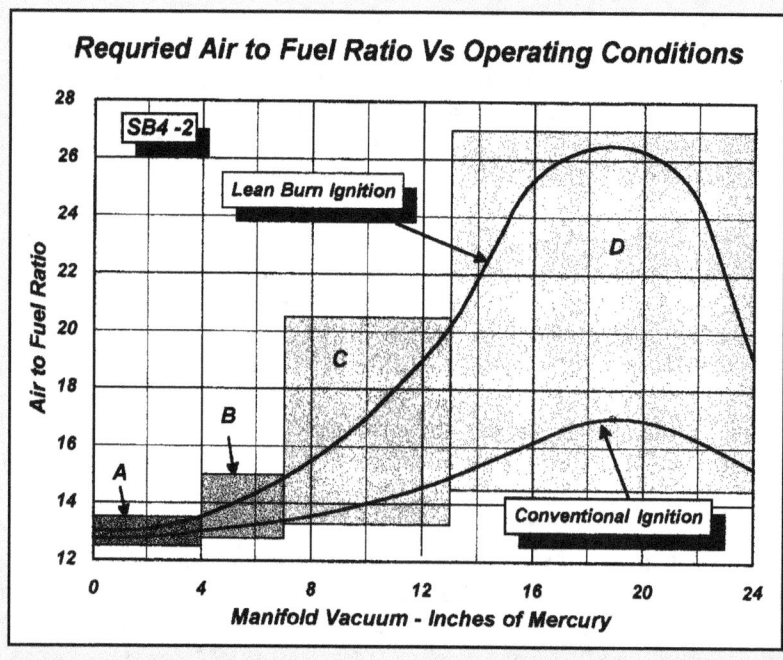

FUEL SUPPLY

There is little point in attempting to calibrate a carburetor that is supplied insufficient fuel. Much is made about fuel systems, as if there is some great mystery involved. This is a misconception. All that is required of the fuel system is to supply an adequate amount of fuel to the engine with a good margin for error left over. The inferred complexity, if that is the right word to use, comes in reliably achieving this goal. At this point, it will pay to consider what happens if the fuel supply is less than adequate. If the fuel pump falls way short of the engine's demand, then the engine goes lean and cuts out. The problem of inadequate fuel supply soon becomes obvious, and the problem gets attention. If the pump is only marginally shy of supplying the engine's demand, we have a potentially more destructive situation. Here, the resulting lean mixture will rob the engine of some of its cooling during the induction stroke. This can lead to melted pistons from overheating, and the problem may be mistakenly attributed to carb jetting. The golden rule with fuel pumps is to start with too much pump and back off from there. Stick with this rule and you will avoid some costly engine failures.

FUEL FLOW REQUIREMENTS

We can make a provisional assessment of the amount of fuel needed by an engine from the Brake Specific Fuel Consumption (BSFC) figures commonly seen. A good engine will, at full throttle, use about 0.4 to 0.43 lbs of fuel per horsepower per hour. That means a 1 horsepower engine running flat out for one hour will consume about 0.4 lbs of fuel. Exceptional motors get into the high 0.3s. Some very fuel-efficient compounded turbo piston aircraft engines have brought this figure down to 0.32. However, most modified engines are far from being as fuel efficient. As a result, even some of the better ones often use as much as 0.5 lbs of fuel per hour for every horsepower they make. This 0.5 lbs per hour per horsepower should be considered the absolute bottom limit for the rate at which we supply fuel to the engine.

Using this figure lets work through an example. Assume we have a 500 horsepower engine. What is the minimum amount of fuel flow needed to satisfy its demand? To come up with the answer, multiply 500 times the minimum fuel flow per hour. That will be 500 x 0.5 = 250 lbs per hour. So our 500 horse motor needs a minimum of 250 lbs of fuel per hour supplied to it. A pump that delivers 250 lbs. per hour on a test rig will not do the job because of loss experienced in the vehicle's fuel system. We need to have a safety margin here, and 50% is as low as you should come for this. Our fuel pump requirement now looks like 250 lbs x 150% or 1.5 which equals 375 lbs per hour. One US gallon of gasoline weighs right on 6 lbs so to find the gallons per hour we divide the lbs.. per hour required by 6. In our example, that works out to be 375/6 = 62.5 gallons per hour. Putting what we have just learned into a simple formula, we

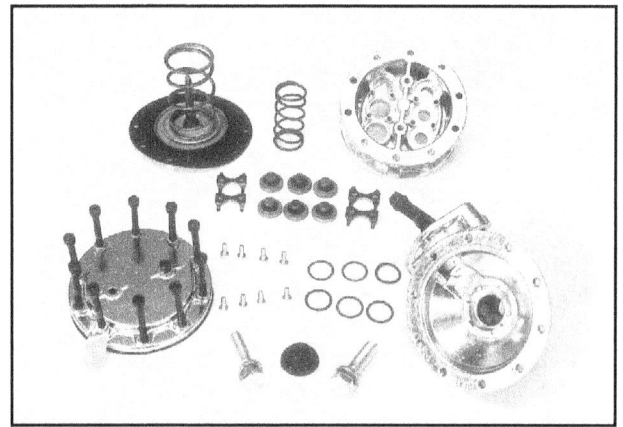

For a circle track application or street where high starting G forces are not seen, this BG-modified Holley 6 port mechanical pump will do the job.

Theoretically capable of satisfying the needs of a 1900 horsepower engine on the dyno, this BG fuel pump is far from the biggest they make. Used in conjunction with the diaphragm bypass valve it is an ideal pump for the serious drag racer, for anything up to about a 1000 horsepower.

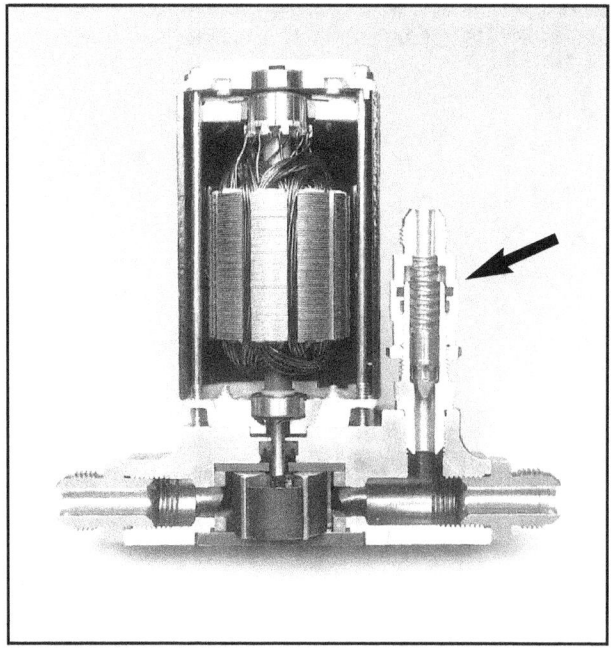

This is a cutaway of BG Fuel Systems biggest pump, the BG 400. It is designed for use on mountain motors and Pro Stock applications. Note the built-in adjustable bypass regulator (arrow).

can say that, with a 50% safety margin on a typical motor, for every 8 horsepower it makes, it will need 1 gallon of fuel flow per hour.

FLOW AND PRESSURE

Many mechanics confuse the importance of flow and pressure. It is entirely possible to have fuel pressure with no flow. Under these conditions, the engine will not run. Conversely, it is possible, given big enough fuel lines, to have a huge fuel flow without much pressure. In the second instance, the engine will run just fine. The only reason we need fuel pressure is to overcome the fuel system's resistance to the fuel flow. If it had a ½-inch diameter needle valve, a Holley carb, which PSI would run just fine on .5 PSI. The problem is, various factors conspire to reduce fuel flow. If the pressure driving the fuel from the tank to the carburetor float bowl is inadequate, then the fuel starvation we are trying to avoid will set in. If there is too much fuel pressure, it will overcome the float buoyancy and open the needle valve and flood the engine.

In practice, we find that there are circumstances that contrive to considerably reduce the effectiveness of a fuel pump. Such a situation arises due to the vehicle's acceleration, which, if its a drag racer, can be as high as 2.5 Gs when it leaves the line. To see what happens, let's walk through one

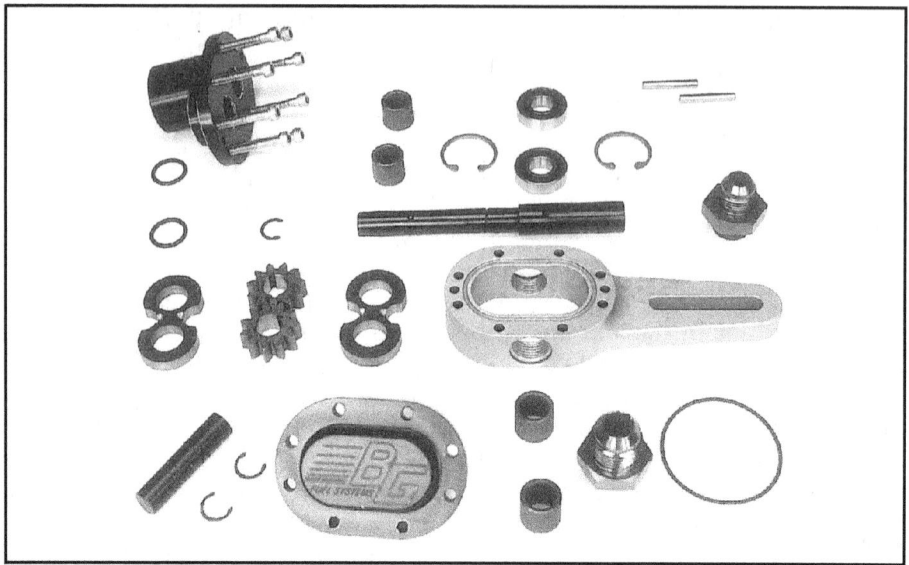

If you are intending to run an alcohol carbureted car then it is worth while considering the use of a very high capacity engine driven mechanical pump of the type seen here. This particular unit is from BG Fuel Systems but other examples are made by several other companies.

possible track scenario. Assume your car has a fuel pump that delivers just a little more fuel than the engine needs at 9 PSI. Under static conditions, such as on a dyno, the engine will perform perfectly. But if the fuel pressure were to drop for some reason, the flow to the carb will also drop and fuel starvation will set in. What could make the fuel pressure drop? Acceleration.

If we were to make a barometer using gasoline instead of mercury, we would, at normal air pressure, have a column not 29.93 inches, as is for mercury, but 580 inches or 48 feet. To pump a column of gasoline 48 feet high takes one atmosphere or 14.7 PSI. The 9 PSI of the pump we are using as an example would only push a column of gasoline to a little over 29 feet. So if our engine was situated 30 feet higher than the pump, it would not get any fuel. If the gravitational force experienced by the fuel were to double, the pump would only push the fuel to 14 ½ feet. Now let us put this pump in a car that leaves at 2.5 G. What this means is that the column of fuel between the tank and the engine experiences the effect of two and a half gravities. As a result, it backs off the pressure. The amount it

When mounted, a typical unit looks like this.

backs it out is equal to 0.3 PSI per foot per G (0.3 psi/ft/G). Typically, the fuel tank is about 10 feet behind the engine, so a moderate launch of only one G reduces the 9 PSI that the pump generates at the tank to 6 PSI at the float bowl, and a fuel shortage begins to occur. If the car left at 2 G, which is quite common, the pump pressure is reduced at the float bowl entry to only 3 PSI.

It is evident from what we have discussed here that the fuel pump needs to be capable of quite a few PSI more than is required at the float bowls. For a typical drag race installation, figure about 6 PSI more. This now means that we must select a pump that delivers fuel at the desired rate working

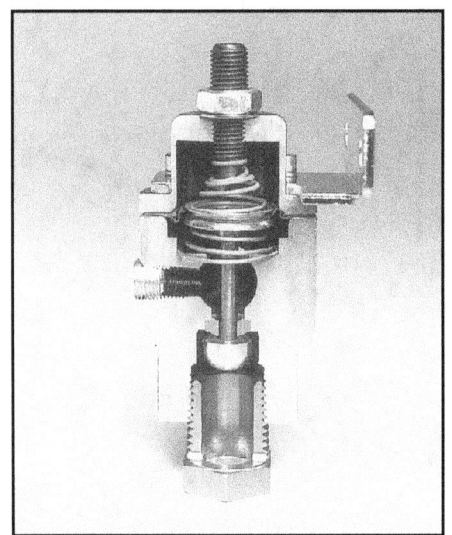

This cutaway shows the internal workings of a poppet valve type pressure regulator. The adjusting screw usually gives about a 6 to 8 psi range of adjustment.

against a pressure of at least 6 PSI higher than the carb needs. The required pump will then need to deliver the fuel pressure required by the carb plus about 6 PSI to compensate for the vehicle acceleration. The bottom line here is for a drag race type application, a low-pressure pump will not work. However, a road, or circle track car will not see such a big acceleration-induced rear-to-front-pump pressure differential because the G forces rarely exceed about 0.7 G. For a circle track car, getting enough fuel at a reasonable pressure gets the job done. A typical circle track car is unlikely to lose more than 2 ½ PSI for any length of time, so an engine driven pump that can suck enough fuel with about a 5 PSI draw and deliver it to the engine at 6-8 PSI will get the job done. For a drag race vehicle, a tank located electric pump of suitable proportions is a must. Do not assume that because you have a popular competition fuel pump, it will be adequate. If you get good at building even small block drag race engines you can put a Holley Blue pump to the edge of its capability.

The first step toward selecting a pump is to check out its flow capability at something close to the pressure at which it will be expected to operate. Holley has some flow versus pressure graphs in their catalog (which you should get), and these are a help if you are shopping on a budget and want to avoid overkill without sacrificing an engine. Conversely, Holley, along with the specialty carb companies mentioned in this book, have high flow, high pressure, pumps to deal with engines up to 1500 horsepower. In this respect, a catalog well worth getting is the BG Fuel Systems one, as this company has some very high output professional style pumps.

Once you have selected a pump it has to be plumbed into the system. Never skimp on fuel line diameter. As a general rule, never use anything less than the size of the ports in the pump. To ensure that the carb receives the desired fuel pressure, you will need to start with a pump pressure considerably higher, then regulate it down by some means. The usual technique is to locate a fuel pressure regulator close to the carb float bowls and, with a gauge in the discharge side of the regulator, set the fuel pressure to that recommended by the carb manufacturer. There is a big variance here (Weber 2.5 PSI, Holley up to 9 PSI) so check what your carb needs.

BYPASS SYSTEMS

Some fuel pumps do not take kindly to being stalled. That is, being turned on and pumping against a stalled outlet. This no flow condition, which occurs just before the engine is started and intermittently at idle, causes the pump to fail earlier than necessary. This can be avoided by using a pump with an internal bypass, or installing a bypass in the system. What the bypass does, is route a certain amount of fuel back to the tank, so that the pump is never stalled. This keeps the pump cooler, the pressure fluctuates less at the regulator and the pump lasts longer. Fig. SB 4-6 shows a basic fuel supply system.

PRESSURE REGULATORS

Pressure regulators and needle valves can be quite critical, more so for street applications than race. Under racing conditions, the fuel flow minimum to maximum does not vary by more than by about a 2 to 1 ratio. However, street driving can call for a 15 to 1 ratio between maximum and minimum. This means that the fuel pressure required for full power is too much for idle and city driving. Instead of the needle valve opening gently at idle, we find it bounces open, takes in a lot more fuel than required due to the pressure it is seeing, then slams closed until the fuel level once more drops and the cycle repeats itself. A good idea here is to install a pressure regulator that sets fuel pressure in relation to manifold pressure. When the vacuum is high, the fuel pressure need only be a pound or so per square inch. With this low pressure fuel level, control is much better. At full throttle, fuel pressure returns to its preset maximum.

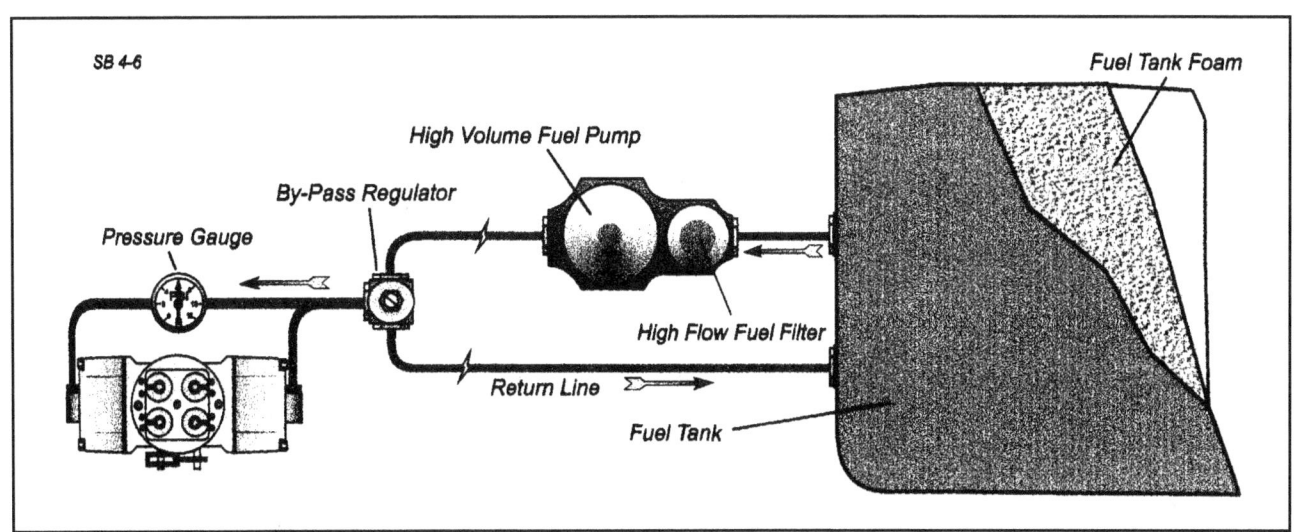

Seen here is a basic fuel delivery system with a bypass pressure regulator built into the system. Some pumps such as those available from companies specializing in modified carbs, have an internal pressure regulated by-pass back to the tank.

How To Build HORSEPOWER: Chapter 5

Carburetors & Intake Manifolds
Induction Basics

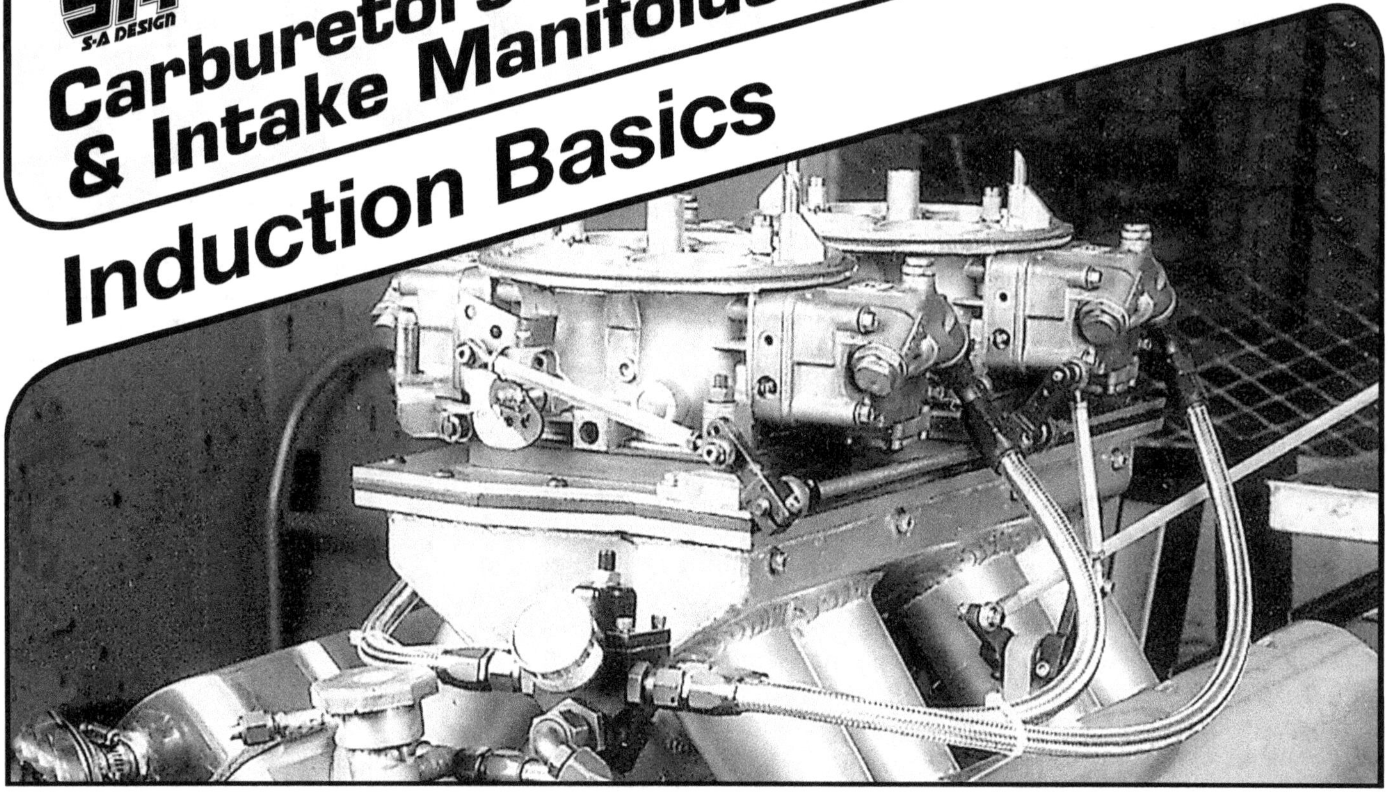

INDUCTION PRESSURE PULSE TUNING

The basics of intake pressure wave or pulse tuning have long been known among knowledgeable engine builders. Also known, is the fact that a tuned length intake is only a positive asset over a narrow band, usually no more than 6-700 rpm wide. In an effort to spread and optimize the tuning effect, some engine builders have developed servo-powered, variable length systems. These enable the engine to stay on precisely the right intake tuned length from typically 6500 to 8500 RPM. Though they are very effective, such systems are extremely complex, to the point where its worth posing the question as to whether there is an easier way. As it happens, there is, and though it is a little less effective, it's a whole lot simpler. The key to its function is the Helmholtz resonator.

BASICS

Although the basics appear simple, when you really get down to it, what goes on in the induction and exhaust system is really complex. There have been countless papers written by research engineers, which usually inundate the reader with almost incomprehensible amounts of data and formulae. I have always believed a race engine builder only need understand enough to produce results that are better than the opposition. This means simplifying wherever possible. Because of the complexities involved, there have been many simple formulae intended to predict induction length, but most produce results little better than an educated guess. Here, I am going to put forward my own method, which I believe to be novel. Unlike many simple formulas, it does take cam timing into account. It appears, with a typically average port taper angle of 1 to 1.5 degrees, to accurately predict the

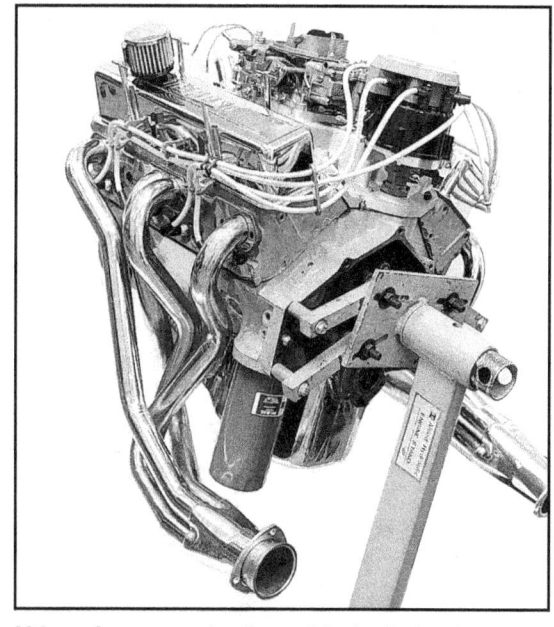

Although we are dealing with the induction system here it should be pointed out that the most powerful influence on the intake is in fact the exhaust tuning length. If it is combined with an appropriate intake length, the result is something greater than the sum of the two.

46 How to Build Horsepower, Vol. 2

induction lengths required to place the positive pressure wave precisely at a useful intake valve opening point.

COMBINED EFFECTS

Before getting in too deep, let us remind ourselves of the basic principles of induction tuning. Essentially, there are three ways to improve airflow into an engine. The first and most obvious is to improve the flow capability of the system by striving for optimal induction tract, port and valve shapes. This we do by spending time on the flow bench testing. The second avenue toward better cylinder filling is to utilize the momentum of the intake charge. By holding the intake valve open after bottom dead center, the speed of the intake charge will, to a certain extent, allow it to go on piling in. The effectiveness of this technique relies very much on using the correct port sizes for the job. Last, we have pressure wave tuning, which of the three methods is the most complex to understand.

In practice, momentum or inertia tuning and pressure wave tuning work very much in conjunction with each other. Since inertia tuning is heavily dependent on efficient, well-developed port shapes, we can see that our flow bench work is also tied into the situation. Fig. 5-1 illustrates how cylinder filling processes interact to achieve our objective. As can be seen, the key is to have a positive pressure wave arrive at the intake valve just moments after it opens. Since piston motion is very limited around TDC, this positive pressure wave gives the air an early start toward filling the cylinder even though the piston has yet to start its downward stroke. An early start to cylinder filling is also aided by the fact that a tuned exhaust system will have produced a negative pressure wave just prior to exhaust valve closure, and this will have scavenged the combustion chamber to the point of reducing the chamber pressure to below atmospheric. Under these conditions, the air flow into the cylinder can start as much as 30 to 40 degrees before TDC. This initial onrush into the cylinder builds additional port velocity,

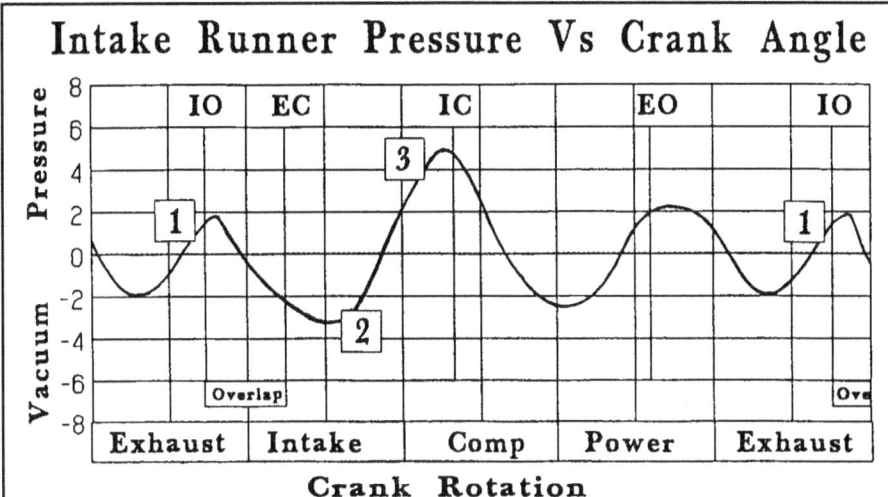

Shown here is the basic pressure wave form in a tuned length intake port. Point (1), repeated every 720 degrees, is a reflected pressure wave. The peak, point (3), is due mostly to inertia ramming, although, if the phasing is right, a portion of it can be due to a returning positive pressure wave. Note that position (1) is the second positive wave from position (3). This pressure wave going positive just prior to the intake valve opening is due to a resonant pressure wave reflected from the open end of the intake. If this arrives at the right moment, as shown here, it will start the cylinder filling process before downward piston motion. The dip in port pressure in the middle of the intake stroke (2) is due to the combined depression caused by the piston at or near its peak velocity on the induction stroke and a negative reflected pressure wave. The rise in pressure starting just before BDC (3) is mainly the result of decaying port velocity being converted to pressure energy plus an element of positive pressure wave. This high pressure at valve closure helps generate a stronger pulse, which after the appropriate number of reflections, arrives as a stronger pulse (1) at the next intake opening.

which is partially sustained throughout the rest of the stroke. This extra velocity then has the effect of considerably improving the inertia filling during the late valve closure period after BDC.

The scenario just described should emphasize the fact that events in the first half of the stroke have a significant affect on successful cylinder filling in the second half. Not so obvious is the fact that propagating a strong initial wave in the intake is somewhat dependent on the exhaust producing a strong negative pressure wave during the overlap period. To see how this works in principle let's look at the propagation of a pressure wave independent of the exhaust system first. In drawing 1 of Fig. 5-2 the piston has just started its way down the bore and, in so doing, produces a negative pressure wave that travels along to the end of the intake tract. Upon reaching the open end, it is both reflected and changed in sign from negative to positive (drawing 2). If this positive wave

With an induction length targeting a peak power RPM of about 7250, an induction system, as seen here might seem only suitable for race applications. However, The lower speed inertial ram effects ...

... in conjunction with the exhaust and the superior low-speed performance due to Isolated Runners (IR) make such systems ideal for street usage. Street rodders often go for such systems for their looks, but the extra drivability proves to be a really worthwhile bonus.

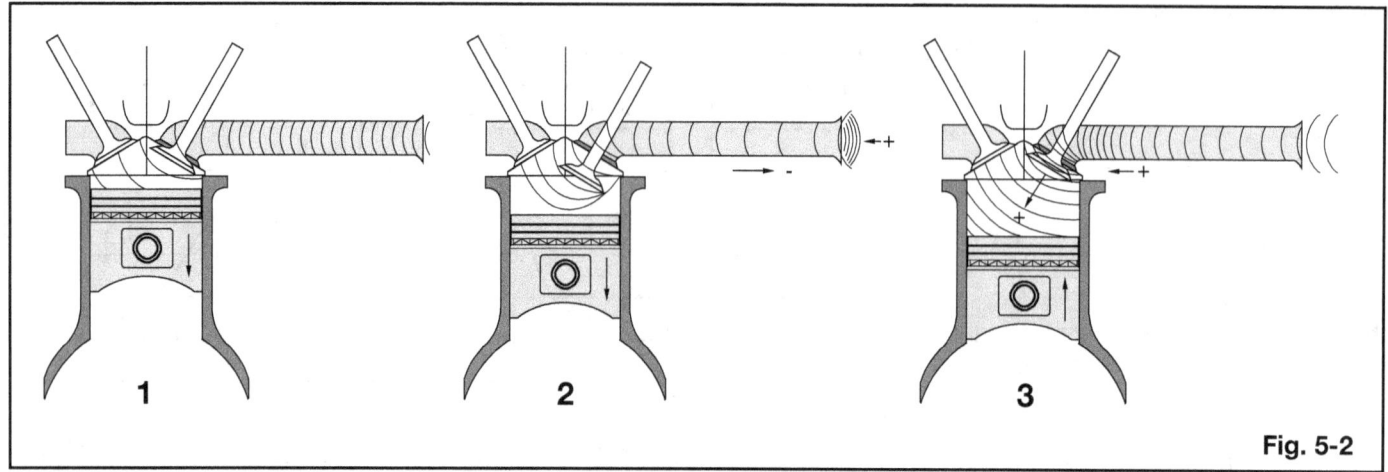

Fig. 5-2

1) At the beginning of the intake stroke, the piston starting its motion down the bore creates a negative pressure in the cylinder. This is communicated with the port and starts a ...

2) ... negative wave that travels down the intake to the open end. Here, it is reflected as a positive pressure wave, which now heads back to the intake valve.

3) If the positive pressure wave arrives just before the intake closes, it will push extra charge into the cylinder.

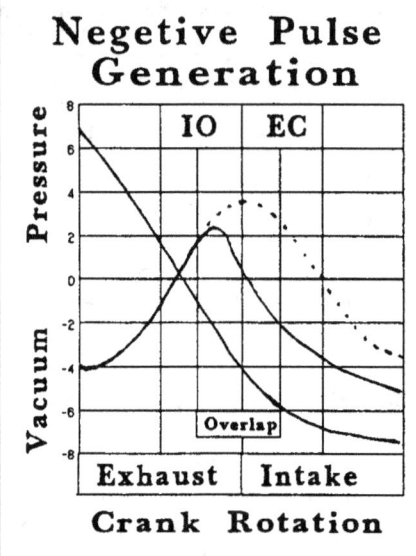

At the intake tuning RPM, a race engine would normally have an intake port pressure going positive as the intake valve opens. However, the exhaust, if tuned appropriately, will be going negative across the overlap period. This is shown by the line passing from the top left-hand side to the bottom right. As the exhaust goes negative during the overlap period, the positive pressure falls into the negative pressure generated by the exhaust. The dotted line shows how the pressure wave would have developed had it not been modified by the exhaust pressure wave.

now arrives at the intake valve just before it closes at the end of the intake stroke (drawing 3), it will push a little extra charge into the cylinder just before the intake valve closes.

This classic example of pressure wave tuning is intended to show only the principle. On a well-tuned engine, the mode of operation is somewhat different and more complex. Starting at TDC on the intake stroke, we will have both valves open on the overlap period. During overlap the exhaust developed negative pressure is transmitted through the chamber to the intake port. This negative pressure wave travels along the intake, is reflected as a positive and, assuming the length is right for the RPM involved arrives back in time to help push in that extra charge just prior to intake closure. When the intake closes any remaining velocity in the column of air causes the pressure to rise on the back of the intake valve. This pressure then travels as a wave up the intake to the open end, where it is reflected as a negative wave. This negative wave travels down the intake to be reflected, still as a negative wave, from the back of the closed intake valve. When it arrives once more at the open end of the intake, it is once more reflected, and due to the open end, it is changed in sign to a positive wave. If the length is right for the RPM the engine is turning at, this positive pressure wave will arrive just as the intake valve opens.

At this point, a number of significant things happen. First, air rushes into the cylinder because the intake port pressure is above that in the cylinder. However, the cylinder is also connected to the exhaust because we are back to the overlap position. This means that the intake is well above atmospheric, while the exhaust is well below. The process of air rushing into the cylinder brings about the effect of the positive pressure falling into the negative one created by the exhaust as shown in Fig. 5-3. Because of the duration and intensity of the exhaust pulse, it is more than able to retain its identity as a negative pulse, so it travels up the intake while a fresh charge continues to flow into the cylinder.

As the induction process continues, so the downward motion of the piston takes over as the source of induction depression. As just described, a pressure wave, be it positive or negative, must travel four times back and forth along the induction tract. It must do this from about the time the intake valve closes at the end of the induction stroke, to about the time it opens again to start the next. Putting this into a basic numerical form, we can say that the time for 4 round trips will be equal to the time for rotation of the engine through 2 revolutions, minus the intake valve opening period, at 720° cam duration. Knowing how long we have and the speed of the pressure wave through the relatively hot intake air, means we can calculate how long an intake tract is needed.

At this point, we are able to determine the intake length necessary, assuming the shock wave peaks must coincide with intake valve opening and closure points. In practice, this is not the case. Pressure cannot be transmitted across a closed valve, so it becomes necessary to assume an effective opening period somewhat shorter than the total off-the-seat timing delivered by the cam. Depending

The most obvious application of tuned lengths is on a tunnel ram system as seen here. The Barry Grant modified Holley Dominators provide the carburetion for this 500 inch 1200 horsepower Pro Stock engine. The remote location of the butterflies on a tunnel ram system means that, at WOT, the runners react as if they have no butterflies in the system to impede either airflow or pressure waves.

how fast the cam opens the valves and how good the low lift flow of the valves is we need to deduct some 20 to 30 degrees of cam timing. Deducting 30 degrees seems to work for a typical flat tappet race cam. To save you going through the math involved, here is what our equation looks like up to this point:

$$\frac{(720 - EDC) \times 0.125V \times 60 \times 12}{360 \times RPM}$$

Where V is the speed of sound in hot intake air (approximately 1250 to 1300 ft./sec., and ECD the effective cam duration. The 60 and the 12 in this formula change the feet and seconds of the velocity into inches and minutes, and the 360 turns the remaining part of 720 into whatever portion is left of two engine revolutions.

The way the events have been described so far are very much a simplification, but nonetheless for a typical high performance four stroke engine, the predicted lengths work so long as a few more factors are taken into account. Of these, probably the most important is the incorporation of the pipe end effect. The reflection of the wave does not actually take place right at the end of the pipe, but about half its diameter out from the end. This means a 2" diameter pipe tunes as if it is 1" longer than it actually measures. To get the correct calculated length, the result given by our formula will have to be shortened by half the diameter of the inlet pipe, or for a rectangular port, half the port width.

At the intake tuning RPM, a race engine would normally have an intake port pressure going positive as the intake valve opens. However, the exhaust, if tuned appropriately will be going negative across the overlap period. This is shown (Fig. 5-3) by the line passing from the top left hand side to the bottom right. As the exhaust goes negative during the overlap period, the positive pressure "'falls'" into the negative pressure generated by the exhaust. The dotted line shows how the intake pressure wave would have developed, had it not been modified by the exhaust pressure wave.

The formula given, predicts the tuned length, based on three pressure waves arriving at the intake valve during the entire 720° cycle of events. These consist of the positive wave generated at intake valve closure and the two subsequently reflected ones, the second of which as labeled in Fig. 5-1 makes the early start of the induction stroke. This can be viewed as a system working from the second reflection. Although the second reflection produces the strongest positive pressure wave at the time the intake opens, it is not our only option nor, in many cases, our best. Using the second wave on a shorter cammed low RPM engine may predict an intake manifold too long to install. In practice we find that employing the third or fourth reflection may be more convenient. To calculate the required lengths for these other reflection values is easy. First calculate the second reflection tuned length, then multiple it by 2 and divide by the required reflection value, and for the final step, subtract the end effect length. The complete formula now looks like this:

Intake Manifold Length L =

$$L = \left(\frac{(720 - EDC) \times 0.25V \times 2}{RPM \times RV} \right) - 0.5D$$

Where :
RV = Reflective Value
D = Diameter of inlet pipe in inches

Here's an example:
A 7000 RPM tuned length is required for a 300 degree cammed engine using a pair of side draft 45 mm Dellorto carbs.

$$\frac{720 - (00 - 30) \times .025 \times 1300 \times 2}{7000 \times 2}$$

$$-(1.78 \times 0.5) = 20 \text{ inches}$$

OPEN VALVE RESONANCE

When the intake valve opens, a different set of pressure wave propagation conditions exist. In the previous case, the pressure waves traveled back and forth along the intake tract much as they do in a organ pipe. However, when the valve opens, a new element comes into play. The volume of the cylinder now causes the system to react like a Helmholtz resonator. The simplest way to visualize the way this device works is to imag-

A single four barrel system, as seen here, may at first appear to have induction lengths too short for effective ramming. This proves not to be the case. Operating on the third reflection, a typical manifold, as seen here, is ideally dimensioned for about an 8000 rpm tuning point. The setup seen here utilizes an air valve instead of a carb as part of a port injected ...

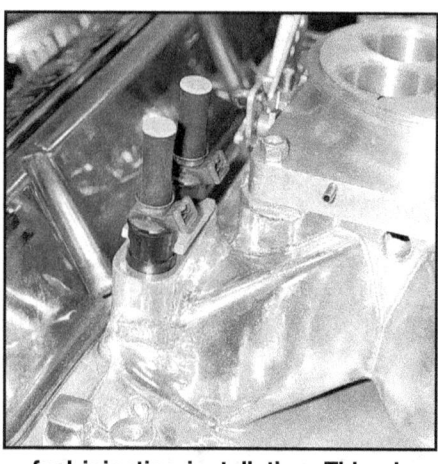

... fuel injection installation. This gives the drivability advantages of precise fuel metering, but not the huge low-speed torque increases of an IR installation.

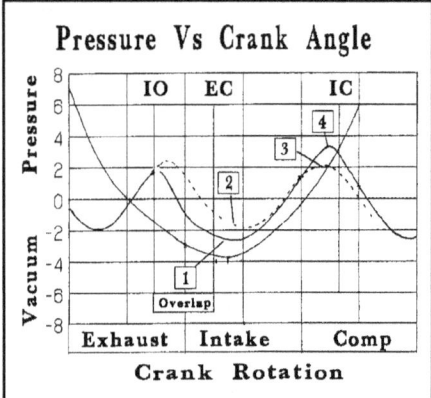

If the negative dip in the pressure wave (2) arrives as the piston created port vacuum is at its greatest, at position (1), it will help boost port velocity in the remaining part of the induction stroke. If the wave also goes positive after BDC (3), it will add to the ramming pressure (4) created by the port velocity. Fig. 5-4

ine the air in the cylinder volume acting as if it were a spring. The air rushing into the cylinder momentarily causes a rise in pressure. This will only exist for a short time before the pressure wave reverses, leaving the cylinder at a slightly lower pressure. This pressure bouncing back and forth is characteristic of a Helmholtz resonator.

Let us now move along to a less than obvious, but very influential, factor affecting cylinder filling. A negative pressure wave occurring during the induction stroke can be made to further augment filling. To understand the mode of function, look at Fig. 5-4. In this drawing you can see how the negative wave arrives at the cylinder at about the same time the piston is creating the greatest depression due to its velocity down the bore. This increases the intensity of the positive pressure wave reflected from the open end of the intake. If this higher intensity pressure wave arrives back at the intake valve just before it closes at the end of the stroke, it will push in additional charge. What with the kinetic energy of the slowing charge changing to pressure energy, plus the positive pressure wave, it is not uncommon to see port pressures just before valve closure as high as 10 PSI above atmospheric. With pressures this high, when the valve is near the seat, you can see how important it is to have good low lift valve flow. When made full use of, pressure wave tuning is like having 10 psi of free supercharge pressure available, it's just a question of harnessing this potential to produce the extra power.

In many instances, it is not possible to harness this effect when the second reflection is used because of the spacing of the waves. Very often the third reflection will generate the conditions required, but the lengths involved are too short to apply to a typical one barrel per cylinder carbureted engine. For instance, 8000 rpm typically needs some 11.5 inches of induction length. Such a length presents a real difficulty with an isolated runner, but not for a plenum-type system where all intake ports draw from a suitably large common source. This statement fits in well with practice. Single four barrel two valve per cylinder V8 engines as per Winston Cup are achieving volumetric efficiency figures of similar magnitude to four valve per cylinder engines by

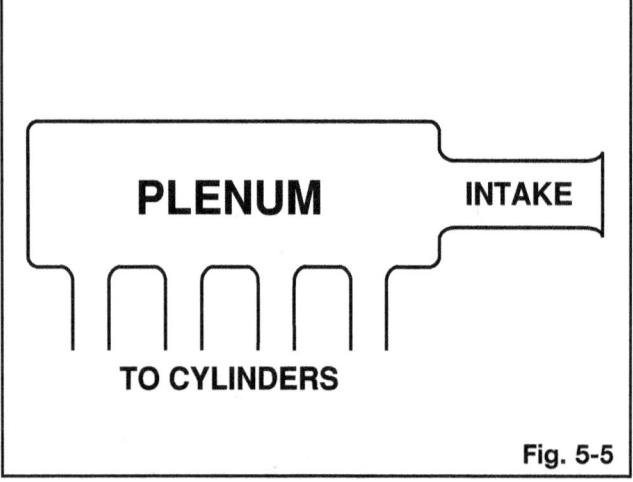

Shown here is a simple plenum for four cylinders. With any more than four cylinders attached to the plenum, the resonating effect is reduced. It would appear that three evenly spaced induction pulses from three cylinders would give the strongest effect. This means that three or six cylinder engines are best able to use this type of pressure wave tuning.

utilizing the third reflection. Power figures from these pushrod carbureted engines are around 125 BHP per liter along with 85 plus ft.-lbs per liter of torque. These results alone justify European 2 liter formula sedans to seriously investigate third reflection plenum type manifolds. Fig. 5-5 shows the basic layout of such a system. The fact that it employs a plenum now means the opportunity exists to broaden the RPM range over which useful pressure wave tuning works.

HELMHOLTZ PLENUM

The Helmholtz resonator has three variables that need to be adjusted to suit the engine we are attempting to tune. By suitable selection of these, we can boost the pressure in the plenum at a time when the pressure wave traveling back and forth in the intake runners are out of phase and are reducing power instead of increasing it. These variables are the plenum volume, the intake pipe length and the intake pipe diameter.

The easiest, to determine is the intake diameter. Although further testing may indicate differently, my own limited dyno testing to date, has indicated that the velocity in the plenum intake pipe should not exceed 180 ft/se., at maximum engine speed. If you are working in cubic inches of engine displacement, this makes the formula for the pipe diameter.

$$D = \sqrt{\frac{CID \times VE \times RPM}{V \times 1130}}$$

For Liters this becomes:

$$D = \sqrt{\frac{Liters \times VE \times RPM}{V \times 18.5}}$$

LENGTH & VOLUME

So far, we have arrived at some working formula for a subject renowned for mathematical complexity. At this point, there are some serious obstacles toward achieving mathematical simplification for the plenum design, yet still achieving precise results. Before getting to deeply into that though, let's set some ground

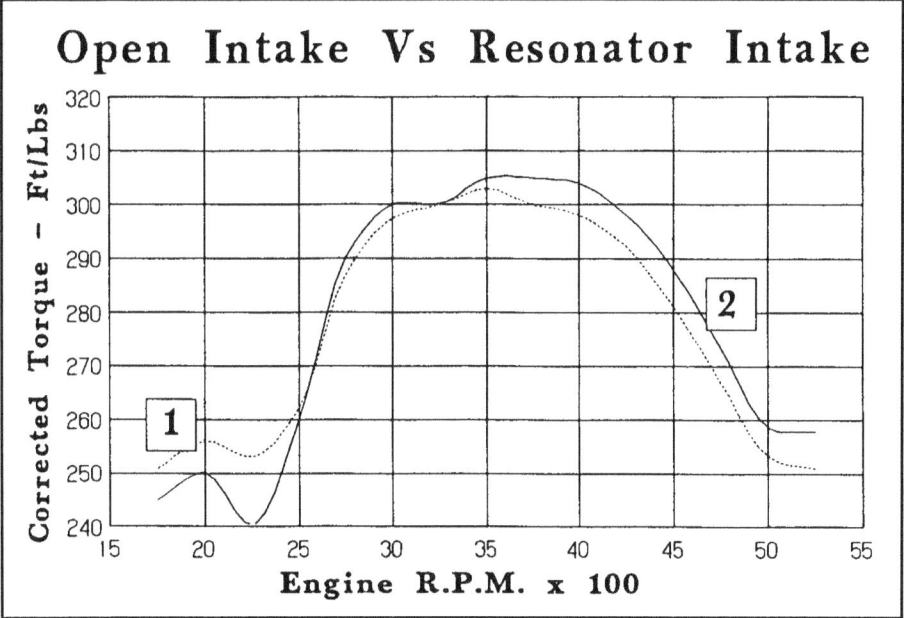

The test engine used here was a stock 305 small block Chevy. Curve # 1 was produced by the use of a snorkle type air filter case. The basic case was 14" dia. X 3.5" high and housed a 11.5" dia. X 3.5". Curve #2 was produced with a 14" dia. X 4" high 360 degree open element filter case. These tests indicate that a measure of tuning, either from inertia or Helmholtz resonating or a combination was occurring at low RPM. This provided a useful boost in low end output but top end suffered because the inlet pipe was to small.

rules. To be effective, a Helmholtz resonator intended to boost power just below the RPM that the tuned intake runner length comes in can only be coupled to a limited number of cylinders. Although it can be made to work in a limited fashion on a V8 (Fig. 5-6), with all cylinders drawing from it, the RPM range at which it occurs is too low for a high performance or race engine. The amount of power boost is also limited. To be effective, a maximum of four evenly firing cylinders should be coupled to a single plenum. In practice, three cylinders per plenum can prove highly functional, so six cylinder engines have an advantage over four in this respect. Solutions for V8s are far more complex. One solution is to use a flat plane crank, then each bank can be treated as a separate four cylinder engine. This is because each bank has two smaller cylinder pulses and one large one from the two cylinders drawing only ninety degrees apart. To a Helmholtz system, this could appear much the same as a three or divided six cylinder setup.

Once the layout has been decided, then it's time to determine the length of the induction pipe and the volume of the plenum. The first stumbling block here is that simple Helmholtz resonator formulae don't predict what's needed in big cammed engines with any real degree of accuracy so a more "cut and shut" method is called for. First a basic "ball park" plenum volume should be determined.

When connected to four cylinders the plenum volume should be about 50 to 60% of the volume of all four cylinders. If the engine is a three or six cylinder unit, then a plenum equal to some 65 to 80% of those three cylinders is needed. For two cylinders the plenum volume should be about equal to the volume of the two cylinders. These volumes will need to go up or down somewhat, depending on the system's required RPM range. However, there seems no pressing need for absolute accuracy here, because the system can be easily tuned to the desired RPM by adjusting the length of the inlet pipe on the dyno. The ability to do this does simplify things for us, but it does not completely absolve us from having to make some intelligent judgements concerning the plenum volumes.

The figures given seem to be good for engines requiring a boost between 5 and 6000 rpm and cylinder sizes of 400 to 600cc (24 to 36 C.I.) To effectively tune at lower RPMsay around 3000 the plenum may need to be

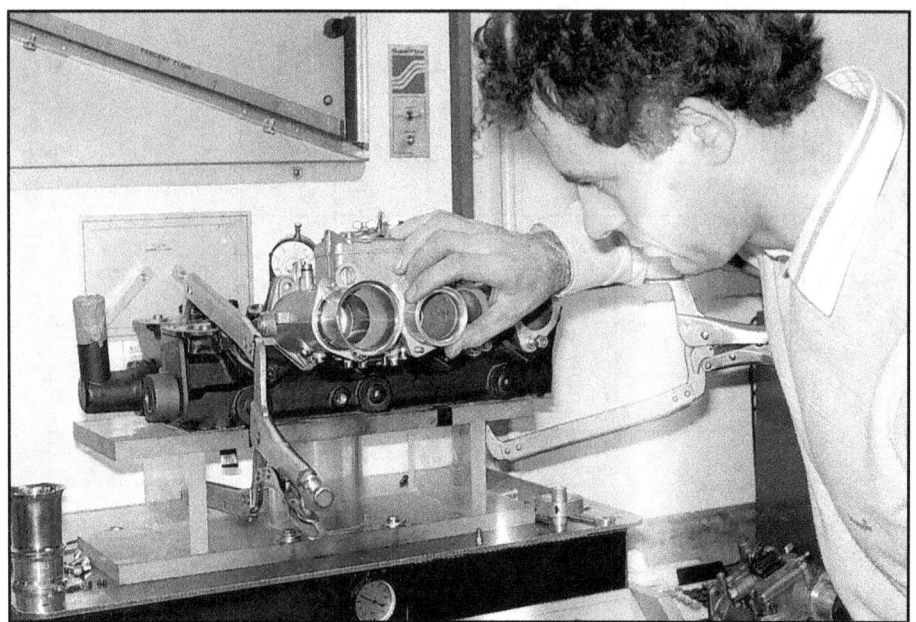

Ram pipes are not just cosmetic or a minor detail of little consequence, as some racers appear to believe. Their form and the effect they have are both critical to overall air flow and to the performance of the booster venturi. Without ram pipes the booster gain can become erratic and its performance can drop significantly.

increased as much as 30% and to tune higher, say 7500 we may need to make it 10 to 15% smaller.

Once a plenum volume of about the right order has been established, then all that remains is to build an adjustable pipe assembly leading into it. As a rough starting point, assume that for 10,000 RPM, the pipe will need to be about 7 inches long. To tune for lower rpm increase the pipe length by about 1.7 inches for every 1000 RPM less. With the adjustable pipe sliding inside the stationary one, adjust the pipe length on the dyno to boost power in the range about 700 to 1200 RPM under the intake runner length tuning speed. Although a small reduction in peak power may be seen the average power in the RPM band typically used will be measurably increased.

PORT AREA

The subject of intake length tends to overshadow the other critical aspect of intake manifold design, namely port area. Whereas selecting the right length for a given RPM only gives positive results over a narrow rev range, choosing the appropriate area has positive effects over the engine's entire rev range.

The sizing of the intake port has a direct influence on the port velocity attained during the induction stroke. If the port is too large, the port velocity will be too low, and much of the ram effect that takes place at the end of the induction stroke will be lost. If the port is too small it will restrict air flow at the higher engine speeds.

Although we are essentially dealing with intake manifolds the simplest method for determining the best area for the intake runners starts within the cylinder head. The prime restriction in any unlimited (not artificially restricted by race regs) induction system is the intake valve area. If the cylinder has 3 square inches of intake valve area, it is pointless feeding it by means of 6 square inches of port area. A little thought here will reveal that any restriction significantly less than the valve will have little effect on overall air flow into the engine. Not only should it be recognized that the intake valve presents an area limitation, but also that it is one of the most unstreamlined components within the engine's breathing system. Because of it's inefficient shape, a valve has only the same flow capability of an unobstructed port with about 80% of the area. Depending on the flow efficiency of the valve, this equivalence ratio will vary up and down slightly, but 80% is a good starting point. To get the velocity induced ram effect as high as possible without causing any more restriction than the valve itself, we need to size the port just prior to the back of the valve to an area that has less restriction than the valve. In a perfect world, the equivalence area would be the target. But this is far from a perfect world, as are the heads we have to work with. The need to put bends into the ports of a cylinder head means that controlling the area of the port has to take a back seat to shaping the port for good air flow. As a consequence of this, the bowl or throat area of a typical two valve per cylinder race-prepared head is larger than we have otherwise predicted is neces-

Ram pipes with large radii at the entrance, such as seen here, can improve airflow, but at the same time have the effect of making the system appear shorter as far as pressure waves are concerned.

sary. The velocity induced ram effect works best when the high velocity occurs right at the back of the valve. In practice, this can rarely be achieved. Howeve,r in the interest of maximizing velocity, the port area just behind the intake valve can drop to the equivalence area at some point a little further upstream of the intake valve. It is this area which gives us the starting point toward determining the intake manifold's port dimensions. If the minimum area just prior to the valve is 80% of the valve area, then the port area needs to increase at the rate of 1.7 to 2.5% per inch of runner length. This represents an average taper of 1 to 1.5 degrees. For a typical four barrel small block Chevy manifold, here are how things look. The intake valve is typically 2.05 inches in diameter. This gives 3.3 square inches of valve diameter. On a well ported head the valve equivalence area will be about 82%, which puts it at 2.705 square inches. The total intake length from valve to plenum will be 11 inches, so the port area will get bigger by 11 x 0.017 for a 1 degree taper or 11 x 0.0255 for a 1.5 degree taper. The 2.705 square inch, are just short of the valve then works out to be 3.21 square inches at the junction with the port runner and plenum. If we had gone with the wider taper angle this would have worked out to be 3.46 square inches.

All the forgoing concerning port area is based on a requirement for maximum horsepower from the engine. If the engines low speed output is of more concern then the ports can usefully be sized smaller.

Ram stacks such as that on this Braswell-modified Holley can serve two useful purposes. First, they help make small improvements in airflow, and second, they can, in use, reduce the effect of booster buffeting by partially shielding the booster from airflow presented at an angle to the carb mouth. For a street motor, stacks around 5 inches or more, can introduce a Helmholtz resonator effect into a single four barrel system which can aid output in the 2-4000 rpm range.

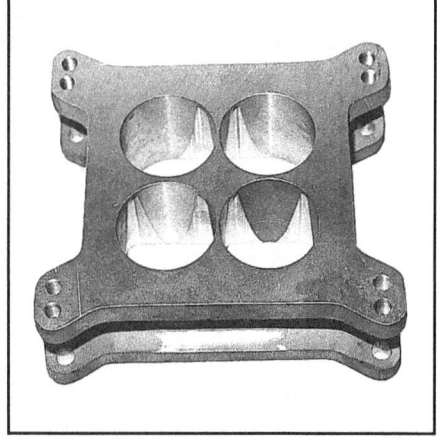

The carb spacer can be a very valuable tuning aid to the single four barrel carbed engine tuner. Its primary asset is that it allows a quick and simple means to alter the plenum volume to suit the engine. Most performance/race single plane intakes are intentionally made with the plenum too small, on the premise that it is easier to add a spacer than to machine off a chunk of the manifold. Also, it is difficult to port a manifold with a deep plenum, so the spacer makes this a more convenient operation. Another issue the spacer addresses is the fuel spray pattern as it leaves the booster. The addition of a spacer usually allows a more homogeneous mixture to develop prior to it being drawn down the runners.

Different length ram pipes are a convenient way to alter the induction length of a system, but it is usually better to increase manifold length. This is because a length increase downstream of the fuel discharge point gives the fuel more time to mix with the air.

How To Build HORSEPOWER: Chapter 6

Carburetors & Intake Manifolds
Holley Carburetors

Without a doubt Holley's range of performance and replacement carburetors represents one of the best value-for-money performance deals in the marketplace today. The most commonly used carburetors, and the ones that we're going to look at here, are their four barrel range. These are made in what is termed a "spread bore" flange pattern, which is a replacement for the GM Quadra-Jet and the "square bore" pattern common to Holley's aftermarket performance units. The term "square" refers to the fact that all the barrels are evenly pitched on both primary and secondary. In addition to these typically street orientated carbs there is the Dominator series. These large body carbs are intended primarily for race applications and feature airflow capacities to 1,150 CFM.

SPREAD BORES

Let's start the ball rolling with our investigation of Holley power and performance potential with the spread bore models. These typically come under the heading of 4165 and 4175 series carbs. Essentially, these carburetors have a pair of small primary barrels and a pair of large secondary barrels. The spread bore bolt pattern fits that of a Quadra-Jet and Carter Thermo-Quad carburetors. Introduced in 1971, Holley's spread bore 4165 carb was available as a 650 and 850 CFM unit. The 650 was intended for use on small blocks, while the larger carburetor was intended for a typical 400 inch plus big block. The basic difference between the 650 and

More high performance and race engines reside under a Holley carb than any other carburetor in the world. One good reason for that is results!

54   *How to Build Horsepower, Vol. 2*

The Spread Bore Holley is a popular replacement for GM Q-Jet carburetor. It's simpler, more easily calibrated, if such is required, and costs a lot less money.

This 750 Holley on a Victor Jr. (very similar results are achieved with Weiand and Holley's 360 race manifold) is one of the author's favorite budget induction combinations. This is good to about a streetable 450 horsepower with a bottom end suitable for a stock or near stock stall speed converter. Worth a mention here is the neat Wire Wizard cable organizer on the HEI distributor. Available from APT (909-686-0260) in Riverside, California, this item puts all the plug cables into the same order as the cylinders.

850 CFM spread bores lies in the secondary venturis. Both sizes of carburetors use a common 1-5/32 inch diameter primary venturi and a 1-11/16 inch diameter butterfly. The secondary venturi"s on the 650 are 1-3/8 inch diameter along with 1-9/16 inch diameter butterflies. The additional flow of the 850 is achieved by using 1 23/32 inch diameter venturis with 1-3/4 inch diameter butterflies.

To quote one of Holley's design engineers of the era, "the 4165 was designed from the outset to be a true replacement for a Rochester Quadra-Jet." That was the target and as far as possible Holley made their spread bore carbs do just that. If your engine is equipped with an old worn-out Quadra-Jet that needs replacement, then getting the right part number for your particular year and model vehicle will mean, in most instances having a carburetor that can bolt on and utilize all the original linkages, emission fittings, and air cleaner.

The model 4175, introduced in 1974, is available only in a 650 size. It differs from the 4165 in that it has vacuum-operated secondary and side-hung float bowls. Also, because of the vacuum secondary operation, it is equipped with jets for accelerator pump function on the primary side only. In addition to vacuum secondary, operation the 4175 differs from the 4165 in that a metering plate replaces the secondary metering block. Instead of using jets, the metering plate has fixed-size drillings, so any calibration changes can conveniently only go one way, bigger. However a 4175 can be easily converted from a plate to a block with the relevant Holley conversion kit.

The later model 4175 carburetors are also available in electronic feedback form. The special float bowl used for this type of carburetor has a solenoid that pulses at 60 cycle/second and, by varying what is known as the "mark space ratio" (time up to the time down), it can progressively alter the apparent size of an auxiliary jet feeding the smaller than normal main jet. This allows the vehicle computer, via an oxygen sensor, to control the mixture and so keep emissions down to federally mandated levels. As was covered in the Holley performance and modification chapter, this type of electronic float bowl can be adapted to many models of Holley carburetors.

The 4175 was originally introduced for application where the engine could be operating at a relatively low RPM and wide throttle opening for extended periods. In this respect, it's ideally suited to recreational and working truck motors, especially those used for towing. Many performance enthusiasts, especially the younger element, often see the spread bore Holley carburetor as something of an emission carburetor and dismiss it as far as performance potential is concerned. In reality, a spread bore can return performance just as good as its calibration. Fig. 6-1 shows a simple build on a small block Chevy which utilizes nothing other than stock parts in the long motor along with a manifold reworked as detailed elsewhere in the book. This combination, plus a 650 vacuum secondary Holley, propelled the author's "economy geared" 4500 lb. truck to 1/4-mile times in the high 14's and trap speeds around 95 miles an hour. Though hardly an out right drag racer, this fully muffled truck did return over 18 MPG on the highway.

Not much may have been said about spread bore carbs compared with some of the other units Holley makes, but don't let this give you the impression that they are anything but a worthwhile carburetor to consider. The fact that you may have installed a spread bore carburetor on your engine may not

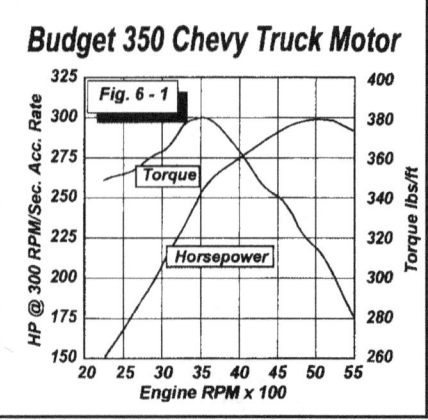

Bolt the right combination of parts together, and it is possible to build a strong motor without recourse to a bank loan. This engine here used a set of pocket ported 186 head castings, 9/1 CR headers, a reworked manifold as per Chapter 12 and a stock Chevrolet 929 cam.

impress the less informed of your hot rodding performance friends. However, it is likely to impress you with it's performance and drivability, and after all, at the end of the day that's what matters.

4150 AND 4160 CARBURETORS

Because the term "spread bore" has been so liberally applied to Holley's Quadra-Jet replacement, its hardly surprising that the evenly space throttle barrel of the 4150/4160 series has led them to be known as "square bore" carburetors. These units have a lineage dating back to the late '50s. Those early carburetors are hardly what we call "high performance" by today's standards with airflow ratings around 400 CFM. By 1958, it became apparent that performance sold cars, and Holley introduced a 600 CFM four barrel. Continually improving cylinder head designs, increasing RPMs, and bigger displacement engines drove up the demand for more carburetor airflow. Holley met this demand by producing even bigger carburetors. The growth in factory race participation in the early '60s brought about the development and introduction of the first double pumpers. This term being used to denote Holleys with accelerator pumps at both ends. The need for two accelerator pumps was brought about by the use of staged or synchronized mechanical secondary throttles. The fact that such a linkage opens all four barrels at once meant pump enrichment would be required for each barrel. By comparison, vacuum secondaries with progressive introduction of secondary airflow meant secondary accelerator pumps were redundant.

Today, we see Holley square bore four barrel carbs range in capacity from 390 CFM all the way to 850, with a special 950 CFM unit designed to be "all performance" topping the list. Because Holley offers such a wide variety of carburetors to the performance enthusiasts, it is a good idea, if you are contemplating using one (or more), to get yourself a Holley catalog. What follows, in essence is a brief description of Holley"s offering in the 4150 and 4160 series range as of 1996.

The smallest Holley four barrel, the 390 CFM unit, is offered in 4160 form in two versions. One is for four cylinder engines, with a power valve appropriate to the low RPM pulsating flow of such engines. The second version is intended for V6s and small V8s.

The next size carburetor, a 450 CFM 4160, unit is designed principally for Ford engines from '61 to '67. This however, does not precluded its use for other applications. For GM vehicles this will mean getting the appropriate linkage kit.

The next step up the flow ladder takes us to the 600 CFM four barrel, which is available in both 4150 and 4160 series form. Some versions of these carbs are model specific, whereas others, such as part number 0-1850, have what Holley calls "universal calibration," al-though the later type are intended primarily for nonemission type of vehicles. Of the range of 600 CFM carburetors, most are equipped with vacuum secondaries. The exception to this is part #0-4776, which is, a double pumper mechanical secondary carb. The 600 CFM Holley in vacuum secondary form is a very popular replacement size for stock and near stock V8s in the 175 to 200 horsepower range.

Ideal for satisfying horsepower levels up to about 300 is Holley's 650 CFM unit. This, at the time of writing, is offered in two part numbers both in 4150 style and both having mechanical secondaries. Following the 650 in flow capacity is the 4150 style 700 CFM double pumper and the 725 vacuum secondary, also in 4150 style.

At this point, we've arrived at the 750 CFM carbs. As an-off-the-shelf performance choice the 750 is probably the most popular size of Holley. Reason, it is an excellent compromise between low-speed booster capability and total airflow

Holley 0-4548 390 CFM four barrel with electric choke and vauum secondaries.

Holley 0-8007 600 CFM replacement carburetor with electric choke and vacuum secondaries.

Holley 0-4777 650 CFM Double Pumper for performance applications up to 300 to 350 horsepower.

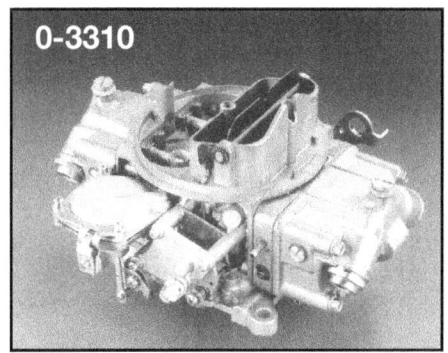

950 CFM rate HP body performance double pumper offers radiused venturi inlets and many features found in performance aftermarket modified carburetors.

capacity for the typical 350 inch engine. It's available in 4150 and 4160 forms. Equipped with a manual choke, it can be had, if so desired, with a four corner idling system as stock (part #0-4779). This popular unit is also offered in vacuum or mechanical secondary form. Again, the Holley catalog should be regarded as your definitive source of information.

Two models of Holley are offered at 780 CFM, both in vacuum secondary form, and, are intended to replace the stock carb on higher output stock type engines with factory ratings in the 375 horsepower range on up. After the 780, comes a single model at 800 CFM. This is a mechanical secondary double pumper 4150 series carburetor. Then we come to the 850, or in this case, the specialized Corvette carburetor an 855 CFM unit. Essentially, we can group these carburetors together. They are the biggest of the group in terms of venturis and butterfly sizes. Part # 04781 is a double pumper with mechanical secondary and it comes stock with four corner idling. This is very much a performance oriented carburetor. It makes no concession to such civilized attributes as electric chokes. However, if the requirement calls for a large flow capacity street carburetor for typically a high output small block or a moderate big block motor then part #0-80436 is a good choice. This unit is a vacuum secondary, electric choke carb, as is the model specific unit intended for the '66 and '67 big block Corvette (part #0-3418-1).

Holley's 950 CFM 4150 series carburetor is a relative newcomer to the game. And one very welcome for racers. Essentially, the 950 is an 850 tricked up at the Holley factory. Because it was intended not to compromise airflow in any way, this outright performance unit has no choke mechanism. The airflowed body design utilizes the 850 butterfly and venturi sizes. Stock features of this carb are four corner idling and dual feed float bowls. In addition to this the 950 is available in both gasoline and alcohol versions, each being equipped with the appropriate needle and jet assemblies.

Most of these carburetors will probably go out of Holley's doors with the progressive mechanical secondary linkage. However, for gasoline fueled engines a vacuum secondary version is available.

The booster design used for the 950 is the dogleg unit with the special double step machined into it. From experience, we have found this double step set-up works very well for V8 engines of 400 horsepower or more. To use a much overworked and usually exaggerated term, which in this instant happens to be an appropriate description, the 950 Holley represents, for a lot of racers, excellent results right "out of the box". This means in most instances it requires nothing other than jetting to achieved near optimum results.

4010 SERIES CARBURETOR

This "Johnny come lately" carb could come under the heading of "Street Performance and Show Pieces." Also one might consider it a later generation 4150 series carburetor that has undergone a number of significant design changes. The most notable of these is that the float bowls are integral with the carburetor body. Access to the float bowls is achieved by taking the entire top assembly, that is the air horn and float bowl tops, from the main body of the carburetor. Access to the main jets is down through the float bowls. The 4010 fuel calibration is much simpler than the Holley carbs most people are familiar with. In most instances, calibration need only take into account main jet changes. If there is a need to make a small change in the fuel curve, then the air corrector jet housed in the body of the booster cluster is simple to resize. It's just the question of taking the booster

How to Build Horsepower, Vol. 2   **57**

We ran this 650 4010 Holley carb on a Victor Jr. and had good results. Top end horsepower matched a regular 4150 series 650 and the low end beat it by as much as 10 ft-lbs.

cluster off, re-sizing as necessary, then reinstalling the booster cluster.

As of '96, this carburetor has not really found much favor with the performance purist. However, this writer's experience with several of these carburetors on the dyno has shown they are capable of delivering good performance. The annular discharge style of booster comes stock with this carb. As a result it represents an effective means of getting good drivability low down because of the strong booster signal it generates.

The 4010 series carbs are available in 600 and 750 CFM capacities. Other options include either manual or electric choke and vacuum or mechanical secondaries.

4011 SERIES CARB

Similar in concept to the 4010 carbs is the 4011 series carbs, which, in essence, represent a simplified version of the regular spread bore carburetors. Again, like the 4010 carbs, the 4011 are made of a different alloy to the regular carb and come in a semi-polished finish. Essentially, few if any, parts of this carburetor are interchangeable with the regular spread bore. The main difference between this and regular Holley carbs is that like it's equivalent 4010 square bore series carb, it has no metering block. Jet changes are made by lifting the whole top of the carburetor off and exposing the jets at the bottom of the float bowl. Air corrector jets are housed in the booster cluster. The boosters are of the annular discharge type. These 4011 series carbs are available in two flow capacities. Namely, 650 CFM and 800 CFM. Either version is available with mechanical or vacuum secondary actuation.

DOMINATORS THE 4500 SERIES CARBURETORS

Every company that is a serious player in the performance business has to have some big guns in its arsenal if it's to compete successfully at the top of the performance league. For Holley, their Pro-series 4500 Dominator range of carburetors is it. These carburetors consist of a completely different, large butterfly body with the metering blocks and float bowls from the 4150 series carburetors. This series of carbs starts with the 750 model. Essentially the CFM of this carburetor was brought down by using a special "skirted" booster. What this does is reduce the flow through the main venturi and encourages more air to go through the booster. It gets the job done, but a more elegant solution to make the carb work on smaller applications would have been to proportionally resize the main venturi and booster. Although the skirted booster is not an efficient way to achieve this goal, it is functional and at the end of the day that's what matters.

The next size up is the 1050 race unit. This carburetor can be equipped, as can Holley's large 1150 brother, with either a conventional short booster or a much more active annular booster. For any application where anything approaching good low speed drivability is required, the annular discharge booster should be your choice. But for high RPM on big inch engines, the conventional short booster may produce better results in terms of outright power.

As far as use on the street is concern the Dominator scores some major points but carries a few penalties. Its number one positive point is that its ideal for an engine requiring a large amount of CFM such as a big block. The biggest strike against it, and this

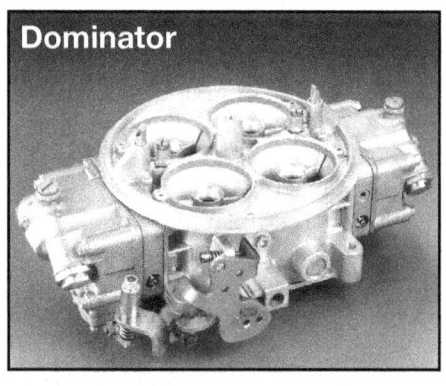

Dominator

may not mean much to the die-hard performance enthusiast, is the fact that it does not have a choke. However, this need not be a total disaster if you have a well set-up engine with a good ignition system. In such a situation a couple of stabs on the throttle to get some pump action going alleviates much of the need for a choke. Add to this, a minimal stationary warm-up time and everything should be ready for business. All this may have the air of inconvenience, but the performance advantages may well, for those serious about performance, offset this.

As far as street drivability is concerned, the Dominator has a major asset in that it has an intermediate circuit between the regular transition circuit and the main circuit. This circuit endows the Dominator with much better drivability than would be expected of a unit with such large venturis and low booster signal at cruise airflow values. When suitably calibrated, the low speed drivability of a Dominator is more than acceptable for most serious high-performance street applications. Indeed for certain uses such as on 500 inch or larger big blocks it would be hard to tell the difference between this and a fuel injection set-up.

Initially, the Dominator looks like an expensive carburetor to use. However, when you analyze what you get in return for your outlay, it becomes obvious that the Dominator is, like most other Holley products, a good value for money deal.

For racing, where large CFM is required, it can well be that the Dominator is the only viable choice. Certainly, if you are contemplating racing any motor over about 400 inches with a single carb, the Dominator must be considered as a prime candidate. It is the only carb with anything approaching adequate airflow for a typical big block. And as such, it produces good results on 454 Chevys, 460 Fords, 440 Chryslers and 455 Pontiacs in the 500 horsepower range on up. If you are contemplating an all out race engine and plan to equip it with dual four barrels then for any self-respecting big block a pair of Dominators should be your choice.

CARBURETOR CFM AND ENGINE DEMAND

Let's talk about carburetor sizing. There's been a great deal of ink expended on this subject in numerous books and magazine features. These have attempted to explain the basic technique for sizing a Holley carburetor to the intended application and have sim-

Here as pair of Dominators are being assembled together with a custom built sheet manifold. This is probably a little on the pricey side for most racers but power costs money - so how fast can you afford to go?

ply re-stated the methods put forward by Holley in their literature. However, if you want to become proficient at sizing Holley carburetors for best results, be it power for the track or mileage and drivability for the street, then you will need to know a little more than just the basics. **It is important to understand that it is not having too much carburetor CFM that is ever a problem**. The real root of all the problems that get labeled "too much carburetor" is, in reality, a question of insufficient booster signal, and consequently, poor fuel atomization and delivery.

Sizing a carburetor to Holley's guidelines produces a carburetor and engine combination where the booster signal is able to adequately, but not necessarily optimally, atomize the fuel at the minimum engine RPM likely to be used. If the carb has a significantly different booster design, it follows that it could also have significantly different atomization capabilities. Everything hinges on how much airflow a booster needs to perform its intended function. This aspect alone can influence matters to such an extent it can significantly modify the choice of carb airflow capacity used. To bring home this important point, let us use an example based on something well-removed from the carb CFM/booster signal situation. Let us assume the fuel is atomized by some means other than a booster induced and amplified signal. A common example of this is a throttle body fuel injection set-up. Here, fuel atomization is dependent on the fuel pressure and the design of the discharge nozzle of the injector. Atomization, therefore, is completely independent of the throttle body airflow. In this instance, we could expect, with a suitably cammed engine, to run a throttle body of 2000 CFM and make good torque as low as one thousand RPM. The bottom line here is being aware of what the immediate goal is. The business of selecting a carb based on CFM alone has always clouded the issue. An example of what can be achieved here is one of the writer's engines. This 350 small block utilized a modified Edlebrock Victor Jr. open plenum race manifold and a Holley carb modified to better atomize the fuel and to give 990 CFM of airflow. Normally, such a setup would be considered a race installation only. This engine idled at 500 rpm and pulled strongly from a thousand. It produced 15 inches of vacuum at idle and cruise. It also propelled a fully dressed 4000 lb car to 110 MPH trap speeds while remaining totally docile on the street. This should adequately demonstrate that ultimately, it is not the CFM that we are trying to optimize but the atomization capabilities of the carb in relation to air-

An Australian race engine builder puts together his first small block after extensive research on the subject. His Holley vacuum secondary carbed 383 street motor was compatible with a stock stall speed converter and pumped out 460 horsepower with a 600 RPM 16 inch idle vacuum.

flow. And with that point in mind, let us progress.

AIRFLOW CAPACITY INFLUENCES

The first step towards selecting a carburetor is to determine a ball park CFM figure for the intended application. Two principle issues affect the initial sizing, and from this point a number of lessor but nontheless important sub-factors modify the optimal airflow capacity of the carburetor needed for the engine. The principle factors are the size of the engine and the RPM it is going to turn. In addition to these primary considerations are other, smaller issues, which cause us to juggle our choice of CFM up or down as the case may be. The most influential of these secondary factors is the booster design used, closely followed by the type of manifold used. Putting this into simple terms if the carb atomizes well, it can be made larger, as it can if a dual plane manifold as opposed to a single plane manifold is used. The type of actuation system the carb has for the secondary butterflies also has a bearing on the final choice. These could be vacuum, mechanical with progressive opening, or mechanical with simultaneous opening. The ratio of primary to secondary size and the absence or not, of manifold heat all play a part in the size selection. When considered in full context by an informed engine builder, all these factors can add up to significantly better results from an off the shelf Holley installation.

COMPUTING REQUIRED AIRFLOW

The first step towards installing the best carb for the job is to make a preliminary selection in the conventional manner, then modify the result based on the relevant secondary factors involved. This initial selection entails determining the amount of CFM the engine is likely to inhale. To do this, we multiply the displacement (CID) by the anticipated RPM the engine is going to be turn to. This result is then divided by 2 if we are dealing with a four cycle engine. What we have so far is the engine's peak airflow requirement in cubic inches per minute. To change that to cubic feet, we divide by 1728. At this stage our formula looks like this.

$$CFM = \frac{CID \times RPM}{2 \times 1728}$$

This formula assumes the engine has a 100% breathing efficiency. On a race engine, where exhaust scavenging is a factor, the VE can exceed 100%. For instance, a well built race 350 with no regulatory race restrictions placed on it's induction flow, can reach 115% VE. However, most Holley equipped engines are likely to be hot street units with something less than 100% V.E. To those of you going through this carb selection exercise, Fig.6-2 will give you an idea of the VE potential of your engine. Using the correction figure (CF) given by the chart, we correct the CFM figures so far calculated. Our formula now becomes:

$$CFM = \frac{CID \times RPM \times CF}{2 \times 1728}$$

So far, everything looks very straightforward and simple. At this point, we have arrived at a carburetor CFM rating which can be used in conjunction with Holley's

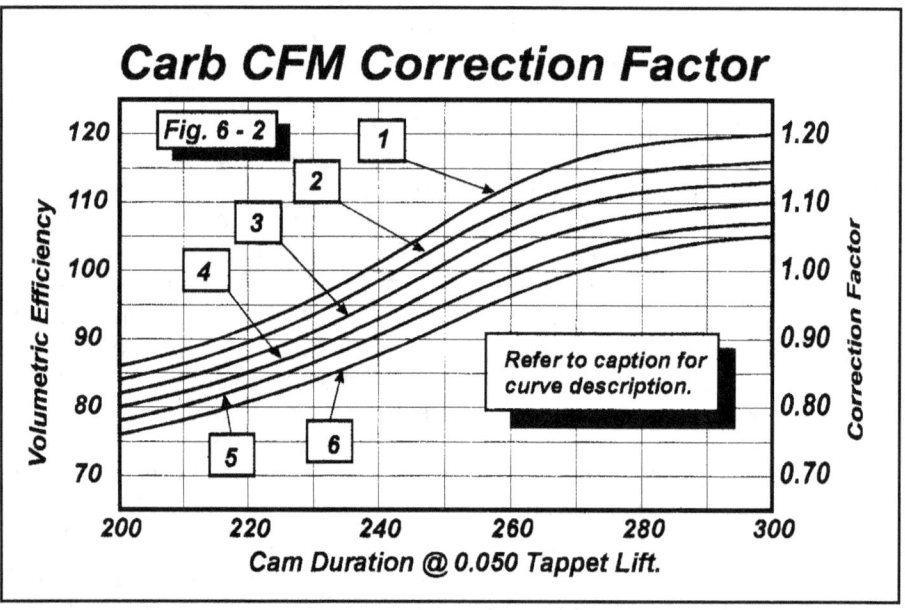

Assuming you are running an unrestricted motor, this chart will help you size your carb more appropriately. The airflow required by the engine, depends primarily on the cam and the breathing capability of the heads. Assuming that the CR and the exhaust system are appropriate for the engine, the head remains as the single most influential factor. For stock heads use curve #6. For pocket ported heads, #5 and for street ported heads, #4. For typical race heads, use curve #3, and for really good race two valve heads in the Winston Cup class use, #2. If the heads are really exotic i.e., inclined valve or 4 valve per cylinder, use curve #1.

Insufficient clearance on the exhaust can easily lose a couple of inches. The intake lash is not as sensitive in this respect. If idle vacuum is lower than you expect and your engine uses a solid lifter cam, go in and check the valve lash.

If idle vacuum is still poor after lash has been properly reset it could be that the cam is mistimed or...

If you feel the cam you've been advised to use isn't going to give the power you are looking for, then it is much better to stay with a short duration cam and add high lift rockers to the valve train.

...the cam selected was too much for the job. It is very common for hot rodders to select too much cam. This is one of the reasons big cam companies such as Competition Cams, run "Cam Select" hot lines.

comprehensive catalog to select a suitable carburetor. Chances are, by doing nothing more than this, the results will be good. However, Holley's recommendations for carburetor sizing are based on the fact that all their four barrel carburetors are sized in terms of CFM using 1.5 inches of mercury pressure drop across them (See sidebar on next page). It is important to appreciate the significance of this to understand what is going on here. In essence, this means that if an engine pulls say, 800 CFM through an 800 CFM carb, it is drawing the manifold pressure down to 1.5 inches of mercury (0.7 PSI) below atmospheric pressure. In other words, it takes almost ¾ PSI of suction to cause 800 CFM to flow through an 800 CFM carb. Full atmospheric pressure is equal to 29.93 inches of mercury, but for the sake of simplification, lets say this is 30 inches. A 1.5 inch pressure drop across the carb means the total air pressure inside the intake manifold at approximately peak power RPM, will only be 28.5 inches. So that's all clear, let's put this into lb/sq. inch. 1.5 inches of mercury is almost ½ psi and, for all practical purposes, we can say that normal sea level atmospheric pressure is 14.7 psi. By dropping ¾ PSI across the carb, the cylinders only see an intake manifold pressure of something a little less than 14 PSI. Three-quarter of a PSI is lost due to the flow restriction caused by the carburetor. This ¾ PSI represents approximately 5% of the available air pressure. If perfect carburation could be achieved without this pressure drop, the engine would instantly gain 5% in power. The reason Holley chose 1.5 inches of mercury pressure drop to quote the airflow of their carbs is because it was a good all-around figure for a high performance street machine, and for a production line vehicle the potential loss in real power was considered inconsequential. Going this route presented minimal problems, so people who are not fully aware of the intricacies of carb calibration could arrive at a working set-up with usually no more than simple jet changes. Holley, rightly so, does not expect their customers to be carburetor design experts. Since Holley assume the customer is not in a position to alter aspects beyond simple calibration, their recommendations are understandably on the conservative side. However, knowing more about the factors influencing carburetion can be a great help toward choosing a more effective carburetor and or installing one without necessarily jeopardizing desirable street driving qualities. It is this aspect of carb calibration that we will now look at.

MINIMIZING MANIFOLD PRESSURE LOSS

It is possible, if enough effort is put into it, to get a Holley carburetor to function perfectly well with only half an inch of pressure drop across it at peak power RPM. With just a little more care than is typically taken by the average hot rodder, it is possible to get decent calibration with less than 1-inch of pressure drop at maximum RPM.

Reducing the full throttle, maximum RPM pressure drop means that the carb used needs to be sized larger than predicted by the equations we have so far shown. Alternately, we could say that we need to re-evaluate the carburetor CFM rating so as to reflect its airflow capacity at a lower pressure drop. The second method is probably the easiest way to visualize the situation.

For the sake of argument, let us assume we have a carb known to be functional with only ½ inch of pressure drop across it. At this reduced pressure drop, the carb will flow less air than at its normally rated pressure drop. Put simply, less suction means less flow. An example here will illustrate how this affects the carburation. Let us assume we have a carb which flows 800 CFM at the normally used four barrel carb rating of ½ inch pressure drop. For a given amount of air flowing into the engine, we could reduce the pressure drop or restriction across the carb by installing a larger carb. How many CFM will this carb be worth at ½ inch of pressure drop instead of 1½. Obviously, it will flow less at the lower pressure drop, so some sort of correction must be applied to the carb's original flow figure to establish it's capability at this lower pressure drop.

As long as the characteristics of the flow pattern do not radically change, the airflow through a carb follows a square law in relation to the pressure drop. If we are coming down from a higher pressure drop rating to a lower, as is the case here, any error that occurs is in our favor. This leaves us with a carb which flows a little more than our simple calculations predict. Working an example is the easiest way to see how this works out in practice.

HORSEPOWER Quick Facts & References

CARB FLOW vs TEST PRESSURE DROP

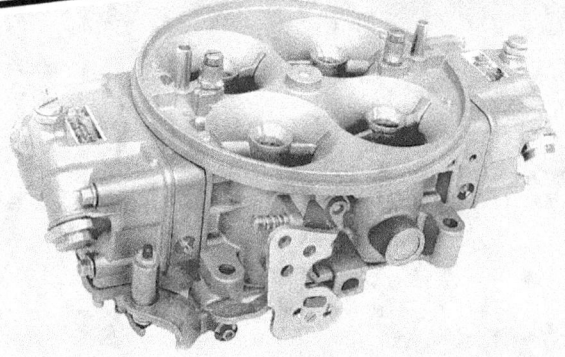

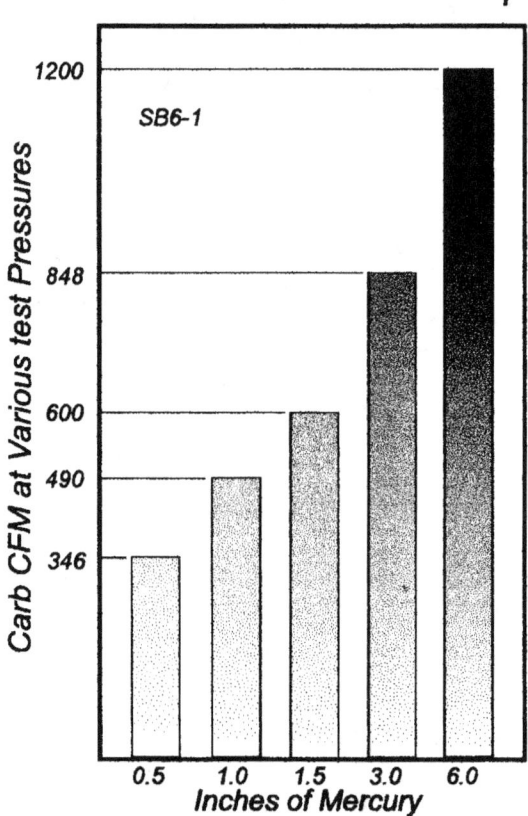

The more the engine is starved of air, the harder it pulls on the carburetor. To get air to flow into the engine, there always has to be some pressure drop, no matter how small across the carb. Minimizing this is what we need to concern ourselves with. In the chart we can see what happens when we subject a 600 CFM Holley to pressure drops other than the 1.5 inches of mercury that Holley uses as the calibration standard. At one end of the range, a 600 Holley would flow about 1200 CFM on a 6000 RPM 700 inch big block. But the pressure drop across it necessary to cause this much to flow would be about 6 inches of mercury. That represents a drop of 20% of the atmospheric air pressure between the outside world and the inside of the intake manifold. At the other end of the scale, if we had a pair of 600"s on a tunnel ram equipped, both carbs combined would only flow about 700 cfm but the pressure drop across them would only be about a half inch of mercury. The bottom line is that the CFM the engine see"s is dependent on the pressure drop across the carbs. If we are looking to minimize this, then we need to think of all our carbs as being smaller than their rated values.

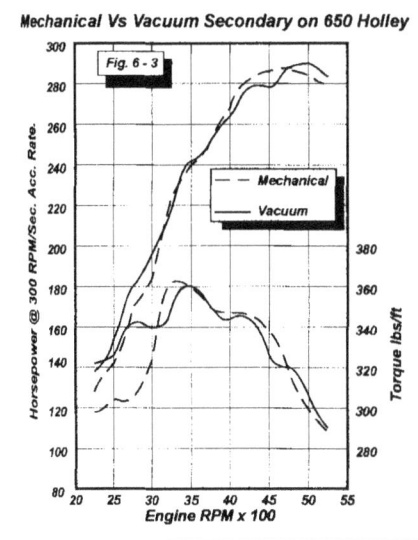

A look at the low-end output of both these 650 carbs shows the "low performance" vacuum secondary carb to be vastly superior up to 3000 rpm and to be about equal from there on up.

How many CFM will an 800 CFM carburetor be worth at ½ inch of pressure drop instead of 1½? Here a simple formula can be used to calculate the carb's new flow rating. This is achieved by dividing the standard pressure drop of 1½ inches by the new pressure drop which in this instance will be ½ inch. When we take the square root of this number, it gives us a number to divide into the original CFM. In practice, it goes something like this.

$$\frac{\text{Carb CFM @ Original Pressure Drop Rating}}{\sqrt{\dfrac{\text{Original Pressure Drop}}{\text{New Pressure Drop}}}}$$

Putting the numbers into this equation gives:

$$\frac{800}{\sqrt{\dfrac{1.5}{0.5}}}$$

This equals:

In practice then, a carb rated at 800 CFM at 1.5 inches pressure drop only flows 462 CFM at .5 inch of pressure drop.

RECOMMENDED READING

RECOMMENDED HOLLEY BOOKS

The book you are now reading was never intended to be specifically on Holleys nor was it intended to be an overhaul manual or parts catalog. What it was intended to do was to help develop your knowledge of carburetion for your performance engine regardless of type. However, more race engines are equipped with Holley carburetors than any other carburetor in the world. To that end, you may find it is useful to become an expert in the many practical aspects of working with Holley carburetors. If this is the case the author can personally recommend the three books shown here. Equipping your library with these books will put you one step ahead of your opposition.

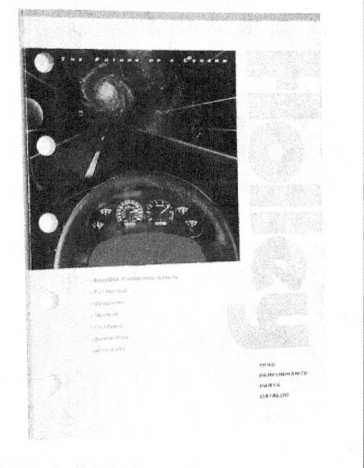

Holley's parts catalog. Without this you will have no idea of the extensive range of induction related parts that Holley produces.

Super Tuning and Modifying Holley Carburetors by Dave Emanuel. Here you have well written book devoted solely to making a most of Holley carburetors.

Jeff Williams book, *Holley Rebuilding and Modifying*. Is a must for the practical work on these carbs.

How to Build Horsepower, Vol. 2

EFFECTIVE USE OF MORE CFM

$$\frac{800}{\sqrt{3}} = \frac{800}{1.732} = 462\ CFM$$

Analyzing the factors that are likely to allow more carburetion than Holley normally recommends, a clear picture of options becomes apparent. First, a carburetor that has annular discharge boosters instead of straight, or dogleg boosters, safely allows about 50 CFM more carb airflow to be used. The use of a "high gain" booster such as the annular discharge type, is far more important on the primary side than the secondary. Indeed, there are many instances where better results are seen when a lower gain booster, such as the dog leg booster, is used on the secondary side. If the intended carb has vacuum secondaries, then annular or high gain boosters in the primary side are all that is required to optimize low end performance from a larger carb.

The opportunity to increase airflow by some 50 CFM also applies if a carburetor that has significantly smaller primary than secondary barrels is chosen. Since any carburation problems are most likely to occur at part throttle when only the primary is in operation attention to this side is the most important.

This brings us to the use of vacuum operated secondaries. These should be viewed as a means of avoiding a low booster signal by limiting the amount of venturi area presented to the engine until it can effectively use it. By letting the carb's vacuum secondary operation system think for us the engine can utilize more carburation capacity without suffering the usual negative side effects.

For many, the vacuum secondary style carb is the epitome of economy street carbs. For the less informed performance enthusiasts this spells anything but performance. True, the vacuum operated secondary carb does offer the potential for better fuel economy and drivability. However, this does not mean that these advantages come with a power penalty. When tested on the basis of like for like in terms of CFM, a vacuum operated secondary 650 Holley held its own against the performance oriented 650 double pumper carb (Fig. 6-3). However, it is questionable if we should be making comparative tests with these carbs and their vastly differing secondary operative actuation methods, at the same CFM. The total CFM has little to do with anything when the vehicle is just cruising along the freeway. What we should consider here, is a test of two carbs giving the same drivability. If we size a non-vacuum carb to give it the same miles per gallon and drivability as a vacuum secondary carb, then we see a big difference. Here, a comparison looks more like a 650 double pumper vs a 750 vacuum secondary. The results on our dyno show it's a no contest situation. The vacuum secondary wins hands down by producing more torque and horsepower (Fig. 6-4). We can say then, there's an advantage to using the vacuum secondary on the street. The advantage of power goes to the vacuum secondary because about a 100 CFM more can be used without mileage and low speed drivability penalties.

Based on our test results, we can say with reasonable confidence, that a vacuum secondary will allow a minimum of 100 CFM of extra usable airflow without disadvantage. This can be a significant factor if the intake manifold being used is a 180 degree type. Because a 180 degree manifold produces sharper pulses at the booster and suffers less vacuum loss due to exhaust reversion during the overlap, we find that with this type of manifold, it is possible to step up the carb CFM by a minimum of 10% over that predicted by the basic sizing formula covered earlier. Indeed, in some circumstances, which are covered elsewhere in this book, increases above and beyond this basic 10% can be successfully made.

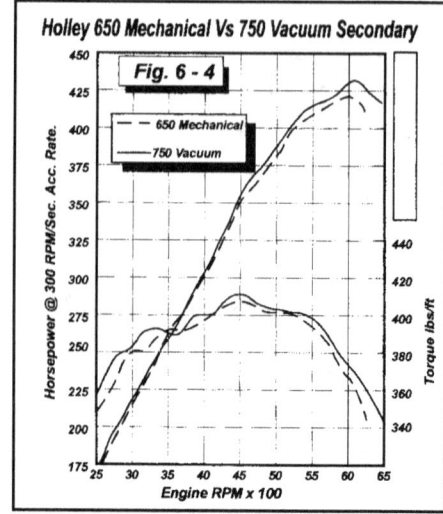

This 383 Chevy motor was equipped with ported Dart II heads, a 9/1 CR, a 280 Comp Cams hydraulic flat tappet cam and 1-5/8 inch headers. The point to note is that the 750 vacuum secondary carb gave better low end and more top end than the 650 Double Pumper carb. Vacuum secondaries are really good for the street.

A 3310 style vacuum secondary carb will give the necessary drivability and response on the street, and you can size it up to 100 CFM larger than a comparative mechanical secondary carb. This offers a performance advantage on the high end without low-speed losses.

CALIBRATING HOLLEY CARBS

HOLLEY CALIBRATION IN ONE PAGE

Step #1 Read this book from cover to cover so that you have a working understanding of how a carburetor and all its various circuits work. This will be the single most effective calibration tool you can acquire and works not only for Holleys but all carbs. This information will allow you to competently set up the idle and transition circuits from a position of knowledge of function.

Step #2 Unless you are prepared to do things the hard way do not attempt to calibrate the full power mixture without some form of mixture measuring device. An oxy sensing air/fuel monitor and a drag strip is the #1 recommendation. Next, is the engine analyzers used in conjunction with a professionally operated chassis dyno. A

There are many ways to get the best mileage and reduce emissions, in most cases, at the same time. Most require diligent calibration of the carburetor's cruise circuits, but here is a system that we tested which does the job for you. Unfortunately, the company building it went out of business, but the concept is worth passing on because it was relatively simple to do. Instead of controlling the mixture by metering the fuel, this system in part, metered air. Here is how it worked. The oxy sensors in the exhaust sensed whether or not there was any unburned oxygen in the exhaust. The signal put out by these was ...

distant third is the drag strip or some timing over a fixed distance and plug reading. Before starting on the carb, set the ignition timing a 2-5 degrees more retarded than you expect the final setting to be.

Step #3 Set the main jet prior to starting your calibration proper so that traces of black smoke can be seen to be coming out of the exhaust as you roll into the throttle. Rolling into the throttle minimizes the effect of the engine's pump requirement, which we don't want to cloud the issue at this point.

Step #4 Reduce the main jet size until you mixture shows 12.5:1 to 13:1 or the car returns its fastest 1/4 mile time. If you are testing with an air/fuel monitor and you find the fuel curve is not a constant, then trim the curve as required by re-sizing the air corrector. On the main jet side (as opposed to idle), this is a very sensitive calibration component and a one thousandth change up or down is significant. Make changes in small increments. If the engine shows a tendency to bog, it could be that you have selected the wrong size carb, in spite of all the good advice you have available within these pages, or the pump enrichment is incorrect. If your carb is a vacuum secondary unit, it could be opening the secondaries too soon or, if there is no sign of a bog, too late. You may need to change the diaphragm springs accordingly. The fol-

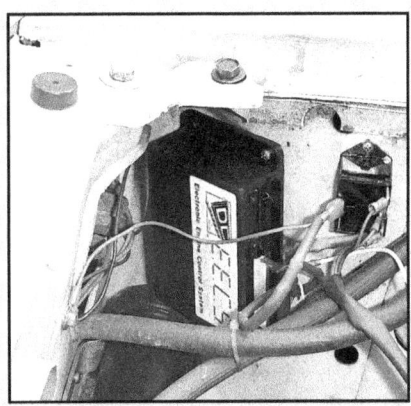

..... fed to this box, whose circuits determined if there was sufficient oxygen in the exhaust to indicate that the engine was in a lean burn mode. If there was not it sent the appropriate signal...

lowing color codes list the springs from fastest/soonest to slowest/latest: White, yellow, red, purple, green, orange, plain, brown, black.

Step #5 If the bog is due to an incorrect amount of pump shot, determine whether it is too much or too little. If you have an air/fuel monitor as we advised then you will already know the answer to that; if not, have someone experienced watch the exhaust as the car leaves the line. If no exhaust smoke is apparent, it is likely that the pump is not delivering enough fuel. If there is more than just a slight trace, too much is being delivered. The pump shot is calibrated both by pump jet size and the stroke produced by the pump cam on the throttle shaft. Try re-jetting first. If this does not produce results, try a change of cam or cam position: First, the position situation. It could be that with a non-trans braked car (which has full throttle well prior to leaving), that the staging rpm requires the throttles to be rotated far enough to use up some of the cam's

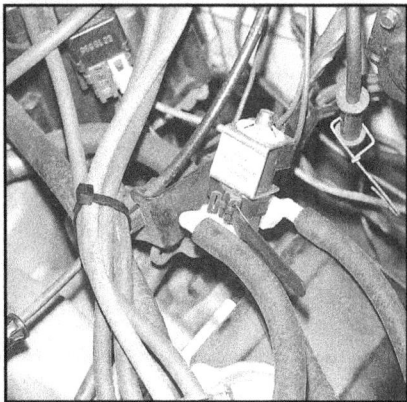

... to this valve, which bled air into the manifold to lean out the mixture by the right amount. This system worked well. We tested it for both emissions and fuel economy. It dropped CO and HC emissions by between 15 and 40% depending on where in the operating range we were running. Mileage did not show a big increase, with only 0.53 improvement. However, it should be pointed out that the engine had been previously dyno tuned with mileage in mind and the car was already delivering some 18.7 average.

pump shot stroke. If you suspect this to be the case, rotate the cam back from its current position or file some material off the lead in on the cam profile. If you suspect the cam has insufficient stroke then here are the color codes from small to large. Black, white, red, blue, orange, green, pink.

Step # 6 Once the mixture is as close as you can get it, then you should finish your tuning procedure by power timing the ignition at the drag strip. Progressively add more timing until the car runs its best. Usually you can go a few degrees past where you found the "initial" best point without performance dropping off. Retard from this point. The idea is to use the minimum advance to get the job done.

How To Build HORSEPOWER: Chapter 7

Carburetors & Intake Manifolds
Performance Mods For Holleys

A stock Holley carb can represent an excellent investment for a stock or near stock engine, but for even a moderately modified engine, something out of the ordinary is often needed. Why? Because, with the exception of a few models, a stock Holley was never intended to maximize performance on engines equipped with big cams, open plenum manifolds, large port heads and so on. Few of these performance attributes ever exist on a stock motor, so the basic but versatile Holley design needs to be re-engineered to suit the needs of a high performance engine. The main areas requiring attention are the idle and transition circuits, air flow capability, booster signal strength and float bowl performance under high G acceleration. Although all these factors are very much interrelated, we will, for simplicity's sake, separate them so it can more easily be seen why they need to be modified.

AIR FLOW

For a well-specced out V8 some 2 CFM of carb air flow is needed per horsepower that the engine is capable of developing in every other respect. The horsepower figure referred to here is the one that the engine would make if given all the carburetion it could handle in the form of, say, a tunnel ram with two appropriately sized four barrels. For most of us, a 2 x 4 tunnel ram installation is less than practical, while a single four barrel is just about the reverse. Unfortunately, utilizing a single carb can cost power because total carburetor airflow is compromised. Based on a requirement of 2 CFM per horsepower, a 650 Holley appears to be only good for some 325 HP. Not quite true, but on our 2 cfm per horsepower rating, adding another 650 CFM of carburetion would only add, at most, some 6 horsepower to an engine already producing 325 HP. From that stand point our 2 cfm per horsepower is a generous racers' rating. In practice, a 650 Holley could be used on an engine of much higher power but it would, if pushed to the limit, significantly cut into the engine's full potential. For instance if a 650 were used on an engine that was able to physically make 500 horsepower, it would pull some 2 inches of mercury vacuum in the intake manifold at peak power. That means the density of the air entering the runners is 7% down. Adding 300 CFM to our hypothetical engine would step up the power to about 530 horsepower. So why don't we put on a carb with all the air flow in the world? No reason at all, so long as it still carburetes, and that means delivering a well-atomized mixture of

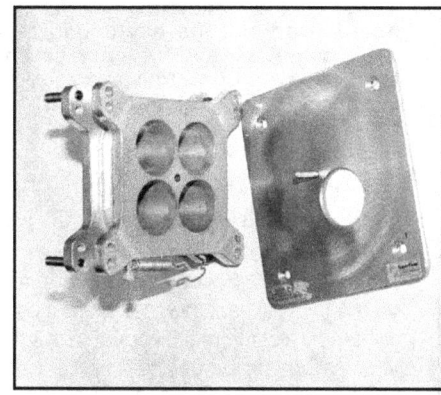

Most flow benches only have enough flow capacity to test one barrel of a Holley carb. This fixture from Superflow allows each barrel to be selected in turn.

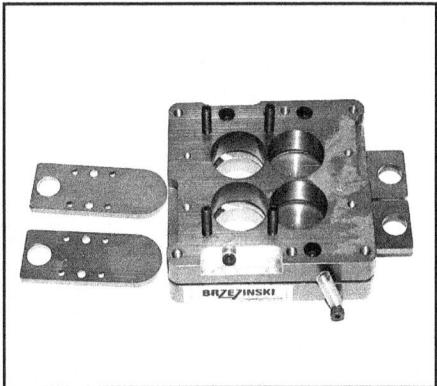

This flow fixture from Brzinski Racing can flow test any one or more carb barrels in whatever combination the user desires..

In this view, the different sizes of various Holley carbs can be seen. The 850 body on the right has only a minimal venturi shape to it. This, plus the use of a booster of indifferent performance, results in its poor low speed performance. Center is the body for the popular and highly functional 650 Holley and far right is the 390 CFM body.

fuel and air in exactly the right proportions. In the real world, the problem is that high air flow from big venturis means a lower venturi signal and in turn less signal for the booster to "boost". The situation is degraded even more if the booster design is such that it only produces minimal amplification of the main venturi signal. This scenario is common not just to Holleys, but most stock carb designs. To get additional power without sacrificing low-speed output the knowledgeable carb specialist will take what ever measures possible to increase air flow **and only increase venturi size as a last resort.** By going this route, all the top-end benefits of a large carb are accrued while the low end performance of a smaller CFM carb is not only retained, but in many instances enhanced. Done right, there are, at worst, only very minimal performance compromises over a high-flow carb with no bottom end performance, so making the right moves results largely in a win-win situation.

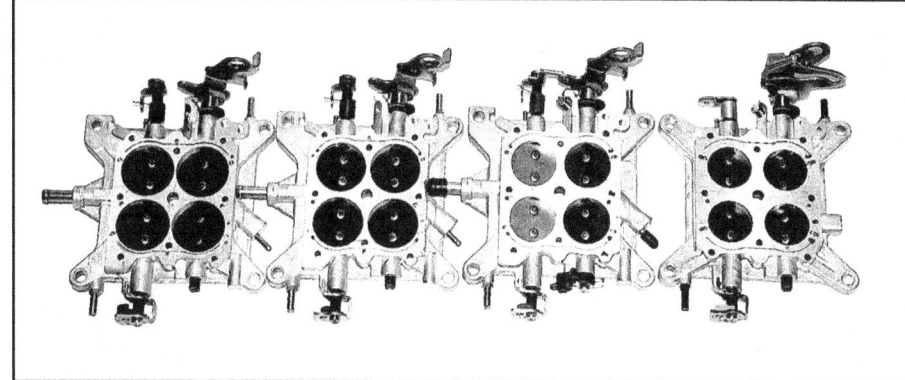

Along with various venturi sizes, there are different butterfly diameters. The 850 uses the base plate on the far left, while the smallest butterflies are in the 390 base plate on the far right.

It's hard to believe that anything comes for nothing, so you may ask where Holley went wrong on its initial carb design if it allows big air flow gains to be made. The answer is: they didn't: their goal just isn't the same as ours, as performance enthusiasts. A stock Holley represents one of the best value-for-money carb deals available. If you doubt this for one moment, just check out the price of some Webers or Dellortos, or constant vacuum carbs, such as SUs. Do that, and it is unlikely you will ever complain about the cost of an off the shelf Holley again. However Holley's cost effectiveness was not achieved by chance. It was done by designing only enough carb to get the intended job of producing acceptable performance from a stock motor.

Other than a Stub Stack, a more conventional type of ram pipe, such as this Braswell example can be used as shown on this single four barrel and this ...

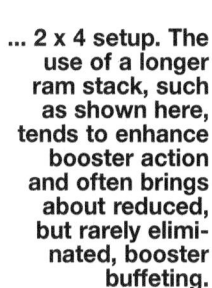

... 2 x 4 setup. The use of a longer ram stack, such as shown here, tends to enhance booster action and often brings about reduced, but rarely eliminated, booster buffeting.

How to Build Horsepower, Vol. 2 **67**

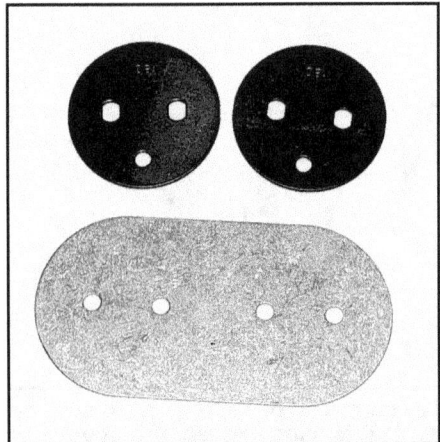

Except on those carbs, such as the 390 CFM unit where the butterflies can be made very large in relation to the venturis, the butterfly represents a restriction well worth reducing. To maximize area and minimize restriction for a two barrel race carb, Braswell Carburetion made up a base plate employing the oval butterfly shown here.

This was installed in a special base plate which required an adapter (right) for clearance...

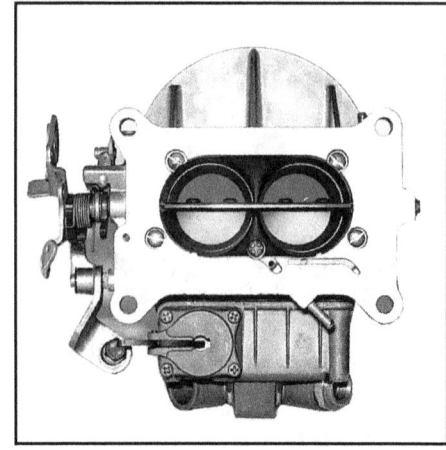

...of the area between the barrels in the main body.

In addition to the oval butterfly, the Braswell two barrel also dispensed with a booster and used annular discharge venturis. This means the main venturi doubles as a booster. For a two barrel application, where there is a high airflow demand over the working range of engine operation, this system works well.

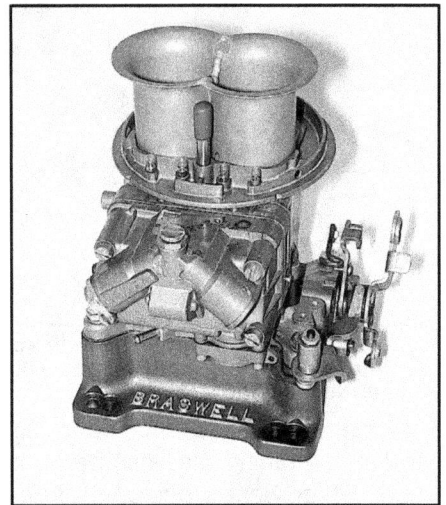

With all the modifications shown, plus an adapter, this Braswell two barrel produced the same air flow as a stock Holly 650 four barrel. This represents no less than a 46% increase over stock. A four barrel equivalent of this carb with a flow capability of some 1200 CFM can under certain circumstances be used. For instance it would be well suited to a high stall speed converter, Trans brake equipped car where low speed operation is more or less academic.

For the most part, performance enthusiasts don't have a stock motor, but nonetheless Holley's street carb cost cutting design philosophy actually works in our favor. Even though a stock Holley may be short on air flow for a performance application, there are a number of steps we can take to improve things. For instance, streamlining the choke horn entry by adding a K & N Stub Stack or, for performance only applications, removing it completely, can add up to 45 CFM. Cleaning the casting flash from the venturis and the rest of the carb body can add a few more CFM but the most significant air flow mods are performed on the butterflies and shafts. By slimming down these components where they pass through the bore of the carb barrels, a very useful gain of around 35 to 50 cfm is achieved ,depending on the throttle bore size. On those carbs equipped stock with the smaller butterflies, usually 600 to 750 cfm size carbs, stepping up to the 850 base plate with it's larger 1 ^{11}/16 inch butterflies is a much recommended move. This maximizes airflow and in many instances produces a small increase in booster signal strength.

BOOSTER GAIN

The whole point of a booster is to boost the signal developed at the main venturi. It is a component that is of major importance to street rodders and racers, who are not only looking for maximum power, but also a high torque output over the widest rev range possible.

For a carb to function as intended, a certain minimum booster signal strength is required to ensure adequate atomization. To this end, it is important to realize that most of a booster's atomization capability comes from its ability to draw hard on both the main jet and the air correction jet. Given the signal to work with, it is primarily these two jets working in concert that provides results. The bigger the air correction jet is in relation to the main jet, the greater the proportion of air contained in the emulsified fuel in the main jet well from which the booster draws. A fuel/air emulsion with a higher percentage of air atomizes better than one with a lower percentage. By using a high gain booster, a stronger draw is seen on the emulsion or main jet well. If no changes are made, we normally find, due to the typical proportioning of the jets, that excess fuel will be delivered. Increasing the size of the air corrector jet compensates for this by increasing the air content of the fuel/air emulsion in the main jet well.

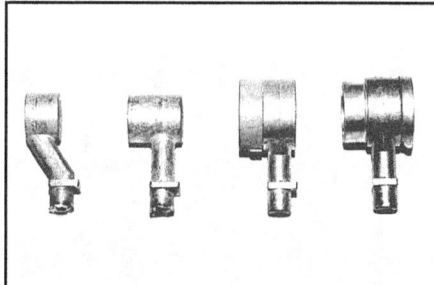

Shown here are the various Holley boosters that are used in most 'square bore' 4150-4160 series carbs for performance applications.

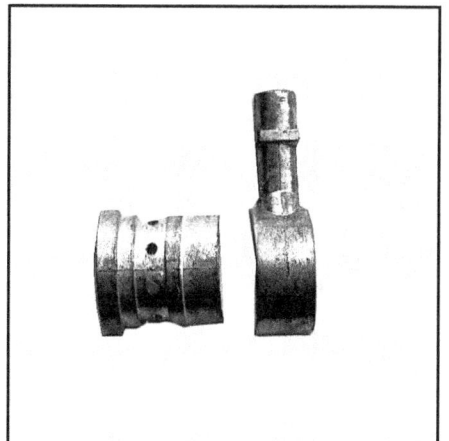

Here we have disassembled an annular discharge booster to show the inner form. The venturi section is a simple press fit in the leg. This design has prompted much work to be done on booster design by the aftermarket. Some did not deliver as much promise as their looks would suggest.

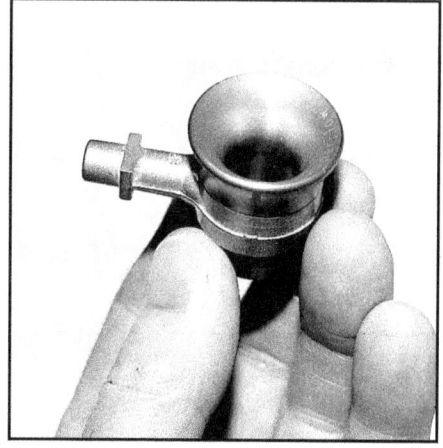

This esoteric appearing design, though functional, did not produce any measurable advantage over modified stock units

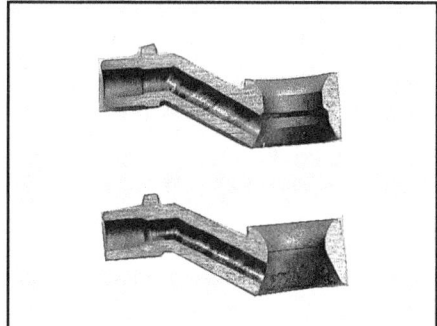

Two modifications are apparent in this shot of dogleg boosters. In both cases, the fuel passage connecting the body to the booster venturi has been enlarged, as this becomes restrictive under high demand situations. In the case of the lower booster, the venturi has been modified by machining a step into the lower side. This produces an improvement in fuel atomization. In some cases, as many as three steps have been shown to be beneficial. Dyno testing has demonstrated that remedying inadequate atomization with a booster having as many as three steps can deliver as much as an additional 12 horsepower in a single four barrel 350 CID application.

The end result is to correct the air/fuel ratio seen down stream of the booster.

In practice, a basic minimum booster signal strength is required to ensure adequate atomization for good low-speed power output. Production carbs achieve this by limiting the size of venturi in relation to the air demand of the engine. Limiting the carb's airflow causes the piston on its induction stroke to draw harder on the booster. Put plain and simply, carb restriction is doing part of the job of generating a booster signal. Improving the booster's effectiveness as discussed allows the use of more carb CFM for a better top end before low-end output suffers due to inadequate signal.

So how do we go about improving booster design? Simple, you start with a basic design and to this you add a substantial amount of carb design experience and an appropriate amount of initiative. Next, you include a lot of flow bench time, and when all that is done, add in the dyno time. Although this may look like the end of the road, we are not done yet. To this already lengthy procedure, we must now add a goodly measure of trial and error, more flow bench and dyno time, and last, but certainly not least, track time must be thrown in. Fortunately, for the aftermarket carb business, Holley has done a lot of the homework on booster technology and achieved a good measure of success in the process.

As you might expect, all boosters are not created equal and that applies to production costs as well as performance. At one end of the scale, we have Holley's most basic booster design, the straight leg booster. At the other end, there is Holley's short annular discharge booster, whose performance is just about a quantum leap from the straight leg design. In addition to this, we have the aftermarket modified boosters such as the Super Booster from The Carb Shop.

Having enough booster signal with which to work is easy under full throttle high RPM conditions. Where a good booster design really comes into play is at part throttle. A typical V8 powering a typical mid- to full-size

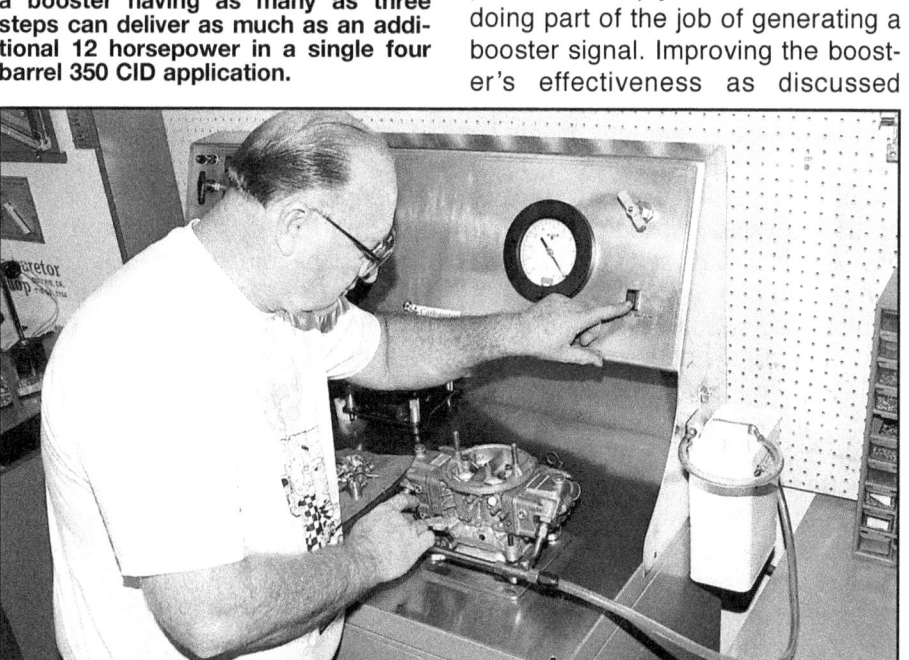

After testing the booster outside of its working environment, it is installed in a carb body and run on a wet flow bench, such as the one seen here. For obvious safety reasons, a special non-combustible fluid which in other respects is closely representative of gasoline, is used for such tests.

How to Build Horsepower, Vol. 2

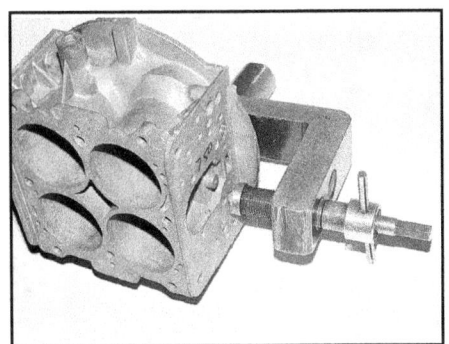

It is unlikely, as an enthusiast, that you will ever install boosters for two reasons. First, it requires a special tool, such as shown here, and second, Holley supplies only a small group of selected shops for insurance reasons.

vehicle down the freeway has to pass some 75 CFM of air into the engine. Opening the throttle for a passing maneuver must result in a quality mixture being fed to the engine. The better it is atomized, the better the low RPM response will be. When tested at a standard 75 CFM flow a stock Holley straight leg booster installed in a 750 CFM carb produced a signal of 4.5 inches of H2O. Replacing this with the stock short annular discharge booster produced 7.8 inches without a sacrifice in flow. Changing the booster again, this time for one of the Carb Shop's Super Boosters produced an 8.8 inch signal. Not only did this booster deliver more signal amplification but its highly efficient design did so with an increase in wide open throttle air flow!

IDLE AND CRUISE QUALITY

With any small block V8 equipped with a cam of more than 275° or a big block with 280°, consideration must be given to transition and idle improvements. To improve both idle quality and low speed, off idle drivability you can install idle circuits into the secondary side of a typical four barrel Holley to make what is commonly known as a four corner idle system. Four corner idle circuits are often seen as a means to improve manifold fuel distribution at idle. In reality, they make little difference to an engine with a high manifold vacuum because most of the fuel under such conditions vaporizes. However, as manifold vacuum decreases due to the use of a longer duration cam,

Although there is a permissible margin of error, it is important that the end of the booster be optimally positioned right at the minor diameter of the main venturi. To check this after reinstalling boosters, a fixture such as this is used.

so the performance of the idle circuit becomes more critical if good idle quality and off idle drivability is to be retained.

A cam having more duration and overlap than stock causes the engine to lose some of its ability to draw a high vacuum. This is due to residual exhaust flowing out through the open intake valve during the overlap period and polluting the fresh charge. Increased exhaust pollution of the intake charge makes the mixture harder to ignite, thus necessitating the need to richen it up, which in turn makes greater fuel flow demands on the idle circuit. This coupled with the low vacuum makes it necessary to open the butterflies a greater amount at idle to get the required air flow. In so doing the primary butterfly starts to uncover the transition slot too early in the driving cycle from idle to cruise. This can lead to poor drivability or even a pronounced stumble just before the throttle is open enough to bring the main jet circuit into operation. As to how much butterfly opening is too much, it is generally accepted that if a .040-inch feeler gauge can pass between the butterfly and body, it is open too much. To an extent, this can be compensated for by opening the secondary butterfly by means of its stop. This is accessed from beneath the base plate.

If resetting the secondary stop to hold the secondaries a little further open fails to cure poor idle and off

When dealing with smaller venturi carbs, we find that the annular discharge booster occupies quite a large portion of the area. This does not stop them functioning, as in bigger venturis but the need for them is no longer there unless we are dealing with a very small engine.

idle drivability due to excessive butterfly opening, other steps must be taken. One of the best all around solutions is to combine two tried and tested fixes. The first is simple, while the second is not and requires the use of special machining fixtures such as used by professional carb shops. The simple modification to improve drivability when progressing from idle to the transition circuits is to drill a hole in each butterfly so that a portion of idle air can pass through this hole. With the hole in the butterfly, it will be necessary to reduce the amount the butterfly is open so more of the transition slot is available for it's intended use. There is, of course, a limit as to how big a hole can be put in the butterflies. Although it is functional with primary side only idle, the full potential of this mod becomes evident when the secondary side is also equipped with an idle circuit thus producing a 'four corner idling' carb. This has many more benefits than just a more even mixture distribution at idle. First, there is twice as much idle airflow available, so each set of butterflies is nearer closed, leaving a greater length of the primary barrel's transition slot available to perform its function. In addition to this the secondary butterflies can also be drilled thus allowing all four butterflies to have the minimal amount of opening thus leaving the maximum length of transition slot for off idle to cruise driving. If a long duration cam has been installed the difference that four corner idling can make is like night and day.

TRANSITION CIRCUIT MODIFICATIONS

Another relatively common problem with engines having a long duration cam is that the motor often generates more vacuum just off idle than at idle itself. This increase in vacuum leads to an overly rich mixture which, in most cases produces lazy throttle response. This can be fixed by appropriately jetting the fuel supplied to the transition slots. The usual technique is to install jets similar to those used for air corrector jets. Based on experience most pro carb builders will use previously drilled or screw in replaceable jets sized to suit the characteristics produced by the camshaft used. Once done, the response to the throttle, when driving on the transition circuit, is often much improved. For that matter so is fuel consumption and emissions.

Once the fuel to the transition slot is near producing the desired mixture it can be fine tuned by changing the idle system air corrector jets. As with the main circuit larger leans out the mixture and smaller richens.

FLOAT BOWL MODIFICATIONS

A high output drag race car with a well set up suspension can leave the line and sustain, for as much as one second an acceleration rate in excess of 2.2 G. Indeed, for maybe a tenth of a second while the suspensions 'anti squat' is active the acceleration may be as high as 5 G! This can play havoc with the float action and the fuel level it is supposed to control. This may cause the fuel to uncover the main jets in the rear float bowl/bowls and cause a temporary lean out. Also a large drop when the needle valve opens can cause a substantial amount of float bowl fuel foaming. This can be another reason for leaning out the mixture. The engine may just about recover from this only to be leaned out all the way

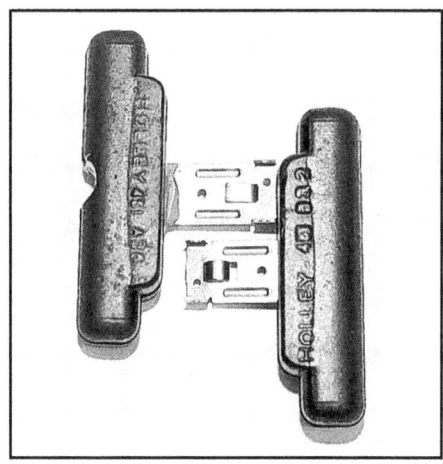

The Carb Shop long arm float steps up the leverage the float exerts on the needle valve by about 18%. This allows higher fuel pressure to be used to the float bowl and if required more fuel flow to deal with higher power requirements.

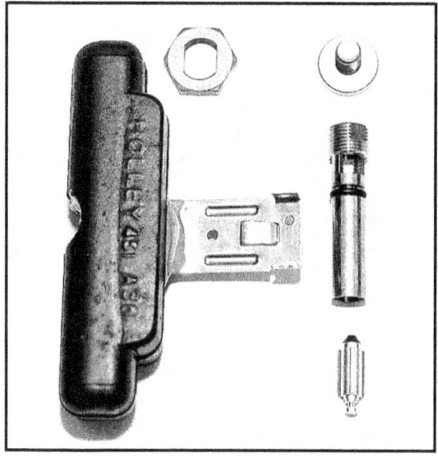

Shown here is the bottom feeder needle valve assembly together with a long arm float. The notch in the float is to clear the extended needle valve.

around due to insufficient flow from the pump.

An electric pump operating from the vicinity of the fuel tank has to overcome a lot of back pressure due to the vehicles acceleration. The fuel in a 10 foot line running forward to the engine will experience 6.0 psi of back pressure due to a 2 G launch. The fuel pump must have adequate pressure to overcome this and still supply the engines demand for fuel. For this reason, the pump should deliver a high pressure right up to the carb and then have that pressure regulated, by one means or another, to a lower pressure that won't overcome the float's ability to close the needle valve, a subject we will deal with in a moment. However, another problem can arise here. With high fuel pressures and hot fuel, the fuel pressure drop through the regulator or into the float bowl can cause the lighter, more volatile elements to flash to a vapor. This causes the carb to momentarily lean out then to flood. The cure is a cool can installed in the high pressure line between the fuel pump and regulator.

So much for the diversion on fuel pressure, now let us consider how it applies to needle valves. When the engine's demand for fuel is high, the fuel, of necessity, must enter the float bowl at high speed. The fuel streaming like water out of a hose pipe creates foam. This aeration of the fuel causes the mixture to lean out and as a consequence the engine looses power. The fix is simple. The stock needle and seat assembly is replaced with the Carb Shop's 'control' package, which features a bottom feeding needle and jet assembly. By extending the needle valve outlet the fuel now enters the float bowl at the bottom below the fuel level and it cannot produce foam from this source.

The bottom-feeding needle valve takes care of the foaming but for race applications high fuel pressure needed for good results often calls for further improvement of float control. This can be achieved by use of the Carb Shop's 'long arm' float. With this type of float, the leverage of the float over the needle valve is increased so the float/needle valve assembly can deal successfully with higher fuel pressures.

The last factor we need to deal with in the float bowl is fuel slosh. High acceleration rates from the start line can cause the fuel to uncover the rear most jets of a single carb, or the front jets of a pair of sideways mounted carbs. Part of this problem is that the fuel may already contain a high percentage of foam so the jet draws an air fuel mix instead of straight fuel. The bottom feeding needle valve is often a cure for this, but if this proves not to be the case a jet extension or slosh tube will fix the problem. By extending the jet we are effectively moving the fuel pickup point into a region of the float bowl that will always contain fuel even under hard acceleration.

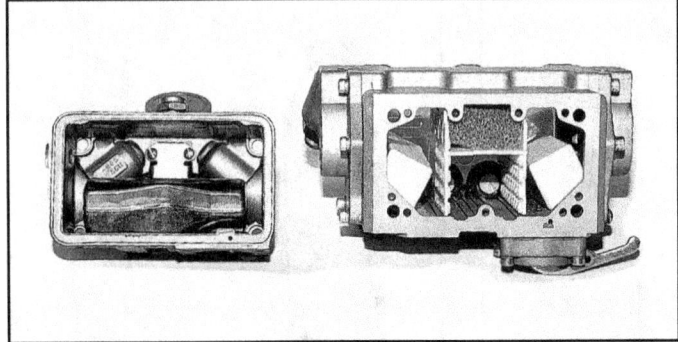
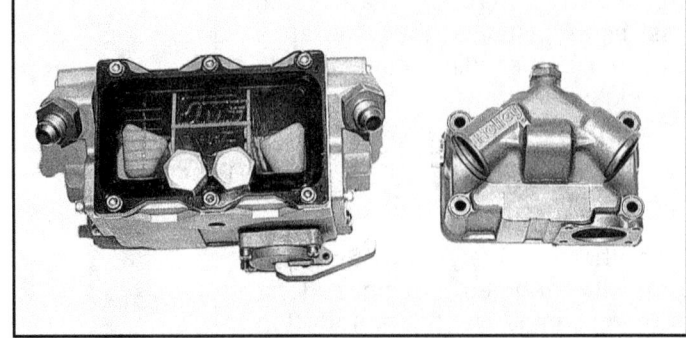

McClintic R-D-M built these Pro Bowl float bowls in an effort to end fuel foaming. Although proven functional they were, because of cost, used mostly by pro racers for serious gasoline dragster applications.

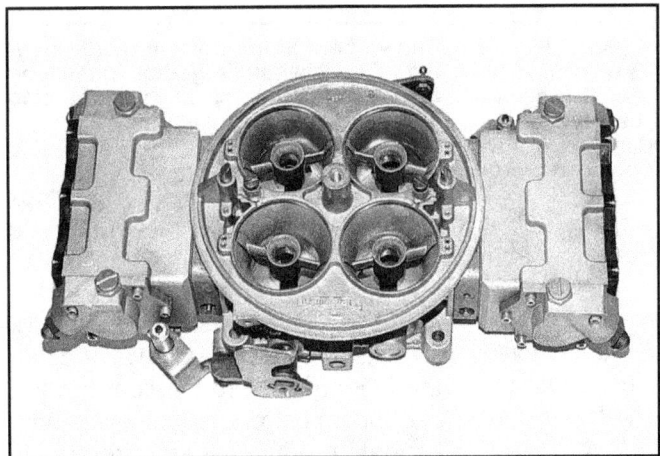

A Dominator equipped with Pro Bowls is a formidable looking carburetor. Pro Bowls feature dual inlets, needle & seats and quick-change jet plugs.

RAPID RECALIBRATION METHODS

There is nothing more futile than buying a Holley carburetor, be it stock or custom prepared, and then failing to calibrate it accurately enough to get the best from it. Just because the carb you bought was recommended for your installation, either by Holley or an independent carb builder, does not mean the jets and other calibration points are correct for your engine. These people cannot determine precisely what your engine needs, but they can, due to their expertise, come workably close in many respects. The calibrations that come with a carb should be looked upon as a good starting point only. What, with the action of uneven induction pulses around the plenum and G forces imposed upon the car, we find that optimum jetting is usually 'staggered'. Let us make no bones about it, getting the calibration 'right on' is worth big power. Often, the amount of power gained from having the jetting casually correct to fully optimized can be as much as the carb had offered in terms of extra power in the first place. An example here will certainly not go astray. Using our dyno instrumentation to verify the mixture ratio being delivered to the engine, it was established that an over all 13:1 existed, which for a small block Chevy on a single four barrel carb is just about typical. By dropping half a jet size on one end and increasing half a jet size on the other end of the engine, which left us with the same overall air fuel ratio, the engine picked up no less than 16 horsepower! This should illustrate the need for accurate calibration. Part of the problem with achieving accurate carb settings, is the amount of time it can consume. With this in mind let us look at methods that offer more rapid calibration.

HOLLEY'S ELECTRONIC CALIBRATION

One of the best ideas to come out of Holley was their unique Mile-a-Dial and Quarter-mile-a-Dial systems. Unfortunately, these are just about out of production. It was good idea that failed, probably because it was ahead it's time. Unfortunately, both pro engine builders, who traditionally are anti-electronics, and tech magazine writers as a whole failed also to realize it's worth. This in turn meant that the performance enthusiast at large remained uninformed, and the idea died. However, the concept worked so well that it's inclusion is well-justified within these pages. Even if the system cannot be had from Holley, the mechanical parts, such as the float bowls, metering blocks, solenoids etc. are still available. If a simple electronic signal generator, producing a 12 v stepped output with a variable mark space ratio (Fig. 7-1) is produced, then everything once again becomes a practicality.

Here are the basics of the system's function, which is best understood by referring to the carb cross section (Fig. 7-2). The solenoid (1) moves up and down by virtue of the 5 pulse per second output of the signal generator. By altering the amount of time it is on and off, the solenoid spends more or less time keeping the jet at its base open. If the percentage of time the signal is on holding the jet open, is greater, more fuel will flow. If the signal holds the solenoid on its seat more time, then less fuel flows. The fuel, which is sourced directly from the float bowl, passes through the control jet (2) to a passage (3) that bypasses the main jet (4) so additional fuel can flow

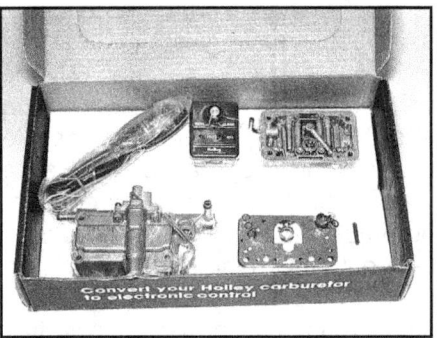

This is how Holley used to sell their electronic control carb conversion kits. All but the wiring loom and the pulse generating control box are still available.

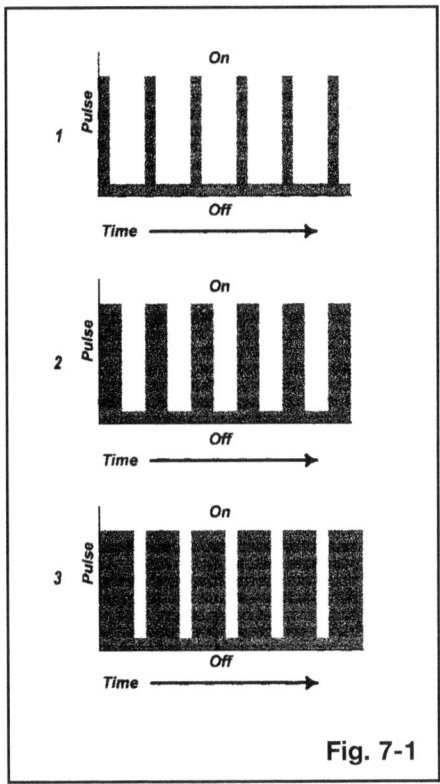

Fig. 7-1

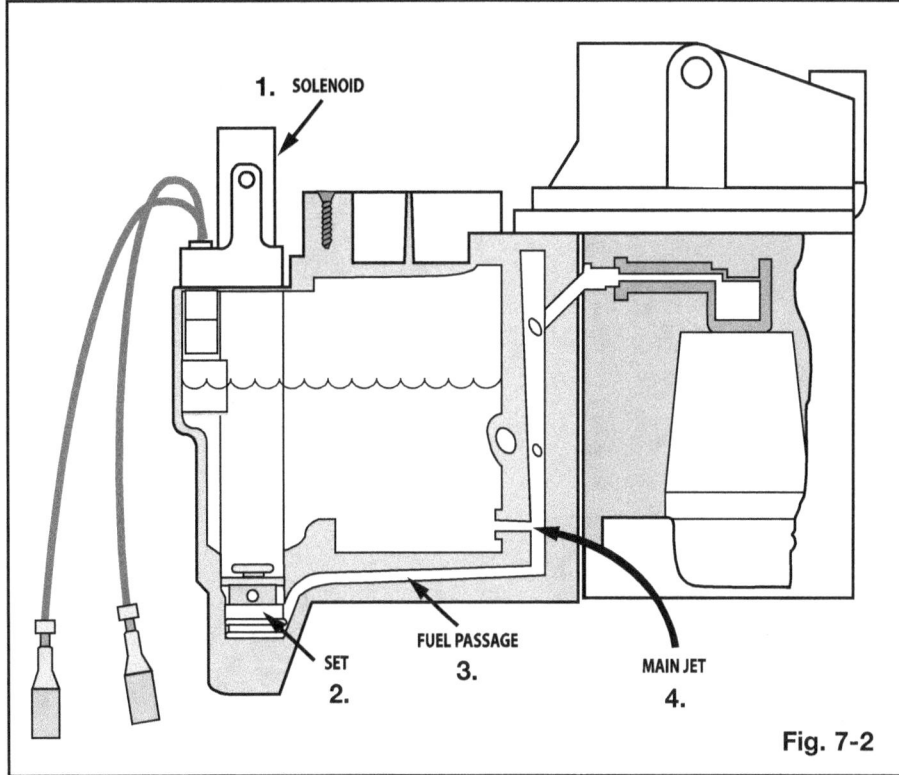

Fig. 7-2

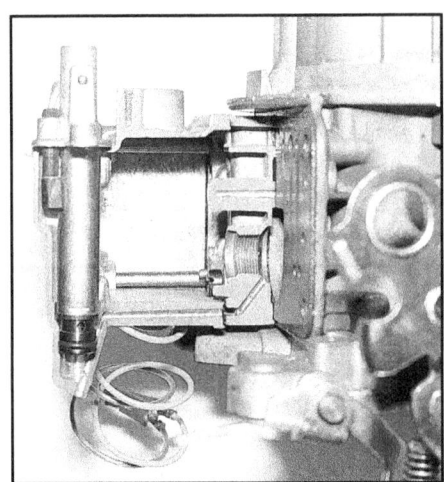

This cutaway shows it all. The solenoid on the left controls the flow of extra fuel to the power valve thus richening up the mixture by an amount dictated by the solenoid duty cycle.

independently of the main jets. If the solenoid is closed all the time, the main jet and power valve restriction channel are the sole source of fuel. As the duty cycle is adjusted at the signal generator control box, the mixture can be richened by about a half a jet size per "click". By setting the regular jetting about 2 jet sizes too lean, excellent control over the mixture can be had at the touch of a finger. This is the system that has been used in the Vizard dyno cell for years because it allows much more accurate carburetion. This has been very important because product testing for magazine articles needs to be done in an exacting manner, otherwise a disservice will be done to the manufacturer of the product being tested, the magazine publishing it and the reader. The author has seen so many cases of dyno tests that are outside the range of test accuracy and give the reader completely the wrong results because of lack of attention to accurate calibration.

The advantage of such a system is that it not only allows near instant recalibration of the carb to do the original optimization, but also a finer calibration can be achieved. This makes correcting for weather conditions at the track a really simple job, especially if you have a means of computing the new size required as shown nearby. Also, with such rapid calibrations being possible, it's far more likely that the time required will

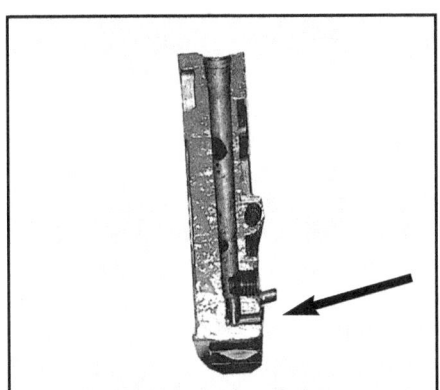

This cross section shows the drilling immediately below the threaded main jet hole that supplies the supplemental fuel from the control solenoid.

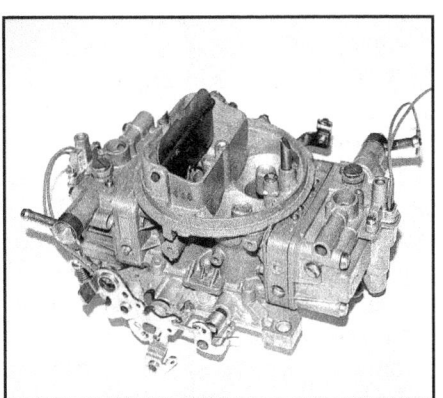

These Quarter-Mile-a-Dial float bowls and metering plates have been installed on the ends of various flow capacity carbs and have ...

... seen literally thousands of pulls on the author's dyno. Their precise and rapid calibration meant getting equally precise and rapid results.

How to Build Horsepower, Vol. 2

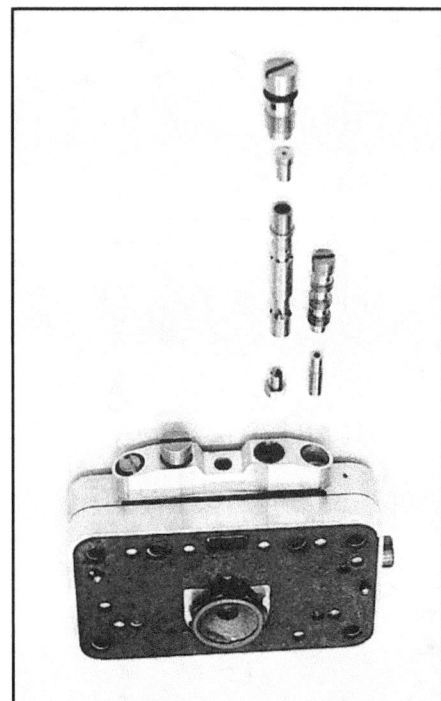

The Weber jet kit from Edelbrock combines the utility of the Holley with the sophistication of a Weber. Using Weber calibration parts, it allows all circuits and the fuel curve, via the emulsion tube, to be precisely calibrated.

In addition to the normally accepted jet changes, the power valve restriction channel can also be calibrated with the Weber jet plate.

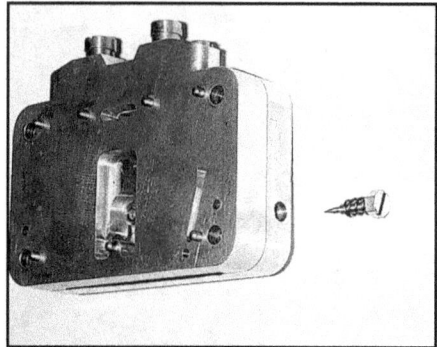

Not only is the idle circuit adjustable by the regular mixture screw, but also the idle/transition circuit has it's own miniature jet, emulsion tube and air corrector.

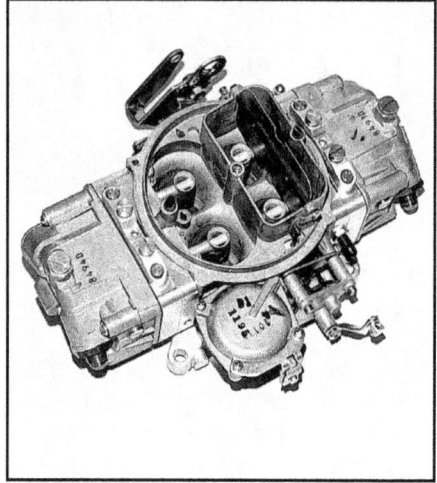

Ready for testing on the author's dyno, the prototype Weber jet plates are seen here mounted on a 650 vacuum secondary Holley.

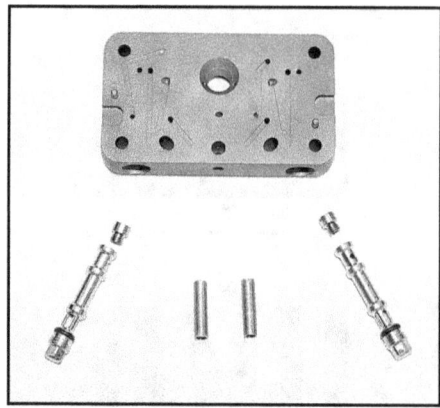

The Carb Shop's Speed Block designed by Louie Hammel represents the easiest to use rapid calibration system we have tried. In ten minutes, the change from stock to Speed Block can be made. Where street driving fuel economy and low emissions are a priority, one Speed Block on the primary side of the carb will get the job done.

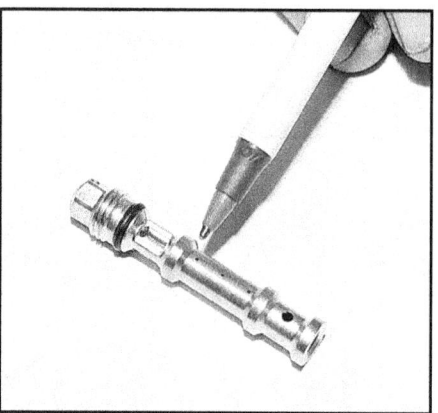

If the mixture is a little rich during low speed full throttle use, enlarging the hole indicated here by as little as .005, will usually cure it.

be spen,t rather than giving up when its close, as is so often the case with the conventional 'drain the float bowl, spill the fuel, breath the fumes, create a fire hazard and change the jets' method.

WEBER JET PLATES

Introduced in 1986, the Weber jet plates looked all set for a great future because they functioned so well. Essentially, what this jet plate did was to replace the Holley metering blocks with a new metering block that used Weber calibration parts. Because the new metering block was spaced out farther from the carb body and the jets externally accessible from the top, jet changing was much faster and did not require draining of the float bowl. Indeed, the main jets could be changed while the engine was running. This setup was originally sold by Red Line, a big Weber importer, but they soon found that to sell something like this, they needed to be in the Holley business. As a result of poor sales the idea was taken up by Edelbrock, who now sell this excellent means of calibrating the Holley carb. The Weber system gives a Holley the same calibration flexibility as a normal Weber carb. As such it allows easier and more precise calibration of every circuit in a Holley carb, not just the main jet.

CARB SHOP SPEED BLOCKS

This system, introduced in 1995, looks like it will succeed where others have failed. First, it is relatively inexpensive for what it does. Second, it utilizes a racers existing Holley main jets. Like the Weber jet plate, the Speed Blocks can accommodate a jet change without draining the float bowl or even stopping the engine.

If you buy Speed Blocks direct from the Carb Shop, the idle circuit will be calibrated to your application based on their experience. However, if purchased through a speed shop the idle fuel jet will be calibrated for a typical 350 in the 300-400 horsepower range. In practice we find the idle jet cali-

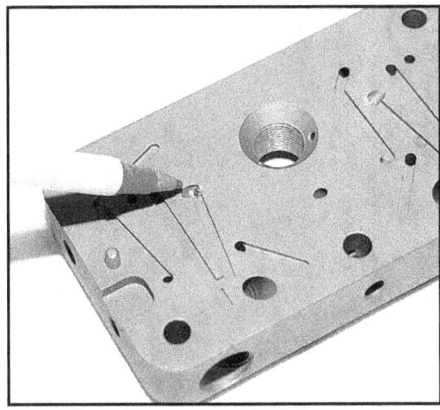

If the idle jet (indicated) needs changing from the one normally used for general applications, it should be drilled larger. Each increase in size should be no more than .002 until only two turns out of the mixture screw is required for a smooth idle.

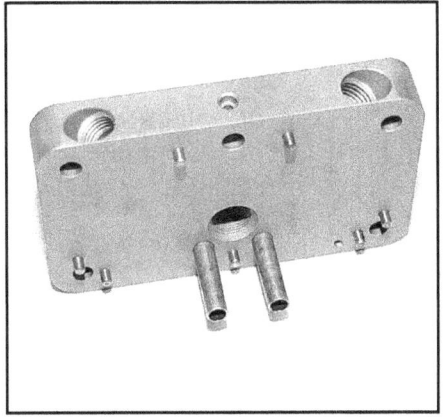

With conventional metering blocks, a jet extension is used to prevent the jet being uncovered during a hard launch. For the Speed Block, simple pressed in 'slosh' tubes, as seen here are used.

bration is quite flexible. Although it won't be optimal the 'stock' calibration will work with cams up to 235 to 240 degrees duration at .050 lift. If the idle jet size needs changing, it is almost always for the bigger. The best way to achieve this is to enlarge the idle jet .002 at a time with a jet drill held in a pin chuck (pin vice). Continue enlarging it until the best idle vacuum is achieved when the idle mixture screws are about 2 turns from seating.

The Speed Block tends to pull over on the main jet sooner than a stock Holley metering block so when the change is made, expect the jetting to require down sizing by 2 to 3 jet sizes. Because the main jet, like it's Weber counterpart, is attached to the end of the emulsion tube the practicality of

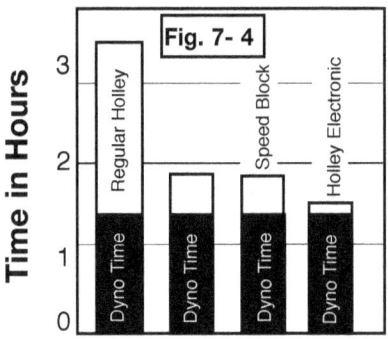

How Much Time Do You Want To Spend Jetting?

This chart assumes 20 pairs of jet calibrations are changed. After each change, the engine makes three accelerated power pulls and the results are computer logged. With speedier ways of jetting, you should question the desirability of doing it the traditional way.

altering the full throttle fuel delivery curve exists. Although only one emulsion tube style is offered it does allow the required leeway in trimming the fuel curve. This is done by changing the hole sizes or adding more holes in the relevant position. Fortunately, the 3 hole emulsion tube supplied covers most V8 applications. If the full throttle mixture curve does prove to be out, it is usually due to low end richness. This is usually fixed by enlarging the top hole by .005.

FINE TUNING WHEN THE WEATHER CHANGES

So you dyno your engine at the beginning of the race season and got the jetting as close as humanly possible. Hopefully a note was made of the atmospheric conditions, otherwise all your efforts will only produce maximum performance on a day having identical atmospheric conditions. In North America, more than any other place in the world where motor racing flourishes, the atmospheric conditions at the track undergo such drastic changes. These are caused not only by extreme temperature and humidity changes over a spring to autumn race season, but also by large variations in track altitude and to a lesser extent barometric changes. If weather and altitude variations are combined, they have a dramatic effect on air density, and consequently, density altitude. For the record, density altitude is the altitude you would have to be on a 'standard day' to equal where you are under the conditions that prevail. As an example, let's consider Houston at the beginning of the year. The combination of elevation and cool dry air can produce a density altitude equivalent to as much as 300 feet below sea level. At the other end of the scale Denver, which is at 5,000 plus feet, can, on a hot humid day, appear equivalent to 10,000 ft. Such a variation represents a substantial change in jetting requirements. This altitude range means a change in air density from Houston to Denver of over 26%. If all your engine has got right down to the last horsepower, counts, then the carburetion must be jetted for prevailing conditions, which are even variable through out race day. Chances are, you won't get an opportunity to optimize jetting on race day, so you will need to know beforehand exactly to what degree the jets may need to be changed. This is where a weather station and it's associated calculator/computer comes into it's own.

THE DENSITY GAUGE

The first commonly used simplified weather station was the density gauge. It has been around for many years and basically com-

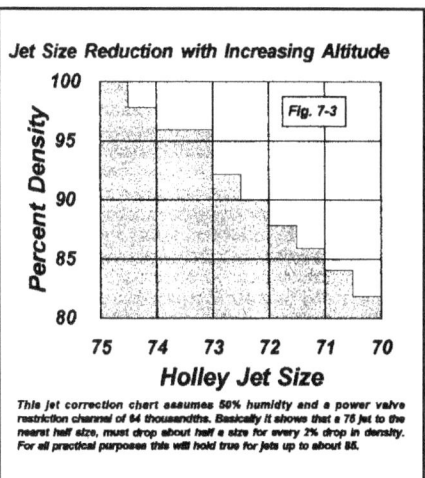

This jet correction chart assumes 50% humidity and a power valve restriction channel of 64 thousandths. Basically it shows that a 75 jet to the nearest half size, must drop about half a size for every 2% drop in density. For all practical purposes this will hold true for jets up to about 85.

How to Build Horsepower, Vol. 2

bines the effects of both altitude and temperature. It does not take into account the amount of water vapor that may be in the air. When a comparison of the amount of vapor the air will hold in relation to what it does hold is made, it is referred to it as the relative humidity. What we actually want to know is the water vapor content of the air. Since any water vapor in the air will be at atmospheric pres-

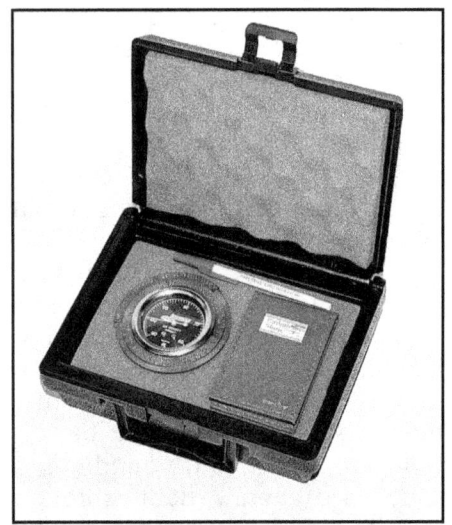

sure, we can assume the partial vapor pressure will have the same effect on power as dropping the air density a like amount. For example, if the barometer shows 29 inches of atmospheric pressure and our wet and dry bulb thermometers and hydrometric tables indicate that 1 inch of this is due to water vapor, we have, since water does not burn, only 28 inches of air pressure to work with.

How much water vapor affects re-jetting accuracy to compensate for atmospheric conditions depends on the air temperature, as hot air can hold more water vapor than cold air. If corrections are made when the air is either cold or dry, the effect of leaving out vapor corrections are inconsequential. But when conditions get hot and humid, the water vapor content becomes a significant factor. What this means is that the density gauge is a good start, and under certain conditions, more than adequate for the job as long as you know how much to correct the jets by. As a first approximation, you can use the chart in Fig. 7-3. However, a better solution, if funds allow, is to spend a little more money and get one of the computerized weather station, as shown on this page.

R. S. A. DENSITY

A computer program we have made much use of is *Density* by Patrick Hale of Racing Systems Analysis. This excellent program (shown below), which can be loaded into a lap top computer and taken to the track, is very comprehensive. It allows the new jet size to be computed not just for Holleys, but any fixed jet carb. In addition, to calculating the new jetting requirements, it also tells you how fast you should be going for the prevailing atmospheric conditions based on previous runs at other tracks under known conditions. If your car does not run

close to the speeds predicted, then you need to look for a problem other than the jetting. This system requires you to supply your own instrumentation, which can be had very inexpensively if you look around in hardware, surplus and believe it or not, furniture stores.

B & G WEATHER STATION

Bruce Huggard of B & G has produced a range of weather stations. His least expensive system has (top right) served us well for a number of years for correcting the track results of many 'on board dyno' tests. The budget system, as you would expect, contains budget equipment, but we have found it to be completely satisfactory. If you feel inclined to step up and purchase the deluxe version, you will get slightly more accurate, but much more durable, instrumentation. With either set up, the specially programmed Sharp calculator has much to offer the racer, engine builder or crew chief. There are some 45 specialty programs built into the unit including jetting for carbs or mechanical fuel injection, be they on gasoline, methanol or nitro. The computer will also calculate altitude density, jet sizes, tires sizes, gearing, fuel line size required, CFM and much more.

HORSEPOWER Quick Facts & References

BOOSTER PERFORMANCE

Much booster development can be done on a conventional flow bench but the final analysis is ...

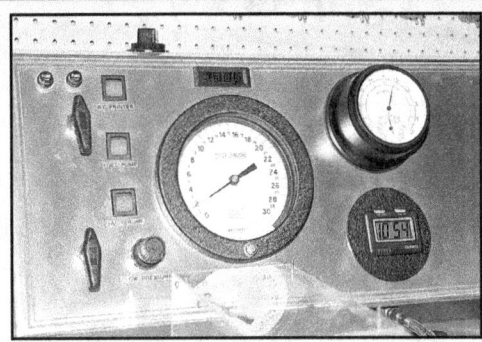

...how well it atomizes test fluid on a wet flow bench. The Carb Shop is one of the pioneers in this area and has one of the few wet benches in the industry. Shown here is the control panel displaying some of its functions.

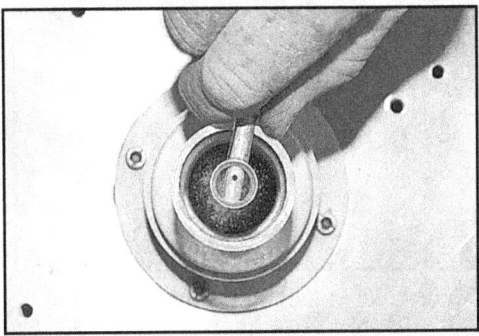

A straight-leg booster, the most common Holley design, is being tested here under simulated low RPM conditions. The larger fuel droplets are easily seen. These only undergo a partial combustion process and as a result, reduces low end output at the expense of increased fuel consumption and emissions.

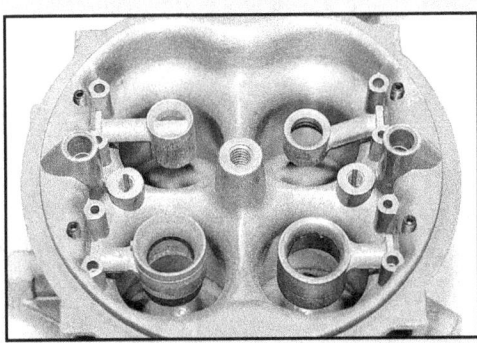

No, this is not some trick carb configuration. This is the author's specially modified booster test carb outfitted with various boosters to show a few of the different designs available. In the top right hand corner is a super speedway double step dogleg booster designed to optimize fuel atomization in a 350 Winston Cup style motor from 5500 RPM on up. Lower right is one of Holleys best all rounders, the short annular discharge booster. Top left is the lowest gain of all stock boosters, the straight-leg booster. Steer clear of this one for a big venturi, high flowing carb. Lower left is The Carb Shop's Super Booster. This booster allows the use of more carb CFM before loosing bottom end.

What do high gain boosters do in practice? As demonstrated by this Vizard-built 383 small block Chevrolet engine, they spread the power curve of a larger cammed motor both up and down, as well as adding considerably to the torque and horsepower. This particular motor had a power curve starting under 1500 RPM (less than the converter stall speed) and going on to 6750. The only parts approaching exotic were all in the Competition Cam's quiet ramp street roller cam valve train. The rest of the engine spec included a set of Vizard ported World Products Dart II iron heads, a Helgesen/Vizard intake manifold based on a 360° Weiand Street Ram and a set of Silv-o-lite Cast KB pistons yielding 9/1 CR mounted on budget Torque Tech 6 inch rods. The result is over 450 ft-lbs and 465 horsepower!

Barry Grant, another big name in the carburetor business, also finds a wet flow bench an essential tool for maintaining technological parity.

HORSEPOWER Quick Facts & References

FLOWING MORE AIR

A carb specialist's #1 development tool is the flow bench. Brad Urban of The Carb Shop spends a great deal of time refining various components in an effort to get more flow without increasing the size of the venturis.

Slab milling the threaded side of the butterfly shaft as seen here and...

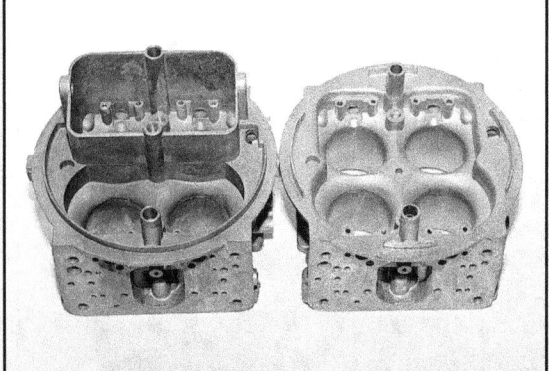

For applications where power is the prime directive, the stock carb body is modified (right) to enhance air flow as much as possible. However, if a choke ...

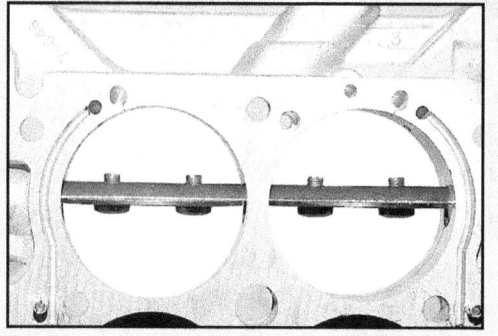

Seen here are the stock butterflies and shaft. They present a considerable restriction to air flow.

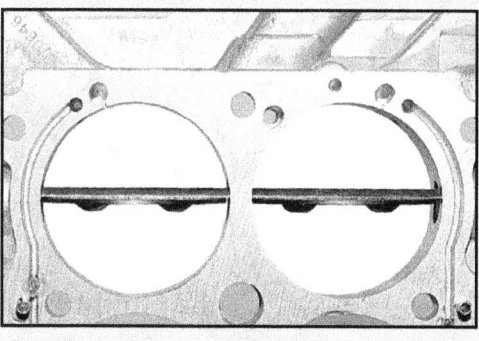

After the butterflies and shafts are reworked as seen here top end power is enhanced because air flow is increased 30 to 60 CFM depending on the carb concerned. This mod also allows individual induction pulses to communicate better with the booster. This helps produce slightly better atomization for increased low end output.

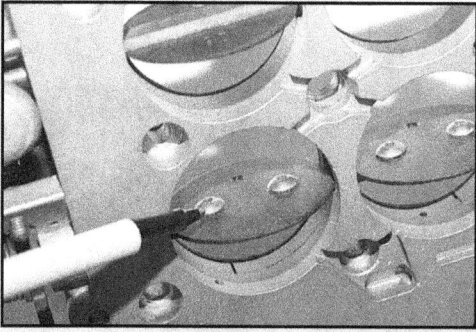

...employing low profile button head screws significantly cuts the obstructive area presented to the airflow by the shaft and butterfly.

...is required for regular street use, then the K & N Stub Stack gets about 80% of the air flow increase given by a fully machined air entry on the body, but still retains the choke mechanism. In addition to this, it also produces an increase in booster signal to increase fuel flow in approximately the same proportion to air flow increase.

FOUR CORNER IDLE

These are the holes that must be duplicated in the secondary barrels for four corner idling.

The Carb Shop uses this special fixture to locate and drill the new secondary barrel idle mixture delivery holes in the desired position.

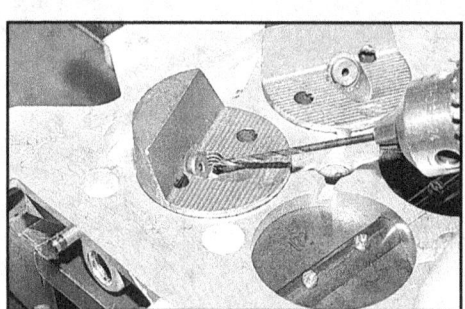

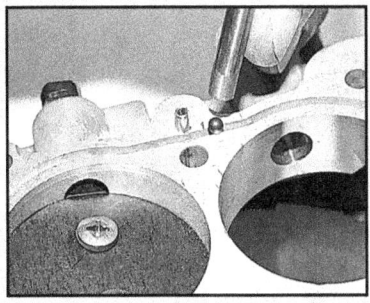

For each idle adjustment screw to operate independently of its neighbors, it is necessary to block the channel connecting the front and rear barrels. This is done by tapping a soft lead ball into the channel.

At this point, two options are open to us. The simplest is to use a second primary metering body on the secondary side. This has all the idle circuits and a power valve ready to go. To get the power valve system to work on all carbs but the 850, the hole shown here must be drilled. This connects engine vacuum to the power valve diaphragm.

Some drag racers prefer to run a carb without a power valve in the secondary claiming better response for cars not equipped with a transbrake. In this case, the existing secondary metering blocks are modified. First the idle screw hole is drilled to accept the tip of the idle screw.

Next, the "as cast" hole is tapped to suit the idle adjustment screw thread.

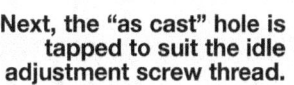

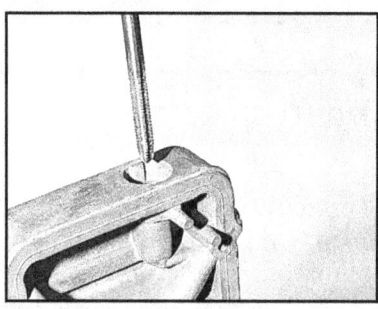

For each side, this hole must be drilled to allow fuel into the idle screw passage.

After drilling the metering block, the corresponding connecting hole in the body must be drilled. This also makes the connection with the idle air bleed.

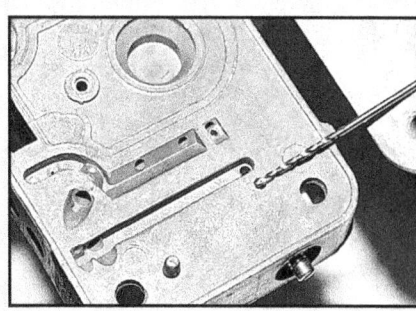

The final operation is to drill the secondary idle air bleeds to match the primary.

And here, with idle adjustment screws in both ends, is the finished job!

How to Build Horsepower, Vol. 2

HORSEPOWER Quick Facts & References

TRANSITION CIRCUIT FUEL METERING MODIFICATIONS

Fuel flow to the transition slots when driving just off idle can, in a big cammed engine, be too much. This is fixed first by drilling...,

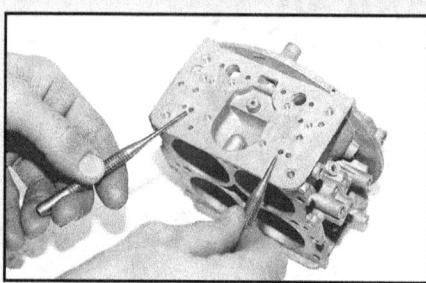

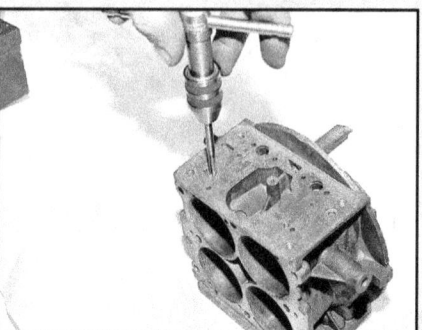

... and tapping the holes, shown here.

This allows a screw-in calibrated jet to be used to tune the circuit for best throttle response and drivability.

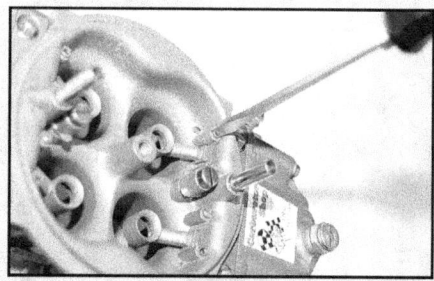

When the idle fuel restriction jet has brought the idle mixture reasonably close to that desired, the final trimming can be done by incremental increases in the idle air corrector.

COMPUTECH SYSTEMS INC.

This system (shown below) is very comprehensive. It comes equipped with a thermal printer that prints out your computations, thus retaining a record of what is needed or was done. Including the required weather/jetting programs, there are some 16 programs that compute 40 functions that the well-equipped race team will need to know. Most of these functions are similar to those produced by the B & G weather station/race computer. The comprehensive manual supplied takes the first-time user through the various routines, which are quickly learned. Although we have only used this computer/weather station for a short while, it has been impressive both in terms of function and original cost.

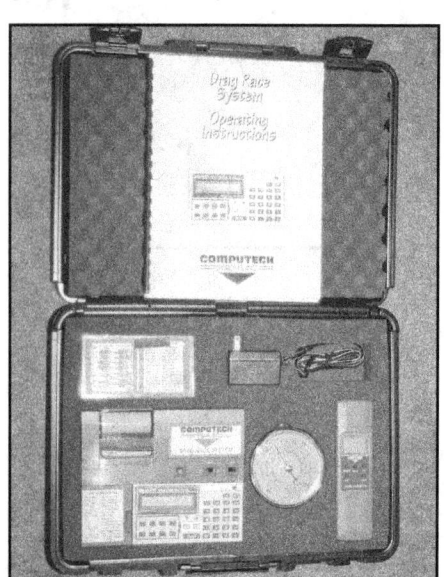

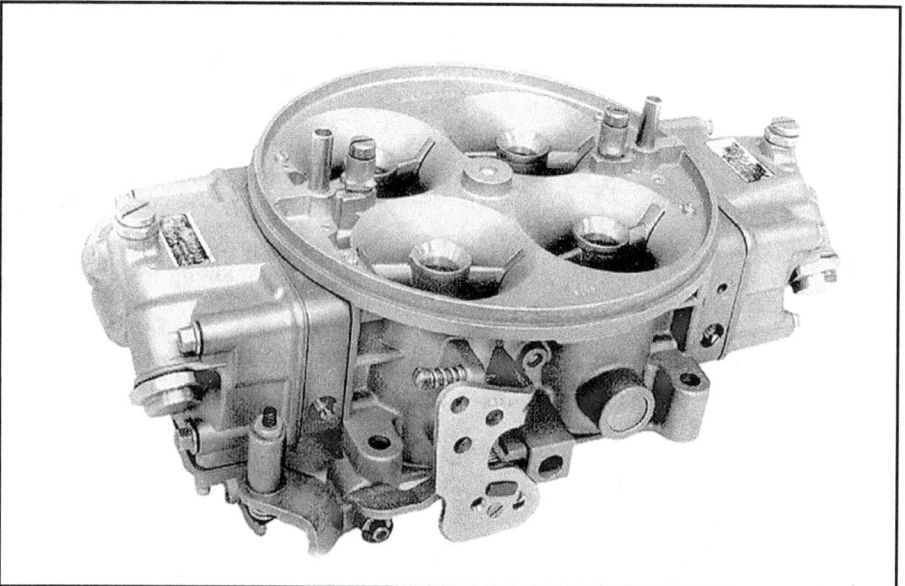

The modifications shown on the 4150/4160 carbs can, for the most part, be carried out on the Dominator series Holley carbs. This Carb Shop Dominator is from their Terminator series and flows over 1400 CFM yet still delivers reasonably good low-speed drivability with outstanding high-speed performance.

THINGS TO CONSIDER

POWER VALVE RESTRICTION CHANNEL CALIBRATION

In the carburetor world, the main jet is so named because its main responsibility is to calibrate the full power fuel demand of the engine. In the case of a Holley, it is misnamed. What is commonly know as the main jet is actually the principle metering element for cruise mixture. The power valve restriction channel is actually the main jet, and, only comes into operation when a vacuum operated power valve opens it. Fortunately, there is a large window of operation for achieving the correct overall full throttle calibration by working almost exclusively with the main jet but it is not the correct nor best way to achieve results. Ideally, the best way to achieve optimal part and full throttle mixture is to calibrate the main jet so that the cruise mixture before the power valve comes in is best for fuel economy. This keeps plugs cleaner, cuts bore wear, gives a faster engine warm up and saves fuel, which can be important if a long race is involved. Ideally the power valve restriction channel and main jet should be optimally calibrated under the average atmospheric conditions the vehicle is likely to see. Doing so will produce a more sensitive main jet calibration and generally allows for finer tuning at the track. To do your initial or principle calibration via the power valve restriction channel here is what you need to do. First, drill out the power valve restriction channel and drive in a lead plug. Drill the plug to a respectable amount smaller than will ultimately be required. Next calibrate the main jet to get the best part throttle drivability and fuel consumption. This will usually mean mixture ratios of around 17:1. Once this has been achieved, go back to the power valve restriction and open it up until maximum output is achieved. It will normally be found that jetting done in this manner results in a larger than normal power valve restriction channel and a smaller main jet.

DYNO TESTING

Dyno tuning the engine in an effort to get precise calibration is a highly recommended move made by informed pro racers. However, an engine's jetting requirements on the track can be significantly different. Often, it is the case that, regardless of weather conditions, there is a need to step up jetting as much as 4 sizes all around to get the best performance. The reason for this is that the vehicle installation is not a duplication of the dyno installation. Booster buffeting due to ram air being fed directly to the carb is one major reason for a difference in jetting. Another, is that the G forces affecting the float bowl function. A third factor is that a 2 G start will have a tendency to drive larger droplets of fuel toward the back of the engine. Just how much of a part this plays in the situation is really dependent on the droplet size. If a fuel droplet is less than about .005 mixture distribution will be relatively unaffected by vehicle G forces. Conversely, if the fuel droplets are as large as .030, which they can be if the booster/main venturi choice is poorly made, the situation will change. Such large fuel droplets will have a measurable tendency to richen the back pair of each set of four in a 2 x 4 tunnel ram and the back cylinders of a single four barrel installation. Another factor is that the dyno cell exhaust is not representative of what is used in the car. Eliminate these variables, and you will find dyno to track jetting falls much more in line.

RESULTS

What we have looked at in this chapter represents some relatively advanced carburetor modifications. They are far removed from the grind and shine that once, with the exception of a few knowledgeable professionals whose carbs we could barely afford, pervaded the aftermarket carb industry. Modern, affordable flow benches and dynos have been instrumental in changing the level of technology employed in the performance industry. The accompanying graph shows how much extra output, when tested on an appropriately specced motor, a fully modified carb can deliver. The test carb was extensively modified by Carb Shop and was tested on a mildly modified 350 small block Chevy. The test engine was deliberately chosen to fall into this category because such an engine would normally be well-suited to a stock 650 Holley. Also, the choice of an Edelbrock Victor Jr. rather than a stock or even an aftermarket 2 plane was deliberate. The rational behind this is that the flow restrictions of a stock or after market 2 plane manifold would not allow the engine to see the benefits of the greater carb flow. Also, as we have seen from previous tests, the heat input from a stock manifold would cause too much of the more finely atomized fuel to be vaporized, thus cutting the engine's volumetric efficiency. This would invalidate the modified carb's ability to show the advantages of both better airflow and fuel mixture preparation. From the test results shown here, you can see that the Super Booster equipped Carb Shop unit picked up substantial amounts of power everywhere in the rev range. Since the carb is not working at anything like its peak airflow capacity, we can deduce that the substantial low-speed gains are a clear indication of the value of good mixture preparation.

How To Build HORSEPOWER: Chapter 8
Carburetors & Intake Manifolds
Performance Mods For Q-Jets

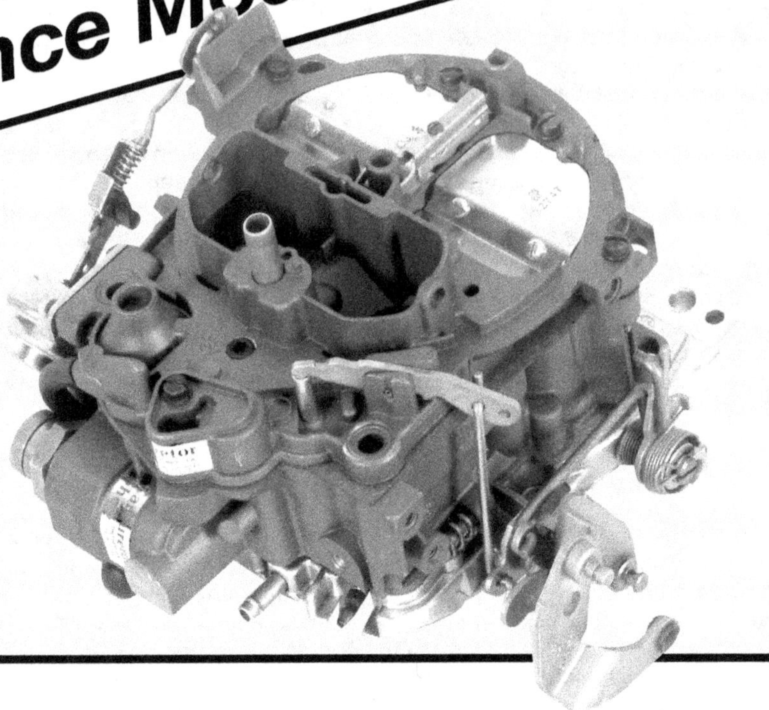

The performance potential of the Quadrajet carburetor is very much understated within the performance fraternity. It is a carburetor that can produce excellent results and comes stock on more cars than any other carb in the world. This being the case, one may ask why it is not seen on performance applications to a far greater extent than it is. Whereever people and high-performance cars gather, you will see but one Q-Jet for every twenty Holleys. Why? Probably for two reasons: symmetry and complexity. Once a carburetor and manifold combination becomes successful at the race track it does in turn, become emulated on down the ranks. The Holley's symmetrical style and ease of calibration made it a drag race success and the rest was just a matter of time.

The Q-Jet's four barrels comprise of two pairs, primary and secondary, and they are of vastly differing size. This asymmetry does not lend them to pairing for use on a tunnel ram style manifold. With such a setup, there would be two big barrels and two small barrels over each set of four runners for the typical port layout seen on most V8 engines. The 'square bore' Holleys on the other hand have four barrels of uniform size with centers that position them directly over the runners of a tunnel ram manifold. In other words, their symmetry makes them appear right for the job. The fact that they looked the part and went fast, meant their future success was all but set in concrete. If we couple this to the fact that the calibration rational for a Holley is far simpler than a Q-Jet, then we can see that the natural trend would be to go to Holleys. Although a Q-Jet may not be the best choice for a 2 x 4 tunnel ram installation, it certainly can produce results with the best when it comes to the more commonly used single four barrel installations.

There are two principle areas in which Q-Jets excels. First, they have

With the advent of fuel injection, the Q-Jet was phased out of use by GM in favor of fuel injection. To service the millions of vehicles needing spare Q-jet parts, Edelbrock took over the manufacturing rights of this carb.

good performance capability because it is difficult to have too much CFM on any engine of 200 CID or more with this carb due to its air-on-demand design. Second, if you know how, it can be calibrated, both at full and part throttle, very accurately. In addition, if you intend to do the work yourself, you can build, from a used core, a thousand CFM carb for a lot less money than buying a new and probably professionally reworked Holley. If class rules dictate that you should use a Q-Jet or if you want to build a stock appearing 'stealth' motor, this chapter has what you need.

AIR FLOW

Stock Q-Jets can have either 1³⁄₃₂ primary venturi's or 1⁷⁄₃₂. This differentiates between carbs factory rated at 750 CFM and at 800. However, since the factory does not sell carbs based on CFM but application, it seems that these ratings are somewhat loose. As a Q-Jet comes from the factory, it's airflow, based on our flow bench tests of a number of models, can show anywhere from 750 to about 830 CFM. A typical 'out of the box' performance Holley application uses a carb around 750 CFM. Unless the booster mods described elsewhere are done, using a much larger carb on a small block could reduce low and even mid-speed torque, drivability and economy even though top end output would benefit. With a Q-Jet, no such compromise exists. A Q-Jet can be modified to deliver over 1000 CFM. It can then be installed on an almost stock 350 and reap whatever benefits there may be had by producing top-end horsepower without sacrificing any low-end. The advantages of a carb with a high CFM of air flow shows to good advantage on a two-plane manifold because the carb capacity is effectively divided in two by the manifold design. Assuming the manifold runners themselves are not restrictive, then the high-performance dual plane manifold and a reworked Q-Jet make ideal stable mates.

AIR FLOW AND BOOSTERS

In an effort to develop as strong a booster signal as possible, the Q-Jet

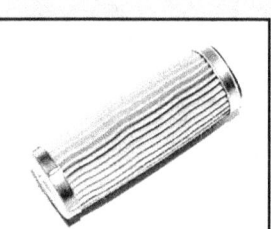

Early Q-Jets were equipped with a sintered bronze filter. If your unit has such a filter, it should be replaced with a high flow paper filter such as shown here.

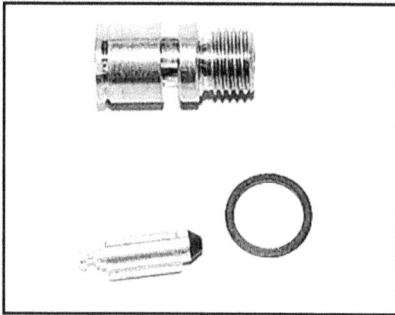

The ideal size of needle valve for any carb is one that will flow slightly more fuel than the engine's peak demand. The Q-jet is no exception. The needle valves from the Carb Shop are appropriately sized to suit the power output of the engine.

This plastic baffle/filler fulfills an important role. Its use reduces the problem of the engine rich stalling under heavy braking.

designers opted to use, in most applications, a double booster to achieve greater amplification of the main venturi signal. As to whether or not this was necessary is a moot point, but in the process of so doing the design ended up with a very thick sectioned fuel emulsion transfer passage from the main carb body to the fuel discharge point in the inner booster. This, plus a few other bulky casting sections, results in a needless reduction in the primary side air flow.

The Q-Jet's butterfly and shaft have excess bulk for the size of the throttle bore. Just thinning the butterfly shaft and the butterfly itself alone before doing anything else can increase the primary side flow by some 3.5%. Working on the primary venturis to thin down various sections with a fine file and a small die grinder is tedious, but produces significant results. After the butterfly mods have been done, work on the boosters, as shown nearby can net an increase in the primary flow of as much as 9%. The bottom line here is that careful work on the primary side alone can net in excess of 30 CFM and the god news is is that all this comes with an increase in booster signal.

Some really big air flow gains can be made on the secondary side of a Q-Jet. Some come about by tightening up on production tolerances, and

HORSEPOWER Quick Facts & References

MORE FLOW AND MORE SIGNAL

This is where work on the airflow starts. Compare the reworked primary side with the stock one to see what was done.

After knife edging, the primary butterfly should look like this. Be sure to leave a thin section of the edge untouched to preserve the fit in the throttle bore. If you want to go as far as possible here, the Carb Shop can bore the throttle apertures from 1.375 to 1.420 inches diameter. This results in about 20 CFM more airflow. The same mods to both throttle shaft and butterfly should be performed on the secondaries.

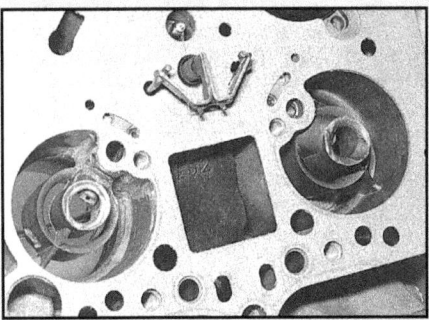

The boosters are reworked as shown here. Again, a comparison of the two primaries will show the difference. If you are prepared to spend the time, the thin 'wings' opposite the fuel transfer passage can be removed to good advantage.

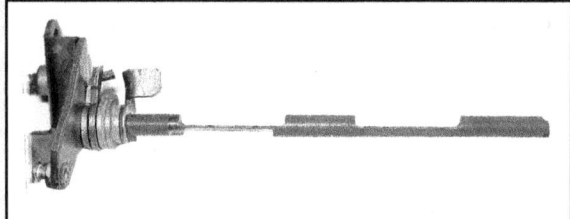

The throttle shaft can usefully be thinned down as seen here. A medium cut file will make short work of this little job.

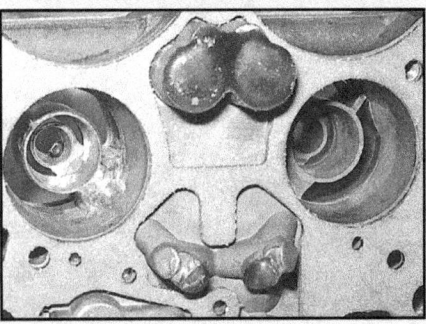

This view from the underside shows what needs to be done in the booster exit area.

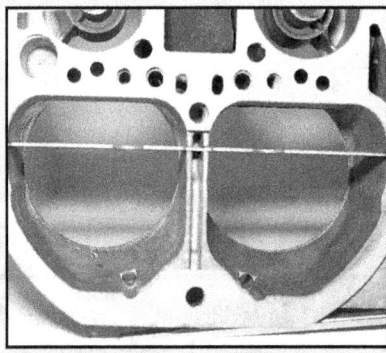

There is not a lot that needs to be done in the secondary bores of the carb body. One consideration here is the removal of intrusive material at the body to throttle plate junction. This area usually needs some casting flash removed.

Looking up the secondary barrels, a ridge will be seen where the throttle bore changes shape. This ridge should be blended out as shown here.

On the secondary side, airflow can be improved by employing the tried and tested techniques we have shown in these pages. Applying a generous radius to the edge adjacent to the air valve is worth 10 to 20 CFM.

This side view of the butterfly shows the knife edging required. It is also worth noting that a vertical butterfly is not always the best for maximum flow.

others by a combination of air valve adjustment and reworking the components concerned. Because of its large diameter, and the flow resistance offered by the air valve prior to it, slimming the secondary butterfly and shaft do not return as much as is seen on the primary side. Reworked as shown in the nearby photos, you will find about 4 to 6 CFM increase.

Having knife edged the butterflies, it would seem that they should now be installed so that when fully open, they are vertical to present the least resistance to flow. This can be a case of things not always being as they seem. Because the air flow direction is disrupted by the shape of both the air valve and the form around it, the air does not pass uniformly down the barrel. For this reason, a perfectly vertical blade does not guarantee the best airflow. Although setting the blades at an appropriate angle, slight though it may be, is worth doing to get the last CFM of air, the biggest gain by far comes from setting the air valve to the optimum position. This proves to be one mod that cannot be done without the aid of a flow bench. Depending on how optimal the original was, it is possible to pick up as much as 70 cfm on the combined flow of the secondary. When a Q-Jet's mixture distribution is checked on an engine, it can sometimes be the case that the butterflies in the secondary need to be in a position other than that which delivers maximum air flow. In such cases, the butterflies may need to be off the vertical simply to help redirect fuel for a more even cylinder to cylinder distribution.

If we combine all the mods we have dealt with here, it is possible to boost a Q-Jet to some 1070 CFM, and if you opt to have the primaries enlarged by a professional carb company such as the Carb Shop, then that number could go as high as 1090 CFM.

FUEL IN

As such, the Q-Jet does not have any big problems with fuel supply even for high-performance use. This does not mean, however, that you can dismiss this area as needing no attention. There are a few aspects to consider if maximum performance is to be

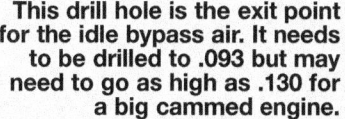

IDLE SYSTEM MODIFICATIONS

For most purposes short of all out race applications, the idle feed down the hole indicated needs to be drilled to .036. This will deal with cams up to about 235 degrees at .050-inch lift.

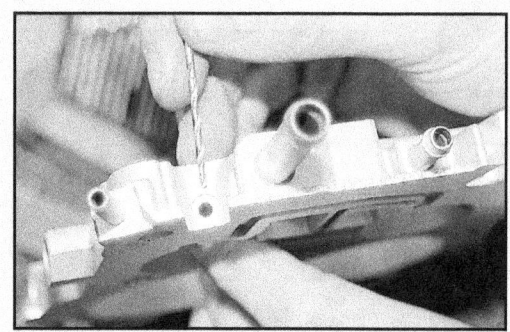

Carefully drill through the idle speed screw adjustment hole with an .089 drill. This will suit most cams but very long ones may need up to .093.

This drill hole is the exit point for the idle bypass air. It needs to be drilled to .093 but may need to go as high as .130 for a big cammed engine.

had. First, the inlet to the float bowl may be equipped with a sintered bronze fuel filter. This filter will only flow a little more fuel than a good stock engine's requirement. To avoid fuel starvation, replace it with a large inline fuel filter. Having eliminated a restrictive filter from the system the next job is to see that the fuel pressure supplied to the float bowl is adequate. Assuming at this stage that the needle valve has adequate flow capacity, the float bowl should be fed with fuel at 4 to 6 PSI. Ideally, the fuel should be brought close to the carb at a higher pressure, then reduced to the preferred pressure just prior to entry into the float bowl. Next, make sure the needle valve is large enough but not excessively large, for the job in hand. This can be done without a lot of extensive track testing by checking fuel flow through the open needle valve with the float dropped ¼ of an inch from the closed position. Estimate the horsepower the engine is likely to produce, then select a needle valve/fuel pressure combination to deliver the required amount. Every 90 horsepower you expect your engine to make will need 1 US pint of fuel per minute. If you estimate your engine will make 550 horsepower, then it will need 550/90 pints per minute. That works out in this instance to 6.1 pints per minute. If you don't want to go

HORSEPOWER Quick Facts & References

TRANSITION & CRUISE CIRCUITS

For the transition circuit to draw enough fuel when a low vacuum, big cam situation exists, the transition fuel circuit will need to be fed with more fuel. This is done by drilling the feed jet down this hole to a larger size. With a hot street cam, try an increase of .020 and up to .040 for a race cammed engine. This jet feeds ...

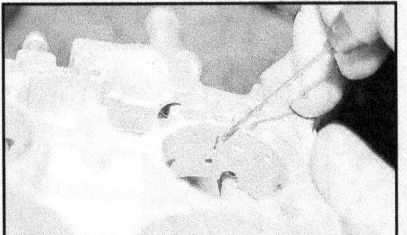

... the transition slot. This does not need lengthening as is sometimes advocated.

Part throttle mixture is controlled by needles, which are raised and lowered by manifold vacuum acting on the power piston.

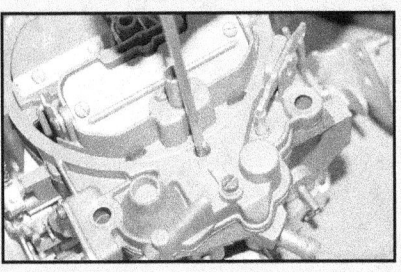

A hole drilled in the top of the carb through a factory fitted plug allows access to the power piston. Using this tool ...

... the piston can be adjusted up or down to alter the cruise mixture.

Primary fuel metering rods are in three basic styles with various tapers calibrating the part throttle fuel curve. Their size at the largest diameter is stamped on the shank. On the bottom is a P type needle, which generally has a slow thin taper. This is good for an application where one of the other needles proves too lean as this circuit starts to feed. Center needle is a K type and is probably the most likely to work for a hot street application. It has a faster taper and they tend to be fatter toward top. This is good for a typical 230° at .050-lift street cam. The needle on the top is a B type and has a double or blended taper, instead of stepped taper. The B type is a good choice for the shorter cammed hot street motor. For street use, a 73 jet is a good starter, but for all out race cams you will find it necessary to use a jet .005 to maybe .010 larger, but leave the needle tip size at the stock .026.

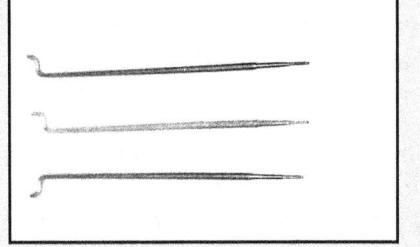

through this routine the Carb Shop can supply, based on estimated horsepower, a suitable needle valve for your application and tell you what pressure should be used.

Once sufficient fuel has been supplied to the float bowl, we have to make sure it stays in there. A rapid rate of change of acceleration (jerk) can cause the fuel to slosh. This can happen during a drag race start or switch back cornering on a road course. The simple fix is to install a vent tube in the bowl vent about an inch and a half high. If that doesn't do the job extend the vent with a suitable fuel resistant hose to some higher and more remote location. You need to be aware that the vent locations can experience buffeting in much the same way that boosters do. This will affect the float bowl's basic pressure, and in turn, it will alter the mixture. This adds up to just one more reason why you should run an air filter on the engine.

Another problem you may have to deal with when underhood temperatures get really high is the effects of heat soak and the vapor lock it can cause. Putting aluminized heat reflecting wrap around the fuel lines does not look pretty, but it helps performance. If a carb atomizes fuel well, too high of a fuel temperature will reduce performance even if it is below the point of causing vapor lock. A cool can is a good move here for a drag racer, but this is not always practical for longer distance events. There are a lot of band aid fixes but the preferred method is to feed the carb with cool fuel. This will allow a higher CR to be used before detonation occurs, save fuel, make more power and fix vapor lock once and for all. The fix is to rig up a small auxiliary fuel pump that takes fuel out of the float bowl and returns it to the fuel tank. The fuel tank is not only a large heat sink but also has enough surface area to radiate the heat picked up by the fuel when it is at the hot end of the vehicle without an undue rise in overall fuel temperature. Installing a temperature probe into the float bowl, with a readout in the cockpit, will quickly establish whether or not a fuel cooling system of some sort is needed. If the fuel goes over 170° F then it's time to give this some consideration.

One last point to consider, is fuel surge during rapid maneuvers. Fortunately, the design of the float bowl and float, is such that these are not usually a problem. A horizontal plastic baffle/spacer at the front end of the float bowl around the needle valve area, is stock on most Q-Jets and will usually fix any tendency to stall from flooding during heavy breaking.

Cornering forces do not seem to have a significant effect on fuel delivery, but drag race starts in a fast light car can affect things. The float is well shaped to control the amount of fuel in the float bowl, but not necessarily where it is in the float bowl. Checking the arc of the float travel and filling in the vacant volume of the bowl with fuel tank foam, secured with a minimum of epoxy resin seems to cure the problem.

IDLE SYSTEM

Little, if anything, other than adjustment ,is required of the idle system until a cam of significantly greater than stock duration is used. Once .050-lift figures progress past about 220 degrees, then the idle feed may need some attention. At about 220 degrees, an idle feed of about .030 is needed. This needs to progress to about .036 for cams up to about 235 degrees. If really radical cams in the 270 degree range are used, then the idle feed may need to go as high as .050 if a large 'idle air by pass' is used, but consider .040 to .045 more normal.

With low vacuum, the butterfly will need to be further open to supply the engine with the air it needs, thus inappropriately using some of the transition slot for idle. As with the Holley, we can drill a hole about a 1/16 in each butterfly to allow the butterfly to be set nearer the normal closed position, so the transition slot works as intended. Although this can be easily done, there is an alternative. There is, already built into the carb, an idle air bypass circuit. It is a simple matter to enlarge this already existing system.

TRANSITION AND CRUISE CALIBRATION

Tuning the transition circuit essentially only involves two factors. The first of

THE MAIN CIRCUIT

Seen here, are a pair of primary (upper) and secondary main metering jets. The full throttle calibration will be done partially by the size of the needles used and ...

... partially by the size of the jets they dip into. The area of the annular orifice that remains, dictates the fuel flow.

The starting position of the secondary metering rods in the jets is controlled by the needle hanger . Although the range used on different stock vehicles amounts to some 2 dozen or more, only a limited number are available. These are supplied by Edelbrock in their race calibration kit which contains 5 hangers graduated in .020-inch height increments.

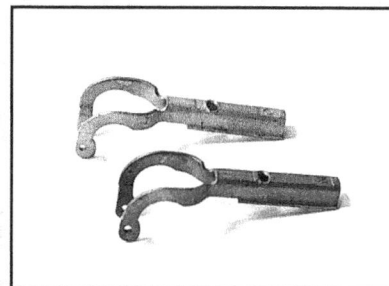

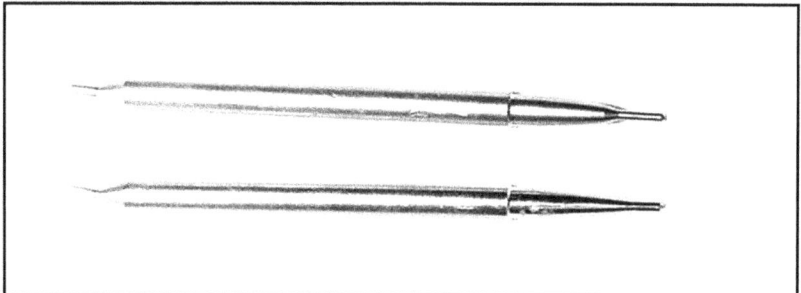

Here are two extremes of metering rods, from lean on the top to rich for the one on the bottom. The difference in tip diameter can be clearly seen.

The small jets seen here, are for the primary and the large ones for the screw-in replacement for the secondary. The sliding aluminum jets in the secondary will need to be removed and replaced with these conventional screw in jets. The stock jet size is 135 and a good starter for a screw in jet is 138 with a DA rod and a B hanger.

How to Build Horsepower, Vol. 2

HORSEPOWER Quick Facts & References

ACCELERATOR PUMP CIRCUITS

The accelerator pump discharge nozzle is situated here. Enlarging this will be the most likely first step toward curing a 'bog' on initial acceleration.

Locating the pump linkage so that it picks up the hole nearer the pivot point, increases the quantity and speed of fuel the pump discharges.

Shown here is the accelerator pump piston. There are two aspects to consider here. First, the spring on the piston shaft. The stiffer this is, the faster the pump well contents will be discharged. Second, the stroke of the piston dictates how much fuel will be discharged. The stroke needs to be maximized. This can be achieved by grinding the end of the shaft to shorten it's overall length. However, it must not be shortened so much that the lip of the piston rises above the fill slot at the top of the piston's bore in the carb body. Almost all piston shafts will tolerate shortening by .030, but some can be taken as far as .090.

Although it may not appear so, this well is part of the accelerator pump system. It is a supply reservoir for the secondary enrichment circuit. The level of fuel in it influences the enrichment as the secondary air valve comes into operation. It receives it's fuel supply from ....

.. the main float bowl via this drilling. If the engine leans out a short while after the secondaries have come into action, it may be that these holes are not replenishing the reservoir fast enough and will need enlarging.

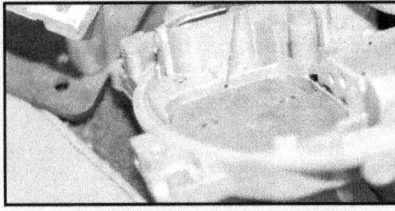

This hole here is the discharge point for the secondary enrichment circuit. Depending on the carb model, this hole may be above or below the air valve. Below the air valve gives a harder initial draw. If the motor goes lean immediately, the secondary starts to come in, then this hole will need enlarging. If substantially larger jetting is needed here it may be found that...

... a restriction can occur upstream of the jet and limit it's fuel supply. The well that the draw tubes dip into shrouds the end of the tube. If it proves to be close shorten the tube by about .050.

these is to make sure that, at idle the primary butterfly is not so far open that it is prematurely activating the transition slot. The way to check this, is to set up the carb to give the best idle possible, then remove it and check the butterfly position. When viewed from the manifold side the ideal position for the primary butterflies is when the transition slot is just showing by about .010 below the butterfly. If it is further open than this, you will need to enlarge the idle air bypass circuit, or drill a hole in each butterfly as described in the Holley section of this book. Having made this change, it will more than likely be necessary to increase the fuel flow to the transition slot circuit. This can be achieved by enlarging the transition slot fuel feed orifice as shown in the nearby photo. For most street applications, this is only likely to need a small increase in size. Only make any increases if the engine appears to stumble into a lean condition when driving slowly at very small throttle openings. To make changes to both the idle and transition fuel feed jets, you will need to go to a tool supply shop as you will almost certainly need long series drills, as the jets are positioned toward the bottom of the holes housing them.

Because of the Q-Jet's small primary venturis, a typical V8 pulls the main jet fuel system into operation earlier than with a Holley. At cruise, the primary butterflies are open enough to pull fuel from the main jet, but a full power rich mixture is not required. When at cruise, a certain amount of manifold vacuum exists. This will be heavily dependent on the cam duration. Obviously, the bigger the cam, the less the vacuum under cruise conditions. Fuel to the venturi discharge point is fed via the primary main jets, but the amount supplied depends upon the position of the metering rod in the jet. The rod is controlled by the power piston. When the vacuum drops to near zero, it releases its pull on the power piston and the spring beneath it lifts it up. This action is equivalent to the power valve in a Holley. However, the combination of spring and tapered needle actually allow a progressive enrichment action to take place. For a high-performance motor, the power piston needs to start initiating enrichment at about six inches of mercury and be all in at three. This can often be achieved with the GM power valve spring #7037851, but probably the best way to go is to get yourself an Edelbrock race calibration kit which contains 5 different springs covering the range from 3 to 8 inches of mercury depression. Some stock equipment springs may be way off what is required, so it pays not to assume they will be close. For a short or a well set up medium cammed engine with plenty of vacuum, a spring coming in at 6 inches of vacuum will be fine but a longer cammed motor may cause the system to enrich the mixture even at small part throttle openings. The cure here, is to reduce the amount of force the spring delivers consistent with it still being able to push the piston to it's full travel. If one of the lighter Edelbrock supplied springs is not immediately in hand, up to two turns can be cut from the end of the original spring, as measured from the wire tip at the flattened end. Taking off much more than this, may prevent the power piston making it through its full upward travel. This will cause the mixture to fail to richen up as much as desired at full throttle. The essence of what we are doing here is to make sure that, at the vehicle's typical light throttle cruise speeds, the power piston is held down to keep the mixture lean. When wider throttle openings consistent with faster driving are used, the mixture needs to go rich for power, so the spring must push the power piston and hence the primary metering needles to the top of the available travel.

Fine tuning the mixture for best cruise diving and economy by changing needles and jets can be a long, drawn out process. The stock power piston assembly has a degree of up and down adjustment which is preset at the factory. By drilling out the plug that is, on most models, directly above the power piston, access is gained to raise or lower the position of the piston by a small but significant amount. On some carbs this action is achieved by an adjusting screw on the base plate situated between the two primary barrels. In either case, this adjustment should only be used to do the final tuning of the system not for large changes in fuel flow.

THE MAIN CIRCUIT

Between 70 and 74% of the air entering the engine through a Q-Jet does so through the secondaries. Since this is the case, we can also surmise that an equal portion of the fuel must also pass via this route. This makes the fuel calibration of the secondary side of far greater importance than the primary, although this in no way implies that careless primary calibration is permissible.

Primary main circuit calibration at cruise was dealt with earlier and you may have understood what was needed from that discussion. Essentially, the primary side needs to be jetted to give the desired mixture at full throttle because all primary needles are 26 thousandths at the tip that is in the jet at full needle lift. Getting the full throttle mixture is easy. It is just a case of changing jet sizes, and that usually means going up, until the desired mixture is achieved. Unfortunately, going up enough for a higher output engine may make the mixture too rich at cruise. This being the case, go back and read the section on transition and cruise calibration so that compensation can be applied via needle selection.

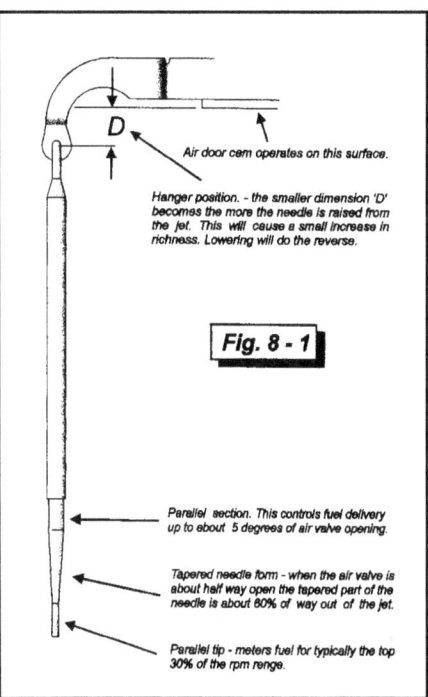

For most performance applications, a medium or a long tip to the secondary metering rod, will most likely be required. A check on various needle diameters (Fig. 8 - 2), shows that the differences are relatively minor in most areas, except the tip. However, you need to be aware that for a given change in size at the tip the mixture only varies about a third of what it does halfway down the taper. With long tip needles, the tip starts the metering at about 75 degrees of air valve opening. The medium length tip delays this to about 80 to 85 degrees and the short tips to about 90 degrees.

On to the secondary side, the first move is to pry out the sliding aluminum/stainless jet plate that the needle goes into and tap the hole to accept screw-in secondary jets. The stock jet is .135. As a starter, replace this with a .138 jet and attempt to calibrate from here with needle profiles. If the system is optimally calibrated, you can save the jet changes for altitude/weather corrections, as this is easier than trying to find another slightly richer or leaner needle. Also, we have to consider that the needle will, at between 60 to 75% of peak power RPM, be fully lifted. This means that only the size of the jet or the power tip of the needle will make any difference. At this point, it would be worth checking Fig. 8-1 to get an idea which part of the needle is in operation at any particular part of the power curve. Once the basic idea has been absorbed from this chart, you will have to superimpose the effect of the needle hanger. If you start calibrations with the medium height hanger, small

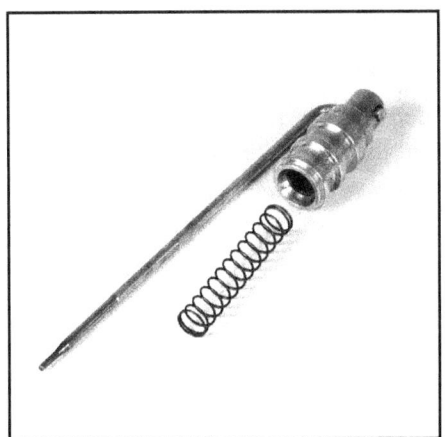

The power piston has vacuum acting on it to pull it down. When the vacuum drops due to throttle opening, the power piston spring lifts the piston and the needle is raised out of the jet to richen the mixture.

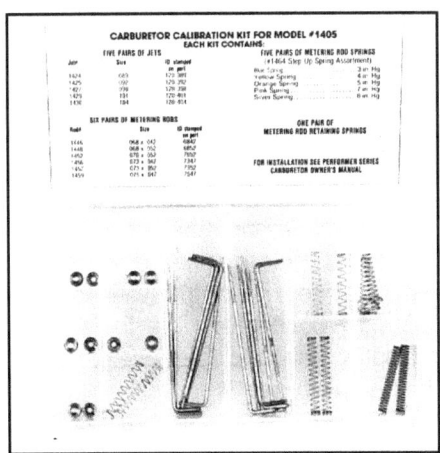

This race calibration kit from Edelbrock can be expected to be of great assistance to anyone setting up an engine for maximum performance.

Fig. 8 - 2

Recommended Q-Jet Secondary Metering Rods.

Marked As.	Part #	A	B	C	Tip
CC	7042356	0.135	0.1095	0.3030	M
CJ	7045780	0.1342	0.0964	0.0400	S
BE	7034377	0.1332	0.1114	0.0413	S
CY/DA	7046004	0.1334	0.0964	0.0443	M
AU	7033665	0.1348	0.1051	0.0530	L
BD	7034365	0.1335	0.1068	0.0580	M
AT	7033658	0.1353	0.1082	0.0670	L
CG/AS	7045778	0.1353	0.1082	0.0777	M

Dimension 'A' is the top part of the needle which meters the fuel at small air valve openings. 'B' is the dimension at the middle of the taper and 'C' is the power tip diameter. S, M, and L signify short medium and long power tips. If an off the shelf needle exists for your application, then the chances are, you will find it among these listed here. As a starting point for a strong street small block, try an AU and for a big block a DA.

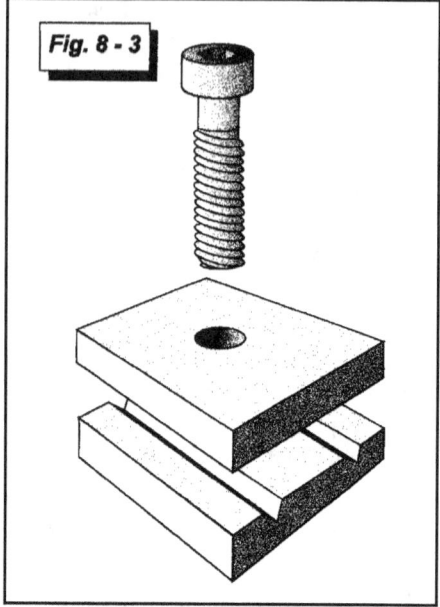

Fig. 8 - 3

If you find it necessary to produce your own needle profiles it is easier to file a flat and get it accurate, than to put the needle in a lathe and reduce the relevant area. Filing a flat on both needles at the same time while they are held in the grooves of this clamp sounds a dicey way to produce an accurate part, but in practice it works out very well. When the initial filing is done on the needles, the form of the flat produced changes in width a great deal for only a few thousandths of metal removal. It is this that allows the filing operation to produce such well matched pairs of needles.

mixture changes in either the plus or minus direction can easily be made in the rev range prior to the air valve reaching the full open position.

Having explained the changes in calibration that the hanger can bring about, let us now concentrate on the needle. If we assume that jet changes are only to be made to compensate for the weather, then we will have a situation where all main jets are likely to fall between about .135 and .140. From here on. it really is a question of getting the needles right. The chart Fig. 8-2 lists the needles that are most likely to work in a performance application. In probably ninety five out of a hundred cases, a suitable needle for a typical V8 application will be found among this selection. If, however, the situation arises that the correct needle cannot be found, here is a technique that is used successfully by the author, but highly frowned upon by carb specialists. First make up a needle clamp as shown in Fig. 8-3. Select two needles you know to be slightly too lean and hold them in the needle clamp's V grooves. Put the body of the needle clamp in a vice and using a small fine file and/or emery cloth file a flat on the appropriate part of both needles that need to deliver more fuel. Having the two needles side by side allows anyone with reasonable filing dexterity, to produce needles of very similar form. There may be some guffaws at this, but remember, an accurate needle that produces the wrong mixture is about as useful as a set of rubber wrenches. However a slightly less accurate needle that produces the correct mixture is, after all, doing precisely what we want of it. Getting a pair of needles right by this method can often be quicker than sorting through dozens of needles, trying to find what you think is needed. The only snag to going the filed needle route is that it will wear jets more rapidly, though not at a rate that is of any consequence to a racer. So long as an eye is kept open for jet wear then filing the needles will work just fine.

ACCELERATOR PUMP CIRCUITS

Unlike most carbs, the Q-Jet has more than one accelerator pump circuit, although some are less than obviously so. Let us start our pump calibration on the obvious, that being the pump injecting into the primary barrels.

The accelerator pump discharges into the primary barrels only because the secondaries have an integral acceleration enrichment system that comes into action when the air valve opens. Because only about 25% of the air passing into the engine goes through the primary side, the accelerator pump does not need to be that big to deal with primary airflow enrichment. This is fortunate because, short of boring out the pump piston bore and fitting a larger piston, there is not a lot that can be done. However, what can be done is usually more than adequate.

The first move if the pump shot proves inadequate, is to drill out the discharge nozzle that directs the fuel into the primary barrels. This puts fuel into the engine faster, which is just what is needed for those larger volume two plane intakes, but unlikely to be enough for a single plane race style manifold. If the discharge nozzles are enlarged too much, the shot will be lazy and will not break up so well when it hits the booster OD. By all means, make the discharge hole larger but don't overdo it. Just how much is overdoing, is not so easy to say as it varies with the strength of the duration spring on the piston rod. If, after drilling the pump discharge holes to around .033 to .035, any throttle lag or flat spots have not been cured, turn your attention to the duration spring. Here, the stronger the spring, the more pressure the fuel in the pump well is put under. This speeds up the discharge and causes the fuel to break up better on impact with the booster. Just for the record, a 67 Cadillac spring and pump assembly part #7037504, has a reasonably strong spring and a lower retainer position which will help gain some pump stroke. If you fail to locate a piston and spring assembly that will do the job, then a suitable one can be obtained from the Carb Shop.

On the secondary side of a Q-Jet, we have what can best be described as an induced pump action. When the secondary butterflies are opened, any engine vacuum that exists, is applied to the air valve to draw it open. A fuel feed jet is positioned in each barrel such that after only a small amount of air valve opening it becomes subject to what ever manifold vacuum exists (usually 1 to 2 inches of mercury). This pulls a substantial amount of fuel out of these jets just in advance of the air flow, thus performing in the same manner as an accelerator pump. Calibrating this system for a modified engine almost certainly means enlarging the relevant fuel passages to increase the pump action.

Always a first move, if the mixture goes lean, just as the secondaries tip in, is to enlarge the jets at the point they discharge into the secondary barrels.. The fuel for these enrichment jets is supplied from a reservoir on either side of the float well. Fuel is fed into these two reservoirs by a hole drilled into the wall separating them from the float bowl. The size of these holes dictates how quickly the fuel is replenished in the reservoirs. It normally takes about 15 seconds to fill them from empty. Although the initial shot of fuel represents the biggest input, fuel does continue to flow through the jets into the secondaries at a decreasing rate until the air valve is well open. If there is a tendency for the motor to lean out before the air valve has fully opened, it could be that the reservoirs are running low on fuel. The obvious cure is to drill the communicating holes from the float well larger. A good starter size for these is .040 which is suitable for engines in the 350 to 400 horsepower range. If that does not provide a complete cure, then there are two other aspects you should investigate. The first of these is the air valve adjustment. If the transition to the secondaries shows a slightly lean condition as the air valve opens up, then increasing the preload will cause a stronger draw on the jets. A second possibility is that the tubes that dip into the channels that communicate with the reservoir are shrouded by the end of the drilled hole they are in. If it is suspected that this may be the case, then shorten the tubes by about .050.

HORSEPOWER Quick Facts & References

THE AIR VALVE

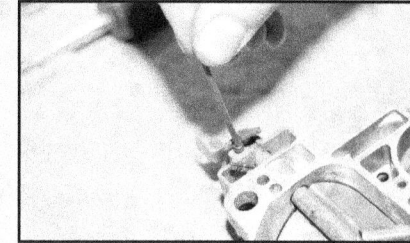

To adjust the tension on the air valve door, slacken the locking screw here and ...

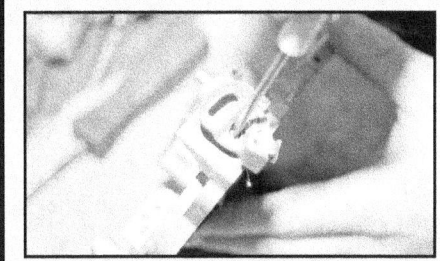

...perform adjustments on the slotted adjuster here. Typical settings are between a half and one turn of tension.

THE AIR VALVE

There are two criteria that get, whether they warrant it or not, attention as far as the secondary air valve is concerned. The first and most important is the preload supplying the closing torque on the air valve return spring. The more resistance there is to opening this valve, the greater the pull on the fuel jets by the slight down stream vacuum created by its flow resistance. In turn, a higher opening load restricts the air slightly more. These two factors combined, influence, as well as needle/hanger and jet calibrations, the mixture delivered while the air door is in the process of opening. Once the air valve is fully open, it has no affect on mixture regardless of the return springs preload. While excessive preload is to be avoided there is little to be gained by trying to find the absolute minimum return spring preload setting. Any self respecting V8 should be able to pull the air valve fully open well before peak power RPM. What this means, is that any gains only occur on the way to full open, so we see only small mid-range gains. All this means that you should not dismiss the value of setting the air valve for optimum results, but you should keep things in prospective. Having covered what we are likely to achieve lets move on to actually setting the air valve up to achieve the desired results. First preload the air valve spring by ¾ of a turn and try out the car to see what happens. If the engine goes slightly too lean from the lower mid range on up to the upper mid range, then set the preload ⅛ of a turn tighter and re-test. If it proves necessary to use more than 1⅛ turns to rectify the situation go back to ¾ of a turn, then fix the problem by means of more jet and needle/hanger changes.

If the mixture looks Okay to very slightly rich, then back off the air door preload by ⅛ and re-test. A half a turn of total preload should be considered the minimum amount. If at half a turn of preload, the mixture is still too rich then once again it is the jet and needle/hanger combination that needs to be changed.

Now, for the second aspect, which seems to have an unwarranted amount of attention applied to it and that is the angle of primary opening that takes place before the secondary butterflies start to open. In this writer's opinion this appears much of a to do about nothing. If you require full throttle extremely quickly you will hit the gas pedal so fast that the butterflies transition through their opening sequence faster than the air valve, so from that aspect it is not needed. If you are progressively opening the throttle, such as the exit from a slow corner then the modified linkage will only mean that you push on the gas pedal a little less. Either way, whatever mods you do to the linkage can be duplicated by your foot on the throttle pedal with a lot less fuss. So for fast opening linkage we have two words—Forget It.

How To Build HORSEPOWER: Chapter 9
Carburetors & Intake Manifolds
Other Performance Carbs

That Holley' outnumber all other carbs used in competition by better than 2 to 1 seems appropriate. In this chapter, we will consider if only briefly in some instances, other functional high performance carbs.

CARTER AND ITS DESCENDANTS

In many respects, the Carter/Edelbrock/Federal Mogul carb operates along the same lines as a Q-jet. The primary side utilizes a jet with a needle centered in it. The needle's vertical position is controlled by engine vacuum and raises or lowers the needle according to vacuum and consequently, air flow into the engine. Full throttle mixture is dictated by the size of the jet and the diameter of the needle tip. Part throttle is determined by needle taper, jet size and spring characteristics. The secondary side uses a spring loaded air valve with the same operating principles as a Q-Jet's secondary. As the throttle is opened, the air demand of the engine opens the air door an appropriate amount. As it opens, a fuel port position just below the starting position of the air valve supplies the fuel required to cover the transition to near full throttle. As full throttle is approached, the main jet/booster system takes over the job of supplying atomized fuel in the correct proportions to the engine.

As can be seen, the Carter and its clones, all bear a striking resemblance to a Q-Jet, so it is hardly surprising that the Q-jets calibration techniques transfer directly to the Carter, Edelbrock, Federal Mogul clones. If the section in this book on Q-jet calibration does not help you get precisely where you are going, then your best bet is to obtain the owners manual for your carb from Edelbrock.

As far as air flow capacity is concerned, this carb, as available from Edelbrock, can be had in 500, 600 and 750 cfm sizes. The 600 and 750 versions are available with either electric or manual choke systems. The 500, intended primarily for dual quad installations, has a mechanical choke. So how well do the Carter clones work? The writer's limited experience here has shown positive results. but talking to people within the performance industry, it appears that this carb's greatest fans are among the people who run chassis dynos for a living. The comment so often heard, is that the carb can be calibrated to hold very precise air/fuel ratios over the entire working range. This results in good mileage, drivability and power with no apparent compromises.

PREDATOR CARBURETORS

The Predator's mode of operation put it squarely into the arena of a type known as a constant vacuum carburetor. The originator of this type of carb was the SU designed in England at the turn of the century. The SU carb developed into one of the most precise means of mixing and delivering a fuel/air charge to a gasoline burning power plant ever designed.

Unlike a fixed jet carb such as a Holley, the constant vacuum carb generates a virtually fixed amount of vacuum to draw fuel from the fuel system. The usual technique for achieving this is to divorce the action of the throttle from having absolute control over the airflow into the engine. The rectangular body of the Predator has a pair of throttle plates in the lower part of it's body and a pair of spring loaded air valve doors at the top. Opening the throttle fully, does not cause the air valve to open fully.

Instead, it opens only by an amount dictated by the return springs and the amount of air the engine is demanding. Located between the air valve doors, is a fuel discharge bar. This bar is situated at a low pressure point between the air valve doors and experiences a depression in a similar way to the boosters in a Holley carb. This depression causes fuel to flow through the hollow fuel discharge bar and on into the engine. A fuel cam, actuated by the air valve shaft, determines how much fuel will flow into the fuel discharge bar. As engine rpm increases, the amount of pull on the air valve goes up and it opens farther to meet the engine's demand. As this happens, the fuel cam moves around to a part that allows more fuel to flow into the engine, thereby holding the mixture to the desired proportions.

Calibrating this type of carb is about as simple as it can get, short of giving the job to someone else to do. As it comes from the factory, the Predator has three different fuel cams. All appear to initially deliver about the same amount of fuel for a given amount of air valve door opening. At the mid-point the cams start to differ inasmuch as each step up is intended to deliver more fuel for those engines having a higher demand, than the base fuel cam can contend with. From this writer's experience it was found that a typical 300 to 385 CID engine, delivering in the 375 to 500 hp range, the intermediate cam gets the job done. As far as accuracy of "out of the box" calibration is concerned, the Predator does far better than average. The system eliminates the need to go to the track or dyno with dozens of calibration jets, as in 95 cases out of a 100 one of the fuel cams will work. It appears that only when engines are much smaller or larger than the norm, is there a problem with calibration. Even so this can be fixed by getting a "blank" cam and filing it to suit.

Another advantage of the Predator is that it tends to compensate for weather changes due to temperature and pressure to a greater extent than a fixed jet carb. The humidity element, though, has exactly the same effect as it does on the more common types of carbs.

On paper the Predator looks capable of delivering an accurate air fuel ratio over a wide range of operating conditions. This, along with it's 930 cfm airflow capability, is just what is needed for good power, drivability and economy. In practice, it delivers, when appropriately set up, good economy, usually excellent street drivability, but disappointingly mixed results for outright power. This however is not because it's capability to deliver a precise and well atomized air/fuel ratio is compromised. The overall mixture ratio seen on the dyno may vary by as little as half of that of alternative carbs, so mixture calibration can be better than most. Experience has shown that, sometimes the Predator will out horsepower a competitive carb while giving similar low speed performance. To match the low speed performance, a fixed jet carb has to be significantly smaller, so it will often fail to deliver as much top-end power. On many occasions though, the Predator

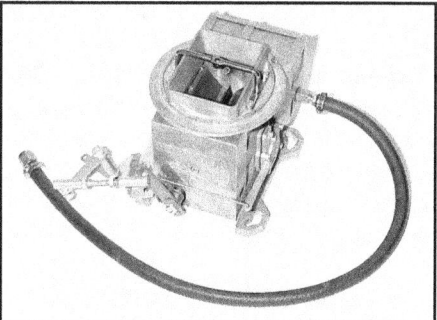
The Predator's squared-off appearance can make it look a little odd for a carb, but form generally ...

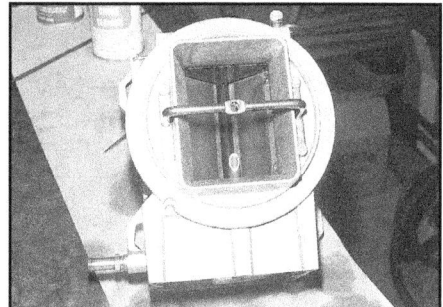
... follows function and the big entry air valve seen here, does have a lot to do with it's shape. The doors to this air valve are pre-loaded and ...

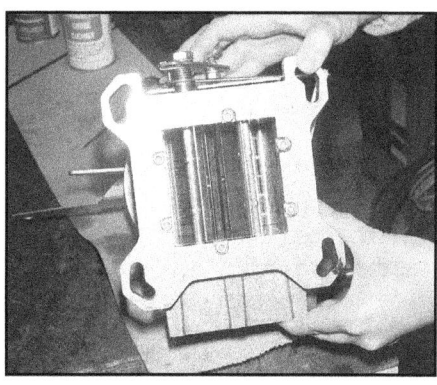
... when the throttle plates are opened draw the doors open an appropriate amount. Fuel is sucked out of the spray bar between the air doors.

On a Victor Jr. manifold, we found that the Predator produced best results when used with one or two 2 inch spacers. Regardless of the number of spacers, we always found throttle response to be very good.

The float bowl not only contains the float, but also the full throttle fuel metering cam. This cam ...

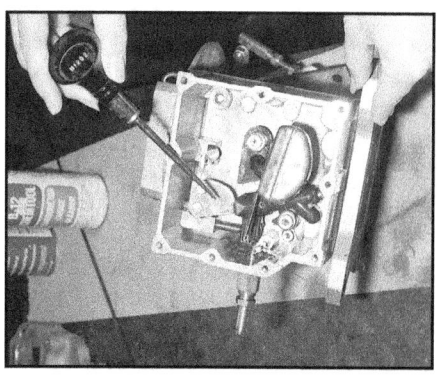
... must have a profile that delivers a fuel curve to match the engine's requirements. To an extent, the Predator is self compensating in terms of the mixture it delivers, but not completely so.

appears to fail to allow the engine to deliver the expected top end output. In reality, it seems unfair to say failed, because the cause for reduced output seems to be the Predator/manifold combination. This seems the most likely reason, considering the fact that almost all the manifolds a Predator is likely to be used on were designed for the fuel discharge pattern of a

Holley or Q-Jet. A Predators fuel discharge pattern, with it's spray bar extending the width of the carb, is significantly different. The fuel distribution with the Predator can be sufficiently different, to completely counter any theoretical advantages it may have over more conventional carbs. Our small block Chevy tests, which used Lambda sensors in each exhaust pipe, have shown cylinders with as much as two ratios different to that given by a Holley, even though the overall ratio differed by no more than half a ratio. The bottom line here, is that a manifold which worked well for a Holley carb may be far less than ideal for a Predator.

Although making general statements based on relatively small numbers of tests is a dubious past time, it appears that the manifolds that the Predator shows worst on are single plane manifolds that have undergone a lot of development with Holleys. After some thought this won't seem without some expected logic. However installing a Predator on a two plane manifold often puts it on the winning side. The usual case here is that it delivers all the expected drivability, along with an increase in output. Again this is not an unexpected result. A single plane manifold divides the airflow capacity of a Holley in two whereas the open interior of a Predator plus its considerable overall air flow capability allows the engine to breath far better. The atomization that the Predator delivers, keeps the low end output in line with a fixed jet carb, and the throttle response it gives is excellent. Our experience to date suggests that the Predator/two plane manifold combination works best on engines having high-flow ported heads and relatively short cams of some 260 to 275 degrees of seat duration.

All the forgoing does not mean that the Predator has no place on an all out race engine. What it does mean is that with almost all single four barrel, single plane intakes you need to be aware that a fuel distribution problem may exist. If this problem arises and is suitably addressed, Predator carbs can be expected to give competitive race results.

Apart from distribution, the fuel discharged from the Predators spray bar may be over atomized at full throttle especially on bigger or very high rpm engines. The simple fix for this, is to use a fuel with less of the volatile front end hydro-carbons. If you are not restricted by race regulations, or a budget, you may want to consider using a pair of Predators on a tunnel ram manifold.

Although we have no dyno figures to back up this statement, it would appear the Predators fuel distribution pattern, if the carbs are mounted with the throttles longitudinally, will not be significantly different to a Holley. This being the case ,the fuel distribution is unlikely to be different, so good results should ensue.

SU CARBURETORS

We have included this type of carb in what may be considered a V8 orientated book for several reasons. The first is that it spawned a number of functionally successful carbs including the Kendig/Predator. Among these carbs are a multiplicity of high performance Japanese motorcycle carbs. Despite being ignored for years by the performance motor cycle enthusiast and the aftermarket motorcycle industry at large, these carbs finally were proven by an initially small group of knowledgeable engine /carb specialists to be near unbeatable on the race track. At first it was believed that such carbs were only good for low emission good drivability situations. For racing, the typical slide plate/needle and jet race carbs were seen as the way to go and, as such, their poor low speed performance was seen as something which just had to be accepted as the price for outright performance. Of course, those who sold racing carbs liked to keep it that way and it was therefore, only with a degree of resistance from the performance industry at large, that the stock constant vacuum carbs made it to the forefront. A few racers prepared to try something different, but based largely on logic, found they had more than just the racer's edge over the opposition using what could be considered as conventional race motor cycle carburetion. This point is made to demonstrate that even in a high tech arena such as motorcycle racing a constant vacuum carb could show very competitive and often unbeatable performance against any other form of carburetion. The SU from which these carbs were developed, have been used on many British sports cars and high performance sedans since well before WWII. Some of the better known are Jaguars, MG's, Cooper Mini's and both the big and small Austin Healey sports cars.

Although the factory recognized they had a good piece for high performance, their appreciation of their own product's potential fell far short of reality. As a result, they never went to any great lengths to develop the SU to it's full performance capability. Efforts to remedy this by the author fell on fields of indifference that so often seem the hallmark of large companies, especially British ones! In many case, it seems companies, and not always big ones at that, fail to adopt an idea, not because it was not a good one, but simply because it was not theirs.

An SU's principle of operation is relatively simple. The throttle position determines the driver's demand for power from the engine. By opening the throttle, engine vacuum is communicated, via suitable ports, to the area above the piston in the bell shaped chamber on the top of the carb body. This not only raises the air valve piston by an amount dependent on the engine's air demand, but also raises a tapered needle out of it's jet. From this, you can see that the accuracy of the mixture ratio delivered to the engine is largely afunction of manufacturing accuracy of the carb itself. If the nee-

Shown here is a one-off triple 2 inch SU installation on a Toyota Land Cruiser, which the author helped a friend build. The intake runners were flow bench developed, and there was a story in that alone. The carb/manifold added about 35 horsepower to the top end, but what it did for the low end was close to spectacular. Idle was a rock steady 450, and torque and drivability from here on up was like a steam engine. In short the engine was just about unstallable.

dle is tapered to the appropriate form in a suitably accurate manner, the SU will deliver a mixture accuracy rivaling and sometimes exceeding that of many production fuel injection systems. The biggest single problem with SUs, is that they often lack the airflow capability to produce competitive power outputs on engines much over about 100 CID. To a degree, this problem can be cut down in size by using more than one carb and applying the same techniques to improve air flow that have been shown elsewhere in this book.

Vizard is seen here using the head of a Snap on screwdriver to find TDC prior to adjusting the valves on the 850 Mini Autocross racer. The use of Big SUs on this type of engine is almost universal because the results achieved are hard to beat.

At full lift, this edge is still hanging down into the air stream. By rounding it off as seen here, a little more air flow is achieved. Depending on the carb model, it is usually between two and four cfm.

FINDING MORE FLOW FROM AN SU

Essentially, even the smallest SU at 1 ⅛ inch throttle bore size, can be made to flow equivalent to ⅛ inch bigger than it really is. When we get up to the 2 inch carbs, these can be made to flow the equivalent of a 2¼ inch SU, if such a thing existed. To put some numbers to this, so you can relate to a typical Holley, the single barrel of a 2 inch HIF 8 SU can deliver well in excess of 300 CFM at 1.5 inches of mercury.

The first and simplest move with any carb, is to slim down the butterfly and shaft. The next move is a little less obvious to see without having a carb at hand but we'll give it a try anyway. Inspection of the intersection of the bore of the air valve piston with the air passage leaves some sharp edges that prove to be a great impediment to flow as the air passes the piston-trailing edge. This area is best visualized as the mouth of a carb having a sharp edge at the intake and no ram stack. In practice, that is just how it functions. By progressively changing the round section of the air passage to a rectangular one with rounded corners as it passes the region of the air valve some very substantial increases in air flow are achieved. Some tuners working on SU equipped race cars have adopted the practice of boring out the entire length of the carbs air passage to a round cross section. By doing so the 'hump' at the jet is removed. This causes a substantial reduction in draw at the jet and reduces the accelerator pump effect that is produced as a result of the relative air flow efficiency of the air

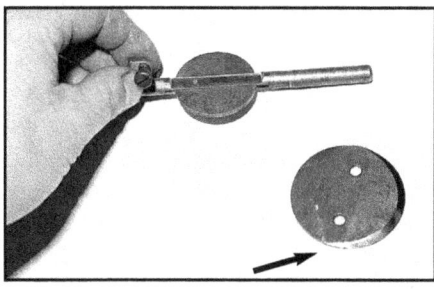

The butterfly and shaft on an SU presents a considerable restriction. Slimming down the shaft, as seen here gains a major amount of extra flow, and when this is done in conjunction with the knife edging of the butterfly the results instantly apparent.

valve section compared with the fuel discharge at the jet. As a point of reference the airflow section needs to be slightly less efficient than the fuel discharge efficiency from the jet. Without this, the carb will need to be calibrated richer than required for full power to compensate for reduced accelerator pump action. The accelerator pump action is brought about by the oil damping of the air valve piston. As the throttle is snapped open, the motion of the piston is held back by the dashpot damping. This causes the depression at

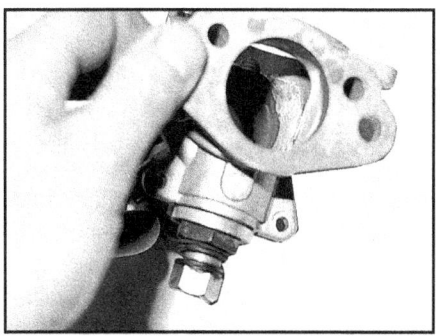

The biggest airflow increase on an SU is achieved by 'squaring off' the bore as seen here. This mod, though time-consuming was one of the features necessary to step up an HIF 6 SU from 240 cfm (on a four barrel carb rating) to over 300!

the 'venturi to go up substantially. During this transition phase, the carb is not ,strictly speaking, acting as a constant vacuum unit. The sudden spike in vacuum increases the fuel flow from the more efficient fuel jet faster than from the aperture formed air valve piston and the hump in the air passage at the jet. As a result, fuel flow momentarily increases by a greater proportion than the air, and the mixture becomes suitably enriched to deal with the acceleration phase of operation. If the air passage is bored out, the air component becomes more efficient than the fuel and acceleration enrichment is reduced.

RAM PIPES

The SU, like so many carbs, is sensitive to ram pipe or velocity stack design. Without the correct entry into the mouth of any carb, much airflow can be lost. Here we can use the SU's response to ram pipe design as being representative of almost any carb. First, ram pipe design should be considered as being two aspects only loosely tied together. The first consideration is length, and the second entry form. In most cases, where the carb is a single unit feeding a number of cylinders the entry form is the most critical. This is usually so because most production vehicles have too little in the way of carb CFM to satisfy the needs of even a stock engine. If an engine is significantly under carbed, then it will inevitably respond to even the smallest increase in airflow by delivering more power. As far as length is concerned, we find that inertial ramming, plus any effect of the length acting with the volume behind the carb to form a Helmholtz resonator, influences the system. Here, we are talking of a carburetion system where the carb or carbs feed at least two cylinders, although the results we will discuss are specific to one carb for four cylinders. First, let us deal with carb entry form. The basic form of an undeveloped ram pipe is as shown in the adjacent drawings Fig. 9-4 to Fig. 9-5. From these drawings, it can be seen that any sharp edge at the mouth of the carb, causes a contraction of the flow which leads to the carb appearing smaller than it really is. So, as if we didn't already know it, sharp edges are bad news for airflow. Let us move along to Fig. 9-6, and see what will most likely be our best approach to eliminate the contraction at the carb entry. For this test we are considering the change in flow by adding a ram pipe to the entry of a carb having a sharp edge as per drawing 1 of Fig. 9 - 6. By adding a plain un-flared section of pipe, the flow is effectively reduced by some

How to Build Horsepower, Vol. 2

6.7%. By increasing the radius at the end of the ram pipe, we reduce the 6.7% deficit to a 2.8% gain. However, increasing the radius on the end of the parallel pipe much past the ⅛ inch radius shown, returned very little in the way of additional air flow. At a ¼ inch radius, no measurable gains were seen at the velocities normally associated with a carb in use. The next series of tests (4 to 7), involved using a flared pipe as the basic form with which to work. Adding a radius to this, proved very effective with flow increases of as much as 5.5% being seen. The results delivered by the last form of ram pipe (11), are revealing. Initially at least, they seem out of step with the results of the other designs, especially if it is taken into account that a radius much above ¼ inch delivers no extra flow. Test 11 seems to contradict the ¼ inch radius limit. The key here, is that all but test 11, have the end of the ram pipe well removed from the surface of the carb mounting flange. As such, it has been found that these ram pipes pull a considerable amount of air from the leading edge roll over. The form of test 11 is such, that there is minimal opportunity to pull air from behind the leading edge thus indicating that a pipe flaring out into a large flat surface is about the best way to go. if this is not practical, then, based on experience, flaring the pipe to about double the original diameter and subsequently adding a turn over of some ¼ radius is about as effective as can be hoped for.

LENGTH TUNING A SINGLE CARB INSTALLATION

Although we are dealing with an SU here, much of what is shown will carry over to other single carb installations. If you remember what was discussed in chapter 5, it will also be seen that the SU is reacting in much the same manner as the single Holley carbed induction system resonating as a Helmholtz resonator. Fig 9 - 7 shows the forms of ram pipes tested. The 2½ and 4 inch long ram pipes were off the shelf items and both gave close to a 5% increase in flow. the 17½ inch long pipe was the result of a number of dyno tests to establish the best length for a single diameter parallel pipe for the test engine. The last example was an effort to find as much torque increase as possible regardless of form. The only reason for the bend in the pipe, is that without it the pipe would exit the engine compartment. On the dyno each of the ram pipes produced the results shown in Fig. 9-8. Analyzing these results, we find that the addition of the 2½ inch ram pipe produced almost 5 horsepower more than no ram pipe. This, on an engine of initially only 63 horsepower, is a sizable increase for such a simple change. This alone should establish the worth of taking care over how the air enters the engine, regardless of the type of carburetor involved. Moving on to the results given by the 4 inch ram pipe, we see that this proved effective at filling a few dips in the power curve that were seen with the 2½ inch ram pipe. Most notable was the filling of the dip between 4000 and 4750 RPM. Moving on to the long ram pipes, it should be made clear going in that this was intended to be an exercise in boosting low end torque to reduce city driving gear changes. As can be seen, there was a substantial increase in low end output, although from 3500 to 5500 were it was once again even, the long ram pipes lost out to the shorter ones.

If you are interested in top end power for outright performance, it does, as is so often the case, look like a choice will have to be made. However, all the story has not yet been told. As this writer has so often stated, a successful engine is not one that employs one or two trick parts but one which is a combination of compatible parts. Subsequent tests established that the long induction system proved to be less sensitive to the unwanted side effects of a longer duration cam. As a result, it was found that a cam with some ten degrees additional duration could be used before any low-end output reduction was measured. This was not the case when a short ram pipe was used. On one engine, it was found that the long style intake permitted the use of a 300 degree race cam without hindering the vehicle's capability of negotiating a traffic island in top gear!

The tests on tuned lengths just described ,resulted in the production of the unit shown in Fig. 9 -9. In practice, it was found that at certain RPM, it pushed so much more air into the engine that the SU carb air valve piston would reach full lift prematurely. Ideally, this piston should reach full lift only at peak rpm. If full lift is reached too soon, the carb's ability to meter fuel in the correct proportions is compromised. To counter this, it proved necessary to use a stronger spring in the carb dashpot and in some cases two springs were needed.

SU NEEDLE SELECTION

Before attempting to recalibrate an SU carb, it is important to know which part of the needle profile affects the operating range. The first ⅛ inch is the idle circuit, the next ½ to ¾ inch is cruise and the remaining is full power. SU issues an extensive list of needle profiles showing the size in ⅛ inch increments down it's length. For those SU users in the USA, Advanced Performance Technology has a booklet part # SU-CHART which lists the dimensions of some 700 needles.

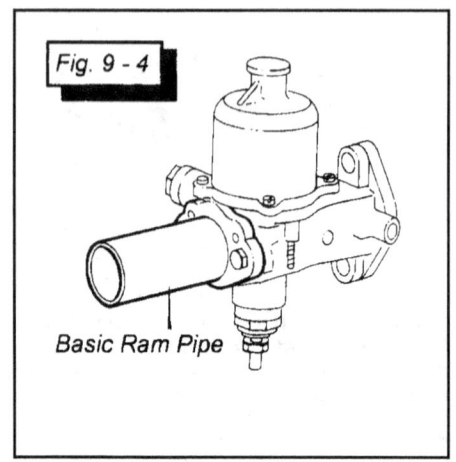

Basic Ram Pipe

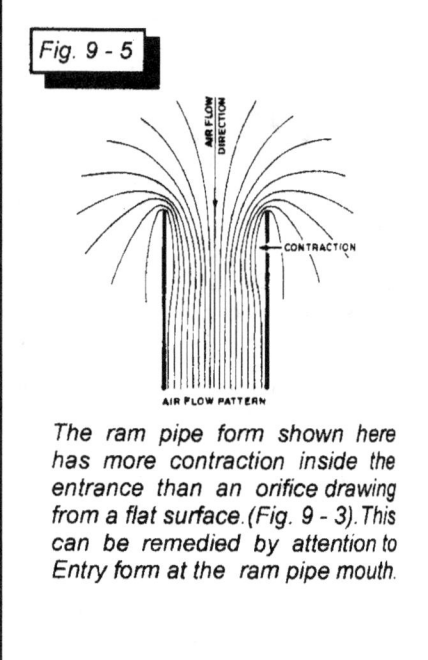

The ram pipe form shown here has more contraction inside the entrance than an orifice drawing from a flat surface.(Fig. 9 - 3). This can be remedied by attention to Entry form at the ram pipe mouth.

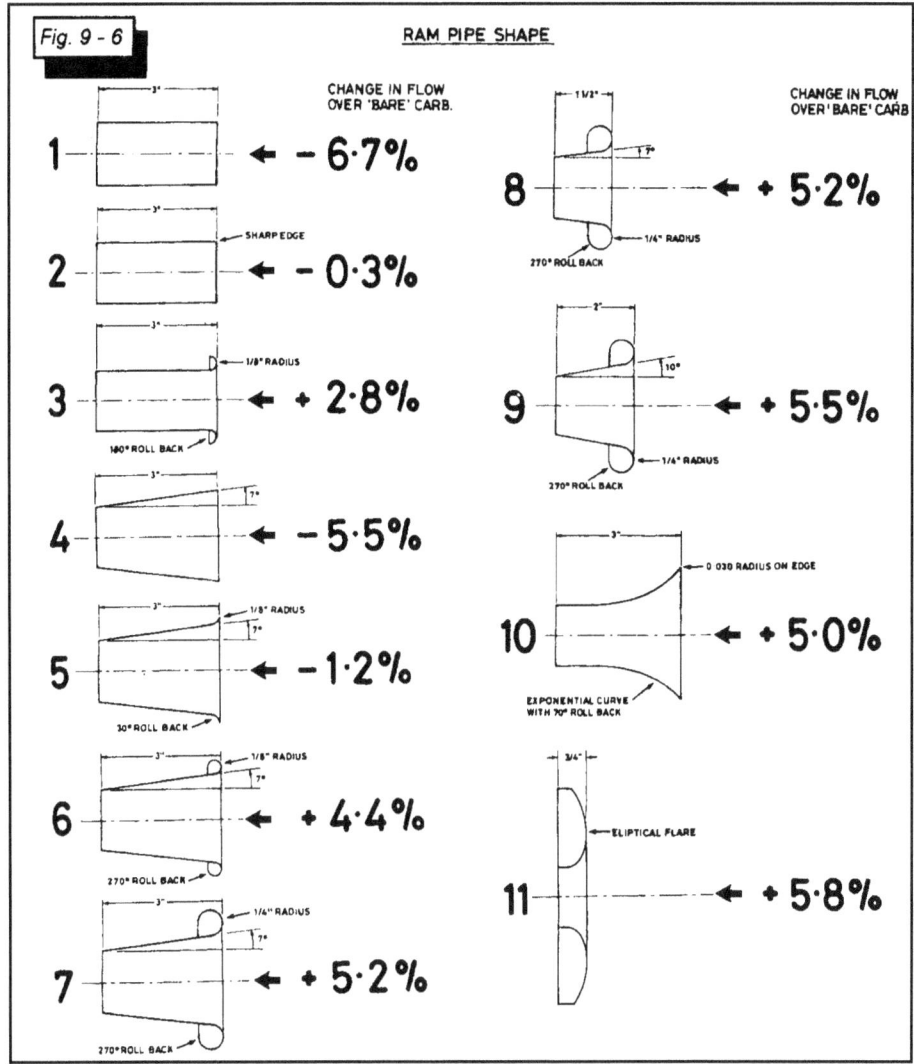

Fig. 9 - 6

DELLORTOS MIKUNIS AND WEBERS

Under this heading, we are going to look at carburetion exotica. If you are buying used speed parts, you may come across carbs such as Solex and SK which look very similar to those named in the heading. These carbs are functional, but the advent of fuel injection and the lack of backing from their parent companies saw them fall by the wayside. However, much of what is discussed here also applies to these two extinct types of carb.

What we are going to look at here can best be described as the pinnacle of carburetor development for the gasoline fueled internal combustion engine. These are carbs designed for independent runner (IR) applications and have the capability of having all the normal fuel circuits precisely jetted. In essence, such carbs deliver as close to fuel injection results as can be achieved without actually having fuel injection. In most cases, these carbs give away little, if anything in terms of total engine output. Where they loose out is almost always in terms of fuel consumption at part throttle and even then, it is often marginal. In many instances they will actually show a significant increase over a typical factory plenum type induction fuel injection system. Also, a comparison between an IR system with butterflies in each port versus a plenum fuel injection system, shows the advantage most certainly going to the IR carb system. There are a number of reasons for this. The first is that Plenum type fuel injection systems are almost always equipped with an air valve with inadequate flow for maximum performance. This can be remedied in many instances by fitting a larger aftermarket air valve in those instances where an appropriate one is available. However, in most cases, these are still short of flow. If a carb of suitable proportions is available, this limitation is removed. If the engine concerned has a larger individual cylinder displacement, such as a typical big block V8, then large enough carbs are not really available. When used as an IR system, this limits carburetion to a cylinder size, with currently available carbs, to about 70 CID (1200cc) or about 110 horsepower per barrel, which ever comes up first.

As far as drivability and low end output is concerned, especially when a larger cam is used, a system with a butterfly in each runner is preferable to open ports and a plenum situated butterfly. Unless a fuel injection system with port-situated butterflies is used, the carbs will outperform the fuel injection. The reason for this becomes apparent if we study what happens when a common set of butterflies controls the air for a number of cylinders. When the butterflies of a common plenum V8 system are closed, the manifold will be subjected to the vacuum drawn by the induction strokes of the pistons. When an intake valve opens, it will initially be in the overlap phase, so the exhaust valve will also be open. Since all 8 cylinders are connected to a common plenum, one of the other cylinders will be at peak draw about half way through it's induction stroke. This cylinder will find it easier to draw the exhaust from whichever cylinder is in it's overlap phase, than it will to draw air through the almost closed butterflies of the plenum air valve. This means that if low-end output and good manifold vacuum are required, the duration of the cam for a plenum type system must be kept shorter than for a system with port located butterflies. The need for a shorter cam on such a setup, as for, say, a typical 350 CID V8 can cost as much as 50 horsepower. With a system having a butterfly located in each port, one cylinder cannot influence

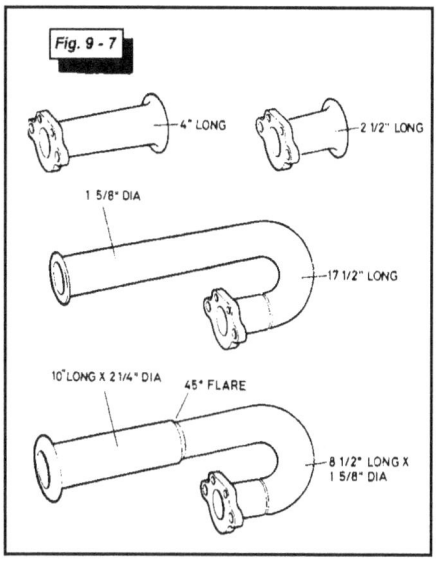

Fig. 9 - 7

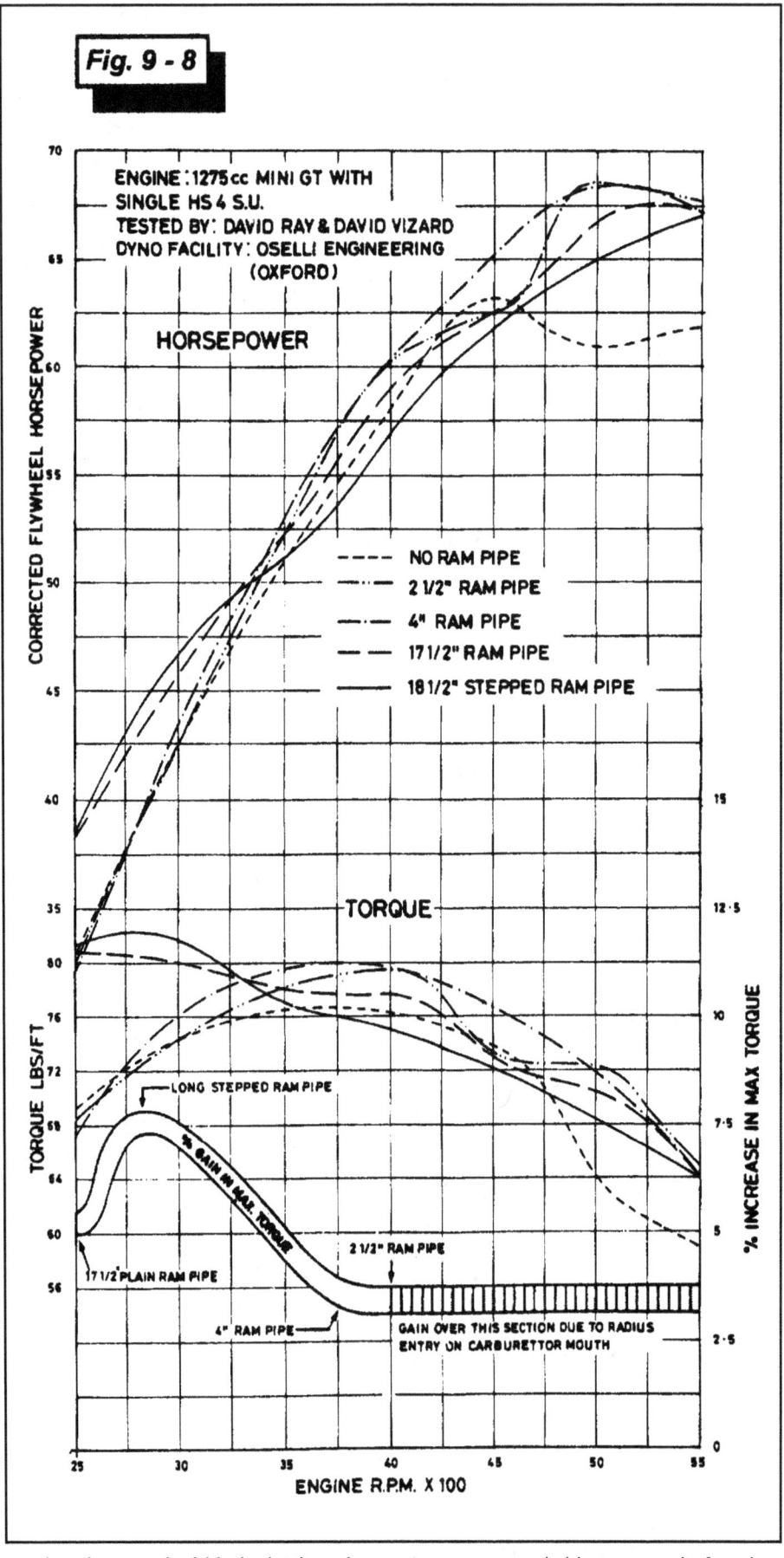

Fig. 9-8

popularity of such systems was limited by their high cost compared to, say, a single four barrel Holley or the likes. However, in recent years many more people have come to accept the price of a sophisticated fueling system and have been prepared to pay out for electronic fuel injection. Additionally, such systems have been popularized by the fact that many of the more moderately priced performance cars are equipped with fuel injection as original equipment. Having accepted that a sophisticated fuel system is going to cost more than a conventional single four barrel, many people have lost sight of the fact that four twin choke carbs and a manifold now cost marginally less and is easier in many instances to set up than fuel injection. Unfortunately, this little known fact may come to be accepted only after the fate of the big IR type carbs has already been sealed. As this is written, the date for the demise of the big Mikuni carbs is already set, with production likely to end in late 1997, and Webers could possibly go the same route not too much later. Still, all may not be lost. Due to the sustained popularity of big air cooled flat four VW engines, the demand for big downdraft carbs continues. These large four cylinder VWs have a similar cylinder displacement to a typical V8 consequently VW tuners have run into the same shortage of carburetor air flow as V8 tuners. Since the 48 IDA style Weber was firmly entrenched as a means for providing carburetion for the flat 4, it followed that if more air flow was needed, the most logical move was to develop carbs along the same lines. This is precisely what happened. Two companies, Gene Berg Enterprises (714-998-7500) and JayCee Enterprises.(714-848-9898), each saw the need among VW racers for a much larger version of the 48 IDA Weber and independently developed appropriate units. The Berg carb has the same bolt pattern as the 48 IDA, but utilizes 58 mm (2.28 inches) throttle plates for a 56% increase in area. This unit utilizes it's own body, throttle shafts, butterflies venturi, and boosters (auxiliary venturis), but takes regular 48 IDA calibration components such as jets, emulsion tubes, air correctors etc. Depending on the size of venturi used, the flow of this unit is up from the typical 320 to 330 CFM per barrel (as measured on our flow bench), for a 48 IDA to some 480 CFM.This makes a 700 horsepower V8 IR installation a practical feasibility.

With a 62 mm throttle body size, the

another. As a result of this the intake valve, in it's early opening phase, experiences far less vacuum than in the case of the common plenum. This allows the engine to use a much bigger cam before low speed drivability becomes unacceptable.

The benefits of an IR carburetion system are considerable. In days past the

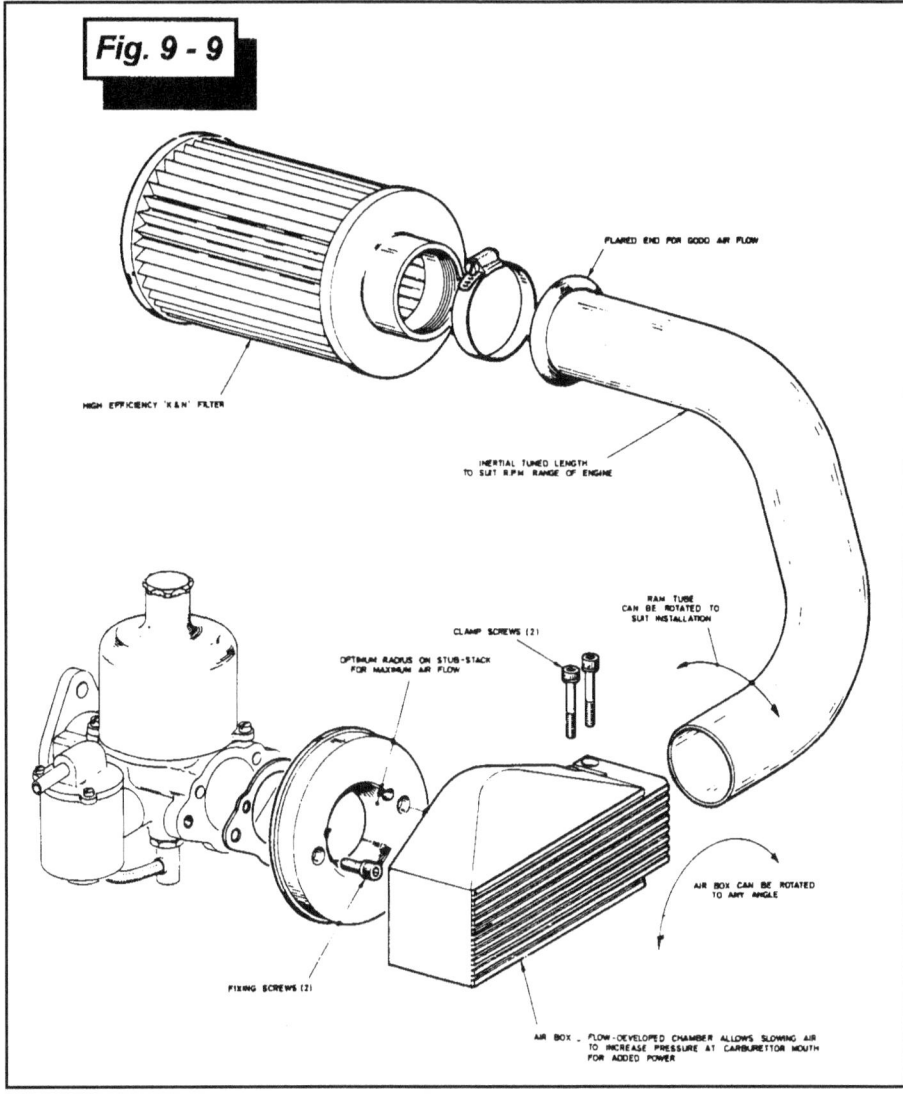

Fig. 9 - 9

carbs from JayCee enterprises are somewhat larger than the Berg units. To accommodate these larger bores, the mounting bolt holes have been moved outboard of the position originally occupied by those on the IDA. The pitch of the throttle bores remains the same. Like the Berg carbs, the JayCee carb utilizes many Weber calibration components. Where it differs most, is in the body and associated parts. An entirely new investment cast body houses 62 mm (2.44 inch) diameter butterflies and venturis up to 50 mm (almost 2 inches). The flow, at some 560 CFM, and area, gives the carb the ability to deal with the air flow demand of a 110 horsepower cylinder in an IR configuration. Used on a tunnel ram manifold in a non IR application, even four 48s would deliver enough air for 1200 horsepower while the bigger carbs discussed here, could cater to twice that amount. Still the virtue of these carbs is not in a tunnel-ram application but an IR one.

Even though these carbs are expensive, they have proved capable of emulating the output of fuel injection systems costing half as much again. Unlike the injection systems, carbs do not need a computer or computer expert to set them up. With a dyno, chassis or engine, and a handful of jet's you are in business.

IR CARBURETION IN PRACTICE

The theoretical advantages of an IR system are more accurate calibration, no inter-cylinder distribution problems, a tuned intake length working on the second wave reflection, better drivability and significantly better low- and mid-range torque. Add to this, the engine's ability to tolerate a longer duration cam and you can see a lot of things fall in favor of an IR setup. To show that such a system can be made highly functional for applications from tow vehicle to race car, the first example we will look at is a motor the writer built for personal truck usage. The engine was a 350 CID small block Chevy sporting ported heads, a 9:1 CR and 1⅝ diameter headers. The cam was a hydraulic flat tappet item with 256 degrees of intake duration and 262 degrees of exhaust. These duration figures are actually shorter than most stock Chevrolet cams but the engine was only required to make about 350 horsepower. Maximizing torque for low- and mid-range operation along with good mileage, were the primary goals. Carburetion for this engine was by quadruple twin choke 48 mm down draft Dellortos. This size Dellorto is produced by enlarging a 45 mm Dellorto. This involves the factory machining out the throttle bores below the venturis to accommodate larger butterflies. The upper body and venturi area remain as per a 45 mm unit. As a result, the 48 Dellorto does not flow the numbers the 48 Weber does, but a set of these are more than adequate, in IR configuration, for outputs up to some 450 horsepower. The figures in the graph Fig 9-10 show, in part, how successful the engine was at meeting it's goals. The term 'in part' is used here because the excellent low end output was not recorded. The reason being, that the dyno was unable to pull the engine down low enough against it's very substantial low end torque output. At 445 lbs/ft the engine's output proved to surpass that of several pro built supercharged engines that have been on our dyno.

On a higher output motor, tests were run using a set of 48 mm IDA Webers. These tests were part of a development program to produce an engine with highly repeatable figures for testing the effect of crankshaft vibration dampers. The idea was to determine if, and by how much, crank vibrations affect power output. Since no previous test results were available to establish just how much the power might change it was necessary to develop a stable and repeatable test engine with suitably high output. The engine in Fig. 9 -11 was the result. Because of cycle to cycle distribution problems, the single four barrel was not able to produce a stable output, whereas the lack of fuel distribution variations was instrumental toward delivering a consistent test engine. For this unit, the compression was kept low enough to minimize thermal degradation of the engine's output as it progressed through it's test sequence. The result is, that the overall torque output is lower than would normally be the case. However the test does

The 300 CFM per barrel of a 48 IDA Weber may be a big number for most engines, but for a V8 it is barely enough, so killing off 20 or 30 with a poor choice of air filter is a substantially counter-productive move. The only filters on the market able to supply the needs of...

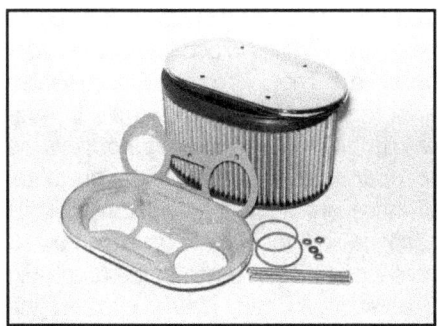

...an engine producing 70 -80 horsepower per cylinder is the big K & N unit shown here. This has enough area for about 250 to 300 horsepower without measurable loss. Four of these will be fine on a 1200 horsepower engine.

show how much extra power the Weber installation gave over a single 650 and 850 CFM 4 barrel. To put this into perspective, many tests done by other test facilities have shown that a typical plenum fuel injection installation often only matches the top end output of a good single four barrel installation on an equally good intake. Here we are not talking about a comparison of a $4000 fuel injection system with a single stock $250, 750 CFM Holley on a $150 Edelbrock Performer, which, however good a value for money such a combination may be, is hardly a fair match. What we are talking about here is a reworked 1000 cfm $1000 Holley on an equally highly developed $750 intake. Tested against a typical plenum fuel injection set up, the Holley more often than not wins out in terms of top end power. The fuel injection scores at the low rpm levels; usually producing 30 to maybe 40 lbs-ft. more torque. Peak torque however, may not be significantly different. Drivability with the fuel injection is also usually markedly better. If all the forgoing is taken into account, then the tests using very finely calibrated electronic carbs on manifolds

Seen here is a 48 Dellorto cut away to reveal some of its inner workings. The two vertical tubes are the air correctior/emulsion tube/main jet holders. The fuel transfer passages in the 'wings' of the boosters connect with the well that these are in. The space around them is....

... the float bowl. A dual float assemble with floats positioned in both the left-and-right hand sides of the carb is designed to minimize the effect of high cornering forces on the fuel level. If the fuel sloshes to one side of the carb, one float becomes more buoyant at the expense of the other, so the effect cancels out.

Changing from a 750 Holley on an Edelbrock Performer, a known functional combination especially at lower RPM, to the Dellorto setup ...

having the benefit of basic porting and port-matching shows the IR carb installation to be very effective when compared to it's single four barrel counterpart. To show the value of an IR setup on a purpose built engine, Fig. 9-12 is worth a long look. Seen here, is a practical high performance street unit. This utilized a set of ported AFR aluminum heads which, in conjunction with flat top pistons, gave a 10.5:1 compression ratio. A streetable roller cam of some 285 degrees seat duration was used along with 1¾ inch headers. Using 92 octane Chevron for fuel, this motor pumped out 518 horsepower and 469 lbs.-ft. of torque. Here we

...-seen here produced an almost constant 45 ft/lbs throughout the rev range on this 350 small block Chevy. At the top end this...

.... produced a 50 horsepower increase. Along with the increased output came reduced part throttle fuel consumption, a glass smooth 400 RPM idle and sprint car like throttle response. On the down side, calibration takes more than just a casual knowledge of carburetor function.

A truck installation with all the hood clearance available is ideal for a down draft carb setup. All that was required for this installation on the author's truck was the production of the air conditioning bracket seen in front of the right front carb. Comments at the gas station while checking oil ranged from, "bet you can't drive by a gas station.....to "wow". Only the second comment was right.

rest our case for the carbureted IR engine.

CALIBRATION

A major point needs to be made here. if you have spent the money on the type carbs we are discussing, you should have also set aside the budget to set them up correctly. Other than being a sheer fluke, they are never correctly jetted straight out of the box, regardless of what the supplier may tell you. Setting up means a) knowing precisely what mixture ratio is being delivered under any and all load/speed conditions and b) knowing how much power a given fuel/air ratio produces. This means oxygen sensors (lambda sensors) CO analyzers and a dyno of some sort be it an on-board, chassis, or engine dyno. Anything less produces correspondingly inferior results.

CALIBRATION TECHNIQUES

The principles for calibrating any of the carbs we are talking of here are basically the same. We will start where most people unfamiliar with the types involved make the most common mistakes. All the carbs we are dealing with here have removable chokes (venturis). This often prompts even experienced engine builders using this type of carb for the first time to assume that the reason the removable chokes are used is to allow the installation of the largest one possible. Consider this: If the factory had intended only the largest size to be used, they would have built it that way. If the choke is too large for the application, the signal at the booster will be too low and consequently, atomization will suffer. The extent with which this causes power to suffer is dramatic and a case example will serve to illustrate the point. A well known and respected engine builder who had, a short time before his visit to our shop, had the distinction of having built both the world's fastest piston engine aircraft and top fuel dragster brought in a prototype 1600cc two valve per cylinder race engine. This was equipped with a large pair of side draft Mikunis with the largest chokes possible installed. The rational was that nothing should impede the flow of air into the engine. The first pull on the dyno revealed the engine capable of only 117 horsepower and our engine building friend considered he had a major disaster on his hands. Reducing the choke size

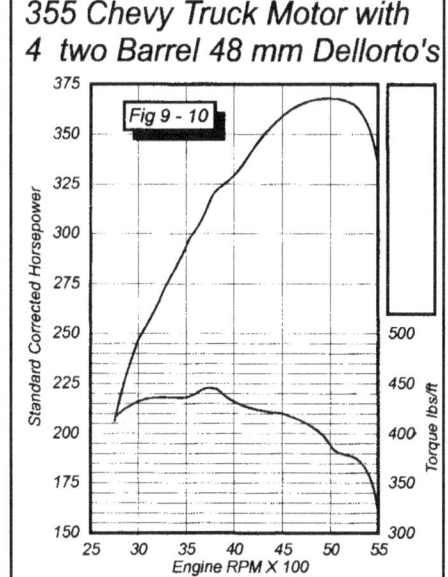

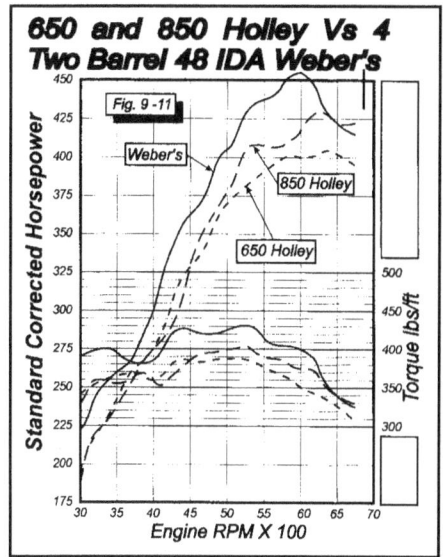

used to the correct size increased the output to a little over 160 horsepower! This serves to illustrate that over-sizing chokes can create a disastrous drop in power and, just for the record, the engine finally made 197 horsepower. In practice, we find that the optimum choke size is affected by two factors. The first is the largest choke size the carb body can accept and still function properly with. This normally proves to be between 82 and 85% of the butterfly size. Use any more than this and power will almost certainly drop. If the engine needs a larger choke size, then it means a carb too small for the job is being used. For most of these carbs, the best airflow and atomization combination occurs when the choke size is close to 80% of the butterfly size and the best working range from 72% to 80%

The second aspect determining the optimum choke size, is engine airflow demand. If the rpm at which peak power occurs, is realistically estimated, the following formula predicts a functional choke size to close limits.

Where:
CV = Cylinder Volume in cc's
RPM = peak power RPM

(To convert cubic inches to cc's multiply by 16.39)

$$\text{Choke in mm} = \sqrt{\frac{CV \times RPM?}{2600}}$$

Having made your calculations, always use the nearest size smaller as a starter. Once the engine has

These big side draft Webers on 'Blower Bob' Benton's blown 350 flowed a combined 1000 CFM, so the airflow requirement for the application was well covered. However, because such carbs rely, not on a a power valve, but for induction pulse induced enrichment for a full power mixture, some innovative calibration was required. The end result of several hundred hours of development in this area, was near fuel injection performance. Power, if you are interested, was close to 600 horses, and a like number of ft.-lbs. with a set of quiet mufflers in place. All this power came with a sub-500 RPM idle speed, as befitting for a true street motor.

As driven on the street, "Blower Bob's" 1970 Camaro could perform rolling burnouts on DOT legal street slicks, and at LA County Raceway, in Palmdale, on a 7000 foot altitude density day, run almost 130 mph in the lights. Not bad for a car with true grocery getting capabilities!

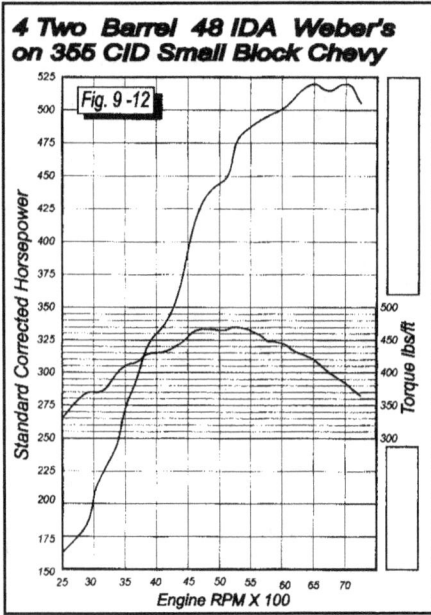

Fig. 9-12 — 4 Two Barrel 48 IDA Weber's on 355 CID Small Block Chevy

been fully set up on the predicted size, you may want to try a size or two larger but no more. This formula is unlikely to be off by more than a mm or two.

IDLE SYSTEM

Calibrating the fuel side of these carbs becomes relatively straightforward if the functional principles explained elsewhere in this book have been absorbed. Starting with the idle adjustment system, turn the idle adjustment screw in until it bottoms and back it out two turns. This should be close to correct if the idle jet is correctly sized. If the engine runs rich, the idle jet may need to be reduced and visa versa. The idle jet also controls fuel delivery for the transition, or, as it is called with these carbs, the progression circuit. The simple test for this is to bring the engine speed up about a 1000 above the idle and check the mixture delivered. Based on the result, the jet should be sized up or down as required. A look at the idle jet holder of all of the carbs we are concerned with reveals that the idle jet holder is actually a smaller more simple version of the emulsion tube in the main jet system. If out on the road the mixture goes rich or lean toward the end of this circuits span of influence (about 10 degrees of opening), then change to a jet holder that introduces more or less air as needed. Once these calibrations start to fall into place, return to the idle adjustment and reset to give the best idle. After this verify the transition/progression calibration to determine if any more changes are needed. Repeat the process as required until a satisfactory performance is achieved. The idle should be much smoother and more stable, with much less of a tendency to 'lope' than with a single or multiple four barrel plenum type system.

MAIN JET CIRCUIT

Usually, much of the main jet calibration is done without the carb's filters being installed, so as to simplify jet changes. If the engine normally runs with filters (and they all should), then if overly restrictive filters are used, it will cause the main jet circuit to richen when they are installed by the equivalent of 1 or 2 main jet sizes. This must be accounted for by dropping the jets when running the filters. If maximum performance is to be had, never remove ram pipes to accommodate air filters. Ram pipes of various lengths are available and should always stay clear of the filter case by no less than the rated size of the carb.

If the choke sizes have been appropriately selected, the main jet circuit usually becomes easy to calibrate. There are three aspects that need to be dealt with: the main jet, air corrector jet and the emulsion tube. In probably half the calibration cases, the emulsion tube installed by the carb supplier will be satisfactory for the application. In those instances where it is not, you need to change it as necessary. If you skipped Chapter 3, go back and read it to understand the intricacies of the emulsion tube and how to select a more appropriate one if currently incorrect. However, the best way to establish that the emulsion tube is suitable or not, is to set up the main jet/air correction system so that at some point, the mixture is known to be correct. The following technique works almost across the board and has served this writer well over many years. First, install a 180 air corrector jet into the emulsion tube and choose a main jet size from the Fig. 9-13. Run the

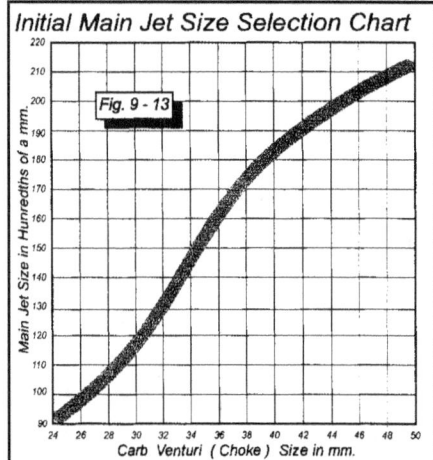

Initial Main Jet Size Selection Chart — Fig. 9-13

engine and determine the mixture status at the lower end of the RPM range used. Change the main jet as required to bring the mixture within the maximum power range of 12.8 to 13.2:1. Once this point is established, run the engine up in the RPM range to establish the mixture trend. If the mixture stays a the desired ratio through out the RPM band, then the job is finished. The chances of happening on the correct calibration this easily though, are relatively remote. More than likely, the fuel will richen or lean out as RPM increases. If it shows a tendency to lean, reduce the air corrector size and do the reverse if it richens. If the air corrector requires altering by more than three sizes, expect to re-evaluate the main jet size at the lower starting point. 3 jet sizes up on the air corrector may require you increase the size of the main jet by 1 size to hold the low end mixture at the desired ratio. Continue to evaluate until it is correct at both ends of the range or the air corrector falls outside the nominally optimum working range. This working range normally falls within 120 to 140% of the main jet size. If the air corrector changes appear to do little, or the suggested range is exceeded, it indicates a need to re-evaluate the emulsion tube. At this time, an emulsion tube selection based on the methods described in Chapter 3 will need to be installed and the calibration process re-started.

ACCELERATOR PUMP CIRCUIT

There are two aspects of the accelerator pump circuit that need our attention: the rate of the fuel injection and the duration of the injection period. In almost all instances, the type of carb we are dealing with here has a fixed volume accelerator pump. The rate of injection is controlled by the size of the pump jet and the system spring stiffness. The amount of fuel injected is usually set by some form of calibrated bypass or spill valve, which in the case of a Weber, is situated in the bottom of the float bowl. The key to accelerator pump calibration is for it to deliver the minimum amount of enrichment fuel to get the job done. Initial calibration should be with too little fuel delivered in a short, sharp shot. A good starting pump jet is two or three sizes less than one third of the diameter of the main jet. This will in most instances produces a slight stumble. Go up in jet size until the stumble clears and a clean sharp pickup is produced. If this fails to produce the desired results, drop back a size or two, and extend the pump duration by whatever means is applicable to the carb type being used. Continue this process until the desired results are seen. If your calibration results in black smoke being apparent in the exhaust, too much fuel is being injected. It is more often than not, too big a jet rather than too long on pump shot duration.

CHOKE SIZING: TOO BIG DOESN'T PAY

Our flow bench tests show how important it is to size both the carb throttle body and the chokes (venturis). In the case of the 40 D.C.O.E sidedraft, the flow increased very minimally when the choke size was increased from 34 to 36 mm.. However, the signal at the auxiliary venturi dropped by over 50%. Conversely, selecting a carb that is too large and then having to choke it down, is also bad, though usually to a lesser extent. In this case we saw how a 45 D.C.O.E. with 32 mm chokes actually flowed less than a 40 D.C.O.E. with the same size chokes.

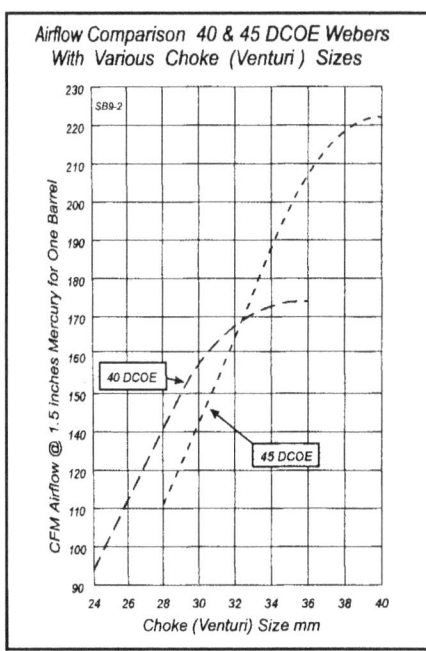

These 48 IDA Webers allowed this, another engine built by the author, to make almost 500 street drivable horsepower from 355 cubes. However, 48s are close to their limit at this level and...

....a larger carb set based on a Berg 58 mm 'Weber' such as shown here or ...

... alternatively, a 62mm unit produced by JayCee Engineering.

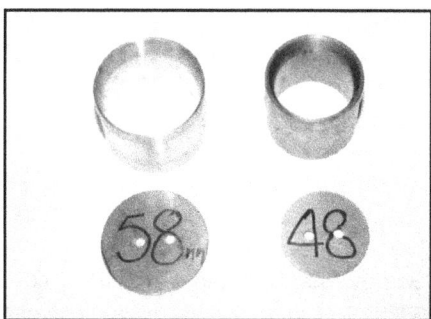

With throttle body sizes from 50 to 58mm, the Berg unit is ideally placed for the big inch VW market, the modifying of which this company excels in. Venturi sizes are available from 38 mm to 50 mm.

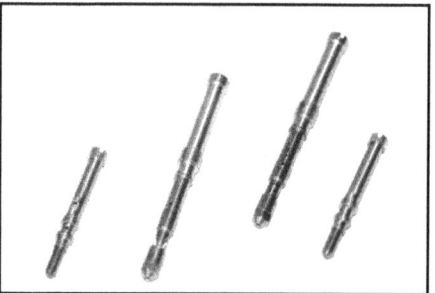

Calibration of these big Weber clones follows the same routine as the originals, except everything will usually, but not always, be proportionally larger. Probably the most difficult aspect of tuning these carbs will be getting the emulsion tube right.

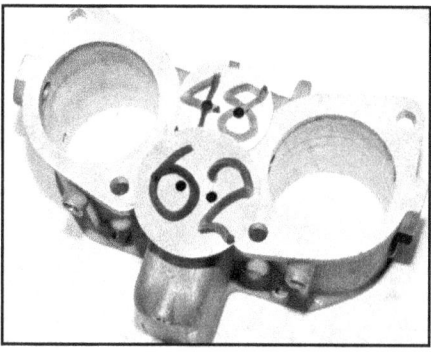

The JayCee Engineering carbs, with their 62mm bodies, represent the largest flowing down drafts available as of '96. They appear to be ideally suited to very high output small blocks up to say 400 inches and big blocks up to about 500 inches.

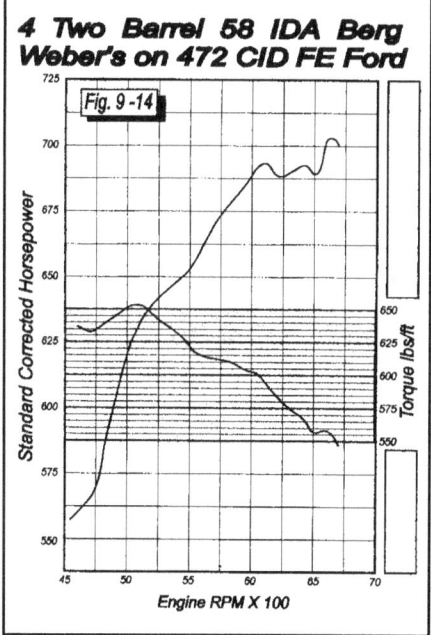

Much work is said to have been done on the fuel circuits to make them "user friendly" and it is claimed that these carbs are easier to set up as a result. The figures on a 427 Ford to go into a Cobra, shown in Fig. 9-14 speak for themselves. This engine, built Kuntz & Co. (Gene Berg 714-998-7500) at 652 ft.-lbs. and 702 horsepower will turn this 2400 lb. car into a wild ride.

How to Build Horsepower, Vol. 2

How To Build HORSEPOWER: Chapter 10
Carburetors & Intake Manifolds
Manifold Design Basics

Some aspects concerning charge temperature and its effect on power have already been covered, but the primary concern up until now has been air temperature as seen by the carburetor. Although inducing cool air aids output, the power of an engine can be greatly affected by the thermal treatment of the air after it has passed through the carburetor. Though water heating is sometimes used, most stock intake manifolds have exhaust heat applied to them in one form or another. With most V8s, this takes the form of a crossover passage beneath the intake manifold. It's sole purpose is to heat the incoming charge. A look into most manifolds will reveal ribbing on the floor of the plenum. This ribbing exists for two reasons. First, it catches puddled fuel and reduces the amount running down into the ports, especially at cold start up, and second, it provides more surface area for fuel to pick up exhaust heat. Knowing the factory engineers are smart enough to rarely do anything without good reason, it's worthwhile considering what the likely benefits of exhaust heat are.

Exhaust heat certainly doesn't help power, so this can be ruled out, but positive aspects do exist. The exhaust heat delivers a much faster warm-up time, and this significantly reduces emissions. More pollutants are put out during the first 60 seconds of running from cold start than the following 20 miles of highway driving. The faster the cold start cycle can be dispensed with, the better. Many late model V8s from about 1975 onwards, had devices which directed as much exhaust as possible through the under-manifold exhaust cross-over passage by means of a thermostatically controlled restrictor in one side of the exhaust system.

When at cruising speed, the exhaust heat still provides benefits, inasmuch as it ensures, as near as possible, that the cylinders receive an even fuel charge, because most of it is vaporized before leaving the intake manifold. In such cases, intake heat leads to good fuel distribution and more effective burning. This much we have already touched on in previous chapters.

POWER AND HEAT

When it comes to maximum output, intake manifold heat is a major power robbing feature. This poses the obvious ques-

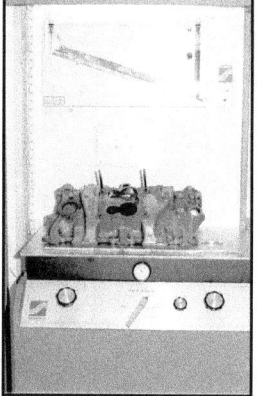

Due to the low flow levels achieved, it is doubtful that GM used a flow bench to develop the stock Q-Jet small block Chevy manifolds until at least the 80s, when the aluminum smog ones became more common. For the racer, a flow bench program is essential.

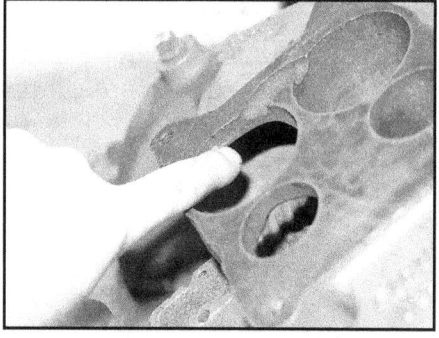

The development of the odd looking DV manifold seen during the next few pages started here, where the air and fuel fight to make it around this sharp edge, which is also too close to the exit of the carb barrels.

A lot of the development of the plenum shape of this manifold was done using a length of cotton to test for flow direction and velocity. A simple yet very effective tool.

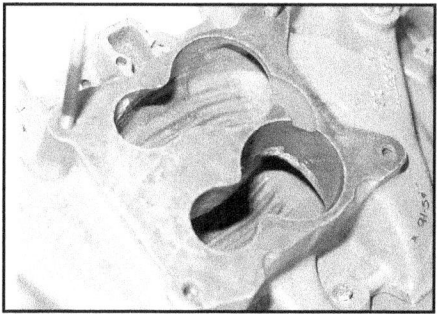
First move was to cut out the space between paired barrels so, air/fuel mixture issuing from the carb could flow in either direction. This movement between runners ...

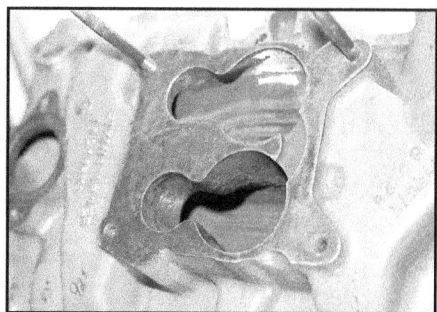
... was further enhanced by rounding off the area at the bottom of the original holes at the point they joined the main part of the runner.

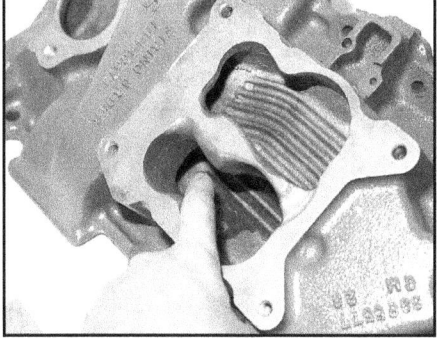
As far as possible, care was taken to transition from the down runner to the one leading to the ports with as large a radius as possible for superior flow. It has been said that rounding of this area can reduce mixture quality because the original corner was a fuel shearing point. This was not found to be the case in this instance.

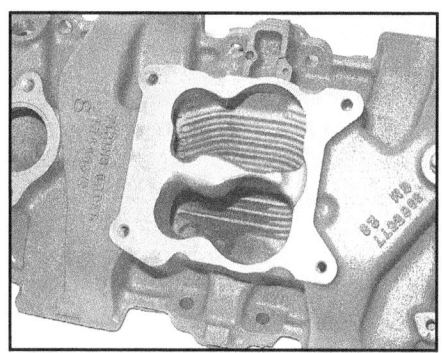
Here is a bird's eye view of the finished plenum to help replicate it if you plan to hop up your own manifold.

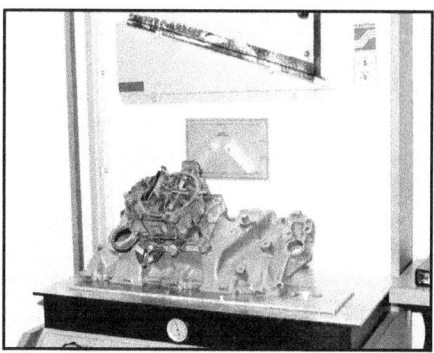
On the flow bench in its final form prior to dyno testing, the DV modified manifold delivered the flow figures shown in Fig. 10-4.

tion as to how much power a typical manifold, heated by exhaust or water, loses. At first sight, it would seem simple to run a test to establish how much power is lost, but, unfortunately, the situation is a little more complex than it appears if the full advantages of its deletion are to be realized. Changing the operating temperature of the intake manifold changes three different operating conditions. The most obvious is the density of the air or charge weight being drawn into the cylinder. However, it also affects mixture distribution and the engine's octane requirement. To establish nearer the true worth of eliminating manifold heat, all these points need to be considered. This makes giving a concise answer a little difficult, or to be more precise, expensive. However, some experience in this area has allowed some test shortcuts which produce figures that are realistically representative of the situation. The engine used for these tests was a moderately modified 350 CID small block Chevy, which was used primar-

Fig 10 -1

Intake Manifold Temperature Test

Test engine:- 355 small block Chevrolet.   Tested by:- David Vizard.
Dyno:- Superflow.   Fuel:- 91 octane unleaded.

RPM	Test #1 Tq	HP	°F	Test #2 Tq	HP	°F	Test #3 Tq	HP	°F	Increase* Tq	HP
2500	348	166	105	356	169	76	360	171	77	12	5
3000	343	196	106	351	201	77	355	203	77	12	7
3500	337	224	105	347	231	77	351	234	78	14	10
4000	325	247	107	333	254	79	336	257	79	11	10
4500	312	267	108	320	274	79	324	277	79	12	10
5000	292	278	108	298	284	79	303	288	80	11	10
5500	267	280	109	277	290	80	282	295	80	15	15
6000	244	279	110	252	288	80	257	294	81	13	15

Ambiant air temperatures:- #1- 104° F   #2 - 105° F   #3 - 108° F.
* Indicates the increase given by test #3 over test #1.
All figures are rounded to the nearest whole number.

Most intake manifolds have too much heat for anything approaching normal weather. The heat applied to most stock manifolds is appropriate for an Alaskan winter, so for anything less reduce the manifold heat as required.

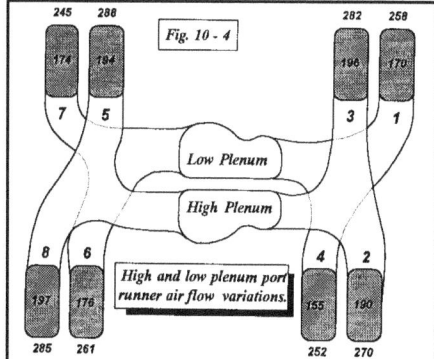
Shown here are the "bare" flow figures for a stock Q-Jet small block Chevrolet manifold before and after applying the modifications shown in the nearby photos. In addition to the plenum mods, the manifold runners were given a cursory clean up. This involved minimal enlargement. This manifold performed better than any aftermarket manifold tested to date. It would produce the top end of the best with as much as 30 ft.-lbs. more at the lowest rpm used.

From the outset, the modified manifold was intended to run with a spacer, so all cylinders had all carb barrels to draw from. The principle intention was to allow this to happen without the use of a large plenum that would damp induction pulses and reduce atomization capabilities.

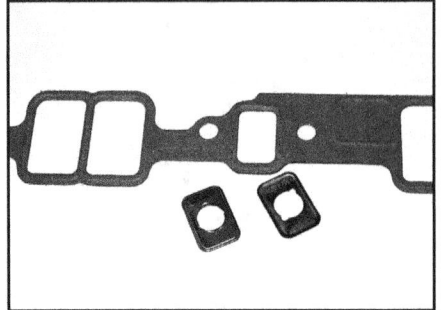

Heat is to be avoided for any performance application, and the easiest way to keep heat out of a stock manifold is to replace the stock type gasket which has exhaust cross over holes in it, with a set of performance ones without.

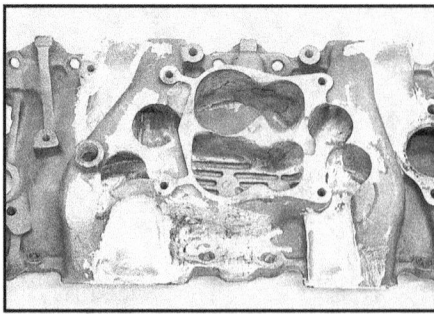

Some of GM's later aluminum manifolds are easier to work with than the cast iron items. Seen here, are some of our partially completed efforts toward building a super stealth manifold. The intent was to build an engine that externally appeared and sounded stock, but performed like a race car. It was specifically intended for money match racing a long way from home.

Apart from cutting holes in the top of the manifold, we also cut into the lower part to make changes to the runners.

ily as a dyno mule motor. This engine was equipped with a relatively long period, wide lobe center line angle cam, and some HTBHP modified cylinder heads based on production 186 castings. These delivered a compression ratio of 10.2:1. The induction system utilized an electronic 650 Holley, that fed the mixture into a Weiand 8004 two plane intake manifold with a temperature sensor installed in #2 intake port runner. Steady state power runs were made and stabilized air temperature measurements were made at each power/rpm increment.

TEST RESULTS

During these tests, two facts became evident. The first is that, when opening the throttle, even after the engine has been idling for only a short time, it takes about 30 seconds for the induction system to drop to within 10% of it's final temperature. From this point on, the intake charge temperature drops very slowly. This cooling is brought about by the flow of hopefully cool fuel and air through the manifold, plus the cooling due to fuel evaporation. The latent heat of evaporation, of gasoline is sufficiently high to produce enough cooling to drop the intake charge temperature below that of the inducted air. However, it is not uncommon for the temperature to take a minute or more to reach near stable conditions after going to full throttle. This little fact should indicate the worth of cooling a drag race engine's intake manifold with dry ice immediately prior to making a pass down the drag strip.

The relationship of air temperature versus power is clearly shown in Fig. 10-1. Blocking off the exhaust heat, caused the temperature at the port runner to drop by 30°F. This resulted in the power and torque climbing by approximately 2.5 %. To put the value of this into prospective, you need to be aware that a typical effective aftermarket, two plane manifold for a small block Chevy, only produces about 5% increase and most of this happens from about 3000 rpm up. Eliminating excess heat produced 2.5% increase **everywhere!** The bottom line is that better thermal management can help an effective intake manifold produce about a 50% greater gain and that is worth thinking about.

CR INCREASE

Although power increases due to charge temperature reductions are worthwhile in themselves, the full possibilities are yet to be achieved. The 10.2:1 CR used for the test engine was chosen because experience had indicated that this was about the limit for a 91 octane fueled small block Chevy with a heated induction. What is so often overlooked, is that the higher the intake temperature, the more octane an engine requires at any given CR. By reducing the charge temperature, the CR could now be raised before the detonation limit would once again be reached. For #3 test results, the compression was raised.

Normally, compression increases would be done a little at a time, until detonation was experienced. Such a test procedure is expensive, and is not a problem to do when someone else is funding it. This was not the case, but from previous experience testing fuels, octane boosters, additives and cylinder heads, some reasonable estimates were made as to how much more compression could be tolerated before detonation became a factor. The 30° temperature difference seen between the heated and unheated Weiand 8004 manifold, represents about 2 octane numbers in octane requirement. At 10.2:1, the engine was just on the point of detonating. It was estimated that, with the reduced intake temperature, this could safely be raised to 10.6:1. When tested with the higher CR, the output shown in column #3 was produced. This shows a gain of up to 15 ft.-lbs. of torque and 15 horsepower over the original peak output with the heated manifold.

ALUMINUM VS IRON

Virtually all aftermarket manifolds are made of aluminum, which unfortunately has a high rate of heat conductivity, much higher than the stock cast iron item. Operation of a typical engine in a cold climate, normally means some sort of intake heat is required. However, because of aluminum's high heat conductivity, the need for exhaust heat is reduced, as it will quickly pick up heat conducted from the rest of the engine. Usually, enough heat will soak through from the heads of a typical V8 engine to meet the needs of intake heat for cruise conditions. This leaves the only real consideration being, how quickly the engine will warm up if the exhaust heat is blocked off. It would seem that for conditions down to about freezing point and high humidity, an aluminum manifold does not need a heated cross over passage. If the type of carb and manifold design puts the

When it comes to making stock appearing manifolds perform, Brzezinski Racing must be one of the best in the industry. Since they are required for race purposes, the manifold mods are geared toward making more top-end output. To do so entails machining out the plenum as an initial move. From here the ...

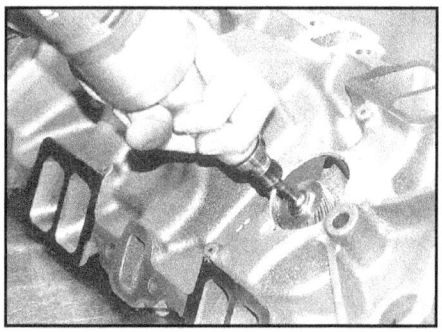

... manifold has access holes cut in it to allow it to be ported. By the time Brzezinski's skilled porters have finished with it, this GM manifold is fully ported and represents a big increase in airflow.

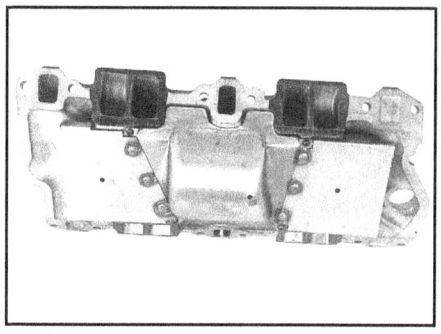

These plates serve to cover the plugs welded back into the access holes, and to help shield hot oil from the underside of the manifold.

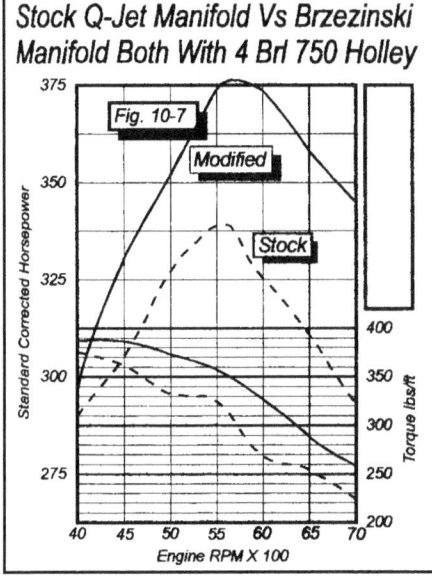

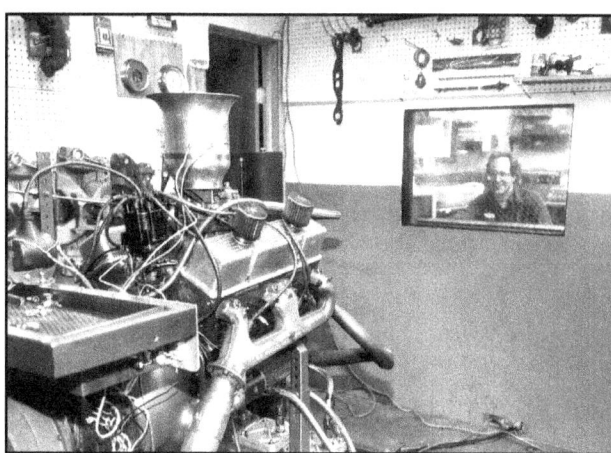

It is on the dyno and the track that the Brzezinski manifold proves itself. Power gains are spectacular for any manifold, not just a modified stocker. The power figures seen in the graph Fig. 10-7 show what a fully ported manifold is typically capable of producing.

carb well clear of the engine, as is the case with many inline fours and sixes, then some form of winter heating may well be needed to prevent carburetor icing. Here the best choice is water heating. A modification well worth doing to an exhaust heated intake manifold is to close the exhaust passage by welding it shut and then connecting it to a source of hot water. In the summer the hot water can be shut off.

The way heat and subsequent fuel vaporization affects fuel economy is easy to see. For street manifolds, a great deal of thought needs to be given to fuel economy, because most driving is done at part throttle. Additionally, manifolds which produce the best mileage are, by their very nature, cleaner running in terms of emissions. But intake heat is not the only factor that effects mileage and performance. Runner shapes and the manifold volume, as seen by the cylinder, also have a major impact on how well the manifold functions. Were it not for compromises forcing the issue, designing an intake manifold would be relatively simple. It would be just a question of connecting one carburetor barrel to each cylinder with a manifold having runners as straight as possible. Add the correct length to tune the system at the desired RPM, and we would be in business. Unfortunately, the real world dictates that compromises must be struck. Such things as cost, convenience, hood clearance, ease of maintenance, emissions etc., all affect the final design of the intake manifold.

MANIFOLD DESIGN

Since a single four barrel manifold is the most common, let's analyze a typical stock piece to see where it falls short in terms of a performance manifold. First, a brief description of a typical stock manifold. Not surprisingly, most are made of Detroit's wonder metal, cast iron. The profile must be low enough to fit under the hood of whatever vehicle in the line-up has the lowest hood line. Apart from this, the factory wants to make it as cheap as possible and they are not going to put any more design time into it past the point it allows the engine to meet it's marketing department mandated power output. This philosophy is one of the fundamental differences between what the factory and the hot rod industry produces. The factory works on a basis of adequate power for the job. Most hot rodders work on the assumption that you can never have enough power. These two view points bring to bear an entirely contradictory set of criteria when it comes to the design of engine parts.

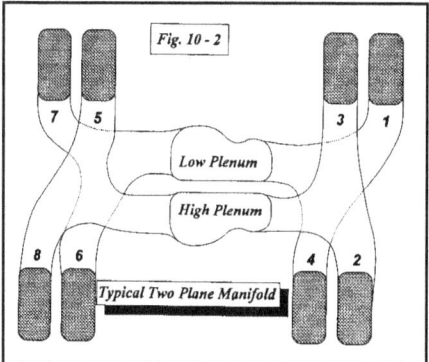

Shown here is the port routing on a typical Chevrolet two plane intake. Each plenum sees an induction stroke every 180 degrees so there is no overlapping of cylinder to cylinder induction cycles.

How to Build Horsepower, Vol. 2   **107**

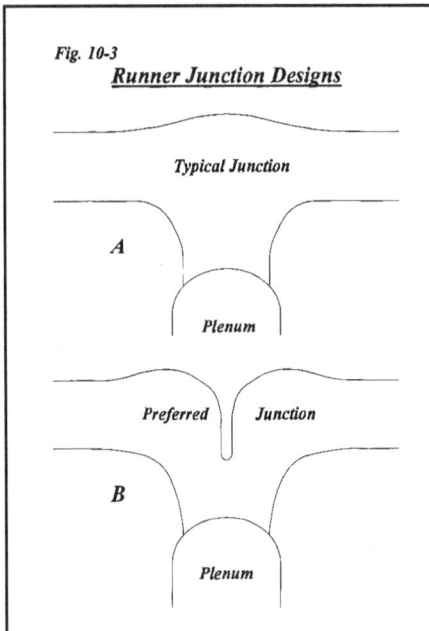

Fig. 10-3
Runner Junction Designs

With the top runner design, the intake momentum from one port runner starts to rob energy from the other at high rpm. This becomes an additional factor reducing the high output potential of a two plane manifold. If the junction is designed as shown in B, the high rpm output will be improved.

THE 180° CONCEPT

So much for the basic design philosophy, now let's dissect a typical stock intake manifold. If it is for a V8, it is most likely a 180° design utilizing a single four barrel carburetor. For a production engine of moderate output, such a design has much to commend it. But first, for those not familiar with the concept, let's analyze how a 180° manifold works.

Essentially, a 180° manifold divides a V8 engine into two four cylinder engines. A four cycle V8 engine has a firing pulse every 90°. The port runner routing on a 180° manifold is such that it connects the cylinders that fire 180° apart. Due to the firing order of a typical two plane crank V8, this means that two barrels of the carb feed cylinders in both banks. This leads to several runners having to cross over their runner counterparts from the opposite bank. Since each half of the carb is isolated from the other, the engine runs, in effect like a two barrel carb on a four cylinder engine. It is worth considering why so many original equipment V8 manifolds are made this way, since a single plane manifold, which has all eight cylinders connected to a common plenum, is easier to make. Needless to say there are good reasons, that will become apparent later. For now, let's analyze the negative effects of choosing this style of manifold.

If you look at some of the nearby drawings Fig. 10-2, you will see that in a 180° or two plane manifold how some runners cross under others. Looking down from the carburetor flange reveals a high and low plenum. The high plenum feeds those runners which pass over the runners from the low plenum. The high runners approach the port in such a way as to produce a good transition from the manifold to the port in the cylinder head. Unfortunately, the runners that must take the lower route, have less than a satisfactory approach to the cylinder head port. To maintain a low overall manifold height, it is necessary to compromise the approach angles of the runners from the low plenum. The net result is reduced breathing efficiency on those cylinders. Apart from this, another factor comes into play which can limit the top end performance of a two plane manifold. On many stock manifolds, the runners from opposite sides of the engine, join before the turn to meet the plenum under the carb. Cylinders #2 & 3 and #5 & 6, on a Chevrolet manifold are examples of this. As RPMs increase, we find, at these junctions an increasing tendency for one cylinder to rob air from the one directly opposite, rather than pulling all it's charge from the plenum.

If there is room, the runners need to join the plenum as shown in Fig. 10-3B rather than Fig. 10-3A. The plenum itself also presents another problem on the stock intake manifold. Unfortunately, it is a problem difficult to cure if the manifold height remains a constraint. Looking into the plenum from the carburetor flange shows that the high port plenum has very little vertical length before making the turn into the port runners. On the other hand the low plenum has more than enough vertical length in which to direct the mixture into the runners. A few factory manifolds were designed with a view to reducing this problem. These are commonly known as 'high rise' manifolds.

REDUCED CARB CAPACITY

In addition to usually poor runner shape and routing, a two plane manifold compounds it's high RPM breathing problems by halving the amount of carburetion seen by any individual cylinder. In practice, this isn't quite as bad as it may first appear. In a two plane configuration, there is no overlapping of the induction pulses, but in a single plane, quite a lot of overlapping occurs. If all other aspects are equal, a carburetor appears to the engine, to be about 15 to 20% smaller on a two plane than a single

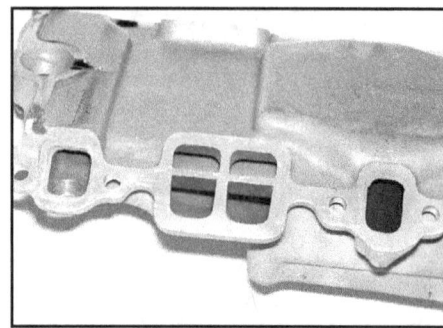

There are numerous unconventional designs on the market. This one from Offenhauser, divides the runners of a four barrel carb so that only the top portion of the runners are active while the carb is operating on the primaries. The intent here is to maintain high port velocities, to supply a better quality of mixture to the engine. The idea has some merit but the execution appears to need some refinement.

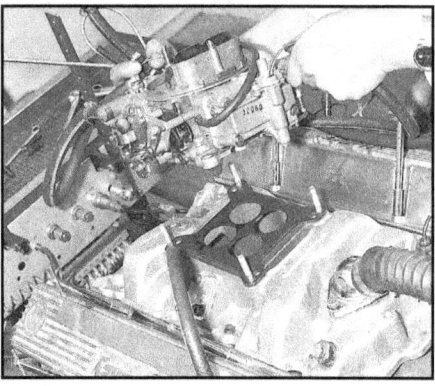

With aluminum manifolds conducting heat at 4 times the rate of cast iron, a thick insulating gasket is of greater importance. If vertical space permits, a 1/2-inch thick Phenolic spacer/gasket is preferred.

plane. This may not make much difference at low RPM, but it does at higher RPM.

When tested on a flow bench, a stock small block Chevrolet intake produced the runner to runner flow differences shown in Fig. 10-4 (page 105). This manifold also produced a roughly similar trend, when the power of each cylinder was determined by means of a Morse test. We could have expected a closer relationship between these two factors, but for the fact that the mixture to the center four cylinders was generally richer than that going to the end ones.

With so many points against it, why are so many original equipment V8 manifolds of the 180° design? Unlikely as it may seem, at this point, there are some very good reasons. By splitting the induction system into two halves, the volume of the intake, as seen by any single cylinder is also halved. This means there is much less damping of the induction pulse and, as a result, the booster functions better and returns much better fuel atomization. This

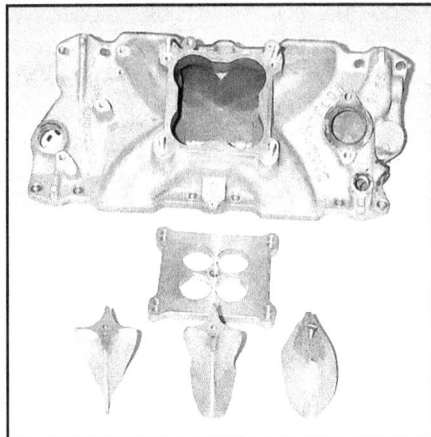

Another idea from Offenhauser. This manifold has a number of 'stuffers' which serve to alter the form and volume of the plenum. Our tests found that the stuffers do indeed change the way the manifold reacts and a degree of tuning to suit the application was apparent.

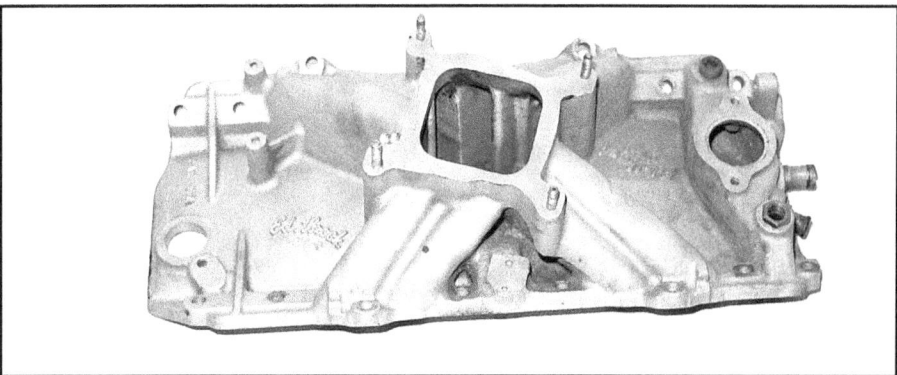

This big block 'X' type manifold was not one of the authors favorites by any means. The twisting of the carb may have been a good idea but the routing of the runners in the form seen here was most certainly not!

has a big influence on output at low rpm. All this leads to better low end output and fuel economy so often associated with two plane manifolds. All these features are just what is needed for a good street motor and that is after all what the factory is building.

BUYING THE RIGHT MANIFOLD

For the typical street rodder interested in a strong day to day transport engine with moderate to fairly good top-end output, a well designed two plane manifold represents a good choice. But the aftermarket proves to be a conglomerate of people whose manifold design capabilities ranges from minimal to highly competent. Among the more competitive companies, manifold design is far from stagnant and what could be the best manifold today may not be the best tomorrow. With this in mind, it pays to research what's out in the marketplace, and what features you should be looking for. You need to have at least a working knowledge of what is good and what is not, so pay attention to what comes next!

Let's analyze the runners first. Air flow is, obviously, an important criteria for anything related to the induction or exhaust system, and the intake manifold is certainly no exception. However, simply putting an intake manifold on a flow bench and producing good air flow figures, will by no means guarantee that it will be a good power producer. The reason is that if made large enough, any runner will flow lots of air regardless of shape. But big runners will, by their nature, introduce a number of unwanted characteristics. Among these will be the

The SP2P manifold from Edelbrock was a small cross sectional area design intended to boost the low end output for true street applications and tow trucks. An advertising 'war' developed between this manifold and the more unconventional Holley 'Z' manifold said to be designed by the late and much respected ....

inevitable low port velocity and a high manifold volume. Both features will soften induction pulses at the booster which in turn impairs atomization. Big port runners then are to be viewed with a certain amount of reservation. They are only likely to work at the top end of the RPM range. A manifold intended for a broad power band must produce good flow figures by virtue of an efficient shape. This allows the use of ports with a moderate cross-sectional area. Such a design strategy inevitably leads to runners that curve gently from the plenum to the cylinder head ports. Unfortunately, these types of manifolds are the hardest to design and make casting patterns for. It is easier to compromise runner design by making a simpler form, with much enlarged cross-sectional areas at the point where any sharp turns are required. Within limits, this is an acceptable technique and more than one manifold manufacturer has got away with it for years. But competition in the manifold business is stiff and this means later generation designs are having to concentrate on more efficient port runners regardless of how much harder they are to produce. Some of the more

........Corvette designer Zora Arkus Duntov. The 'Z' manifold had a runner connecting the back ports together. A quote from one of Holley's top engineers 'We don't know why it works, it just does' When the author conducted a shoot-out between these two manifolds the SP2P was much better at the low end and the 'Z' much better at the top. Seems the 'war was between advertising personnel rather than manifold designers.

modern designs, such as Edelbrock's current Performer manifold (as of 1995), are displaying larger runner curvature from the plenum area and reaping the benefits of the results. Increasing the air flow by improved runner efficiency means, either manifold volume can be reduced for improved low end potential, plus a little upstairs, or volume can be held constant to produce low end equal to stock, but with a greatly improved top end output. Of course, there are occasions when low end power counts for everything. These days, with the popularity of trucks, many owners are looking for improved low end output for towing, plus better mileage. Such requirements led to the development of the Edelbrock SP2P manifold which was a low volume, small cross-sectional area manifold. It enjoyed a great deal of popularity during the gas crunch era of the 70s, but as drivers became accustomed to the higher prices charged at the pumps, so it's popularity waned. By 1990 most intake manifold manufacturers were attempting to design their two plane manifolds to produce the

How to Build Horsepower, Vol. 2

Seen here is two of Edelbrock's dyno cells. After the flow bench work is done much effort is put into dyno testing to fine tune for the application.

bottom end power of a stock intake. Most failed, to a greater or lesser degree to meet this goal. The top end increases targeted, were achieved by a combination of more efficient port design and larger cross sectional areas. For a typical street performance intake to produce more bottom end power without reduction in volume or cross sectional area would mean special attention being paid to fuel distribution. A typical stock V8 manifold in this respect, is nothing more than moderate, but there are power gains to be had in this area. The criteria for designing an intake is to have flow efficient runners with shapes, especially in the plenum area, conducive to good mixture preparation and distribution. A visual inspection of an intake manifold should, at a first approximation, at least give an idea of it's flow potential. Our experience here is that if it doesn't look that good it usually isn't. However, guessing its mixture distribution capabilities is another thing altogether. Here, for the most part, you are forced to rely on the manufacturer's expertise at manifold design. Judging by the design expertise put into some of the manifolds tested on the HTBHP dyno, that's a sobering thought. Fortunately with stiff competition in the marketplace manufacturers are continually updating designs in an effort to upstage the opposition. All the foregoing means that it is important to understand, as far as possible, what is potentially an effective design. This will allow you to avoid buying a less than adequate manifold, which is more commonly done than most people realize.

FUEL DISTRIBUTION

Although complex, air management problems within a manifold can pale to insignificance compared with fuel management. Even with all the modern equipment, hand sorting and correcting mixture distribution problems to give good results at all throttle and RPM conditions becomes exceedingly complex and trying. In the final analysis, it often comes down to a cut and try technique for a satisfactory solution. To demonstrate the complexity of successfully managing air and fuel interactions, some tests run at Iskenderian Racing Cams are worth relating. In an attempt to even up the mixture between cylinders, air valves were installed in those runners that were carrying a rich mixture. The intention was to bleed air into these runners to compensate for the richer mixture they carried. In an effort to achieve the best results these valves were positioned as close to the cylinder head as possible. When put to the test, it was found that opening any one air valve resulted in all the cylinders running leaner. This demonstrates that the air moves around within the intake manifold far more than might normally be supposed and that any one cylinder can pull air from as far away as half way down the runner of another cylinder. With interactions as strong as this, it becomes easier to understand why uniform fuel distribution is not the simplest of goals. The question now is how is it best achieved?

The most basic rule toward developing good mixture distribution is to pay attention to good fuel atomization. This is a point that has been brought up many times before but its importance cannot be overstressed. If atomization is good, the finer droplets of fuel will more nearly follow the pattern of air distribution within the manifold. This means if it enters the plenum at the correct fuel/air ratio, it should come out of the ports still having the correct fuel/air ratio. The more fuel puddles within the manifold, the less likely it is that each cylinder will receive the same mixture ratio. Short of redesigning the carb, the first step toward obtaining good atomization is to make sure the carb selected is not too big for the job. The requirement for good part throttle and low speed output is a strong argument for a vacuum secondary carb. It is obvious that at low speed, an engine's demand for air will be much less, and drawing it all through two barrels instead of four will result in higher venturi gas speeds and better booster operation. Granted, many race cars use four barrel carburetors with synchronous butterfly opening. Although their performance is obvious, it shouldn't take much to see that the application is very different. The operating range of these engines is from 4500 RPM up, so there is no low-speed requirement of any consequence. What works on a race car should not be viewed as necessarily desirable for a street machine. The bottom line here is that for a given air flow, the signal at the booster venturi should be as high as possible. At low RPM this can either mean running all the air through two boosters of typical capability or making sure there is high enough booster signal per CFM of carb flow by utilizing high gain boosters.. Some stock carbs, the 850 Holley among them, have poor booster signal per CFM of flow. The result is a tendency to produce very poor low-speed performance. However, nothing is impossible to improve upon and, as discussed in an earlier chapter, hopping up the air flow and improving the booster signal is a practicality. Such a move often improves the low end significantly.

PLENUM AND RUNNER DISTRIBUTION

Regardless of whatever moves are made at the carburetor, there is always going to be liquid fuel in the manifold. Getting good fuel distribution largely becomes a question of dealing with puddled fuel in an effective manner. The first aspect to consider here is that any fuel puddling will be affected not only by airflow but also by both gravity and vehicle accelerations. Since the center of the manifold plenum is high, there will be a tendency for the fuel to flow down into the runner, favoring some more than others. Apart from any natural tendency toward uneven distribution, a car that leaves the line hard is going to create a raw fuel bias to the back cylinders.

For the most part, the plenum floor is where we deal with mixture distribution problems, though changes in runner design can have an effect. First, let's consider the floor. Very often the key to evening out fuel distribution, or at least avoiding raw fuel going down the runners into the ports, is to make sure that the floor of the plenum is lower than the start of the runner. Creating some kind of fuel trap that discourages liquid from flowing from the plenum floor into the runner is always a good move.

WALL AND PORT FUEL FLOW

All we have discussed so far on fuel management is leading up to the fact that there are two distinct forms of fuel flow within an intake: fuel that is airborne and fuel that runs along the port walls. These are known as port and wall flow respec-

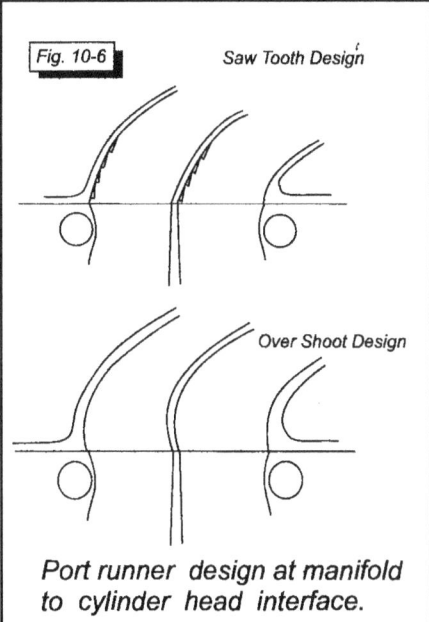

Port runner design at manifold to cylinder head interface.

Here are a number of means of taking the fuel, which tends to run on the outside port wall, and redistributing it more evenly throughout the port. The 'sawtooth' arrangement is one possible solution, but it inevitably costs air flow. An alternative is to "overshoot" the cylinder head port. This achieves better distribution and, if correctly done, enhances air flow.

tively. Normally, one would expect that the greater the proportion of airborne fuel, the better because it would be in smaller droplets and therefore burn better. In contrast, wall borne fuel will have much greater difficulty mixing with the incoming air. Even when it does leave the surface, it is riding and mixs with the air it is likely to produce large droplets. In reality, the relative merits of wall and port flow

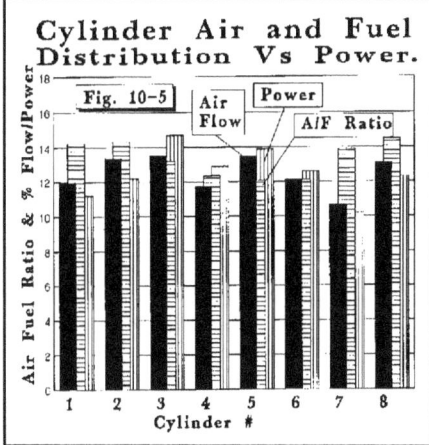

This graph shows the distribution of air and fuel in a typical 180 degree manifold. The air distribution figures are from the flow bench, and the fuel ones are derived from having an oxygen sensor in each cylinder. The power supplied by each cylinder was determined by a 'Morse' test. Note how cylinder #7 had poor airflow and ran lean. This resulted, as would be expected, in a low output from this cylinder.

are not clear and there is plenty of contradictory evidence. For instance, Ford Motor company engineers conducted some clever experiments where they measured the effect of various port to wall fuel ratios. The results indicated a surprisingly small variance in power and economy between one extreme and the other. In direct contrast are the experiments done with vortex generators. When there is a problem with excessive wall flow, the use of a vortex generator has shown relatively big improvements to part throttle fuel economy. Unfortunately, vortex generators of the type shown nearby severely hamper air flow and result in a substantial loss of power. There is still a lesson to be learned from this, and some performance manifold designs have incorporated saw tooth shape ridges on the outside turns to re-introduce wall borne fuel into the air stream. Edelbrock pioneered some manifold designs that incorporated this type of feature. However, it seemed a popular move by most hot rodders to grind them out, as they were seen as an

impediment to airflow. We have never tested a manifold with this sawtooth ridge design on the HTBHP dyno, but there does seem some justification for building in some form of "overshoot" on any manifold that has to make a turn into the cylinder head. Take a look at Fig. 10-6. Here is a runner with a saw-tooth form and one with a certain amount of "overshoot". Putting overshoot into a single four barrel manifold, especially where the runner makes a relatively abrupt turn into the port, achieves two things. First, it tends to redirect fuel to the opposite side of the port, and second, it allows the air to transition from the manifold to the cylinder head with less flow loss. Unfortunately, with the close proximity of paired ports such as we find on a many V8s such a technique can only be applied to any great effect to the outside cylinders. On the positive side though these are the ones that need it most.

VORTEX GENERATOR

The drawing below shows the form of a vortex generator designed for a round port. The original intent of a vortex generator was to cause a large number of random disturbances in the air to promote better fuel/air mixing just prior to ignition. As can be seen from its design, it is likely to achieve this without difficulty. Studies of wet flow through vortex generators shows a strong tendency to redirect the fuel flow in toward the middle of the port. This means that much of the wallborne fuel flow prior to the vortex generator now becomes airborne. Just how much fuel stays airborne after passing through the vortex generator is a subject of conjecture. Even if a portion of the fuel does reattach itself to the port wall, the fuel/air mix is still likely to be much better on arrival at the cylinders.

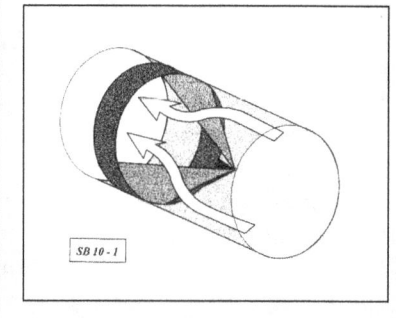

How To Build HORSEPOWER: Chapter 11

Carburetors & Intake Manifolds
High Performance Intake Systems

Most readers will be inquisitive as to how much of an increase in power an induction change will make. We've already dealt with the improvement that is likely to be seen by changing to a high efficiency air filter assembly. Such an induction change is generally easy to make, so even for the least experienced mechanic, it is far from daunting to do. However, when we start moving into the realms of carburetor and intake manifold changes, things become a little more complex. In most cases, this is going to involve draining the coolant system, and for most V8s, removing the distributor to access the intake manifold for removal. For this reason, most people need to be a little more sure of what they're going to achieve by manifold change. In many instances, manifold changes are dictated by virtue of a change from a two to a four barrel carburetor. In such instances, it is not just a single component change that we're dealing with. Nonetheless we will deal separately with carb and manifold. Our first step is too analyze how much difference is likely to be seen by replacing a two barrel carburetor with a four barrel unit on a relatively stock motor. Fig. 11-1 shows the result of just such a change. The base engine used here was essentially a blueprinted street unit. The intake manifold used for both before and after tests was a cleaned up, factory four barrel QuadraJet intake manifold. This was used because of the basic similarity of the intake runners of the two and four barrel factory manifolds. Because of this, it was concluded that we could duplicate a two barrel manifold relatively easy by utilizing an adapter plate to adapt the two barrel carb to the four barrel manifold. Approaching things this way, meant that only a carburetor change was made as opposed to a carburetor and manifold. As can be seen from the figures in Fig. 11-1, the four barrel carburetor started to pay off about mid-range and by the time the engine reached it's peak RPM, power was up by over 30 horsepower.

MANIFOLD CHANGE

For whatever reason intake manifolds seem inordinately alluring especially to the less experience hot rodder. Very often during the installation of an intake manifold much of the rest of the induction system will be changed. This comes

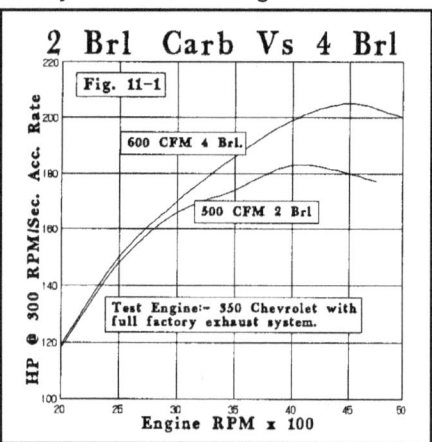

Two barrel carburetors are used on V8s for no other reason than production costs. No V8 of any consequence should use a 2 barrel carb unless mandated by race regulations designed to limit the power of the engines. Shown here is the power increase on a near stock 350 small block Chevy. It becomes significantly greater as the power potential of the base engine increases.

RPM	1 B/Line	2 +Int	3 HP Inc	4 +750	5 HP Inc	6 B/Line	7 +Int	8 HP Inc	9 +750	10 HP Inc
2000	118	116	-2	116	0	129	126	-3	127	-2
2500	145	145	0	144	1	164	160	-4	160	-4
3000	174	178	+4	179	1	199	203	+4	202	+3
3500	194	202	+8	203	1	235	242	+7	243	+1
4000	197	206	+9	206	0	266	277	+11	278	+1
4500	197	205	+7	206	1	284	296	+12	299	+3
5000	181	188	+7	189	1	289	302	+13	306	+4
5500	-	-	-	-	-	284	296	+12	301	+5

Fig. 11-2

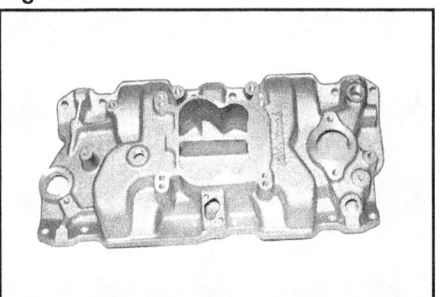

The original Edelbrock Performer manifold had squared off runner forms as seen here. This made for easier pattern making, but flow had to be achieved by larger, rather than more efficient runner design. The later Performer...

...used more efficient runner shapes, which can more easily be appreciated from ...

... this shot of the runner casting core form. This is the upper plenum set of runners and from this shot, the progressive curves to the cylinder head ports can easily be seen.

about not necessarily for change's sake but because certain parts are simply not reused. Probably number one on the list of parts that are not subsequently reused are the power robbing components that make up the stock air filter system. Usually, the intake manifold will be installed right along with other performance enhancing induction system parts. However, because the intake manifold looks like the 'fastest' part, very often it will be credited with the power increase delivered, when in fact, a large portion of the increase has been brought about by a freer flowing, and probably cooler running induction system ahead of the intake manifold itself. To put things into perspective, it is worthwhile looking at the gains given by a typical intake manifold change on stock, or near stock engine as opposed to the power brought about by changing the intake manifold and other components. Just how much gain can be expected from an intake manifold change depends upon a number of factors. Not the least of these is the spec of the original engine, how much it's starved of air and how much better the replacement intake manifold is. If we analyze an engine's prime sources of flow restriction we find, in most instances the worst restriction occurs about 1 inch before and after the intake or exhaust valve. Changing to a high-performance intake manifold will make no difference to the restriction caused by the valves, although it can be expected to make a moderate reduction in overall restriction. The greatest gains will come about if the inefficiency of the original manifold rivals that of the valves.

Gains seen from an intake manifold change depend primarily on how much more air it allows the engine to inhale. In addition to this is the influence of fuel distribution and mixture quality. Any added power achieved is due only to the combined improvement in these areas over the stock manifold. If the existing

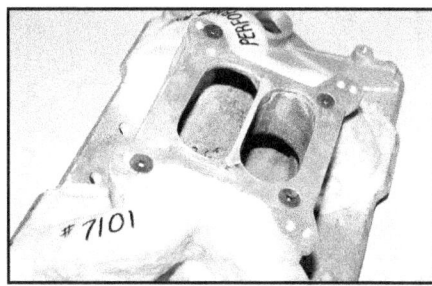

Prototype Manifolds are usually built up of existing casting parts, such as the carb pad and the cylinder head manifold face and valley cover. Onto this, a fiber glass (or similar) and resin model is made and dyno tested. Usually, these models are so well insulated from engine heat that they freeze moisture in the air around the runners.

air demand of the engine is not particularly high because of poor flowing heads, a restrictive exhaust, short cam timing and other flow limiting factors, a change in manifolds isn't likely to add much extra power. If these factors are appreciated, it will be seen that there's no magic involved. To demonstrate the point, take a look at the test results in the chart in Fig. 11-2. The figures in column 1 are for a stock motor dumping it's exhaust through a low restriction dyno cell exhaust system. These figures were produced on a 650 CFM Holley carburetor installed via an adapter plate to a stock intake manifold. For column 2, a Holley Contender manifold was installed. When tested 'bare' on the flow bench, this manifold typically showed a 20 to 30% increase in air flow over the stock manifold, depending on which runner was tested. As you can see from column 3, it really didn't show any increase in output until 3000 RPM, and its greatest increase was at 4000 rpm where it was 9 HP over the stock intake. For column 4, the 650 Holley was replaced with the 750 vacuum secondary Holley. An insignificant

If you are successful at engine building, it is possible to have more low-end torque than the car can put to the road, as is the case seen here with the author's 4000 pound 12½ second, Trans Am. The cure, if one is available, is to install a higher (numerically smaller) rear end ratio.

The Weiand 8004 manifold, in both its early and current (as of '96) form is an item that we have found to be good on engines from 350 up. If you are building a 350 with a quarter-inch stroke in it, to give 383 as a true street motor both the Weiand 8004 and the Edelbrock Performer are worthy of consideration.

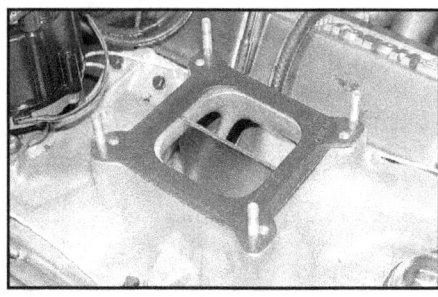

Some manifolds can be quite fussy over the way they are setup. For instance, this Weiand manifold is supplied with a divider plate for optional use. We have found that without it some engines will drop as much as 50 ft.-lbs. With it, the manifold usually produces the sort of positive results you would expect.

change in output strongly suggests the engine required no more airflow than the 650 Holley was capable of delivering to the engine. The fact that the 750 did not show a significant loss anywhere in the rev range, is a good argument in favor of vacuum secondary carburetors for street applications. The figures shown in column 6 were produced by a mildly reworked version of the engine in the previous columns. This engine differed from that in column 1 in that the heads were street ported and had larger valves. In addition, the stock cam was re-timed to give optimal results. It's interesting to note that these two changes produced well over an 80 horsepower increase, even with the same stock intake manifold and 650 carburetor as used in column 1. Making the change to the Holley intake produced the results in column 8. Here, you can see that the peak gains went up to 13 horsepower, as opposed to the 9 horsepower given in column 3. The reason being that valve restriction has been reduced, so the benefits of the intake manifold were greater, as were the benefits of the larger, 750 CFM carburetor. The added flow of the 750 Holley produced up to 5 horsepower increase at the top end of the RPM range. Because it was a vacuum secondary carburetor, it produced this extra power without any major detriment to the low-end output of this engine.

MORE CUBIC INCHES

When making a manifold change, it is hardly surprising that the bigger the engine, the greater the possibility of making extra horsepower. Looking at the larger displacement engines, that is 400 cubic inches or more, we find that stock, they tend to have carburetors the same or only slightly larger than the typical small block. As a consequence, there is often much more power to be gained on the big block sized engine from changing the intake manifold and carburetor than a small block.

If a change of carburetor for a big block engine is contemplated, it is important to note, that it is often difficult to establish the CFM rating of the stock carb. Without knowledge of the existing carb's capacity, it often gets inadvertently replaced by a smaller carburetor than the original. For instance, many QuadraJet carburetors, as used on big block Chevrolets, have flow capabilities in excess of 800 cfm. Correctly calibrated, the Q-Jet is a fine carburetor and it does little to enhance the engine's per-

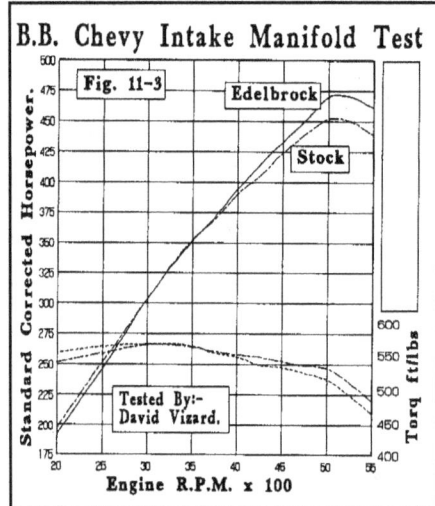

The Edelbrock Performer for the 454 big block Chevy in only a moderate state of tune proved to be worth about 22 HP at the top end, while losing about 15 ft.-lbs. at the bottom of the used RPM range. This, and the considerably reduced manifold weight, helped the car, which had an over abundance of low-end torque, to launch with less tendency to blaze the tires.

formance potential by replacing it with a smaller carburetor. Having made that point, let's see what the potential gains are from installing an aftermarket intake manifold on a typical big block Chevrolet. Fig. 11-3 shows the numbers generated by a 454 big block Chevy. This engine utilized the same QuadraJet carburetor in both the before and the after tests. This carb was stock, apart from some butterfly shaft and venturi clean up work to enhance flow. When flow tested on the flow bench, it produced a little over 900 CFM of flow. Although GM makes a number of different manifolds for the big block, the differences between them are usually brought about by differing hood clearance requirements. Replacing the stock manifold, we find that in this particular instance the aftermarket manifold, a two plane Edelbrock item, reduced torque up to about 3000 RPM, and from there it went on to increase output, eventually giving some 22 horsepower increase. A first impression may be that sacrificing low-end torque for more top-end output may appeared a bad move, but with a well-tuned big block in a typical sedan, we find there is usually so much low-end, that traction can be a problem. It actually helps to bleed off some low-end torque simply to allow the car to get a grip on the pavement. On the other hand, if the engine is to power a heavy truck then, the loss of any low end output could well be a penalty.

SMALL ENGINES

Two or four barrel carbureted V8s may constitute a majority, but they certainly aren't the only applications that we should consider in a book of this nature. Although fuel injection is rapidly taking over from carburetors on small four and six cylinder engines, we still find a large number of high-performance carburetors being used. The reason for this is twofold. First, if an engine comes stock with a carburetor, it is inevitably too small for anything much above stock output. Second, if the engine is fuel injected, it is usually for mileage and emission reasons rather than power. Very often factory fuel injected cars have throttle butterflies barely any bigger than a typical two barrel carburetor. As a consequence, for outright performance and race applications, it's often a less expensive deal to replace the entire fuel injection system with a set of high performance carburetors such as Webers or Dellortos. Making a change to such carbs means investing a lot of money, because it always involves a complementary change in manifold. Just how much power gain is made by going to a sophisticated set of carburetors on an independent runner induction system depends on how starved of air the engine was in the first place. In addition to any gains brought about by freer breathing, we must add the fact that an IR system pressure wave tunes far better than a typical stock carb and intake manifold. Since most European engines tend to be in the 90 to 150 cubic inch range, we'll use a 122 inch Pinto engine to demonstrate the potential of a set of side draft carburetors on both a mild, as well as wildly modified engine. In Fig. 11-4, we see the before and after curve produced by a mild street modified engine. Curve #1 was produced with the stock two barrel down draft Weber carburetor of some 280 CFM capacity. The baseline engine was tested with a low back pressure dyno exhaust system typical of that used on the street. As can be seen, the side draft Weber 40 DCOE carburetors boosted the output of the engine throughout its working range. When essentially the same engine is modified to a higher spec in terms of the head, cam, CR and exhaust, we find that the increase given by a set of appropriately sized side draft carbs is, as expected, far greater. In Fig. 11-5, an engine in near race trim produced curve #1 when tested with the stock two barrel carburetor. When this carb was replaced with a pair of 48 DHLA Dellortos, the power output climbed by almost 40 horsepower along with an appreciable torque increase.

IR SYSTEMS AND V8S

Using an independent runner system, as just described, on a four cylinder engine is not limited to just such applications. When the small block Chevy and Ford V8 first became a popular source of power for specialized European originated sport and GT cars they were commonly used with down draft Weber IDA type carburetors. There are numerous reasons for going this route. First and most importantly, it was known that these carburetors deal with high cornering Gs without necessarily suffering from fuel surge and the resultant fuel starvation of a number of the engine's cylinders. In addition, some European engine builders were far more familiar with these sophisticated carburetors than they were with the fundamentally simpler Holleys. The fact that every circuit on a Weber can be calibrated with the relevant jets, emulsion tubes and air correctors meant that good results could be virtually guaranteed without the need for a major carburetor development program. Last and

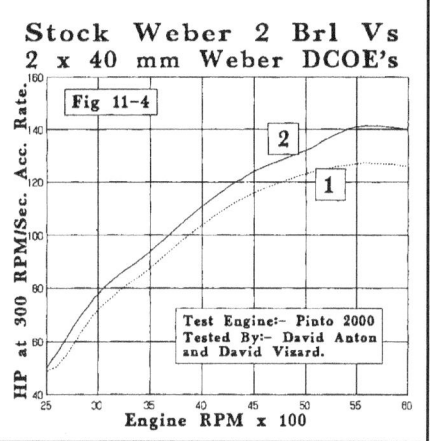

With any big block engine, unless it is a really short cammed unit with more or less stock heads, there is always a problem getting enough carb and manifold air flow.

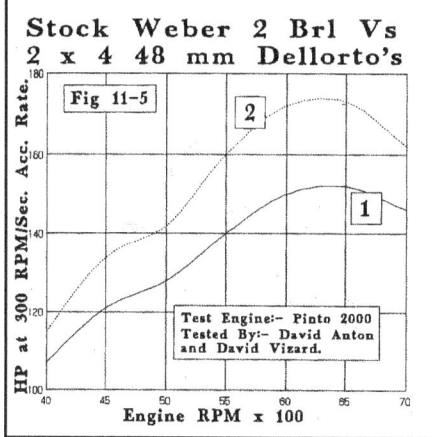

A pair of side drafts on a 4 cylinder street motor helps output everywhere. It is just like adding cubic inches, except there is no mileage penalty as long as the carbs are correctly calibrated.

On a race 4 cylinder engine, a big set of side draft carbs is worth a lot of extra output both in terms of torque throughout the RPM range and top-end power.

Even a reworked 1300 CFM Dominator, such as this Braswell unit, is hard pushed to supply the goods. The 454 shown here, which was basically a 600 ft.-lb., 600 horsepower engine really needed about 1500 cfm.

most importantly, it was known that their high air flow capacity, as much as 375 CFM per barrel, is well-suited toward making a lot of horsepower from the engine. Also, another point in favor of an IR system is that there are no fuel distribution problems and because every cylinder is guaranteed the same mixture, power, torque and fuel efficiency are up.

To many enthusiasts, a V8 carbureted IR system looks like a calibration and installation nightmare. In reality, it is in most instances significantly easier to go this route than it is to install a programmable fuel injection system. Once the carb calibration is understood (as described in a previous chapter), setting these carburetors up becomes relatively straightforward, especially if a chassis dynamometer of adequate capability is at hand. The performance gains, especially for street and road race applications, achieved by IR installations are significant.

Going hand-in-hand with improved low-end output is the superior idle quality produced by an IR system compared to a plenum system. The reason for this becomes apparent when we look at engine vacuum at idle. When a number of cylinders are joined, as in a typical single four barrel induction system, the plenum volume is drawn down to a partial vacuum. If there is a significant amount of overlap, then a cylinder just starting it's induction cycle connects the entire intake system to the exhaust via the overlap. Because there is a partial vacuum in the intake, a certain amount of exhaust will be drawn into the intake and pollute the incoming charge. This necessitates increasing the idle speed and richening the mixture to compensate.

With an IR system, the vacuum created in the runner, largely exists only when the piston starts it's downward stroke. Prior to this, there is, compared to a plenum type intake, almost no vacuum existing in the intake port during the overlap period. As a result, reduced exhaust pollution of the intake charge occurs from this source. This means that the idle mixture used, can be much leaner as the fresh charge is more easily ignited. Also, the ill effects a big cam can have on part throttle operation at low RPM, are substantially reduced. It is not uncommon to achieve a smooth 600 RPM idle on a V8 equipped with a moderate race cam.

Considerable experience on both the street and race track with IR systems, has always shown them in a very favorable light. As a project, a 350 cubic inch small block Chevy was built using four 48 DHLA down draft Dellortos for (would you believe) a working truck motor. Low end pulling power, mileage and drivability were prime requirements right along with power. On seeing this installation, the most common response was that the engine couldn't possibly have any low-end power because of the massive 2200 cfm of carb capacity. Additionally, it was reasoned that the engine must have been really fuel hungry as there were, in effect, eight carburetors on the engine. This goes to show how a little knowledge can often be a dangerous thing. In practice, fuel consumption was excellent because the same, precisely calibrated, well-atomized fuel mixture was delivered to every cylinder. Indeed, the mixture calibration was almost as accurate as a good fuel injection system. Consequently, mileage was about 7% better than a good vacuum secondary single four barrel induction system. As far as the huge number of CFM is concerned, we have to remember that since this is an IR system and each

Here is a close up of the Braswell carb mounted on yet another Mag Masters polished intake. Note the annular discharge boosters. These were instrumental in delivering a power curve that would allow 5th gear to give strong acceleration from as little as 1500 RPM.

cylinder only sees the 350 odd cubic feet/minute that's actually attached to it. Therefore, the atomization at low speed, because of the very sharp pulse seen at the booster, was very good. As a result of this and the induction length involved, the low end torque delivered by such a carburetor set-up was about the same as adding some 50 extra cubic inches to the engine without the corresponding increase in fuel consumption.

At the end of the day, the result was an extremely high torque engine giving very good mileage during normal day-to-day usage. When the throttle pedal was floored, performance was very Corvette like, i.e. 14.2 seconds for the quarter mile with a 102 MPH trap speed just as it is driven on the street. Not bad for a 4800 pound truck that turns in good mileage.

In terms of airflow, the 48 down draft Dellortos, which are basically bored out 45s, lag behind the airflow given by the 48 Webers and their larger brethren. Because of their price and the more than adequate airflow for applications up to 45 to 50 horsepower per cylinder, the DeLortos make a good set-up for street use. But if more top-end power is the goal, then the greater airflow of the Webers or some of the carbs discussed in Chapter 9 are needed. If hard cash is not an obstacle, the bigger carbs such as the 48 Webers are more than capable of producing good low-end output when used in a short cammed motor and correctly set-up, especially in terms of venturi size. Fig. 11-6 shows the power curves produced by one the author's truck motors, in this instance a 9:1 unit, with both a four x 48 Dellortos installation and a 600 Holley. With increased compression and a little more cam, a similar engine to this (chapter 9) made about 20 horsepower more along with more torque. With more exotic heads and roller cams, some really high, but streetable outputs, can be achieved. A set of 48 IDA Webers on one of the author's fully prepared 350s produced good low-end, almost <u>470 lbs.-ft. of torque, over 510 horsepower</u>, and with 3000 total CFM of Weber carburetion.

MANIFOLD COMPARISONS

Although there are a tremendous number and variety of performance intake manifolds, by far the greatest portion are made for the small block Chevy. This market probably represents as much as 75% of all performance manifolds sold worldwide. As can be expected, there's a great deal of sales competition within this market, and there are a lot of diverse designs for the hot rodder to choose from. One may ask if all these different approaches to developing horsepower work equally well? <u>Based on our experience the answer is that they most certainly do not.</u> Dyno tests from a great number of intake manifolds over the past 20 years indicate that there are probably as many that do not work as there are that do. However, because of the design changes that occur at relatively frequent intervals and the fact there are so many manifolds available, it is impractical to test them all. This leaves us with only one viable option, that being to tell you which of those tested do work. However, because a manifold does not appear on our list does not mean that it doesn't work, it could equally mean that we have not had the opportunity of testing one.

Following is a list of intake manifolds known to function well on a 350 cubic inch or larger small block Chevy engine. An important point to note here is that since the 350 is the most popular displacement in use, most manifolds are developed on that size engine. When equipping a smaller engine than this with an intake manifold, you should be aware that very often these manifolds won't show any improvement until correspondingly higher RPM. And in some instances this maybe a higher rpm than you are prepared to run your engine to. For instance, a particular intake manifold may only deliver extra power on a 350 from 3000 RPM up, and below that may show a small loss. On a 300 cubic inch engine that same manifold may not show a gain until 4500 RPM and the low-end loss may well be even greater than that seen on a 350. In which case, unless you are intentionally building a high RPM 300 inch engine, changing the intake manifold for one with dubious low end performance may not be the best way to go, unless it was accompanied by compatible torque improving changes in other areas. The usual reason for loosing low end output is that the carb booster signal has become inadequate because the manifolds usually greater volume has damped the induction pulse. This leads to poor atomization and, well, we have covered that story in earlier chapters. The moral here, is if you're building a street motor, one of the first rules of the game is to make sure that you are building the most practical, cost effective bottom end possible. This means cubic inches is almost always the way to go.

Our experience indicates that some manifolds can be rather fussy to use. That is, they are sensitive to the specification of the engine. The manifolds recommended in SB 11-1 (below) are not, for the most part engine spec sensitive. This makes them a far safer bet for building an engine that for one reason or another will not have the benefit of being set up and sorted on a dyno. On the other side of the coin, we have found one or two manifolds that in many instances will drop a considerable amount of hp over stock. During some dyno tests we've seen a loss of as much as 50 horsepower For this reason, it is suggested that unless you are prepared to do you own testing, stick to the manifolds recommended here for near fool proof results.

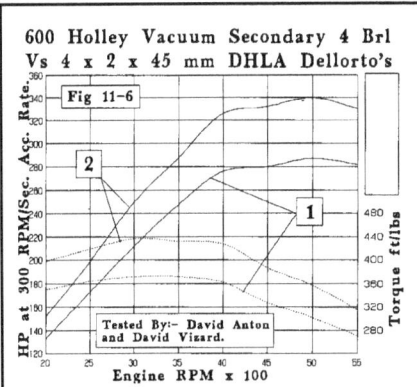

What you see here is the typical torque increase given by a set of carbs on an IR induction system. In this back to back test, only the induction was changed and, in this instance, the torque went up by some 70 ft.-lbs. However the cam spec required for an IR induction system is a little different to a single 4-barrel induction system. With an appropriately speced cam of the same intake duration, another 10-15 ft/lbs can be had.

SB 11-1
Here is a list of two plane manifolds that are known to work well as of 1996. This represents about 1/3 of the manifolds that have been very thoroughly tested. In alphabetical order they are: Chevrolet LT1 factory manifold, Edelbrock's Performer and Performer RPM, Holley Contender, and Weiand's 8004. For a typical street 350 in the 250-300 hp range these manifolds will deliver an increase in power from about 3000 rpm-3500 rpm mark upwards with the peak increase around 12-20 hp.

How To Build HORSEPOWER: Chapter 12
Carburetors & Intake Manifolds
Modifying & Building Manifolds

The view held by many performance enthusiasts is that most intake manifold manufacturers are producing close to 'state of the art' pieces. Unfortunately, this rather idealistic view is a little removed from reality. Such a viewpoint must be tempered by the fact that the larger intake manifold manufacturers are primarily in business to sell large quantities of functional, cost effective merchandise. At the end of the day good business means making money. If a product is already a strong seller it is bad business to redesign both it and the expensive casting patterns needed to produce it. The possible loss of a number one position as a horsepower producer does not cause mainstream manifold companies to change their intake manifold designs. It is the loss of their position in terms of sales that eventually brings about a design change.

In the performance field, engine development moves along at a rapid pace. An intake manifold that may have been a top performer a year or two ago may now be lacking whatever it takes to be a part of an engine combination with winning potential. For a company producing large quantities of intakes, this can bring about a conflict between good business practice and good race practice. The manufacturer will not want to change a high sales volume manifold, but serious racers, who are a minority group, are always demanding whatever the latest technology can produce. In an effort to get an edge over the competition, race engine builders are researching manifold designs and bringing about design changes over a very short period of time. The usual technique employed is to base a new manifold design on a good existing off the shelf design. This has brought about a small, but nonetheless thriving, industry of manifold modifiers. These people take an existing manifold and modify it, thereby filling in the gap between last year's and last week's technology. To improve any already functional intake manifold takes a lot of time dedicated to flow bench, dyno

Port matching to the intake gasket is acceptable provided that the gasket ports are about the right size. Bear in mind, they may not be because it is unlikely that the gasket designer employed a flow bench during the design procedure!

When heads and blocks are machined, the manifold will need corrective machining to restore the original fit. Many machine shops are reticent to do this because they do not have the necessary tooling to do a cost effective job. In our shop, we use the Brzezinski 'Roll-over' fixture which makes manifold and head milling a breeze.

and track testing. Getting the ultimate is problematical even for the pros, but making improvements to existing manifolds can be achieved by anyone with a little patience, a die grinder and some welding gear.

MODIFYING STOCK MANIFOLDS

It really isn't necessary to go out and spend hundreds of dollars or more on an intake manifold just to practice intake manifold modifying skills. It is entirely practical to hone such skills and produce a highly functional street manifold without spending more than a few dollars. A great deal can often be achieved by reworking stock intake manifolds, and in many instances, the results can be as good, if not better, than many "off-the-shelf" aftermarket manifolds.

Performance based side draft manifold designs for carbs such as Webers, SUs, Strombergs etc. rarely present problems in terms of physically carrying out the modifications, as all areas of the runners are accessible. For 360 degree V8 intakes, the situation is often a little more difficult. Some of the runners have curves that make access difficult, but rarely impossible. However, modifying a 180 degree two plane manifold is usually a lot more difficult, both from the point of view of access, and determining what shapes to employ. If you have some kind of pattern to work to, reworking a stock manifold can be a very inexpensive exercise toward achieving more power.

If the intent is to modify existing manifolds, having a flow bench certainly helps and in the case of a two plane manifold, it is almost a necessity. Using a flow bench, plus suitable reworking materials in terms of grinding wheels, cutters and emery sanding rolls, it is possible to modify a stock small block Chevy four barrel iron manifold to good effect. Using these simple tools, we undertook such a project in the workshop to demonstrate the results possible.

The first step was to spend time on the flow bench to determine not only which way the air went when it came out of the carburetor, but also which way the fuel was likely to go. This was done with pieces of cotton, spray cans of engineer's layout blue, a fair amount of careful thinking and a lot of experience in airflow. The manifold seen on page 125 was the result. Even though this manifold did not flow as much

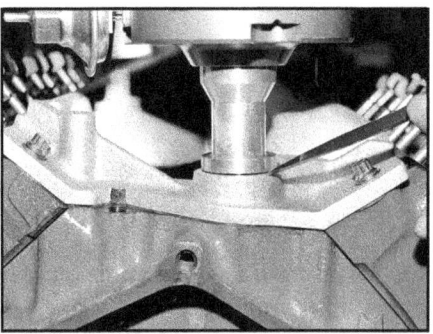
Machining the manifold lowers the distributor mounting pad on many engines. This distributor is bottomed out and still has not seated on the manifold pad. Suitable spacers must be used to rectify this situation.

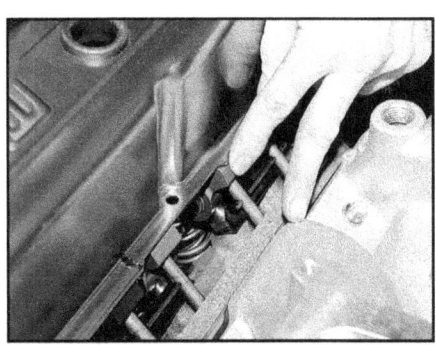
Many manifolds have the top surface of the port runners considerably higher than stock. This often interferes with aftermarket valve covers, such as these aluminum Moroso items. Cutting the covers as shown here allows manifold removal without first taking off the covers.

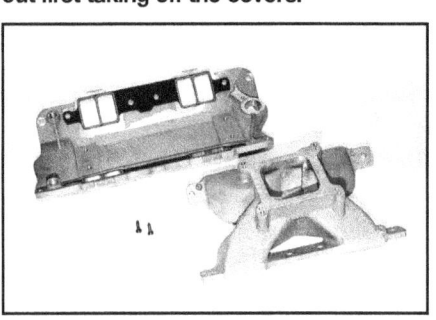
... separated from the base, it can first be matched to the head ports, then the manifold matched to the base. The same technique can ...

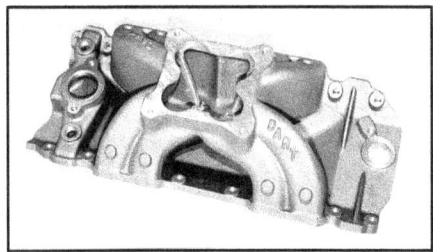
Attention to the form of the leading edge in manifolds feeding paired intake ports, such as Chevrolet, appears to be an important performance aspect. Many of the best performing manifolds are applying learned lessons here. For instance, this highly functional Dart BB Chevy manifold has the curved, laid back form discussed ...

On many Chevrolet manifolds there is insufficient clearance between the oil pressure fitting and the manifold at the point indicated. Check this and cut the manifold accordingly before you start on anything else.

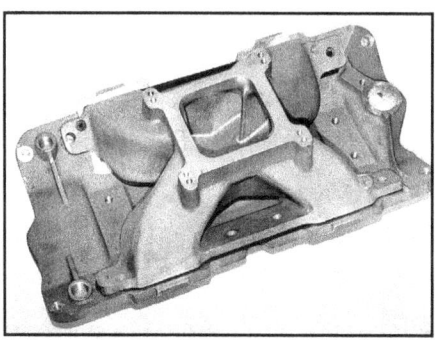
JV, the boss at Brodix, sent this manifold along for us to look at. The concept makes port matching about as simple as it can get. Because the manifold can be ...

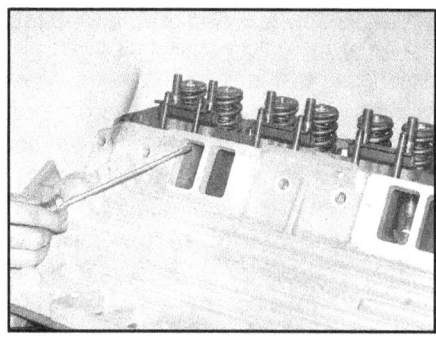
... be used with CB Performance's 4 x 2 Dellorto manifold for a small block Chevy.

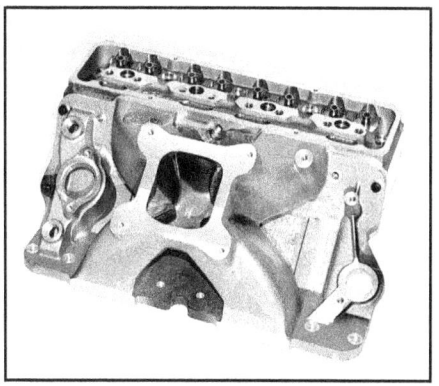
... as does this Brodix S/B Chevy manifold.

How to Build Horsepower, Vol. 2

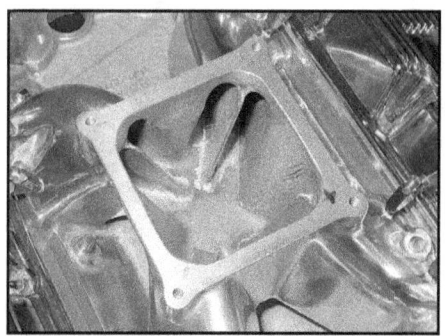

This DV modified BB Chevy manifold has the same type of curve. The one shown here is for use with a Dominator carb and ...

... this one with a modified 4150 series carb having 1000 CFM capability.

air as a typical two plane aftermarket manifold, it produced some very satisfying results. Installed on one of our test engines, it made the same peak power as the best aftermarket manifold we have tested, but on the way up it produced considerably more torque. It has been our experience that in most instances, aftermarket manifolds achieve most of their extra airflow by using ports which are not only a little more streamlined, but also larger. In the case of the manifold we developed here, a lot of attention was paid to both air and fuel management within the manifold. Minimum runner sizes were sought, thereby keeping the overall manifold volume to a minimum. Such a tactic allows a stock carburetor to produce good low-speed atomization because of minimized induction pulse damping. The net result was an intake manifold that, when use in conjunction with a stock automatic transmission, would out perform any commercially produced, off the shelf two plane manifold.

The DV manifold used a half inch open spacer to raise the carburetor above its original position. This allowed a certain degree of carb barrel sharing as per a 360 degree manifold. The shaping of the center part of the manifold into the unusual shape seen in the photos is dictated both by airflow from the barrels and the fact that due allowance was made for airflow to feed either bank from each side of the carb, plus the need to minimize manifold volume. Additionally, it was an attempt to even out the fuel distribution from the carb to the cylinders. Though the center part of the manifold was complex in shape, it did, for the most part, achieve all three goals. The result was just as expected, a sizable torque increase throughout the RPM range instead of just towards the middle and top-end, as is the case with most manifolds.

MODIFYING SINGLE PLANE MANIFOLDS

The 360 degree type manifolds are most often the subject of modifications because they easily produce the best mid- to top-end horsepower for competition work. With that in mind, we'll dissect a typical intake manifold into various sections in an effort to establish some basic techniques that will allow a manifold to be successfully modified. This means having a good idea as to where metal should be removed or added.

Starting at the point where the air exits from the carburetor, we find that most popular race style manifolds, such as the Holley Strip Dominator and the Edelbrock Victor Junior, have an inadequate plenum volume for most 350 cubic inch or more race engines. This appears to have been an intentional move on the part of the manufacturer. Adding a spacer is easy, and most applications need one for the increased plenum volume it produces. But should it not be needed, it takes a lot more to remove the added volume of a cast in spacer. Some versions of the more popular race manifolds already have the spacer volume cast in. Modifying these manifolds is very difficult because the extra height of the carb pad severely restricts access to the port areas that need to be reworked.

In most instances then, the first modification is to add a spacer between the carburetor and manifold. Typically, a two inch spacer gets the job done. There are a number of different types of spacers available. The most common is the open spacer, which does not continue the form of the carburetor barrel into the spacer. Probably the next most common is the semi-open spacer where the carb barrels are continued into the spacer, flaring to an open form about half way through. Then we have the

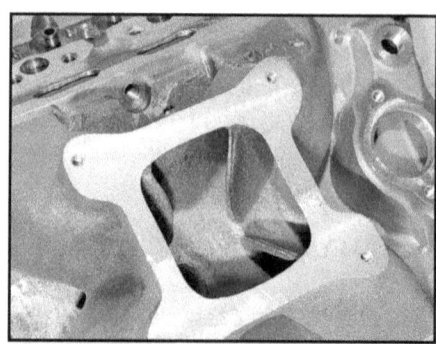

Although a plenum, such as seen on this Brodix manifold, is functional "as is," it is worth while dressing the leading edges of the runner dividers, to present a smooth radius to the incoming air.

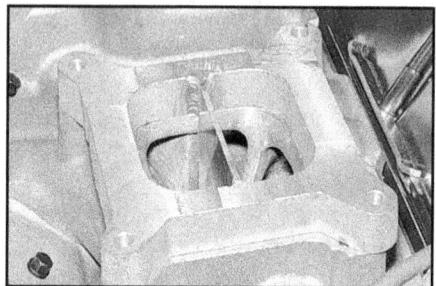

Because of the low vaporization rate and the large quantities of fuel involved, alcohol carbed engines like a strong booster signal. By adding a plenum divider, the induction pulse damping is reduced, and as a result, throttle response in the lower RPM range is significantly improved.

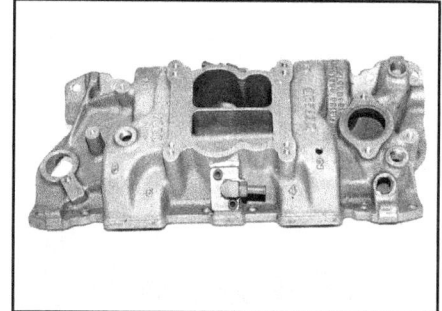

This Weiand manifold was modified for our fuel octane/temperature tests. The exhaust passage has been welded shut and fittings installed to route cold water through instead. Although slower on the warm up, a water heated intake is far preferable to an exhaust heated manifold because it supplies much nearer ideal heating for all weather conditions. Not too hot in the summer because it can be shut off, and not too cold in the winter so icing will be prevented.

type of spacer where the round barrels flare out into a form that matches the manifold's plenum entrance. In term of airflow those spacers that continue the form of the carb barrels usually flow best, but as previously discussed, airflow is not the sole criteria with which we must deal. In addition to airflow mixture quality, fuel distribution needs must be met. In the absence of a flow bench and dyno, the safest choice is to go with an open spacer as it is the easiest to work with toward developing a strong working combination. Although ultimately the more complex spacer may well prove to be the best, they can often take much more time and effort to refine to a fully functional form.

PLENUM AND PORT ENTRANCE

Once high velocity air exits the carburetor, it enters the plenum and undergoes a substantial velocity reduction. As the velocity drops so the pressure rises over that seen farther upstream. This will cause a certain amount of the fuel that may have vaporized to return to liquid form. Conversely, any heat in the intake will reverse this process. In a typical race manifold, we will be dealing with a lot of wet fuel flow and a certain amount of vaporized fuel. Our first job is to try and attain equal fuel distribution within the manifold, and that means equalizing fuel flow down each runner. In this respect, we have to take into account that fuel droplets will not take turns like air. In most intake manifolds, but certainly not all, one of the busiest areas is in the region of the port roof and its junction with the plenum. Without an adequate radius at this point, two things happen. First, fuel droplets do not make the corner, which results in the bottom part of the port becoming fuel rich ,and the top, high flow part, fuel lean. Second, anything resembling a sharp corner at the top of the port is going to cut airflow into the port.

At this stage, it helps to look at the port and plenum junction and view it as if it were an independent ram stack leading out of an airbox. To this end, we need to visualize the wall between the two adjacent ports as the sides of a ram stack having only a very small 'lead in' radius. Flow into a ram stack is greatly affected by how big this lead in radius is. If you look at ram stacks or ram pipes on any purpose built engine, you will see they use a large radius to help the air make the turn into the pipe so as to minimize edge effect losses. If there isn't an adequate radius at this point, the air will not make the tight turn into the runner. The tighter the radius the air has to negotiate, the more it increases an effect known as the vena contracta (see Figs. 9-3 to 9-6 in Chapter 9). This effectively reduces the apparent area at the beginning of the ram stack, and it has the same effect on the port runner

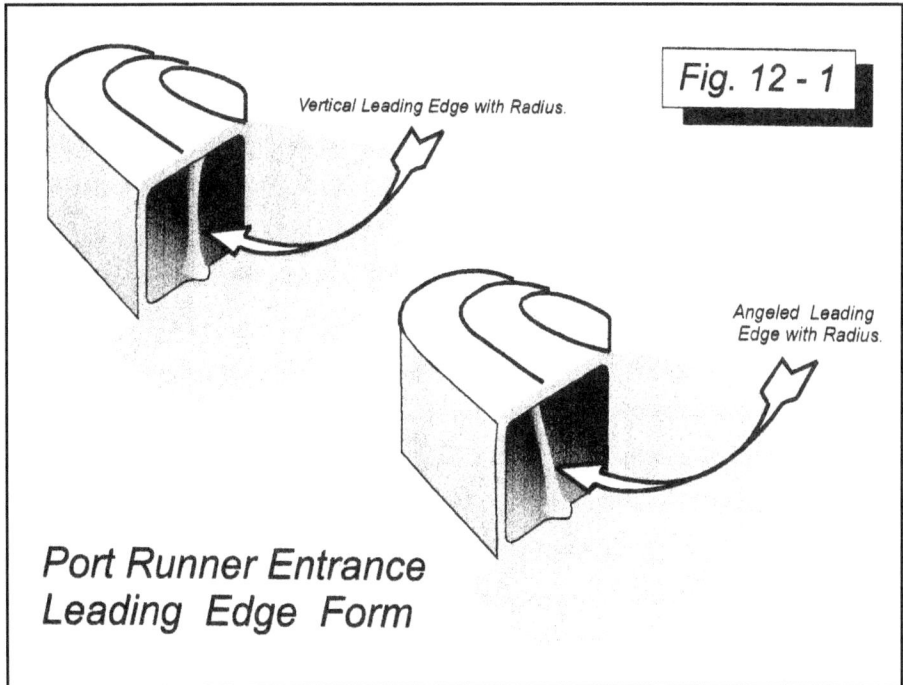

On many single plane manifolds, there is power to be had by cutting the top edge of the divider between each paired set of runners as is shown here.

entrance in the intake manifold. The higher the air velocity, the more important it is to have a large radius at the port runner juncture with the plenum. The first move toward improving flow is to form a larger radius turn at the top of the port because it is normally, but not always, a busy area.

Apart from the use of a large entrance radius, further enhancements to the way the air makes this turn can be made. If the top part of the dividing wall is cut back from the plenum, the air will initially enter a channel two ports wide, thus providing a more progressive speed increase before going down the operative runner. Fig. 12-1 shows how to cut the port at the top to achieve the form we're explaining here. By angling back the top of the runner wall in such a way, we have increased the length of the leading edge of the runner walls. This gives the air a larger entrance area, which in turn reduces the speed over the leading edge of the dividing wall. This makes it easier for the air and fuel to make the turn into the port runner.

PORT EXTENSIONS

This technique of lengthening the leading edge can be continued to good effect. Normally, the leading edge of a runner is about at a right angle to the floor of the plenum. By extending the leading edge in a curve or angling it by adding material to the lower part, we can further increase its length thus aiding port flow even more.

Reshaping the leading edge as just described can also be beneficial in terms of velocity distribution from top to bottom of the port. The more even the port velocity, the better it usually fares in terms of an even fuel content that any particular part of the port maybe carrying. Overlaid on anything we may do is the effect of gravity. This will always bring about a tendency for the fuel to flow more on the port floor. This is not where we want the fuel to be and our efforts need to be directed towards alleviating rather than aggravating this situation.

Let's focus our attention for a moment on the leading edge of the dividing port wall. It's often reasoned that if these edges are sharp, it will produce a 'knifing' action splitting the air on its route down each port. However, in a typical V8 engine with a Chevrolet firing order, only the adjacent cylinders 5 and 7 have air passing down them at the same time. As a result, it could be argued that if knife edging was to achieve anything it would only do so on this pair of cylinders. Flow bench testing indicates that, for the most part, even on adjacent ports with overlapping induction events, knife edging provides a little or no advantage over a generous radius. One of the most successful manifold modifiers in the business, Keith Wilson, modifies production manifolds by welding to produce a thicker dividing wall to allow a more generous radius to be formed on this edge. Keith also uses a curved leading edge at this point. By laying back the

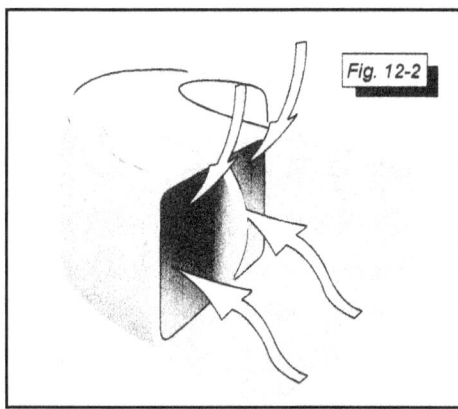

Curving the leading edge of a paired set of runners is a popular move on many race bred single 4-barrel manifolds. Applied to some of the more popular high, semi mass produced cost effective designs of race manifolds, such as those from Edelbrock, Holley and Weiand, it appears to help output in the 5-8000 rpm range.

upper part of this leading edge it functions as explained earlier and promotes an easier entry for the air from the plenum into the port runner. By having the lower edge curve back down in the reverse manner, it would appear that the motion of the air into the port runner has a slight upward bias. This in itself may cause fuel that's on floor, to be more readily picked back up into the airstream. Of course, determining exactly what happens to the fuel and air in the port is very difficult. It all happens with great speed, and it is difficult to see precisely what's going on even when the manifold has plexiglass windows. However, the bottom line is that manifolds modified using these techniques tend to produce significantly more power. Fig. 12-2 shows those aspects of manifold design we have just discussed put together.

MANIFOLD FLOOR

As for the floor of the manifold, several schools of thought prevail. Some successful manifold designers believe that a flat floor is best, and other equally successful designers, the reverse. Although the flat floor theory may hold true in those instances where carb atomization or intake heat provide adequate mixture preparation, there still exists, a good argument for depressing the manifold floor. Doing so means that liquid fuel cannot easily run down the ports. If the fuel is insufficiently atomized, making a depression or grooving the floor will almost certainly help output. If the fuel is already adequately atomized then, depressing or grooving the manifold floor rarely causes a reduction in power. That leaves it as one of those modifications which is reasonably fail safe.

PORT FORM

With any single four barrel carburetor manifold on a V8, it is necessary for the port to make some kind of turn into the cylinder head runner. Regardless of the type, be it Ford, Chevrolet or Chrysler, runners to the outer cylinders will always have close to a 90 degree turn in them. For Chevrolet pattern cylinder heads, where intake ports are paired, even the inner cylinders have a substantial turn, leaving no port directly in line with the plenum. The key to an efficient high flow port runner design, is to make the turn from the plenum with a minimum flow loss and mixture quality degradation. A primary requirement, is to make the port runner turn as gentle as possible. This seems so obvious it makes one wonder why the popular 'X' manifolds of the '60s and '70s ever came into being. Their design rational defies all commonly accepted methods of getting air around a corner efficiently. Subsequent and more expertly conceived designs did show the folly of the X manifold. Such manifolds are often seen for sale at swap meets. Avoid them.

In designing an efficient port, there are a number of factors to consider. First, the port area needs to decrease as it approaches the cylinder head. Thousands of developmental hours have indicated that engines tend to make their best power when the intake port tapers from the intake end to the valve by an average of about 1½ degrees' although research indicates that the higher the engine's operating RPM, the greater this angle may need to be. Engines needing relatively narrow power bands and making power up in the 9 to 10,000 RPM range and above, appear to benefit from taper angles as great as 2½ degrees. Because a straight port is impractical, it also renders a simple taper on the port as equally impractical. Fortunately, practical and effective solutions do exist. The port can change form, as long as the area decreases progressively towards the valve at a rate about the same as a straight port area reduction equal to the desired taper angle.

PORT DESIGN

As the port progresses to the cylinder head, it will of necessity have to make a turn. The turn, to be the most efficient in terms of airflow, needs to have as large a radius as possible on the inside wall. There will be a tendency for the port to be more efficient if it becomes taller and narrower. This allows us to make the inside radius larger as it progresses around the turn. As the turn is being made, the area must decrease to generate the desired taper angle. When reworking a manifold, some track of the port area at any given point along its length must be kept. When it comes to making a turn, priority should be given to removing material from the busiest part of the port, with a bias towards the top and bottom rather than the side walls. Just how much this proves to be the case can be established by velocity probing the runners to find the busiest areas.

The next area to investigate is the runner approach to the cylinder head. Here, it should be borne in mind that ideally, the mixture needs to exit the manifold face as close to 90 degrees as possible. Remember, for the most part cylinder head intake ports go straight in. If the air is still angling across due to the fact that it was misdirected by the port, then flow will be lost. Along with a loss of flow, there will also be a tendency to dump fuel on which-ever cylinder head port wall is on the outside of the turn. A typical Chevrolet port is necked down as it passes the push rods and, as a result, the inner pair of ports are mirror images of the outer. This produces an entirely different approach, and consequently, fuel distribution pattern for each pair of cylinders. Such differences in fuel flow patterns pertain to all single four barrel manifolds for "V" configured engines. However, when a Tunnel Ram manifold is used, we have mirror image manifold port runners. This means the wet flow fuel pattern in the port becomes far more uniform, but reversed between one cylinder and another. A practical countermeasure to offset differing wet flow patterns within a single four barrel manifold is to build a degree of "overshoot" into the runners (see page 111). Unfortunately, very few production manifolds actually have enough material, short of welding them up, to allow this to be done to a significant degree. But whatever is possible is better than none.

After making all the turns the charge must exit into the cylinder head. Here, the main job is to try and make a reasonable match of the manifold's port runners with those in the head. It is not necessary to achieve a perfect match. If the manifold port runners are slightly smaller than the intake ports in the head, then there will be no significant flow loss due to any mismatch of up to .025-inch. The most important aspect here is to make sure there is not a step the wrong way between the intake and the cylinder head. Also, there are reasons to believe that if the floor of the manifold is slightly higher than the floor of the cylinder head port, there will be a tendency to re-introduce some of the fuel back into the air.

TUNNEL RAM MANIFOLDS

Although reworking an existing tunnel ram manifold casting means removing a lot more metal, catering for flow and fuel distribution is a little easier than with a single four barrel manifold. The main aspect to consider with a tunnel ram manifold is that the port runner area and length falls in line with design requirements. Both of these factors are dealt with in Chapter 5. The only aspect that needs to be considered here is that the entrance into the runners should have a generous, but not overly large, radius. If the radius is too small, there will be a flow loss. If it is too big, it will cause the pressure wave reflection to be more progressive. This causes the port to act as if it has a far greater taper angle than it really has. This, in turn, causes the intake to act as if it is significantly shorter than it really is, and much of the effectiveness of the intake length tuning is lost. A 3/8 to 1/2 inch radius at this point appears to be optimum.

TUNNEL RAM PLENUM VOLUME

The single most tunable aspect of a tunnel ram manifold is the plenum volume. The easiest way to deal with this is to have various thicknesses of spacers between the top and bottom halves of the plenum, thereby adjusting the volume. Essentially, we find that if the volume is reduced, it tends to favor the low end which on a drag racer engine may be 6500 to 7000 RPM.If the volume is increased, it will tend to favor the high end. On a no holds barred engine this could be at 9000 to 10,000 RPM. Other than the volume of the manifold we find the only other factor that is necessary to deal with, and this is usually a relatively minor issue, is fuel distribution. However, because each carburetor is positioned over the entrance of four port runners, we find that fuel distribution is, for the most part, relatively even. It is only when we're looking for the last degree of power from the engine that we need to turn our attention to fuel orientation in the runner. Probably the most important aspect of manifold design, other than area and length, is how the mixture exits the runner. To visualize this will require making some wet flow tests, and to be representative, port velocity would need to be reasonably close to that occurring in a running motor. Although we need only test one end of the manifold to be meaningful, such a test would require a flow bench capable of drawing about a ½-inch of mercury (7 inches of water) depression on four wide open carb barrels. This requires a reasonably powerful flow bench. Of the commonly available flow benches, only the more powerful are capable of doing such a test. Also, most

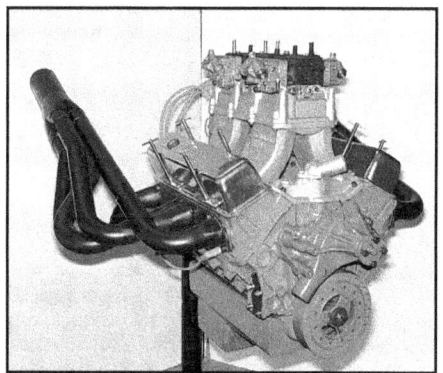

A tunnel ram installation has, without a doubt, more power potential than any other carburetion setup possible. But, like any off the shelf manifolds.......

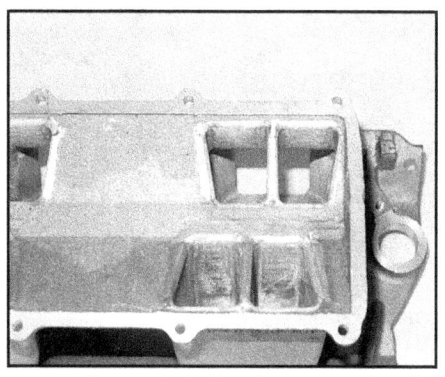

...... work needs to be done to make the most of them. The simplest, most effective first move is to blend the entry radius into the runners.

flow benches cannot deal with wet flow, as it will short out the electric motors. This means making provision to blow through the carbs and leaving the runners open so the wet flow pattern can be seen. Although it has a higher specific gravity than fuel, water is a perfectly acceptable fluid to use for wet flow testing. It is safe and, because of the usually fine airborne droplet sizes involved, will give representative results.

SHEET METAL MANIFOLDS

Professional and serious amateur racing has spawned so many head modifiers, with equally numerous head designs, that often there isn't a manifold that is even close to fitting or more importantly, up to the job of delivering what the engine builder perceives is needed. This is where it becomes necessary to call upon the skills of a sheet metal manifold maker. Such manifolds are made up of formed aluminum sheet, and then welded together. Building a manifold this way is a long and arduous task, and as a consequence such manifolds are expensive. Because they are so labor intensive, they can cost between 5 to 10 times the price of a quality cast race manifold. However, making a manifold from scratch does mean that there is plenty of scope to produce exactly what is believed required.

PORT TAPER

Here, it is worth emphasizing that a universally optimum port taper has yet to be determined. Indeed, such a single angle may not even exist because there are so many variables involved. This, plus difficulties in determining from tests what is precisely needed for the induction system, means we are no nearer than a good estimate based on practical experience. But the computer age is changing this. Computer programs using sophisticated mathematical models are allowing us to home in on more optimal intake angles, as well as lengths and areas, for given applications. A pioneer in its field, the Dynomation program by VP Engineering makes the extremely complex number crunching involved a relatively fast process on a computer with a 486 or faster microprocessor. Using this program, the effect of different port taper angles can be tried without the normally associated cost of real-life testing.

Horsepower Quick Facts & References

BUILDING THE HELGESEN/VIZARD PERFORMANCE MANIFOLD

Here is what it took for the development of the Helgesen/Vizard manifold that we use for our serious street engines. On engines with cams less than 280 degrees of seat (advertised) duration, it will produce the bottom end output of a good aftermarket two plane while typically delivering 15 horsepower more top end than popular out-of-the-box race single plane manifolds.

The starting point for our custom manifold is the Weiand Street Ram, which is intended for use with a Q-jet or spread bore Holley. Take a good look at it so you can identify it at the swap meets (that's where we get all ours). Just for the record, this manifold works well as is with an adapter plate and a square bore 600 to 750 carb installed. But it can be dramatically improved. The first move is ...

...to make up some runner extensions, as seen here, then welded them in.

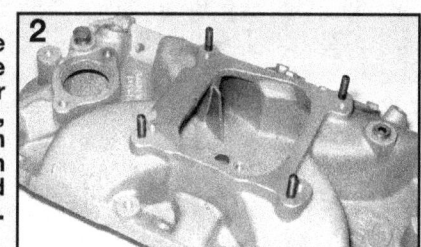

Next comes the porting work. In this instance, the port work required is straightforward. The Street Ram has intake runners of differing areas. The biggest are close to what is needed for a 400 to 500 horsepower small block, while the small ones are too small. If you make use of all the porting tips and manifold design requirements that have been put forward in these pages, you will get the job done right. Essentially, porting involved making short turn radii as gentle as possible, as a first move. Then to even the area of all the ports, the roof and the outside wall of the ports were re-worked. This, together with dressing the runner extensions, as seen here, produces a stock height manifold for low hood lines which will run with or beat any out of the box race manifold while producing all the low end of a two plane. However, if hood clearance permits, these manifolds like a spacer so here...

... is how to make a permanent job of installing one. First, acquire a sand cast (not a die cast) aluminum spacer. These are weldable whereas others are not. Remove excess metal from the lower half as seen here.

Next, position it on the manifold and drill through the spacer into the manifold, so some positioning dowels can be installed.

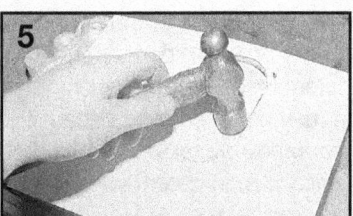

With the dowels installed, locate some tough gasket paper on the dowels and cut the form of the manifold plenum opening with a hammer.

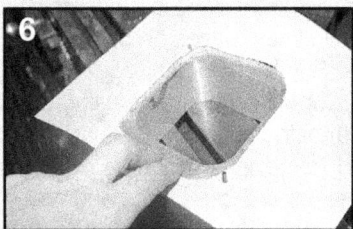

When you are done, flip over the paper template and install it on the spacer, as seen here and transfer the shape to the underside of the spacer.

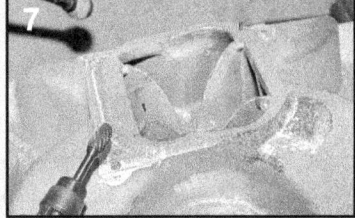

Next locate the spacer back on the manifold dowels and mark around it, then cutter away excess metal as seen here.

The next move for us is to throw the spacer onto the mill and rough out the excess metal. However, you can do it ...

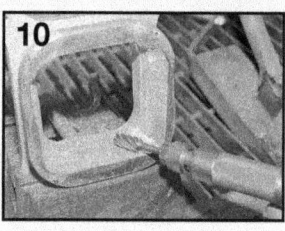

... with a carbide cutter and a die grinder, it just takes longer. Here, we are cleaning up our mill work.

With all the smog and exhaust heat passages machined off, the manifold has to have a lot of holes welded shut. This was done, along with welding the spacer to the top of the manifold.

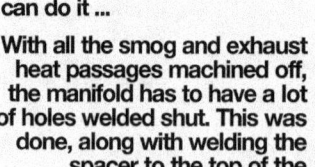

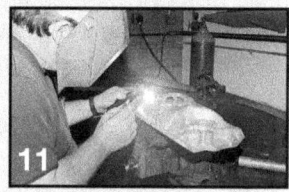

Here is the completed manifold. As a performance advantage and to retain its good looks Sam Davis at Gold Coast Coating applied a thermal barrier to the inside and a ceramic chrome-like finish to the outside. If you want a manifold like this, don't call us, we are strictly R & D. Go find a core manifold and send it to Keith Wilson, he's in business to build manifolds and does a fine job, but don't expect it to be cheap. Until someone decides to cast the HV (Helgesen/Vizard) manifold from scratch they never will be!

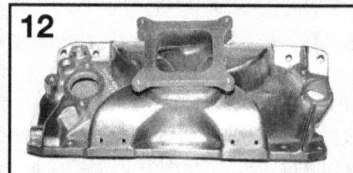

HORSEPOWER Quick Facts & References

CUSTOM MANIFOLDS

Any special, out of the ordinary, engine project is very likely to need something more than just an off-the-shelf manifold. Keith Wilson's (the Wilson in Dart/Wilson) Florida-based company specializes in manifolds and has the distinction of having a number intakes banned from Winston Cup racing because they had too much of a performance advantage.

Part of the art of manifold modification can be to make the manifold look as if it has not been touched. The drag race manifold for a Ford engine has had a Dominator top added to it.

This Wilson installation for a blown 5.0L Ford featured a much modified Edelbrock lower portion with a custom built top half.

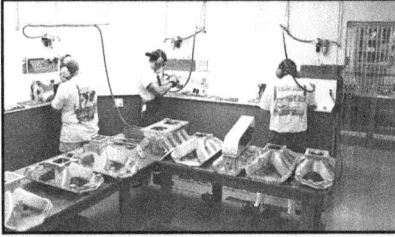

Now that we have introduced you to Keith Wilson, we will walk you through the procedure to produce a state-of-the-art race manifold. As you can see from this view of Keith's shop, he deals in a variety of manifolds. However, the one we are going to concentrate on here is the Dart/Wilson manifold. Because Keith was the designer of this piece, he had control over the cast port shapes and as a result there is less work to do to get it up to speed. The first move is ...

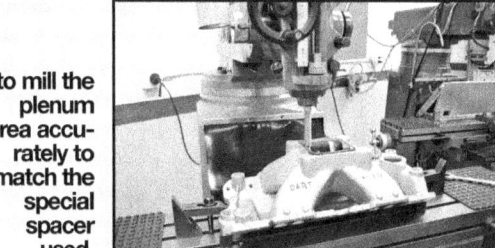

... to mill the plenum area accurately to match the special spacer used.

Next, the manifold faces have to be machined to produce the required height to fit your heads. This, and subsequent port matching operations, may mean sending your heads along to Keith's shop, if they have ports in a non standard position. The first step toward matching it, is to indicate the existing surface flat.

The desired amount of metal is then taken off to produce the ...

... desired fit and port location. The manifold is now ready to start the port matching sequence. the first step is to...

... mark the location of the vertical and horizontal edges of the cylinder head ports on the head (arrow), so they can be transferred to the manifold.

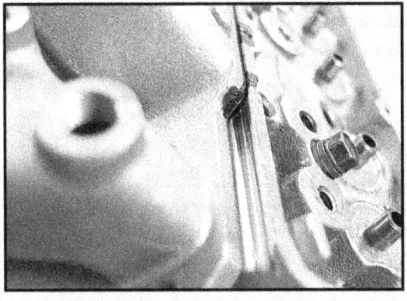

Seen here is the horizontal port matching reference line being transferred to the manifold. Once the lines are ...

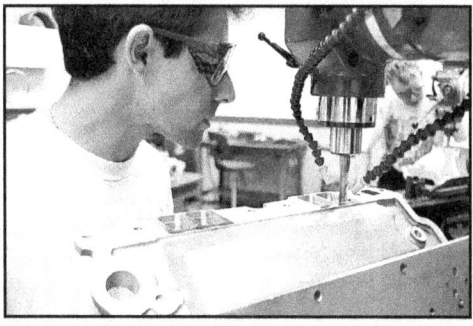

... transferred to the manifold face, the manifold is set up in a mill and cut to the lines.

How to Build Horsepower, Vol. 2   **125**

CUSTOM MANIFOLDS continued

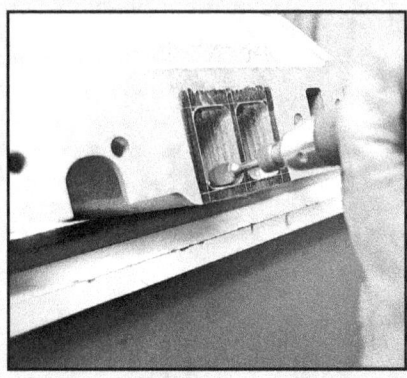

Now comes the hand work. Starting at the manifold face, the ports are reworked as far as possible up toward the plenum. A good eye for what is required is needed because the area must get progressively larger, but the height to width ratio of the port changes, making it a difficult judgment call. Practice and experience count for much at this stage.

Starting at the carb spacer face, the plenum is worked down to the previously done port work and the ...

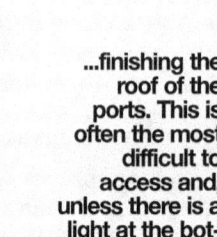

... leading edges of the runners rounded as require. From here, it is a question ...

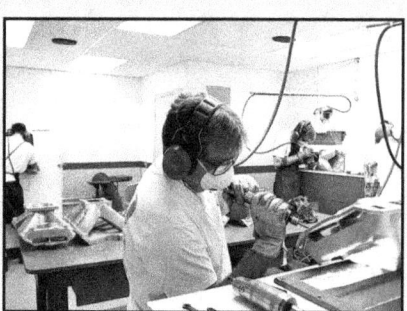

...finishing the roof of the ports. This is often the most difficult to access and, unless there is a light at the bottom of the grinding bench, the most difficult to see.

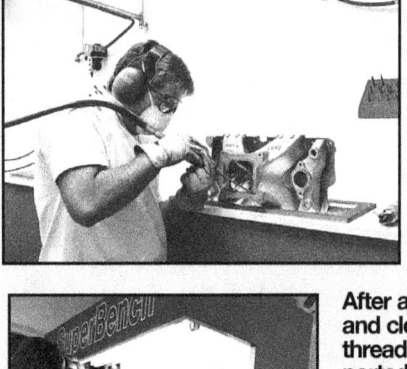

After a thorough washing and cleaning of the threads, the finished ported manifold is flow tested to verify that the ports flow to spec. Knowing the numbers the manifold should flow and checking this way, is fine, but when the manifolds are originally developed, virtually all flow testing is done with carb and cylinder head in the system.

From Keith Wilson's shop, our manifolds go to Mag Masters where Tom works his polishing skills. Our front cover manifold is getting the treatment here, and remember that shine reflects unwanted heat so it is both a performance and cosmetic attribute.

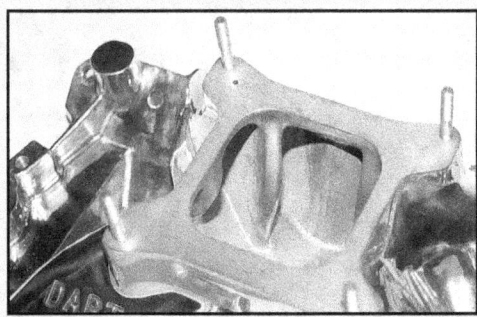

This view of the finished plenum shows the high quality workmanship Keith Wilson puts into his product.

Here, equipped with a fully modified carb flowing a little over 1000 CFM is our Dart Wilson manifold ready for installation on a 383 street/strip small block Chevy.

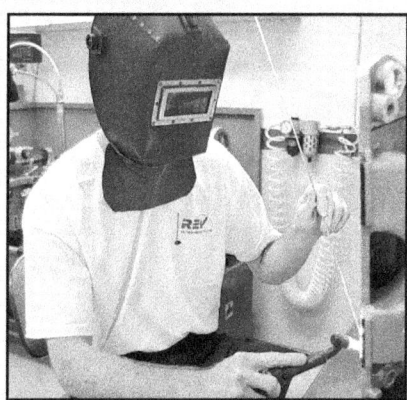

Some manifolds, such as this Winston Cup item, need to be welded to achieve the desired shape. The Edelbrock Victor series is a sound basis for a super performance manifold and requires welding to ...

... allow for the required port size for bigger engines, as well as ....

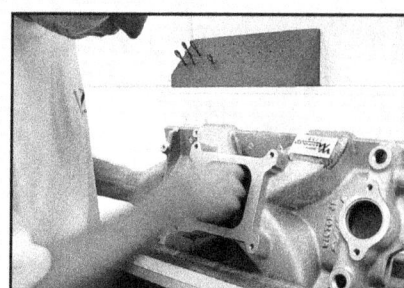

... in the plenum for the extensive modifications to the runner divider walls.

Here is the stock plenum on a Victor Jr. From this, it can be seen ....

...... how much the plenum area has been reworked on the Wilson modified Victor Jr.

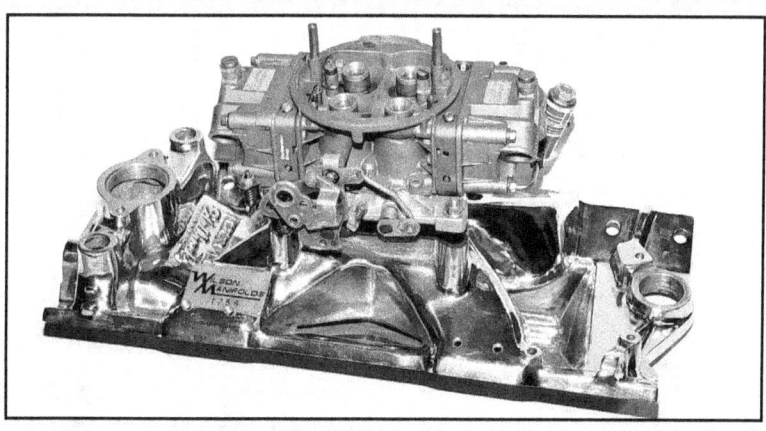

This Wilson modified, Mag Masters polished manifold is destined to go on a 406 Chevy and installed in a 1980 Pontiac Trans Am with a hood shaker air scoop. With only minor mods to the scoop, the Victor Jr. is just about as tall a manifold as can be used.

From experience, it can be said that polishing manifolds and other engine components such as heads, which all seem to have inaccessible corners, is a long an tedious job. The starting point, is to take out major casting flaws with first a course emery drum, then a fine one. This operation is a bit like porting, only on the outside where everyone can see your handiwork.

When major flaws have been dressed out, the manifold (or whatever), is rough polished on this big fiber wheel. Gloves are essential because of the heat generated.

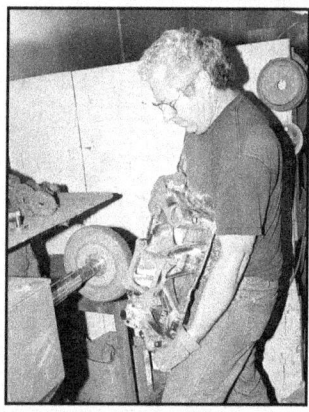

Last operation is to buff the part on a soft wheel with what is often termed 'buffing soap.' The finished results are as you see dotted around various pages of this book.

How To Build HORSEPOWER: Chapter 13
Carburetors & Intake Manifolds
Sources

Here is a preferred suppliers list. Not all of these companies supply catalogs, but those that do and are considered to be required reading are listed in bold italics.

COMPANY	SOURCE OR TELEPHONE #
Edelbrock	Local Speed Shop
Holley Carburetors	Local Speed Shop
Weiand	Local Speed Shop
K & N	Local Speed Shop
Braswell Carburetion	(909) 985-6308
The Carburetor Shop	(909) 481-5816
Wilson Manifolds	(305) 771-6216
Air Inlet Systems	(905) 540-3801
Gene Berg Enterprises	(714) 998-7500
Fast Freddies (Webers)	(714) 540-3801
JayCee Enterprises	(714) 848-9898
BG Fuel Systems	(706) 864-8544
C.B. Performance	(209) 733-8222
Dart/World Products	(313) 362-1188
Brodix	(501) 394-1075
Brzezinski Racing Products	(414) 246-8577
B&G Computers	(602) 274-2537
Gold Coast Coating	(805) 987-9060
Dynojet Research, Inc.	(406) 388-4993
Tech Line Coatings	(214) 923-0752
Harman Enterprises (Intake stacks)	(714) 592-0435
Predator	(908) 367-8487
Mikuni America Corp.	(818) 885-1242
Carter/Federal Mogal Corp.	(810) 354-7700
Computech Systems	(800) 870-8883
Advanced Performance Technology (APT)	(909) 686-0260
VP Engineering (Dynomation)	(515) 276-0701
Racing Systems Analysis (RSA)	(602) 241-1301

More great titles available from CarTech®...

S-A DESIGN

Super Tuning & Modifying Holley Carburetors — Perf, street and off-road applications. *(SA08)*

Custom Painting — Gives you an overview of the broad spectrum of custom painting types and techniques. *(SA10)*

Street Supercharging, A Complete Guide to — Bolt-on buying, installing and tuning blowers. *(SA17)*

Engine Blueprinting — Using tools, block selection & prep, crank mods, pistons, heads, cams & more! *(SA21)*

David Vizard's How to Build Horsepower — Building horsepower in any engine. *(SA24)*

Chevrolet Small-Block Parts Interchange Manual — Selecting & swapping high-perf. small-block parts. *(SA55)*

High-Performance Ford Engine Parts Interchange — Selecting & swapping big- and small-block Ford parts. *(SA56)*

How To Build Max Perf Chevy Small-Blocks on a Budget — Would you believe 600 hp for $3000? *(SA57)*

How To Build Max Performance Ford V-8s on a Budget — Dyno-tested engine builds for big- & small-blocks. *(SA69)*

How To Build Max-Perf Pontiac V8s — Mild perf apps to all-out performance build-ups. *(SA78)*

How To Build High-Performance Ignition Systems — Guide to understanding auto ignition systems. *(SA79)*

How to Build Max Perf 4.6 Liter Ford Engines — Building & modifying Ford's 2- & 4-valve 4.6/5.4 liter engines. *(SA82)*

How to Build Big-Inch Ford Small-Blocks — Add cubic inches without the hassle of switching to a big-block. *(SA85)*

How To Build High-Perf Chevy LS1/LS6 Engines — Modifying and tuning Gen-III engines for GM cars and trucks. *(SA86)*

How To Build Big-Inch Chevy Small-Blocks — Get the additional torque & horsepower of a big-block. *(SA87)*

Honda Engine Swaps — Step-by-step instructions for all major tasks involved in engine swapping. *(SA93)*

How to Build High-Performance Chevy Small-Block Cams/Valvetrains — Camshaft & valvetrain function, selection, performance, and design. *(SA105)*

High-Performance Jeep Cherokee XJ Builder's Guide 1984–2001 — Build a useful Cherokee for mountains, the mud, the desert, the street, and more. *(SA109)*

How to Build and Modify Rochester Quadrajet Carburetors — Selecting, rebuilding, and modifying the Quadrajet Carburetors. *(SA113)*

Rebuilding the Small-Block Chevy: Step-by-Step Videobook — 160-pg book plus 2-hour DVD show you how to build a street or racing small-block Chevy. *(SA116)*

How to Paint Your Car on a Budget — Everything you need to know to get a great-looking coat of paint and save money. *(SA117)*

How to Drift: The Art of Oversteer — This comprehensive guide to drifting covers both driving techniques and car setup. *(SA118)*

Turbo: Real World High-Performance Turbocharger Systems — Turbo is the most practical book for enthusiasts who want to make more horsepower. Foreword by Gale Banks. *(SA123)*

High-Performance Chevy Small-Block Cylinder Heads — Learn how to make the most power with this popular modification on your small-block Chevy. *(SA125)*

High Performance Brake Systems — Design, selection, and installation of brake systems for Musclecars, Hot Rods, Imports, Modern Era cars and more. *(SA126)*

High Performance C5 Corvette Builder's Guide — Improve the looks, handling and performance of your Corvette C5. *(SA127)*

High Performance Diesel Builder's Guide — The definitive guide to getting maximum performance out of your diesel engine. *(SA129)*

How to Rebuild & Modify Carter/Edelbrock Carbs — The only source for information on rebuilding and tuning these popular carburetors. *(SA130)*

Building Honda K-Series Engine Performance — The first book on the market dedicated exclusively to the Honda K series engine. *(SA134)*

Engine Management-Advanced Tuning — Take your fuel injection and tuning knowledge to the next level. *(SA135)*

How to Drag Race — Car setup, beginning and advanced techniques for bracket racing and pro classes, and racing science and math, and more. *(SA136)*

4x4 Suspension Handbook — Includes suspension basics & theory, advanced/high-performance suspension and lift systems, axles, how-to installations, and more. *(SA137)*

GM Automatic Overdrive Transmission Builder's and Swapper's Guide — Learn to build a bulletproof tranny and how to swap it into an older chassis as well. *(SA140)*

High-Performance Subaru Builder's Guide — Subarus are the hottest compacts on the street. Make yours even hotter. *(SA141)*

How to Build Max-Performance Mitsubishi 4G63t Engines — Covers every system and component of the engine, including a complete history. *(SA148)*

How to Swap GM LS-Series Engines Into Almost Anything — Includes a historical review and detailed information so you can select and fit the best LS engine. *(SA156)*

How to Autocross — Covers basic to more advanced modifications that go beyond the stock classes. *(SA158)*

Designing & Tuning High-Performance Fuel Injection Systems — Complete guide to tuning aftermarket standalone systems. *(SA161)*

Design & Install In Car Entertainment Systems — The latest and greatest electronic systems, both audio and video. *(SA163)*

How to Build Max-Performance Hemi Engines — Build the biggest baddest vintage Hemi. *(SA164)*

How to Digitally Photograph Cars — Learn all the modern techniques and post processing too. *(SA168)*

High-Performance Differentials, Axles, & Drivelines — Must have book for anyone thinking about setting up a performance differential. *(SA170)*

How To Build Max-Performance Mopar Big Blocks — Build the baddest wedge Mopar on the block. *(SA171)*

How to Build Max-Performance Oldsmobile V-8s — Make your Oldsmobile keep up with the pack. *(SA172)*

Automotive Diagnostic Systems: Understanding OBD-I & OBD II — Learn how modern diagnostic systems work. *(SA174)*

How to Make Your Muscle Car Handle — Upgrade your muscle car suspension to modern standards. *(SA175)*

Full-Size Fords 1955–1970 — A complete color history of full-sized fords. *(SA176)*

Rebuilding Any Automotive Engine: Step-by-Step Videobook — Rebuild any engine with this book DVD combo. DVD is over 3 hours long! *(SA179)*

How to Supercharge & Turbocharge GM LS-Series Engines — Boost the power of today's most popular engine. *(SA180)*

The New Mini Performance Handbook — All the performance tricks for your new Mini. *(SA182)*

How to Build Max-Performance Ford FE Engines — Finally, performance tricks for the FE junkie. *(SA183)*

Builder's Guide to Hot Rod Chassis & Suspension — Ultimate guide to Hot Rod Suspensions. *(SA185)*

How to Build Altered Wheelbase Cars — Build a wild altered car. Complete history too! *(SA189)*

How to Build Period Correct Hot Rods — Build a hot rod true to your favorite period. *(SA192)*

Automotive Sheet Metal Forming & Fabrication — Create and fabricate your own metalwork. *(SA196)*

How to Build Max-Performance Chevy Big Block on a Budget — New big-block book from the master, David Vizard. *(SA198)*

How to Build Big-Inch GM LS-Series Engines — Get more power through displacement from your LS. *(SA203)*

Performance Automotive Engine Math — All the formulas and facts you will ever need. *(SA204)*

How to Design, Build & Equip Your Automotive Workshop on a Budget — Working man's guide to building a great work space. *(SA207)*

Automotive Electrical Performance Projects — Featuring the most popular electrical mods today. *(SA209)*

How to Port Cylinder Heads — Vizard shares his cylinder head secrets. *(SA215)*

S-A DESIGN RESTORATION SERIES

How to Restore Your Mustang 1964 1/2–1973 — Step-by-step restoration for your classic Mustang. *(SA165)*

Muscle Car Interior Restoration Guide — Make your interior look and smell new again. Includes dash restoration. *(SA167)*

How to Restore Your Camaro 1967–1969 — Step-by-step restoration of your 1st gen Camaro. *(SA178)*

S-A DESIGN WORKBENCH® SERIES

Workbench® Series books feature step by step instruction with hundreds of color photos for stock rebuilds and automotive repair.

How To Rebuild the Small-Block Chevrolet — *(SA26)*
How to Rebuild the Small-Block Ford — *(SA102)*
How to Rebuild & Modify High-Performance Manual Transmissions — *(SA103)*
How to Rebuild the Big-Block Chevrolet — *(SA142)*
How to Rebuild the Small-Block Mopar — *(SA143)*
How to Rebuild GM LS-Series Engines — *(SA147)*
How to Rebuild Any Automotive Engine — *(SA151)*
How to Rebuild Honda B-Series Engines — *(SA154)*
How to Rebuild the 4.6/5.4 Liter Ford — *(SA155)*
Automotive Welding: A Practical Guide — *(SA159)*
Automotive Wiring and Electrical Systems — *(SA160)*
How to Rebuild Big-Block Ford Engines — *(SA162)*
Automotive Bodywork & Rust Repair — *(SA166)*
How To Rebuild & Modify GM Turbo 400 Transmissions — *(SA186)*
How to Rebuild Pontiac V-8s — *(SA200)*

HISTORIES AND PERSONALITIES

Quarter-Mile Chaos — Rare & stunning photos of terrifying fires, explosions, and crashes in drag racing's golden age. *(CT425)*

Fuelies: Fuel Injected Corvettes 1957–1965 — The first Corvette book to focus specifically on the fuel injected cars, which are among the most collectible. *(CT452)*

Slingshot Spectacular: Front-Engine Dragster Era — Relive the golden age of front engine dragsters in this photo packed trip down memory lane. *(CT464)*

Chrysler Concept Cars 1940–1970 — Fascinating look at the concept cars created by Chrysler during this golden age of the automotive industry. *(CT470)*

Fuel Altereds Forever — Includes more than 250 photos of the most popular drivers and racecars from the Fuel Altered class. *(CT475)*

Yenko — Complete and thorough story of the man, his business and his legendary cars. *(CT485)*

Lost Hot Rods — Great Hot Rods from the past rediscovered. *(CT487)*

Grumpy's Toys — A collection of Grumpy's greats. *(CT489)*

Woodward Avenue: Cruising the Legendary — Revisit the glory days of Woodward! *(CT491)*

Rusted Muscle — A collection of junkyard muscle cars. *(CT492)*

America's Coolest Station Wagons — Wagons are cooler than they ever have been. *(CT493)*

Super Stock — A paperback version of a classic best seller. *(CT495)*

Rusty Pickups: American Workhorses Put to Pasture — Cool collection of old trucks and ads too! *(CT496)*

Jerry Heasley's Rare Finds — Great collection of Heasley's best finds. *(CT497)*

Street Sleepers: The Art of the Deceptively Fast Car — Stealth, horsepower, what's not to love? *(CT498)*

Ed 'Big Daddy' Roth — Paperback reprint of a classic best seller. *(CT500)*

Car Spy: Secret Cars Exposed by the Industry's Most Notorious Photographer — Cool behind-the-scenes stories spanning 40 years. *(CT502)*

CarTech®, Inc. 39966 Grand Ave., North Branch, MN 55056. Ph: 800-551-4754 or 651-277-1200 • Fax: 651-277-1203
Brooklands Books Ltd., PO Box 146 Cobham, Surrey KT11 1LG, England. Ph: 01932 865051 • Fax 01932 868803
Brooklands Books Aus., 3/37-39 Green Street, Banksmeadow, NSW 2019, Australia. Ph: 2 9695 7055 • Fax 2 9695 7355

Visit us online at www.cartechbooks.com for more info!

More Information for Your Project ...

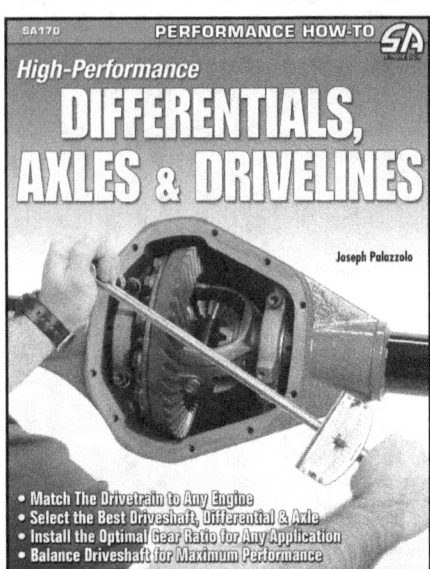

HIGH-PERFORMANCE DIFFERENTIALS, AXELS & DRIVELINES by *Joseph Palazzolo* This book covers everything you need to know about selecting the most desirable gear ratio, rebuilding differentials and other driveline components, and matching driveline components to engine power output. Learn how to set up a limited-slip differential, install high-performance axle shafts, swap out differential gears, and select products for the driveline. This book explains rear differential basics, rear differential housings, rebuilding open rear differentials, limited-slip differentials, and factory differentials. Ring and pinion gears, axle housings, axle shafts, driveshafts, and U-joints are also covered. Softbound, 8-1/2 x 11 inches, 144 pages, approx. 400 color photos. *Item #SA170*

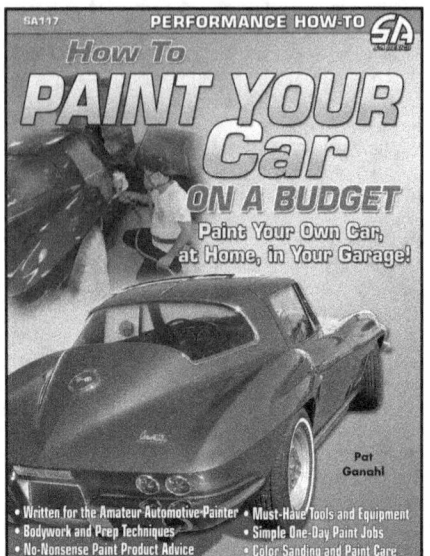

HOW TO PAINT YOUR CAR ON A BUDGET by *Pat Ganahl* If your car needs new paint, or even just a touch-up, the cost involved in getting a professional job can be more than you bargained for. In this book, author Pat Ganahl unveils dozens of secrets that will help anyone paint their own car. From simple scuff-and-squirt jobs to full-on, door-jambs-and-everything paint jobs, Ganahl covers everything you need to know to get a great-looking coat of paint on your car and save lots of money in the process. Covers painting equipment, the ins and outs of prep, masking, painting and sanding products and techniques, and real-world advice on how to budget wisely when painting your own car. Softbound, 8-1/2 x 11 inches, 128 pages, approx. 400 color photos. *Item #SA117*

THE STEP-BY-STEP GUIDE TO ENGINE BLUEPRINTING by *Rick Voegelin* this book is simply the best book available on basic engine preparation for street or racing. Rick Voegelin's writing and wrenching skills put this book in a class by itself. Includes pro's secrets of using tools, selecting and preparing blocks, cranks, rods, pistons, cylinder heads, selecting cams and valvetrain components, balancing and assembly tips, plus worksheets for your engine projects, and much more! Softbound, 8-1/2 x 11 inches, 128 pages, over 400 b/w photos. *Item #SA21*

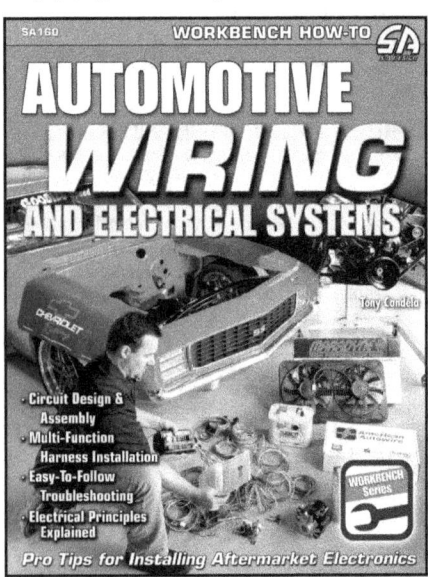

AUTOMOTIVE WIRING AND ELECTRICAL SYSTEMS by *Tony Candela* This book is the perfect book to unshroud the mysteries of automotive electrics and electronic systems. The basics of electrical principles, including voltage, amperage, resistance, and Ohm's law, are revealed in clear and concise detail, so the enthusiast understands what these mean in the construction and repair of automotive electrical circuits. Softbound, 8-1/2 x 11 inches, 144 pages, approx. 350 color photos. *Item #SA160*

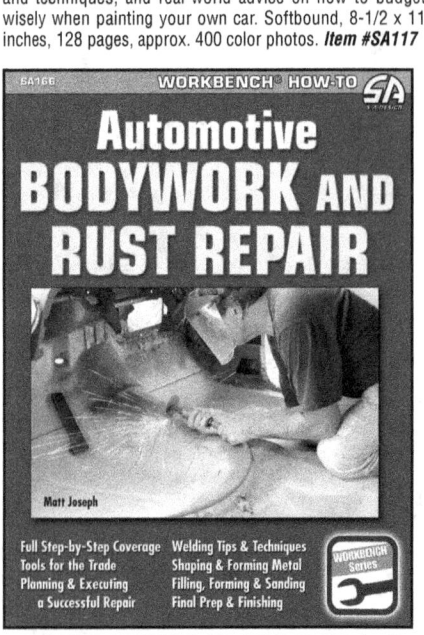

AUTOMOTIVE BODYWORK AND RUST REPAIR by *Matt Joseph* This book shows you the ins and out of tackling both simple and difficult rust and metalwork projects. This book teaches you how to select the proper tools for the job, common-sense approaches to the task ahead of you, preparing and cleaning sheet metal, section fabrications and repair patches, welding options such as gas and electric, forming, fitting and smoothing, cutting metal, final metal finishing including filling and sanding, the secrets of lead filling, making panels fit properly, and more. Softbound, 8-1/2 x 11 inches, 160 pages, 400 color photos. *Item #SA166*

PERFORMANCE AUTOMOTIVE ENGINE MATH by *John Baechtel* When designing or building an automotive engine for improved performance, it's all about the math. From measuring the engine's internal capacities to determine compression ratio to developing the optimal camshaft lift, duration, and overlap specifications, the use of proven math is the only way to design an effective high performance automotive powerplant. This book walks readers through the wide range of dimensions to be measured and formulas used to design and develop powerful engines. Includes reviews of the proper tools and measurement techniques, and carefully defines the procedures and equations used in engineering high efficiency and high rpm engines. Softbound, 8.5 x 11 inches, 160 pages, 350 photos. *Item #SA204*

www.cartechbooks.com or 1-800-551-4754